CULTURE, POLITICS, AND MONEY AMONG THE YORUBA

CULTURE, POLITICS, AND MONEY AMONG THE YORUBA

Toyin Falola
Akanmu Adebayo

Routledge
Taylor & Francis Group
LONDON AND NEW YORK

First published 2000 by Transaction Publishers

2 Park Square, Milton Park, Abingdon, Oxfordshire OX14 4RN
711 Third Avenue, New York, NY 10017

Routledge is an imprint of the Taylor & Francis Group, an informa business

First issued in paperback 2017

Library of Congress Catalog Number: 99-16174

Library of Congress Cataloging-in-Publication Data

Falola, Toyin.
Culture, politics, and money among the Yoruba / Toyin Falola, Akanmu Adebayo.
p. cm.
Includes bibliographical references and index.
ISBN 1-56000-418-5 (alk. paper)
1. Yoruba (African people)—Economic conditions. 2. Money—Nigeria—Cross cultural studies. 3. Yoruba (African people)—Social life and customs. I. Adebayo, A. G. (Akanmu Gafari), 1956– . II. Title.
DT515.45.Y67F33 1999
332.4'9669—dc21 99-16174
CIP

ISBN 13: 978-1-56000-418-9 (hbk)
ISBN 13: 978-1-138-50888-0 (pbk)

For our wives,
Olabisi Florence Falola
and
Omotola Aduke Adebayo

Contents

Preface

This book investigates and analyzes several aspects of money among the Yoruba of Nigeria. It explores the origin, philosophy, uses, politics, and problems of acquiring and spending money. There is no existing book on this subject among the Yoruba, a major ethnic group in Africa, with established connections with the black diaspora in North America and the Caribbean. The strength of the Yoruba as the focus of the study is impressive indeed: a rich oral and written culture; a large and diverse population; an integrated rural-urban society, and a strong economy monetized as far back as the fifteenth century. Conclusions from this study are intended to inform other studies, and certain general principles from this study are expected to influence studies of similar societies in Africa and elsewhere.

The book is conceived in a way that each chapter could be read individually. The study is divided into three parts, each conceptualizing and evaluating the different cultural and political dimensions of money. The first part—money and its uses—has five chapters. They focus on the transition from barter to cowry currency, the idealistic and pragmatic views of money, the impact of monetization on social stratification, accumulation among members of the elite, and the development of savings, banking, and credit institutions. As in most economies, barter was the earliest system of economic exchange among the Yoruba. It was barter that gave the vent for the creation of markets, and it was these markets that enhanced local and international exchange after the adoption of cowries as currency. Chapter 2 examines the economic and cultural uses of money, including the evolution of a complex method of counting and mathematics, the use of cowries in religion and ritual, and the employment of cowries in the *aroko* system of coded communication. From its introduction in the fifteenth century, cowries featured in local and international trade, including the slave trade, in which the Yoruba participated. Two of the consequences of increased monetization were the development of a complex and dynamic view of money (discussed in chapter 3), and the transformation of the system of social stratification (examined in chapter 4). Politics enabled power holders to accumulate substantial wealth, a subject treated in chapter 5, with an elaborate example on the collection of tolls. At the same time the Yoruba developed functional institutions for saving, credit, and banking (the focus of chapter 6), which were further transformed by the introduction of colonial currency. Altogether, these uses of money enhanced the mode of production and accumulation among the ruling elite, and created several problems in the social relations of production.

The second part—money and its problems—investigates social, political, and cultural problems of money, such as the difficult task of money lending and loan repayment, and the effluence of frantic, illegal, or quick methods to acquire money. Two chapters (7 and 8) examine how creditors collect their debts, using all sorts of devices. Some people attempt to acquire money by stealing (chapter 9), counterfeiting (chapter 10), or using their bureaucratic privileges to collect bribes (chapter 11). The problems of money in Yorubaland were indeed fascinating, but they were not limited to the Yoruba or to Africa. Theft, counterfeiting, corruption, and default on loans, the four problems evaluated in this section, are a worldwide phenomenon. They could, indeed, be seen as the result of monetization, capitalization, and materialism. This section of the book raises many issues and answers many questions: What mechanisms did the Yoruba institute for moneylending? How were loans made, guaranteed, and repaid in precolonial and colonial periods? How dynamic were interest rates and what impact did these have on social and production relations? How did colonial currency and other aspects of colonial policy (including taxation, capitalization, and political centralization) promote theft, counterfeiting, and corruption? How did these efforts to create wealth affect the culture and politics of money?

The third part—money and the oil boom—has two chapters. It examines the impact of oil money on Yoruba economy, society, and spending. Nigeria is an oil producer but the wells are not located in Yorubaland. So, how did the Yoruba-speaking people share in the increased wealth from oil (called "oil boom") in the mid-1970s? Chapter 12 answers this question. First, it examines the development of the oil industry in Nigeria. Second, it assesses the impact of the oil industry on the Nigerian state and society. Third, it analyzes the system of revenue allocation to illustrate how a nonoil-producing area shared in oil (and other) revenues collected by the federal government. Above all, this chapter reviews several areas in which the oil boom affected Yoruba society, both positively and negatively. The oil boom lasted only a few years, and was followed by a period of economic slump. Efforts to arrest the crisis led to the adoption of the Structural Adjustment Program (SAP) in 1986. Chapter 13 evaluates the impact of SAP on Yoruba society and shows some of the major changes in money spending against the background of declining revenues. It also evaluates the effects of currency devaluation on personal and communal responsibilities and social payment.

There are two chapters that should be read together: the introduction (chapter 1) and the overview and conclusion (chapter 14). The former presents the central thesis of this book, which is the culture of money, and it also reviews the development of the Yoruba economy. The conclusion returns to this central thesis and ties together the major findings and conclusions on the culture of money among the Yoruba presented in the preceding thirteen chapters.

Acknowledgments

This book is the outcome of several years of study. It benefited from formal and informal discussions among colleagues and friends. The authors owe a debt of gratitude to numerous people from the conception of the book to its publication. To start with, we must thank our publisher, Irving Louis Horowitz of Transactions, and the anonymous reviewers for their interest in the book and their invaluable suggestions. We also thank various publishers and editors of journals for allowing us to draw freely from previously published essays. The journals are: *The Journal of African History*, the *Journal of Asian and African Studies*, *Afrika*, *African Economic History*, *Paiduema*, and *Anthropos*. A large part of chapter 13 was originally co-authored with Professor Tunde Lawuyi, to whom we also pay gratitude. His contribution is hereby acknowledged.

Several parts of the book benefited from comments by different scholars. They include: Professors Ralph Austen of the University of Chicago, Paul Lovejoy of York University, Larry Yarak of Texas A & M University, Femi Taiwo of Loyola University in Chicago, and Felix Ekechi of Kent State University in Ohio, Dr. Chidi Nwaubani of University of North Carolina in Boulder, Dr. Olutayo Adesina of University of Ibadan, Dr. Funso Afolayan of the University of New Hampshire, Dr. Iheanyi Enwerem of Dominican Institute in Ibadan, and Professor Lovett Elango and Dr. Melvyn Fein, both of Kennesaw State University.

We owe a lot of debts to informants and many people who have assisted us in locating informants. On the latter, Toyin Falola would like to thank Segun Faleye, Bolanle Ogundele, Mary Ojoade, and Lati Oni. Akanmu Adebayo is appreciative of the support of Jare Adejuwon, Lanre Amzat, and M. A. Enilola for assisting him in the research for this study in Nigeria. He is also grateful to those who further assisted him from April through June 1998, when he was in Nigeria researching and rechecking some aspects of this study. They include Ademola Adebayo, Dejo Akanbi, and Sola and Nike Ibraheem.

In addition, we are grateful to participants in a number of conferences and seminars where aspects of this book were read. Toyin Falola would like to thank the Center for Historical Analysis, University of Rutgers, for a seminar in 1991. Akanmu Adebayo is grateful to Professor Leonhard Harding of the University of Hamburg, who made it possible for him to present some drafts of this book as a series of lectures to four distinguished scholarly audiences in Germany in 1992. He is also grateful to the Kennesaw Academic Forum to which he presented aspects of this book between 1993 and 1997. Finally, the authors are grateful to Mr. David King of Kennesaw State University for reading the final drafts of the manuscript and to the staff of Kennesaw State University for their bibliographic assistance.

Toyin Falola
The University of Texas at Austin
Akanmu Adebayo
Kennesaw State University
Fall 1998

Conversion Table

Year	Place/Foreign Exchange Market	Local Currency	US $
1826	Katunga (Old Oyo)	Cowries	2,000 cowries = $1 (Spanish dollar)
1853	"Yorubaland"	Cowries	2,000 cowries = $1
1857	Lagos	Cowries	2,000 cowries = $1
1858	Lagos	Cowries	4,000 cowries = $1
1858	Ilorin	Cowries	3,000 cowries = $1
1862	Abeokuta	Cowries	6,400 cowries = $1
1973	CBN* (official) rate	Naira	N1 = $1.50
1975	CBN (official) rate	Naira	N1 = $1.98
1980	CBN (official) rate	Naira	N1 = $1.84
1981	CBN (official) rate	Naira	N1 = $1.57
1982	CBN (official) rate	Naira	N1 = $1.54
1983	CBN (official) rate	Naira	N1 = $1.34
1985	CBN (official) rate	Naira	N1 = $1.01
1986	FEM**	Naira	N2.11 = $1
	SFEM***	Naira	N3.64 = $1
1987	SFEM	Naira	N4.24 = $1
1988	SFEM	Naira	N5.09 = $1
1989	FEM	Naira	N7.58 = $1
	Parallel market	Naira	N11 = $1
1990	Parallel market	Naira	N11.50 = $1
1992	Parallel market	Naira	N13 = $1
1993	Parallel market	Naira	N10.49 = $1
1995	Parallel market	Naira	N21.89 = $1
1997	Official rate	Naira	N84 = $1
	Parallel market	Naira	N92 = $1
1998	Official rate	Naira	N86 = $1
	Parallel market	Naira	N92 = $1

*CBN: Central Bank of Nigeria

**FEM: First-tier Foreign Exchange Market

***SFEM: Second-tier Foreign Exchange Market

Sources: G. O. Ogunremi, *Counting the Camels: The Economics of Transportation in Pre-Industrial Nigeria* (New York: Nok, 1982). Central Bank of Nigeria (CBN), *Annual Report and Statement of Accounts* (various years). CBN, *Economic and Financial Review* (various years). Ekpo Eyo, *Nigeria and the Evolution of Money*, (Lagos: Central Bank of Nigeria, 1979).

1

Introduction

Although the focus is on the Yoruba, one of the major ethnic groups in West Africa, the theme of this book is broadly conceived in African financial institutions. This is easily one of the fastest-growing fields in African economic history in recent decades. Money, monetary policies, the main currency types, and the socioeconomic and political impact of money on the major currency zones of North and West Africa are being studied; and so are the rotating savings and credit systems (ROSCAs), which serve principally as banking institutions in many parts of precolonial Africa.

Most of the issues addressed in the book are fresh while others break new ground in interpretation and definition in showing the connection between what, at present, exists as separate and disconnected themes in the study of African economic history. This study is also timely in view of the impact of recent and on-going political and economic changes in Africa, and in other parts of the world, on African studies as a discipline. The degree of African indebtedness, the political effects of socioeconomic reforms promoted by African states in response to suggestions by the International Monetary Fund (IMF) and World Bank, the imperatives of loan repayment, and the new emphasis on rural development have had great implications for the direction of research in Africa. Moreover, political and economic changes in other parts of the world (such as the collapse of the socialist economic system, constitutional reforms in previously communist societies, and the escalation of ethnic nationalism in many countries) have forced scholars to question old notions and challenge old ideological and theoretical positions. This was partly in order to make sense of the current drastic changes and give direction to the formulation of future policies. The emergence and rapid expansion of feminist studies and the focus on the role of women in the development process also call for an urgent revision of debates thought to have been satisfactorily laid to rest. Indeed, the discussions here are as fresh and as problematic as any topic on African economic history.

This introductory chapter has three parts. The first is a discussion of the idea of money, particularly stressing the cultural and transformative functions. The second is a brief delineation of Yorubaland, the region that is the focus of the study. The third defines the economy of this region and evaluates the transition from "traditional" to "modern" financial systems.

Money

Money has been defined as "anything that can at all times, within a particular national system of markets, be used as a medium of exchange."[1] James Tobin introduces his entry in the *New Pelgrave Dictionary of Money and Finance* with the following interesting statement:

> Among the conventions of almost every human society of historical record has been the use of *money*, that is, particular commodities or tokens as measures of value and media of exchange in economic transactions. Somehow the members of a society agree on what will be acceptable tender in making payments and settling debts among themselves. General agreement to the convention, not the particular media agreed upon, is the source of money's immense value to society.[2]

The importance of this statement lies in the assertion that every society has money and that somehow they all come to an agreement on the media or material that would be used for that purpose. Another important element in Tobin's statement is that money serves a number of functions.

The classical view of money emphasizes this utilitarian value of money. Over the course of debate a consensus seems to emerge on the three functions of money: (1) a means of payment or medium of exchange; (2) a unit of account; and (3) a store of value. Money is able to accomplish these functions because, according to Georg Simmel, it is an objective reality with great transformative powers. Simmel describes money further in these terms:

> If the economic value of objects is constituted by their mutual relationship of exchangeability, then money is the autonomous expression of this relationship. Money is the representative of abstract value.... In this manner, it becomes one of the links and conditions in the series in which it is, at the same time, contrasted: its value becomes dependent upon supply and demand; its costs of production exert an influence, however slight, upon its value.... Money is measured by the goods against which it is exchanged and also by money itself.[3]

He also thinks money transforms (even reduces) relationships. According to him,

> Money is concerned only with what is common to all: it asks for the exchange value, it reduces all quality and individuality to the question: How much?[4]

Going through the works of the "German school" represented by Simmel, Marx, and Weber, one is likely to conclude, as has Viviana Zelizer, that the classical interpretation would function only in a thoroughgoing market economy. Zelizer provides the following succinct summary of the classical interpretation:

> i. The functions and characteristics of money are defined strictly in economic terms. [Money is assumed as] a qualityless, absolutely homogeneous, infinitely divisible, liquid object.
> ii. All monies are the same in modern society. Differences can exist in the quantity of money but not in its meaning. Thus, there is only one kind of money—market money.
> iii. A sharp dichotomy is established between money and nonpecuniary values.... Money is qualitatively neutral; personal, social and sacred values are qualitatively distinct, unexchangeable, and indivisible.
> iv. Monetary concerns are seen as constantly enlarging, quantifying, and often corrupting all areas of life. As an abstract medium of exchange, money has not only the freedom but also the power to draw an increasing number of goods and services into a web of the market. Money is thus the vehicle for an inevitable commodification of society.
> v. The power of money to transform nonpecuniary values is unquestioned, while the reciprocal transformation of money by values or social relations is seldom conceptualized or else explicitly rejected.[5]

Neoclassical theories, which include monetarism, general equilibrium theory, rational expectation theory, and neoclassical Keynesianism, all agree with many of the positions above but emphasize the function of money as a *numeraire*. That is, money is a yardstick "upon which to measure the relative prices (and therefore scarcities) of the various goods that are produced."[6] Keynes especially holds money as the means of contractual settlement and a store of value. As a store of value, money has the following two properties: "i) the elasticity of production is zero or negligible, and ii) the elasticity of substitution is zero or negligible."[7]

The present study benefits only to a small extent from these classical and neoclassical theories. For one thing, these theories emphasize the modern market economies and assume that present and future trends are statistically known or predictable. African economies in the past were not mathematically calculable, neither are they predictable now because of the paucity of statistical evidence and data. This study could only be qualitative rather than quantitative. For another thing, in this study we are interested in money as a *cultural* phenomenon. In other words, money for us in this study is not an abstraction or an objective reality. It is an economic and cultural product and, at the same time, it has transformative powers on the economy and the culture that have produced it. This is why we have chosen to derive our conceptual framework from researches in the economic history of West Africa, and situate our analysis in the general framework of economic history.

Whereas in Western societies economic research dominates the literature on currencies and monetary policies, in Africa until recently the field was virtually the monopoly of anthropologists. This arose partly from the fact that Western or Western-trained scholars have tended to regard African precolonial currencies as "primitive" and left the field to disciplines such as anthropology and ethnology, which study the so-called primitive cultures. Although some progress occurred in the study of African financial institutions, recent anthropological researches have not completely abandoned this notion that Africa's currencies were primitive. In her introduction to the volume on money and monetary policies in West and Equatorial Africa, Jane Guyer compares African currencies to those of Europe and the West. She states that Africa's monies have developed "in a continuous though shifting relationship" to the currencies of Europe. She also boldly states that these currencies "have never been 'primitive' in the absolute sense." Nevertheless, she admits that African currencies "have *always* been—by various dynamics—'primitive' or 'special purpose' relative to the capacities of their contemporary European counterparts."[8] "Primitive money," it should be understood, "consists of a range of recognized objects generally with no other use, whose relative *natural* scarcity ensures a stable money *stock*."[9] Seen this way, it is possible to agree with Jane Guyer that Yoruba (and, indeed, Africa's) precolonial currencies were "primitive." They were not primitive, however, if we go by Thomas Crump's further clarification that primitive money is found in societies "where there is no market in land or labor, where no goods are produced for exchange, and [where the uses of money] are generally non-commercial."[10] Indeed, as will be shown in this study, the contrary was the case in Yorubaland.

Despite this humble beginning, the literature on the development of African financial systems has been expanding. This growth arose initially from the effort to explain the "currency revolution" that resulted from colonialism.[11] More recently, however, the expansion in the literature owes to the complementary factors of the triumph of the capitalists system in the West and in many parts of Asia, and the collapse of the economies of several African countries. Economic historians are paying closer attention to issues of monetization, capitalization, credit, and finance. Under close scrutiny are matters of the coexistence, interaction, and transformation of informal and formal (or traditional and modern) financial institutions. Given the degree of indebtedness on the continent, scholars seem to suggest that the hope for Africa's development is in the complete transformation of its financial systems.

One area that has received attention in the literature is the resilience of preindustrial financial institutions in developing nations. Of note is the discussion on the ROSCAs. Anthropological interest in these associations began in the middle of this century when Bascom published his findings on the Yoruba.[12] Indeed *esusu*, the Yoruba name for these associations and the name used in Bascom's article, dominated the literature until Clifford Geertz coined the phrase "rotating credit association" in an article published in 1962.[13] Geertz was pessimistic about the future of ROSCAs. Considering them as the "middle rung" of the development process, Geertz believed that these associations would be replaced by modern credit institutions. This article was followed immediately by Shirley Ardener's comparative study published in 1964.[14] Ardener documents the existence of ROSCAs in many societies around the world. She disagrees with Geertz's view of the future of ROSCAs. She finds that instead of declining these associations were actually expanding in significance "in reaction to the insecurity of the banking system" and were disrupting the normal operation of the modern banks.[15]

These early studies fostered several others, and the field soon fascinated development economists who have attempted to evaluate the profitability of these associations' savings and lending practices.[16] Nevertheless, anthropologists have continued to work on ROSCAs, the most recent being the volume edited by Shirley Ardener and Sandra Burman.[17] Contributors to this volume present several case studies demonstrating the continued importance of ROSCAs to developmental and other issues affecting women in developing countries. Although the Yoruba experience was not included in this anthology, the volume makes significant contribution to the study of ROSCAs by demonstrating their economic and social significance for women. Our study here returns the Yoruba experience to the center stage and uses the historical approach to demonstrate the coexistence of the modern and precolonial financial institutions.

In her editor's introduction to *Money Matters*, to which we have once referred, Jane Guyer raises a number of issues that are also addressed in this book. She reiterates that "there are enough data to show that however poor African populations are...it is still impossible to be a social adult in most places without the capacity to mobilize sums of money that are quite substantial relative to people's income." She goes on to pose the following questions:

> Under unstable and, in recent years, declining circumstances how are the acceptable levels, compositions, priorities and frequencies of these social payments reworked? With what implications? And how do people build up assets against which claims can be made in case of substantial need?[18]

Yoruba society provides extremely fascinating cases that answer the above questions. Indeed, using the historical approach, this book addresses these and similar questions, evaluates the changing conception of money and monetary obligations, and demonstrates the dynamic character of social payments among the Yoruba.

Yorubaland

The Yoruba inhabit the area which Samuel Johnson, in a classic study, has delimited as lying

> to the immediate West of the River Niger (below the confluence) and South of the Quorra (i.e. the Western branch of the same River above the confluence), having Dahomey on the West and the Bight of Benin to the South. It is roughly speaking between latitude 6° and 9° North, and longitude 2° 30' and 6° 30' East.[19]

In more current political delimitation, Yorubaland could be said to be the area where the Yoruba language is spoken, or is the dominant language, that is Lagos, Ogun, Oyo, Osun, Ondo, Ekiti, and Kwara states of Nigeria, and the central regions of the French-speaking Republics of Benin and Togo.

The people are neither ethnically nor politically homogeneous. Rather, they had been, from time immemorial, organized into many states or kingdoms. The number is not clear: seven, sixteen, twenty-one, and twenty-six have been mentioned.[20] The origin of each of the states has also been the subject of much controversy. The debate is increasingly made complex by two fairly related issues: the existence of more than one account of the tradition of origin of each state,[21] and the contemporary search for legitimacy and seniority by the numerous fractions and factions of the ruling elite in each state.[22] What is not in dispute is the fact that the ruling houses/families in most of the states and kingdoms claim descent from Oduduwa and/or Ile-Ife. Moreover, each of the kingdoms was independent and autonomous in its internal affairs. In other words, each could be regarded as "state actors" in the Yoruba international political system. Each of them had well-defined boundaries recognized by others and respected as such. The states conducted relations bilaterally and multilaterally, and such relations were peaceful or conflictive, depending upon the circumstances.[23]

In essence, the Yoruba state system was highly decentralized. Each of the states had a monarchical system of government. Most of the monarchs could trace their origin, and the origin of their crown and other instruments of office, to Ile-Ife. Indeed, all Yoruba peoples look upon Ile-Ife as their *orirun*, place of origin. This fact conferred some position of significance on Ile-Ife, and the provision that the *orirun* must be kept sacrosanct ensured the survival of the ancient city, even though it remained relatively small and militarily weak. In spite of its extensive size and proven military strength, Oyo was not regarded by all as the power center of all Yoruba. The real issue is that the Yoruba, being decentralized politically and administratively, were neither a federation nor a confederation: each state was independent and guarded its autonomy jealously.

The Yoruba have been described as the most urbanized people in Africa.[24] This urban setting is relevant to the development of monetization and the financial institutions. The urban character of Yoruba society has fascinated scholars.[25] In discussing the origin of large cities, Ade Obayemi's concept of transition from mini to mega state system is still valid.[26] This concept relies heavily and appropriately on the assumption of predynastic and dynastic eras, coinciding with the pre- and post-Oduduwa periods of Ile-Ife history. It recognizes that before the ascendancy of Oduduwa and the creation of a dynasty, there were several mini states in the Ile-Ife area. According to oral tradition, the most notable of these states were Oke Ora under Oduduwa; Idena ruled by Oreluere; Itapa, and later Ideta Oko ruled by Obatala; Ita Yemoo under Yemoo, regarded in the traditions as wife of Obatala; and Igbo Olokun or Ebolokun ruled by Olokun, also regarded as wife of Oduduwa.

These settlements must have been very small, but Obayemi argues that in spite of their size they all had the knowledge of iron, and possessed a highly developed artistic culture. Moreover, the settlements often conflicted over the question of political and cultural ascendancy.

It has been suggested in Ife tradition that at one point (which, unfortunately, has not been dated with any degree of certainty) Obatala's settlement or its cultural system was predominant. Indeed, Obatala is recognized as the "chief priest" and "it is strongly implied that it was during his pre-eminence, or a period when the Obatala title was supreme, that the artistic masterpieces of Ile-Ife were produced."[27]

Urbanization in Ile-Ife evolved out of these mini states by a process of fusion or agglomeration. In a conflict situation such as obtained in the mini state system, the fusion could only have come about by the military or political success of one group over the others. Oduduwa fulfilled this condition when he moved from his Oke Ora settlement and engaged Obatala in a series of battles as recorded in Ife traditions, and was victorious. Oduduwa's name, understandably enough, has been linked with the revolutionary period in Ife (and Yoruba) history that produced a dynasty. It is also reasonable to link his name with the emergence of Ile-Ife as a city. With the Oduduwa phase, urban life began and professionalism developed. Several people have been remembered in Ife traditions either as companions of Oduduwa during the descent from *orun* (heaven), or as his children. They included such professionals as Orunmila or Agbonniregun, the scientist; Ogun, the expert in all forms of metallurgy; Aje, who stood for commerce or wealth; and Elesije, the physician.[28] In other words, several aspects of the economic transformation of Yorubaland began in this early phase of Ife history.

Because Ile-Ife was probably the first urban community in all of Yorubaland, and because the founders of the ruling dynasties in the other kingdoms were said to have migrated from Ile-Ife at different times, the city of Ile-Ife became the archetype of Yoruba cities both in structure and in design. A. L. Mabogunje has described the broad plan and layout of Yoruba cities.[29] First, the cities had walls. These walls were so extensive that they enclosed the dwelling places and nearby farms. The advantage of this was felt during the period of external attacks when the inhabitants of the cities had to rely on food produced on the farms located within the city walls. Archaeological excavations in Ile-Ife and Old Oyo reveal the structure of these walls. According to Bassey Es'Andah, the walls and materials in which they were built in both cities were found to be similar, with the exception that at Old Oyo the city was defended by a system of walls "comprising three more or less concentric walls, and a concentric arc of wall within a large northern loop."[30] The construction of the walls was dated to a period between 960 and 1160 A.D. They were thickly built, and renovated annually.

Gates were provided for entry and exit. Usually, there were four gates located at the four cardinal points. In Oyo, archaeologists have found the outlines of six principal walls, and have recognized gates "to the north-east, north-north-east, north-west, and west-south-west—and leading in the directions respectively of Jebba, Bussa, Kishi/Kaiama/Nikki and Igboho."[31] Each gate was manned by a detachment of the kingdom's military force under a commander or "gate-keeper" (*Onibode*). His roles often went beyond those of security: he was also in charge of the collection of duties and tolls on trade goods and caravans. The gate-keeper was, therefore, an important office to which were appointed brave, trusted, and loyal men. More is said about the role of these gates for toll collection in chapter 5.

All major institutions were located in the center of the city. These were the ruler's palace or administrative headquarters of the kingdom, the market, and the religious buildings (shrines and/or mosques). These three institutions were considered crucial to the prosperity of the city, and in Yoruba traditional concept of warfare conquest was incomplete until they (the palace, market, and shrines) had been sacked. As a result, the three were sited close to each other to enjoy the advantage of joint protection. Other members of the ruling class—that is the princes, princesses, and hereditary chiefs—took up residence around this city center. This was considered necessary because transportation was mostly on foot and these chiefs and noble men had to be in the palace daily. At the outermost ring, separated from the city wall by the encased farmlands, is the residence of the rest of the population. Reviewing this interesting layout, Mabogunje has concluded correctly that "it was the poor who were made to do most of the long trekking within the pre-industrial cities."[32] In addition, it was the poor who bore the brunt of occasional raids to secure captives for slave trading, as such raids could be successfully made without actually sacking the city.

Yoruba cities were composed of compounds and quarters. A compound was the residential unit of an extended family—the abode of at least three generations of several adult heads of a household, their wives, children, and slaves. This compound had a recognized head (the *bale*), a courtyard where children could assemble for moonlight stories and games and adults could hold important meetings, and a shrine for the ancestors. A group of compounds made up a quarter, with a quarter head (or chief) that presided over cases such as theft, adultery, and debt. Some compounds were known for the occupation of the majority of their members such as weaving, metal works, leather works, dyeing, sculpting, and entertaining. In most cases, the compounds concerned preserved the secret of the occupation in cultic rituals. The financial impact of this occupational specialization is addressed in chapter 4.

The above was the general structure of Yoruba cities, but there were local variations. For many years, Ile-Ife was preserved through the *orirun*[33] concept, which forbade the attack on Ife by any of the Yoruba kingdoms. With time, princes and princesses, chiefs and commoners of Ile-Ife grew accustomed to city (urban) life. It is not surprising, therefore, that the princes who later left Ile-Ife to found new settlements proceeded consciously to build urban centers. It can also be safely assumed that in many instances where a particular founder was mentioned in the traditions, he had a large following capable of seizing power in a small community and transforming it into a city.[34] In retrospect, too, it would seem that the possession of a "crown of Oduduwa" by a migrant group presupposed the acquisition of the cultural, military, and political powers necessary for guaranteeing of security for the new settlement and its inhabitants.

Another important factor that aided the emergence of urban centers in Yorubaland was geographical location. Most probably owing to the knowledge of iron, Yoruba cities were founded in the forest as well as in the savanna regions. Possibly because it was easier to build city-states in the more open grassland than in the rain forest, many powerful Yoruba developed in the guinea savanna: Oyo, Ketu, Sabe, Idaisa, Iresa, Ibadan, Ikoyi, and Ilorin among others. If the evidence in the traditions of the kingdoms located in the forest zone is anything to go by, the people faced greater hardship such as forest clearing, menace of large animals and reptiles, outbreak of environment-related epidemics, and flood. Nevertheless, prominent Yoruba cities like Ile-Ife, Owu, Iwo, Ijebu-Ode, Ilesa, the sixteen Ekiti kingdoms, Ondo, Ede, and Osogbo developed in the rain forest region.

The foregoing would explain urbanization before the large-scale disturbances and military revolutions of the nineteenth century. Owing partly to the political and constitutional troubles in Old Oyo,[35] and in part to the *jihad* in Ilorin,[36] many Yoruba cities in the savanna, including Oyo, were deserted. These refugee populations pressed to the south partly to swell the existing cities, and partly to found new settlements, but not to live in villages. Nevertheless, the new urban centers of the nineteenth century used a different set of rules. In some areas, the main measure of power was no longer the crown but militarism. Biodun Adediran has shown that in the latter part of the century Yoruba *obas* had lost their clout, and the power base had shifted to the military class.[37]

Thus, with the exception of new Oyo transformed from *Ago* Oja (that is, Oja village) to a new metropolis because of the presence of Prince Atiba who later became the *Alaafin*, all the major cities that emerged in the nineteenth century (Ijaye, Ibadan, Abeokuta) were primarily military camps. In these new cities the success of the rulers rested more on the possession of ammunitions than on any mythical Oduduwa crown. Indeed, some of the preexisting crown heads were relegated (the fate of the *Oluwo* of Iwo) or had their settlement utterly destroyed (the fate of the *Olowu* of Owu).[38]

The point to note is that at the beginning of colonial rule Yorubaland had two types of urban centers. Most were ruled by kings; others were ruled by brave men and women who derived power from their military or commercial prowess. Despite this fundamental difference, political organization in Yoruba cities was not markedly different. Taking the common denominator, it would seem that sovereign authority in most cities (especially in those that were also the headquarters of the kingdom or state) resided with the *oba*, the *de facto* and *de jure* ruler, with power of life and death over the residents. The *oba* was also the *alase ekeji orisa,* the most powerful, second only to the gods. His authority was exercised directly or through a number of military and civilian chiefs who could not be kings. Even in Ibadan, the most radical of the new states, the ruler could only be promoted to *Bale*, a status lower than king. The *oba* was also aided by other institutions such as the age grades, secret societies, cults, and rituals. He had power over the city, the provinces, and the outlying villages.

So much space has been devoted to the examination of the origin and development of urban centers here because the discussion in this book will focus on urban populations of Yorubaland. Although the economy was intricately linked to the rural sector, particularly agriculture and food production and processing, public finance was an urban phenomenon. Money, credit, and banking were urban based. The town and village were integrated but, as S. Goddard has correctly pointed out, "the Yoruba living in the country traditionally looks upon the town as his real home and owes direct social allegiance to it."[39] Moreover, trade, commerce, and market centers were concentrated in the cities where members of the dominant class (princes and princesses, chiefs, traders, warriors, professionals, etc.) also resided.

Two main features of relations that have not been adequately emphasized in the literature on Yoruba political economy are the importance of the location of the various states and the degree of their economic interdependence. As we have shown earlier in this introduction, the geographical expanse of Yorubaland stretched from the guinea forest in the south to the savanna in the north. This conferred many economic advantages. The entire Yorubaland constituted an integrated economic area, and the various states and kingdoms regarded as politically independent were actually economically dependent on each other. Agriculture and the fertile soil supplied a large majority of the food needs of its population and external trade supplied the balance. The food crops cultivated included root crops (the different varieties of yam, cocoyam, and cassava), grains (such as maize, guinea corn, and beans), tree crops, and vegetable oil. Oyo, the most northerly state, engaged in commercial relations with its neighbors to the north, participated in the caravan trade, and had a cavalry. It also engaged in successful trade and/or commercial imperialism with its southern neighbors including the Egba and the Egbado. The states of the forest zone to the south—Ijebu, Ife, Owu, Ijesa, and the rest—also benefited from the trade relations with the Oyo, which brought essential and luxury articles such as a different variety of salt and natron. So beneficial was this trade that a major market center developed in the hinterland at Apomu where Oyo, Egba, Owu, Ife, and Ijebu traders met to exchange articles. We know, too, that the unequal access to these economic advantages, along with political forces, produced rivalries, and conflicts. The emergence of Oyo into imperial status could not have been accomplished without challenge by the other states. There is no doubt, too, that during the apogee of Oyo's imperial power the hinterland market of Apomu[40] was controlled by Oyo traders. The monetization of the economy contributed significantly to the development of these commercial interactions.

All these were before the advent of the Europeans along the Atlantic coast from the sixteenth century onward. Once trade relations were established with the Europeans virtually everything changed. For one thing, the Yoruba states closest to the coast—particularly Ijebu—derived the greatest benefit from the contact with the new traders and adventurers. Oyo tradition preserves several stereotypes to show contempt for the Ijebu, but one which would seem to have survived well into the modern times, and which demonstrates that the stereotypes were based more on economic than subethnic rivalry, is the view that the Ijebu were shrewd businessmen and women.[41] The coming of the Atlantic trade also affected the direction of Oyo expansion and trade. More specifically, it brought Oyo into commercial rivalry with the Egba directly to the south, the Ijebu to the south-east, and the Dahomey to the west. Whereas the empire was able to overcome the competition with Dahomey and open its own port for trade with the Europeans, the Ijebu and other groups controlled the trade of the entire southeast.

The Oyo were not the only group of traders that felt the impact of Ijebu trade networks and monopoly of trade with the Europeans. The Owu also did. It was probably this trade rivalry that was played out violently at the Apomu market earlier in the nineteenth century over alligator pepper, a sad event that precipitated the Owu War.[42] Ijebu trade monopolies also hurt the Europeans later in the late nineteenth century, leading eventually to British invasion in 1892 to clear the trade route through Ijebu country.[43]

What did the Ijebu traders control that made them the envy of other traders? The answer seems to be the cowries that the Ijebu traders were receiving in large quantities from the Europeans (directly or through Lagos) in exchange for legitimate items and slaves. The surviving evidence reviewed by Robert Smith and Robin Law shows that two Portuguese ships went to Ijebu country as early as 1553, and that some Portuguese traders actually lived in Ijebu-Ode.[44] These traders imported European manufactures and cowry shells in exchange for slaves and Ijebu cloth. The transition from barter and the adoption of cowry shells as currency are subjects examined in chapter 2 of this study. In the next section, however, we examine the major components of the economy of Yorubaland.

Yoruba Economy

In this section, we intend to provide a synopsis of Yoruba economy from the precolonial to the modern, and show some transitions in the currency system from cowries to coins and paper money. We only identify those aspects that relate to the understanding of our central themes regarding money in the chapters that follow.[45] Yoruba economy has always been changing and dynamic, reaching perhaps its most prosperous phase in the mid-twentieth century when it was able to sustain an expanding elite and one of the fastest modernizing regions in Nigeria. Yoruba urbanism contributed to large markets within cities, in addition to the production of various forms of leisure activities. Farming, craft specialization, and commerce were the three essential components of the economy. The use of money was important to this economy, notably to facilitate commercial transactions and distribute access to important privileges.

Agriculture has always been a principal occupation. For hundreds of years it absorbed a large number of people, and it made it possible to create, accumulate, and appropriate wealth. Agricultural implements were cheap and locally manufactured. At its core was farming, supplemented with food production, gathering, collecting, livestock keeping, hunting, and fishing. Yoruba agriculture and other economic activities owed much to, and depended on, the availability and the effective organization of human and land resources. The Yoruba met their labor demands through the lineage or family units (*ebi* or *idile*). The family included everyone who could be ascertained to be related by blood, the dead ancestors, and the unborn children. Many activities, be they economic, political, or spiritual, were performed within this *ebi* or *idile* circuit. Every *ebi* had its rules and regulations. Members of the same *ebi* were resident in a single compound (*agbo ile*) and might also have had a recognized head called the *baale* or *olori ebi*. The *baale* was usually the oldest male member of the *ebi*. He had authority over all members of the family and his functions included seeing to the economic livelihood of members and preserving the harmony and continuity of the family.

It was within this established family system that the Yoruba did their agricultural and other economic works. It is true that families experienced fissions and fusions at different times, but the organization of labor was the same for many years. The *ebi* was always able to divide itself into smaller, more manageable production units without experiencing devastating consequences. Thus, the *ebi* had various household units within it. The household comprised the man, his wife or wives, and their children, relatives, and dependants. The man organized and coordinated the labor of these people. They worked not for wages but were fed and clothed by the household head. It was partly because every household did its economic work that the Yoruba placed a value on large families. A man who wanted to be prosperous had to have many wives and children or, as an alternative, money to acquire pawns and slaves.

Ways had to be devised to expand the labor force to meet the demands of expanding production and market. The *iwofa* system (usually translated as "pawnship") was one of such ways. In this system, a borrower surrendered a young person called the *iwofa* to work for the creditor until the debt was repaid. This enabled wealthy citizens to use their money to recruit labor. The creditors were, however, prevented by customs, laws, and regulations from maltreating their *iwofa* or subjecting them to intense exploitation. In addition, two main cooperative work groups enabled access to labor, especially by the underprivileged. The first was the *aaro,* which involved the rotation of labor by members of the same family, age group, and friends. This was a sort of working club where members rotated their services to work for one another in turn. People of comparable age and physical ability usually belonged to the same group. Cheating and laziness were frowned upon; those who exhibited these lapses were repaid by other members in their own coin. *Aaro* was practiced mainly by farmers who needed extra hands for clearing and hoeing between September and March and weeding between April and June. The second was the *owe*. Like the *aaro*, kinsmen and friends worked together for one person. Unlike the *aaro*, the labor was not rotational though it could be reciprocated at any other time. The *owe* involved more hands than the *aaro*, the number of participants depending on the type of work to be done and the social connections of the person who raised the *owe*. Participants were lavishly entertained with food and drinks as an expression of gratitude and not in lieu of monetary payments for their services. By being able to provide labor without paying for it, cooperative work group reduced the use of money in raising labor.

Where money and power became important was in the recruitment of slaves, which provided the opportunity to exploit labor more than other means. The wars of the nineteenth century produced thousands of slaves, who were used to expand private armies and productive enterprises. Wealthy merchants were also able to buy slaves to expand their economic activities and consolidate their political status.

The family also had another major economic function that reduced the demands for money: it allocated lands to its members. Land was regarded as the inalienable property of the community, held in trust by the political head who was supposed to act as the defender of the people's interest. Every family had a right to own land. This claim to land had a history behind it, some even claiming that they had been in possession of land long enough for anyone to remember the beginning. Professor A. Ojo has given some tentative reasons why the idea of lineage ownership developed.[46] According to him, to surmount the problem of clearing and cultivating primeval forest, a group of people had to work in common and in effect, "family ownership became complementary to the family approach to work." Secondly, it was imperative for members of the same family to flock and work together to present a common force against their enemies. In addition, the dangers of land hunger and natural disasters could best be solved if many people held land in common. Lastly, land had no exchange value "which could have stimulated a more individualized form of land holding."

The right of the individual to land was recognized within each family. This right was derived from being a member of a lineage, and a person belonged to the community by virtue of being born there or being absorbed by a lineage. The individual could use the land for any economic purposes and the right to do this continued as long as he was able to make use of the land. The individual was, however, prohibited from alienating the land.

Yoruba societies welcomed strangers. Those among them who needed land were given it without having to buy it. But such strangers had to associate themselves with some lineages: "the unattached stranger was an anomaly," concluded P. C. Lloyd.[47] He added that "a grant of land to a stranger suggests that he is planning to settle permanently in the community."[48] A few rules accompanied the grant of land to a stranger, as if to by-pass the use of money. He must be of good behavior and must be willing to accept the laws of society and those of the family that gave out the land. As an acknowledgement of gratitude, the stranger was expected to make an annual gift of a small portion of his harvests, and was forbidden from alienating the land.

Manufacturing developed as a branch of the economy, to produce a wide variety of objects for domestic use and aesthetics. Some industries depended on plants, some on animal products, and some on minerals found within a particular locality. Technical skills were high, and products reached both local and distant markets. Craft specialization encouraged the expansion of market and monetization, because products had to be sold and also because craft workers, by ignoring farming, had to purchase food. We agree with Professor William Bascom when he draws the connection between manufacturing and other occupations among the Yoruba:

> Craft specialization makes each individual economically dependent upon the society as a whole. The carver depends upon the blacksmith for tools, and upon the farmer, the hunter, and the trader for food. The blacksmith depends upon others for food, and upon weaver for clothing. The farmer depends on the smith for his hoe, machete, and axe, and on the weaver for his clothing. The weaver depends on the farmer for his food, and on the farmer, the spinner, and the dyer for his cotton thread. Each of these, moreover, must rely upon the herbalist, the priest, the potter, the drummer, the chief, and other specialists for goods and services which they can not provide for themselves.... Craft specialization also meant the development of internal trade and town markets for the exchange of local produce.[49]

This interconnection made the use of money almost inevitable.

Trade has always been integral to the Yoruba economy. Institutions of exchange—markets, trade routes, currencies, and the like—were all available. Most transactions took place in the market place where traders, mainly women, and buyers met physically to conduct business. The currency was the cowry, which performed most of the functions of a general-purpose money. It served as en effective measure of value and a unit of account, which made it convenient to know the value of each good in relation to another and to fix prices to all kinds of products. It also made a deferred payment possible; a person could buy on credit or borrow and use the cowry to pay later. Among other advantages which the cowry had were that it could not be forged and its small size made it very easy to carry. The cowry also made exchange possible over a wide territory. It was used throughout Yorubaland and many other places in Africa.

The price at which a commodity was bought in Yoruba markets was usually determined by haggling. The trader would tell the buyer the highest price possible and would stress the quality of the good, the efforts deployed to get it, and the losses which had been encountered. The trader would often maintain the air of cheerfulness throughout the bargaining process, constantly indicating that the price was specially for this particular buyer who happened to be a "regular customer," and should not be disclosed to competitors and other buyers. The buyer, on the other hand, would scale the price down and down, and at the same time decry the merchandise as poor in quality. The trader kept the cost price and anticipated profit in mind, giving the buyer very little information to use in arriving at what might be considered a fair price. To get a deal, the buyer must be very skilful at haggling and bargaining.

Trading activities were not localized. Intergroup trade linked Yoruba cities and their neighbors. Ecological differences accounted for varieties of articles available in each area and promoted the need for trade. Scattered markets were connected by roads, and traders traveled in caravans to reach them. Along the way, the traders paid tolls to political authorities.

As with other African societies, the Yoruba were affected by their incorporation into the global economy. The Yoruba participated in the Atlantic slave trade, supplying non-Yoruba slaves and subsequently members of their own ethnicity. Lagos became a principal slave port. The slave trade altered economic and social relations, introduced more imported items, and turned slaves into sources of money and wealth. Abolition of the slave trade came during the nineteenth century, but the same period witnessed an increasing use of domestic slaves, and expanding British interest in so-called legitimate trade. Using the suppression of the slave trade as a pretext, the British established control on Lagos in the early 1850s and turned it into a colony in 1861. The British subsequently established control on the Yoruba, making them part of modern Nigeria.

For the greater part of the nineteenth century, the Yoruba supplied palm oil and palm kernels to the international market. The palm oil industry was labor intensive. Those who profited from it used slaves in large numbers, not just to produce but also to transport the oil to the coastal market in Lagos. In the 1890s, cotton and rubber were added. Wealthy merchants emerged in such towns as Lagos, Abeokuta, Ijebu-Ode, and Ibadan. The wars of the period also produced successful warriors who grew rich and famous. Merchants and warriors spent large sums of money on large houses, food, clothes, imported items, and lavish entertainments. The poems about individuals composed during the period emphasized money, prestige, fame, and grandeur.

In the last years of the nineteenth century, cocoa was introduced, and it remained the principal cash crop in the forest region for most of the twentieth century. Cocoa brought money to many farmers, thereby improving their life styles. Many were to invest some of this money in the education of their children. Hundreds of new stores emerged, to sell imported items; new houses with corrugated iron sheets were built; and the consumption of beef—for years the preserve of the rich—became more common. Cocoa also encouraged the use of wage labor, as there was money to pay them. This further monetized the economy, especially in many rural areas. If money was a principal commodity for credit, the cocoa tree served a similar purpose: it could be pawned for goods or loans and the creditor could harvest the crops for years to come until the principal was paid. To prosperous cocoa farmers, there was no need for them to devote much time to food production. As they purchased foods in the market, they further monetized and enabled farmers in areas where cocoa did not grow well to benefit by selling yam, cassava, and other food items. Yoruba land tenure system was transformed. The need for more and more farmlands increasingly led to land commercialization and conflicts. Prosperity from cocoa made the Yoruba a highly developed region by Nigerian standard.

The British introduced coins and pound sterling which eventually replaced cowries. The history of this currency transition has been narrated in some details.[50] The currency situation was at first chaotic. In

Lagos, different currencies circulated: cowries from Mozambique and Maldive; French twenty-franc pieces, gold dust, and nuggets; Spanish and South American gold doubloons and half doubloons; Mexican, Peruvian, Chilean, and Brazilian dollars; British gold, silver, and copper coins. These were currencies brought by different commercial houses. Some were not successful among the Yoruba—for example American Eagle coins, French twenty-franc coins, Spanish and South American gold doubloons—partly because their denominations were too high in value, but they were nevertheless legal tender among European traders. On the other hand, Maria Theresa dollar was accepted.[51] None of these foreign currencies was as popular as the cowry, and their relevance was localized to Lagos where they were used to pay duties to the government. Even then, there were problems—the government had to deal with many cases of counterfeiting and incurred losses in converting these currencies in Europe. In the 1870s, British officials began to talk of demonetization and allowed holders of different currencies to redeem them for British currency.[52]

On May 21, 1880 the British demonetized the Maria Theresa dollars. A notice published on May 11 gave a rather short notice and sounded drastic:

> The public are hereby informed, that in accordance with the provisions of ordinance No. 2 of 1880, which has received the assent of the Governor-in-Council, the only silver coins which will be accepted as legal tender on and after the 21st instance, being ten clear days from the date of this notice, will be British silver coins which will be accepted as legal tender, and in payment of duties, etc.[53]

This was greeted with protest, as many in Lagos complained that ten days were not enough to change their old currencies. However, sanity was introduced into the currency situation. In the years that followed, the British currency system gradually gained a wider acceptability.

As to be expected, new currencies were originally resisted by the Yoruba, due to familiarity with cowries, the problems of conversion, the preference of European commercial firms for barter trade, which enabled greater profit and opportunity to advance credit. The real problem was that the cowry made small purchases possible, in a society where the cost of living was very low. For five cowries, the equivalent of one-twenty-fifth of the British penny, a person could meet for a day most of his basic requirements in essential food items. The British bronze and silver coins were considered too large denominations to make small purchases. Many in fact either hoarded the British coins or converted them into ornaments.

However, the British insisted on the currencies whose supply they could control and took concrete steps to demonetize the cowry. In certain situations it was necessary for officials to persuade the people to change, pointing out that large cowries were cumbersome to carry. New currencies were used to pay people, thereby popularizing its use, at a time when the value of the cowry was undergoing depreciation. For many years, the British allowed the conversion of cowries to the new currencies. After 1899, the supply of cowries began to diminish, creating some problems of access. In 1904, legislation was passed to abolish the cowry currency, although it remained in circulation for many years after. New cowry import was abolished by law while the government could also restrict and prohibit its circulation. Its rate of depreciation became faster afterward, thereby promoting the use of new currencies. In 1906, the government decided to mint coins of small denominations, and one-tenth of a penny was created to meet the demands for small purchases. This was replaced in the 1940s with 1/4d of a penny, the *onini*, to cope with inflation. In general, the inflation of the colonial era undermined the use of cowries, more difficult to carry in large quantities than British coins and pounds. Lebanese and European retail stores were opened in different Yoruba cities, and they only accepted British currencies, thus again restricting the circulation of the cowry. Paper currency, introduced during the First World War in denominations of £1, 10/- and 1/- enabled bigger purchases. The successful introduction of British coins and paper money made possible the establishment of modern banking, which began with the opening of the Bank of British West Africa in 1894. Additional new banks were opened during the colonial period. The European banks dominated the banking industry, although indigenous ones began to be created after 1929.[54]

Thanks to wage labor, the new currencies were available to more people. As people received their pay in lump sum either at the end of the week or month, the acquisition of money was faster and more regular. People had more to spend, and the elite could readily imitate Westerners in habits of dress, music, food, and customs. There were negative consequences, as lamented by one contemporary who listed the "new evils" of the age: "embezzlement, forgery, counterfeiting, low standards of sexual morality, low standards of business and commercial ethics, bribery in official positions and tyranny of petty officials."[55] Many of these were, no doubt, associated with the craze for money.

There were other profound changes during the colonial period. Islam and Christianity spread. Western education became popular, leading to the establishment of the first university at Ibadan in 1948. The reliance on children and wives as household labor reduced as children went to school and wage employment became available. While the lineage was still important, those with reliable wage incomes became individualistic, spending their money on themselves and desire. A rich individual also ensured that his inheritance passed to his children, rather than to the large extended family.

Modern industries emerged after 1945 to manufacture cement, shoes, textiles, and such. Modern means of communication were introduced and, in 1959, the first television station was established.[56] Other changes followed after Nigeria's independence in 1960: millions of people became wage earners, hundreds of new schools were opened, the economy modernized, and rivalry for power, fueled by the desire for personal enrichment, intensified.

Since independence, the Yoruba have witnessed a decline in agriculture and other sectors.[57] Nigeria rapidly began to rely on oil revenues. In the 1970s, there was a boom, and much money was pumped into the economy. This boom did not last and contemporary history has been characterized by economic crises. Instability in politics continues to affect economic performance but at the same time promoting greed and corruption by those who have access to power. Either to cope with inflation or meet the excessive requirements of materialism, the Yoruba continue to glorify and exaggerate the importance of money. In chapter 3 we analyze the ideals of money that have endured for a long time among the Yoruba.

Notes

1. Ross M. Robertson, "Money," in Julius Gould and William L. Kolb, eds., *A Dictionary of the Social Sciences* (New York: The Free Press, 1964), p. 437.
2. James Tobin, "Money," *The New Pelgrave Dictionary of Money and Finance* (London: The MacMillan Press, 1992), vol. 2, p. 770.
3. Georg Simmel, *The Philosophy of Money,* translated by Tom Bottomore and David Frisby (London: Routledge, 1990 [1900]), pp. 120–25.
4. Georg Simmel, *The Sociology of Georg Simmel,* translated by Kurt H. Wolff (London: The Free Press of Glencoe, 1950), p. 411.
5. Viviana Zelizer, "Money," *Encyclopedia of Sociology* (New York: Macmillan, 1992), vol. 3, p. 1305.
6. Paul Davidson, "Money," in Adam Kuper and Jessica Kuper, *The Social Science Encyclopedia* (London: Routledge & Kegan Paul, 1985), p. 536.
7. J. M. Keynes, *The General Theory of Employment, Interest and Money* (London: 1936), cited in Paul Davidson, "Money," p. 536.
8. Jane I. Guyer, "Introduction: The Currency Interface and Its Dynamics," in Jane I. Guyer, ed., *Money Matters: Instability, Values and Social Payments in the*

Modern History of West African Communities (Portsmouth, NH: Heinemann, 1995), p. 2.

9. Thomas Crump, "Money, Primitive," in Adam Kuper and Jessica Kuper, *The Social Science Encyclopedia*, p. 537.
10. *Ibid.*
11. We agree with Jane Guyer that the concept of "currency revolution" has limited applicability because the modern did not completely supplant the traditional, and because "[a]dvances in knowledge about African pre-colonial currency systems suggest that they had more modern 'purposes' and characteristics than was thought in the past." See *ibid*, p. 1. See also Jane I. Guyer, "Wealth in People, Wealth in Things—Introduction," *Journal of African History*, 36, 1995, pp. 83–90.
12. W. R. Bascom, "The Esusu: A Credit Institution of the Yoruba," *Journal of the Royal Anthropological Institute*, vol. lxxxii, no. 1.
13. Clifford Geertz, "The Rotating Credit Association: A 'Middle–Rung' in Development," *Economic Development and Cultural Change*, vol. 1, no. 3.
14. Shirley Ardener, "The Comparative Study of Rotating Credit Associations," *Man*, vol. 94, no. 2.
15. Shirley Ardener and Sandra Burman, eds., *Money-Go-Round: The Importance of Rotating Savings and Credit Associations for Women* (Oxford: BERG, 1996), p. 2.
16. See, among others, T. Besley, S. Coates, and G. Loury, *The Economics of Rotating Savings and Credit Associations* (Harvard: J.F.K. School of Government).
17. Shirley Ardener and Sandra Burman, eds., *Money-Go-Round*, p. 2.
18. Jane I. Guyer, ed., *Money Matters*, p. 24.
19. The Reverend Samuel Johnson, *The History of the Yorubas* (Lagos: C.M.S. Bookshops, 1921, reprinted 1976), p. xix.
20. Biodun Adediran lists the following as the major states: Yagba, Ekiti, Igbomina, Ijesa, Ife, and Ondo in the east; the Oyo, Egba, Owu, Egbado, and Ijebu in the center; and the Sabe, Ketu, Anago, Idaisa, Manigri, Isa, and Ana in the west. See his "Yoruba Ethnic Groups or a Yoruba Ethnic Group?," *History Department Seminar Series*, University of Ife, 1978/79.
21. Samuel Johnson records the two traditions of the origin of Ile-Ife, one claiming migration from the east, the other claiming creation or descent from heaven. See *Ibid*, pp. 3–4; 143.
22. The rivalry between the present *Alaafin* of Oyo and *Oni* of Ife has been so great in the recent past that the history of Yorubaland has received the most fervent reinterpretation, and the issue is seen to have led to the creation of the Osun State out of Oyo State to eliminate the friction between the two *obas*.
23. Much of what follows is taken from Richard Olaniyan and A. G. Adebayo, "Yoruba Intergroup Relations and Diplomacy," in G. O. Ogunremi and A. A. Adediran (eds.), *Yoruba History and Culture*: *Essays in Honor of I. A. Akinjogbin* (Lagos: John West, forthcoming). For more details, see Richard Olaniyan, "Elements of Yoruba Traditional Diplomacy: An Assessment," in Wande Abimbola (ed.), *Yoruba Oral Traditions*: *Poetry in Music, Dance and Drama*. Ile-Ife: Department of African Languages and Literature, 1975, pp. 293–332; and A. G. Adebayo and Toyin Falola, "Intergroup Relations in Nigeria," in Toyin Falola and Biodun Adediran (eds.), *Nigeria: Peoples, States and Cultures before 1800* (Lagos: John West, 1986), pp. 177–93.
24. S. Goddard, "Town-Farm Relationships in Yorubaland: A Case Study from Oyo," *Africa*, xxxv, 1, 1965, pp. 21–29, at p. 21. Other studies of Yoruba towns include W. R. Bascom, "Urbanisation among the Yoruba," *The American Journal of Sociology*, lx, 5, 1955, pp. 446–54; A. L. Mabogunje, *The Yoruba Town* (Ibadan:

Ibadan University Press, 1962); N. C. Mitchel, "Yoruba Towns," in K. M. Barbour and R. M. Prothero (eds.), *Essays on African Population* (London: Routledge & Paul, 1961), pp. 279–301.

25. A. G. Adebayo and M. M. Fasheke, "Social Transformation, Colonial Government Intervention and the Rise of the Urban Crisis," in Sola Akinrinade (ed.), *Nigeria: The Urban Crisis* (Lagos: Jad, forthcoming).
26. Ade Obayemi, "The Yoruba and Edo-speaking Peoples and their Neighbours before 1600," in J.F. Ade Ajayi and Michael Crowder (eds.) *History of West Africa* (London: Longman, 1971), second edition 1976, pp.209–15.
27. *Ibid*, p. 211.
28. *Ibid*, pp. 213–34.
29. A. L. Mabogunje, *Cities and African Development* (Ibadan: OUP, 1976), is used in this study.
30. Bassey W. Es'Andah, "An Archaeological View of the Urbanization Process in the Earliest West African States," *Journal of the Historical Society of Nigeria* (*JHSN*), VIII, 1975, p. 9.
31. *Ibid.*
32. *Ibid*, p. 10.
33. Meaning "the source" or "the original source."
34. This has been shown to be the case in a study of Iwo, a kingdom founded by Parin in the sixteenth century. See A. G. Adebayo, "Origin and Development of Iwo," *The African Historian*, x, 1983, pp. 27–45.
35. This is a well-trodden field of study. For the interesting debate that has developed on many issues on the fall of Oyo empire, see I. A. Akinjogbin, "The Prelude to the Yoruba Civil Wars," *Odu: A Journal of West African Studies*, I, 2, 1965; J. F. Ade Ajayi, "The Aftermath of the Fall of Old Oyo," in J. F. Ade Ajayi and Michael Crowder (eds.), *History of West Africa*; R. C. C. Law, *The Oyo Empire, ca. 1600–1836: A West African Imperialism in the Era of the Slave Trade* (Oxford: Clarendon, 1977).
36. The jihads in the south have also been studied. For details, see Peter Morton-Williams, "The Fulani Penetration into Nupe and Yoruba in the 19th century," in I. M. Lewis (ed.), *History and Social Anthropology* (London, 1968), pp. 1–24.
37. Biodun Adediran, "The 19th century Wars and Yoruba Royalty," in I. A. Akinjogbin *et al.* (eds.), *War and Peace in Yorubaland, 1793–1893* (Ibadan: Heinemann, forthcoming).
38. On Owu, see A. L. Mabogunje and J. D. Omer Cooper, *Owu in Yoruba History* (Ibadan: Ibadan University Press, 1971).
39. S. Goddard, "Town-Farm Relatinships," p. 21.
40. For information on the establishment of the Apomu market, see R. C. C. Law, "The Owu War in Yoruba History," *JHSN*, VII, 1974, pp. 144–47.
41. The derogatory views have been preserved in Samuel Johnson, *The History*, pp. 18–20. However, E. O. Akeredolu-Ale has evaluated the view that the Ijebu "are rather stingy and meanly averse to spending money" and other stereotypes. See his "A Sociohistorical Study of the Development of Entrepreneurship among the Ijebu of Western Nigeria," *African Studies Review*, xvi, 3, 347–64.
42. There are many causes of this war. The most oft remembered was the dispute between the Owu and the Ijebu at the Apomu market over the sale of alligator pepper. Several Ijebu traders were said to have lost their lives and wares during this violent dispute, whereupon the Ijebu and the Ife, in alliance with the Egba and Oyo refugees, sacked Owu completely. For more information, see A. L. Mabogunje and J. D. Omer Cooper, *Owu in Yoruba History*; R.C.C. Law, "The Owu War in Yoruba History," pp. 141–47; Samuel Johnson, *The History*, pp. 206–10.

43. For more details on relations between the Ijebu and their neighbors in the nineteenth century, see O. O. Ayantuga, "Ijebu and its Neighbours, 1851–1914," Ph.D. thesis, University of London, 1965.
44. Robin Law, "Early European Sources Relating to the Kingdom of the Ijebu (1500–1700): A Critical Survey," *History in Africa*, 13, 1986, pp. 246–47; Robert Smith, *Kingdoms of the Yoruba* (Madison, University of Wisconsin Press), third edition, 1988, p. 63.
45. For recent studies, among others, see Ann O'Hear, *Power Relations in Nigeria: Ilorin Slaves and their Successors* (Rochester, NY: Rochester University Press, 1997); and Toyin Falola and Ann O'Hear, eds., *The Economic History of Nigeria During the 19th Century* (Madison: Program of African Studies, forthcoming).
46. G. J. A. Ojo, *Yoruba Culture: A Geographical Analysis* (London: Univeristy of London Press, 1966), pp. 57–58.
47. P. C. Lloyd, *Yoruba Land Law* (London: Oxford University Press, 1962).
48. *Ibid*., p. 64.
49. William Bascom, *The Yoruba of Southwestern Nigeria.* (Prospect Heights: Waveland, 1984); first edition, 1969, pp. 24–25.
50. Among others, see W. Ibeke Ofonogaro, *Trade and Imperialism in southern Nigeria 1881–1929* (New York: Nok Publishers, 1979); G. I. Jones, "Native and Trade Currencies in Southern Nigeria during the 18th and 19th Centuries," *Africa*, vol. 1, 1958, pp. 43–54; and A. G. Hopkins, "The Currency Revolution in Southwest Nigeria in the late nineteenth Century," *Journal of the Historical Society of Nigeria*, vol. 3, no. 3, December 1966, pp. 471–83.
51. See for instance, Otunba Payne, *Payne's Lagos and West African Almanack, 1893* (London: J. S. Philips, n.d.), pp. 43, 54.
52. Public Record Office, CO147/41 (Lagos, Original Correspondence), Griffith to Ussher, April 29, 1880.
53. *Payne's Almanack*, p. 43.
54. See, for instance, P. N. C. Okigbo, *Nigeria's Financial Systrem: Structure and Growth* (Harlow: Longman, 1981), chapter 5.
55. N. A. Fadipe, *The Sociology of the Yoruba,* edited and introduced by F. O. and O. O. Okediji (Ibadan: Ibadan University Press, 1970), p. 326.
56. For an excellent summary, see R. O. Ekundare, *An Economic History of Nigeria, 1860–1960* (London: Methuen, 1973).
57. Two studies have captured theses changes: Sara S. Berry, *Fathers Work for the Sons: Accummulation, Mobility and Class Formation in an Extended Yoruba Community* (Los Angeles: University of California Press, 1985); and Toyin Falola, ed., *Oil and Nigerian Economy and Society* (Lagos: Longman, forthcoming).

Part 1

Money and Its Uses

2

Barter, Cowry, and the Culture of Exchange

After the pioneering writings of the late Marion Johnson[1] and other economic historians of Africa,[2] there seems at first sight to be very little to add to the existing knowledge of the importation, distribution, and use of cowry currencies in West Africa. It has been demonstrated that, to use Johnson's very apt words, "West African cowry currencies...[were] in no sense a 'primitive' money, but a sophisticated form of currency capable of adaptation to the particular needs of West African trade."[3] Toyin Falola and O. B. Lawuyi also contend that cowries functioned much more than a currency. They went on to examine cowries' "symbolic and ritual role" among the Yoruba.[4] In addition, other scholars have shown the east-west and north-south spread of the currency in Africa, and have speculated on its diffusion from one part of the region to another.

This chapter examines the transition from barter to cowry currency. It demonstrates that the same factors that had aided barter also promoted the adoption and acceptance of money as the principle, and of cowries as the medium of exchange. Furthermore, it shows that barter did not completely disappear with the evolution of cowries, but money advanced the frontiers of production and distribution in ways that barter could not (and did not).

Pasiparo: Nonmonetized Barter System

Toyin Falola and O. B. Lawuyi once speculated that "the earliest form of trade in Yorubaland and Nigeria as a whole was probably barter."[5] "To barter," Mike Atchison wrote, "is to exchange goods for goods rather than money. This was common in early days. Presumably, however, the deal was not always fair. Barter is from the old French *barater*—to cheat!"[6] Falola and Lawuyi went further to say that:

> by this system, items of farm produce and properties were exchanged according to some established rates or by on-the-spot bargaining.... Terms of trade were nego-

> tiated; both the buyer and the seller usually believed they had a fair return for their goods. Little is known about the indigenous standards of weights and measures. Quite often the weight and size of an object was determined by comparison with other objects. It is therefore possible that two objects of the same size but different weights be exchanged for one another. Whatever loss one incurred was at one's own risk.[7]

Also misleadingly called "silent trade,"[8] barter is generally understood as a method of trading by exchanging one commodity for another. Bruce Fitzgerald has categorized barter along with several other exchange arrangements called countertrade.

> The most common countertrade arrangements are: *barter*, a simultaneous exchange of goods of equal value; *counterpurchase*, in which a supplier agrees to purchase other, unrelated goods from the initial purchaser; *buy-back*, under which a supplier of machinery, equipment, or factories agrees to purchase goods manufactured with that equipment and technology; and *offsets*, where foreign suppliers are required to assemble, purchase, or manufacture components locally.[9]

Several features differentiate barter from other countertrade arrangements, however. These features are discussed in many studies.[10] They include the following: First, barter was well adapted to a less sophisticated economy because of its comparatively simple exchange mechanism. According to Falola and Lawuyi, barter trade ensured that no excessive surplus existed and guaranteed that the biological needs of people were not entirely at the mercy of nature.[11] Secondly, barter exchange was characterized by haggling or bargaining, "a way of arriving at a fair price by consensus."[12] Furthermore, barter was the earliest basis for the development of "fair value" and fair price.[13] Such concepts as value and price probably developed in the process of bargaining and haggling under barter.

One of the most serious problems associated with barter is that it involves a good amount of uncertainty in the determination of value (say, between kolanuts and salt), and in what is called double coincidence. Many scholars have posed the question: Suppose the salt producer knows nothing about kolanut, or vice versa; or suppose the kolanut seller does not want salt? George Akerlof thinks that in the absence of discernment the unsuspecting buyer under barter could easily be stuck with a "lemon."[14] And if the kolanut seller wants pepper instead of salt, she would have to search for someone who sells pepper but who also wants kolanuts. On the other hand, a set of barter chains could be developed which would guarantee that the owner of kolanut got what she wanted. What cannot be guaranteed is the "value" of kolanuts, which could be affected by the chains of barter exchange and result in the kolanut seller receiving more or less for her produce.

Barter is often considered a primitive system of exchange, and is believed to have disappeared in all societies shortly after monetization. Yet, this is not entirely accurate. In 1983, for example, Mary Rose Noberini and Rochel Berman found barter in a small community in the Bronx, New York. As if surprised, they wrote that "barter is currently being resurrected by representatives of industry, government, and small communities who need help in dealing with economic realities."[15] The following year, the *Economist* reported the practice of barter on a grand, international scale. "On some estimates, 25% of all the world's exports are now bartered—a trade worth around $500 billion a year. Ten years ago, barter's share was less than 5%."[16] Barter was overshadowed by money, but money never really completely replaced barter.

There is, of course, no question about the inefficiency of barter. According to Thomas Mayer, direct barter is extremely inefficient "because it requires that one locates someone who wants the particular good one provides, and just by coincidence happens to have available for exchange a particular good one wants." It is also true that in a modern economy "with millions of products it would require an extensive search to locate such a person..."[17] Can we say the same for small- or medium-sized economies and communities? And why is barter reemerging in today's complex economies and international trade? Are these "few isolated cases" or the first signs of a popular, future trend?[18]

In short, we do not view barter as a primitive system, or merely as "humanity's earliest attempt to deal with limited resources," but as an arrangement that continues to be "attractive during times of economic hardship."[19] We also take barter as "the exchange of objects for one another without reference to money and with maximum feasible reduction of social, cultural, political or personal transaction costs."[20]

In the rest of this section we examine the process of the barter exchange among the Yoruba before monetization. Perhaps it is necessary to differentiate between barter and social or ceremonial exchange of gifts. Neighbors exchanged gifts all the time, but that did not qualify as barter. On special occasions such as naming, marriage, initiation, and funeral ceremonies, gifts were given to celebrants to augment the costs or reciprocate favors. On the other hand, barter was an exchange between two or more parties who might or might not know each other but whose purpose was economic rather than social.

Several factors aided barter among the Yoruba. The first is surplus production. It is difficult to quantify the volume of precolonial production. It is impossible to estimate the size of premoney production. Qualitative assessments give the impression that there was generally only a little bit more than enough to eat. Such minimal surpluses were bartered mostly for subsistence purposes, that is, to meet basic needs of food, shelter, and clothing.

Another factor that aided barter was intergroup relations among Yoruba autonomous kingdoms. Indeed, this is a point that anthropologists tend to stress: that *within* a kingdom or ethnic group, exchange often represents "social and ceremonial gift-giving," whereas *between* ethnic groups, kingdoms, or other political entities, exchange is characterized by barter. As we have shown in chapter 1, each Yoruba kingdom was sufficiently autonomous to allow and support the operation of pure barter.

Yoruba urbanization and division of labor also aided barter. Professionalism developed very early in the history of Yorubaland. The list of professionals/specialists varied from political to economic elites, from agriculture and commerce to mining and manufacturing, and from herbalists and priests to historians and entertainers. These professions predated monetization, and were further advanced by the introduction of money.

The final factor that aided barter was the development of an increasingly sophisticated economy and society. The ostentatious lifestyle of the elite encouraged importation of rare and "luxurious" commodities. Also, the demands of annual or periodic festivals encouraged exchange of items not produced locally but considered an essential part of the ritual occasion.

There were two types of barter in Yorubaland: Goods for goods and goods for services. Although Yoruba economy has been monetized as early as the fifteenth century, existing practices in many communities reveal the resilience of barter in the economy. Indeed, many examples of barter—discussed below—have been deduced from these surviving practices.

In our fieldwork we encountered a variety of barter exchange. Our first series of examples relate to goods-for-goods barter system. Farmers freely exchanged agricultural produce with each other. A yam producer who grew only a limited amount of millet would exchange yams with the millet grower who cultivated only a small amount of yams. Moreover, farmers exchanged crops for hoes/cutlasses produced by blacksmiths. Participants in the long-distance trade also exchanged their products by barter before the introduction of standard money. This must have been the process by which Yoruba traders imported natron, salt, and other commodities of the trans-Saharan trade before monetization.

Our next series of examples demonstrates the prevalence of goods-for-service exchange system among the Yoruba. Ifa priests and herbalists were often paid in kind. They received goats, roosters, palm oil, and other valuable (and edible) items from their clients. Although clients knew that these were in-kind payments for service, they would not question the priests' claims that the items would be offered in sacrifice to the gods. Indeed, the more outrageous the demand, the stronger the clients' belief in the efficacy of the priest's sacrifice or the herbalist's suggested treatment. In addition, the more severe the condition of the client, the bigger the demand of the herbalist.

Entertainers, such as drummers, singers, and magicians, were also paid in kind. The payments varied. A performer at the basic level would not expect much; sometimes leftover food would suffice. This is expressed in the statement *a lu'lu gb'omi eko,* the drummer that received leftover pap. The virtuoso, on the other hand, performed for the wealthy and powerful. Such artists and musicians were paid in expensive clothes, horses, or even slaves.

Yoruba Cowry Currency

Unlike many West African peoples, before colonial rule the Yoruba did not use metallic currencies such as gold and silver coins.[21] The main trade currency was cowry shells, *cypraea moneta,* imported from the Indian Ocean. The available evidence indicates that cowries came through two major routes: the northern route connecting Yorubaland with the caravan trade, and the southern route by way of the Atlantic coast. It is not clear from which of these routes cowries first came to the Yoruba country. The Portuguese were said to have found cowries in extensive use in Benin at the beginning of the sixteenth century.[22] Given the close historical and trade relationships between Benin on the one hand, and Ile-Ife and other parts of eastern Yorubaland on the other hand, the diffusion of cowries from the former to the latter can be reasonably assumed. This speculation is further supported by the similarity in the cowry numismatics of the Edo and Yoruba.[23] According to S. A. Akintoye,

> the earliest contacts between Ekiti, Ijesa and Akoko with Benin were commercial. It is generally believed that these earliest contacts dated to the fifteenth century. Benin traders brought corals, European cloth, cowry shells and European iron imple-

ments and, at a later date, guns and gunpowder, and took away home-spun cloth and camwood as well as beads and potash.... Akure was the *entrepot* of this trade and a considerable number of Edo people soon settled permanently at Akure.[24]

The above clearly indicates that the eastern routes for the spread of cowries to Yorubaland were as important as the southern route through Ijebu country. On the other hand, cowries were known to have been imported to the Western Sudan centuries before the Portuguese set out on their voyages, and before European traders began importing cowries to the Atlantic coast of West Africa. They were known to be the currency in the Niger Bend countries, and to have come there through the trans-Saharan caravan trade of which the Oyo Empire was a southern terminus. Thus, a northern route is also suggested for the diffusion of cowries into Yorubaland. Indeed, earlier attempts to date the beginning of cowry shells as a currency among the Yoruba have led to the suggestion that they were probably introduced about (but not later than) the fifteenth century.[25] Yorubaland combined the practices of stringing cowries as was done in the Bights of Benin and Biafra and of counting them individually, a practice more prevalent in the western Sudan. This shows the diversity of monetary policies as well as sources of the cowry shells.

The participation of Yoruba traders in the Atlantic trade probably reduced the volume of cowry importation by way of the trans-Saharan route from the seventeenth century onward. It has been demonstrated that the slave trade increased the volume of cowry importation to West Africa. It has also been shown that several Yoruba states, including Ijebu, Egba, Egbado, and Old Oyo empire, took part in the slave trade.[26] Trade relations between the Ijebu and the Portuguese were established as soon as the latter reached the Bight of Benin.[27] Although this trade was initially in other commodities, slaves subsequently predominated. The exchange of cowries for slaves, and the popularity of the shells as currency, were soon to pitch the Ijebu in commercial competition with their neighbors in the hinterland. Thus, Oyo expansion in the seventeenth and eighteenth centuries toward the Atlantic coast was due partly to the interest of the business elite to, among other reasons, take control of the sources of the cowry currency. This was also the main source of the rivalry between Oyo and Ijebu traders. This rivalry was interpreted in larger subethnic terms. As could be expected, the Ijebu, being closer to the Atlantic, dominated the trade in cowries until the Oyo opened their own port of trade in the central part of the Bight of Benin.

Before the introduction of modern (European) currency, the Yoruba referred to cowries simply as money: *owo*. However, with the spread of

British metallic currency in the nineteenth and twentieth centuries, a distinction began to emerge between the old cowries and the new currencies. The former was called *owo eyo*, meaning literally loose or numerated money; and the latter simply termed *owo* or the Africanized names of the denominations such as *kobo* for copper coins, *sile* for shillings, and so on. As could be expected, the sources of cowries were shrouded in rituals and mystery. There are several variants of the myth, but generally they reveal that Olodumare, the Yoruba supreme God, reveals the secret of cowries to only a select few:

> They are living things with shells, small in size like snails. To obtain them, a hole was dug in the ground. When the hole has reached a certain depth, a sheep (with a rope tied around its neck) was thrown into it and buried alive. These living things would then crawl up the carcass of the sheep and stick to it. When there were many of them, the sheep would be brought out (with the help of the rope tied to its neck) and the living things sticking to its body would be removed, put into a pot which would be covered to make them die within a few days. After this, they would be taken to a river and would be washed very thoroughly to remove the decay of the cowries. The shells were then put into circulation as money.[28]

The above could be interpreted in two major ways: (1) that the Yoruba "manufactured" their own cowry currencies, and (2) that the business elite adopted this myth as a ploy to monopolize the information about the true sources of their wealth. Our position is a combination of the two interpretations. This is supported by the fact that, although there is only one dominant species of cowry currency in Yorubaland (the *cypraea moneta*), which would suggest importation from the Maldive Islands rather than production from the Bight of Benin, there are certain other species of cowry shells in limited circulation which are similar to the type the Benin were using before the Atlantic trade, a fact that would also suggest internal production along the Atlantic coast. Moreover, the average, lower-class person was discouraged from :looking for money" (*wa owo*) because of the huge expenses involved in the above ritual, and this worked to limit the membership of the affluent upper class.

In other words, whereas cowries could not be counterfeited, people were passing at least two types of shells differentiated by size. This may, in fact, explain the confusion reported by Ekpo Eyo (*via* G. Basden) that "west of the Niger River the larger cowries, that is, *C. annulus,* were preferred, whereas east of the Niger the smaller type from Maldives, *C. moneta*, was in vogue."[29] It can be assumed that both the larger and the smaller types were in circulation in Yorubaland. We encountered both types in our research, but the testimonies of many informants suggest that the smaller type was more acceptable and has higher value than the bigger type. According to Falola and Lawuyi,

> *Cypraea annulus* [imported from Zanzibar] were generally recognized as of less value than *Cypraea moneta*. This was not a consequence of an esthetic judgment or issue of identity, but probably related to the problems associated with transporting heavy materials, since more money and more labor are involved in moving heavier materials across the country by land.[30]

Tables 2–3 show the Yoruba system of numismatics. Like the Yoruba numeral on which it is based, the counting of cowries was a complex system involving extensive use of the mathematical principles of addition, multiplication, and subtraction. This system has attracted many western scholars who have found it intriguing that an illiterate society could develop such an intricate numeral. This has led to some misunderstanding of the origin of the Yoruba numerals. Marianne Schmidl is quoted to have speculated that "reckoning with the cowry shells was basic in the construction of the number system."[31] This is most unlikely; on the contrary, cowry numeration was built upon the preexisting ordinary numerals. The most vivid description of this numeral is still that of Samuel Johnson, and has been quoted in full here:

> From one to ten, different terms are used, then for 20, 30, 200, and 400; the rest are multiples or compounds. Thus 11, 12, 13 and 14 are reckoned as ten plus one, plus two, plus three and plus four; 15 to 20 are reckoned as 20 less five, less four, less three, less two, less one, and then 20.
>
> In the same way we continue 20 and one, to 20 and four, and then 30 less five (25), less four, and so on to 30, and so for all figures reckoned by tens.
>
> There is no doubt that the digits form the basis of enumeration to a large extent, if not entirely so. Five, ten, twenty, i.e. the digits of one hand, of two, and the toes included, and their multiples form the different stages of the enumeration.
>
> Beginning from the first multiple of 20 we have *ogoji*, a contraction of ogun meji, i.e. two twenties (40), *ogota*, three twenties (60), *ogorin*, four twenties (80), *ogorun*, five twenties (100), and so on to ten twenties (200), when the new word *igba* is used.
>
> The intermediate numbers (30 having a distinct terminology), 50, 70, 90, 110, 130 to 190 are reckoned as: 60 less ten (50), 80 less ten (70), a hundred less ten (90) and so on to 200.
>
> The figures from 200 to 2000 are reckoned as multiples of 200 (400, however, which is 20 x 20, the square of all the digits, has a distinct terminology, *irinwo* or *erinwo*, i.e. the elephant of figures—meaning the highest coined word in calculation, the rest being multiples).
>
> Thus we have *egbeta*, a contraction of igba-meta, i.e. three two-hundreds (600), *egberin*, from igba-merin, four two-hundreds (800), *egberun*, five two-hundreds (1000), and so on to *egbewa*, ten two-hundreds (2,000), which in its turn forms the basis of still higher calculations.
>
> The intermediate figures of 300, 500, 700, 900, 1,100, to 1,900 are reckoned as 100 less the multiple above them, viz., *odunrun*, contracted from orun-din-ni-irinwo,

i.e. 100 less than 400 (300), *orun-din-ni egbeta*, 100 less than 600 (500), *orun-din-ni-egberin*, 100 less than 800 (700); and so on to 2,000.

By a system of contraction, elision, and euphonic assimilation, for which the Yoruba language is characteristic, the long term *orun-din-ni* (egbeta, egberin and so on) is contracted to *ede* or *ode*, e.g., *edegbeta* (500), *edegberin* (700), *edegberun* (900) and so on.

But the multiples of 200 do not end with ten times, although that figure is the basis of the higher calculations, it goes on to the perfection (or multiple) of the digits, viz.: twenty times (two hundred); thus we have *egbokanla*, that is igba mokanla, 11 two-hundreds (2,200); *egbejila*, twelve two-hundreds (2,400), and so on to twenty two-hundreds or *egbaji*, that is, twice two thousand (4,000).

With this ends the multiples of 200. The intermediate figures of 2,300, 2,500, 2,700, 2,900 are reckoned the same way as before, viz.: 100 less than the next higher multiple.

As already mentioned, *egbewa* (or *egbaa*), 2,000, forms the basis of still higher calculations; the multiples of *egbaa* are *egbaji*, two two-thousands (4,000); *egbata*, three two-thousands (6,000); *egbarin*, four two-thousands (8,000) on to *egbawa*, ten two-thousands (20,000), which in its turn forms the basis of the highest calculations.

The intermediate figures of 3,000, 5,000, 7,000, 9,000, 11,000 onwards are reckoned as 1,000 less than the multiple above them. the more familiar terms for 3,000 and 5,000, however are *egbedogun*, or fifteen two-hundreds, and *egbedogbon*, 25 two-hundreds.

For those figures beyond 20,000 the contracted forms which are generally used are *okanla* (for egbamokanla) 11 two-thousands (22,000); *ejila*, *etala*, on to *egbagun*, i.e., 20 two-thousands, i.e., forty-thousand.

...Thus we see that with numbers that go by tens five is used as the intermediate figure—five less than the next higher stage. In those by 20, ten is used as the intermediate. In those by 200, 100 is used, and in those of 2,000, 1,000 is used.

The figure that is made use of for calculating indefinite numbers is 20,000 *egbawa*, and in money calculation especially it is termed *oke kan*, i.e., one bag (of cowries). Large numbers to an indefinite amount are so many "bags" or rather "bags" in so many places.[32]

Like all forms of money, the value of cowry shells was not stable. Aside from the late nineteenth century inflation which has been discussed by A. G. Hopkins and Marion Johnson, the value of the currency increased in direct proportion to its scarcity; thus, it had a higher value in the hinterland than along the coast. Table 3 shows the range of value of cowries shells relative to the contemporary British currencies in the mid-nineteenth century. This was not constant, either. A. G. Hopkins has summarized how the value fluctuated widely in the period thus:

The steepest fall was during the first stage, from 1851 to 1865, when the value of one head of cowries (2000 K) dropped from 4s. 9d. to 1s. 3d., as a result of the increased shipment made by the competing German and French firms. During the second stage, from 1865 to 1879 (and to 1883, in the case of Badagri), the value of the cowry fell from 1s. 3d. to 1s. per head. This period of relative stability may be explained by the tendency for net imports of cowry to fall; by an upward movement in demand for cowries following the general expansion of trade in the period

> after the creation of the Colony of Lagos in 1861; and...as a side effect of speculation in the dollar. The third stage, from about 1880 (or 1884 in the case of Badagri) to about 1895, was a period of renewed upheaval and fluctuating exchange rates, during which the value of one head of cowries dropped from 1s. 0d. to 6d.... The changes in this period were not caused by over-issue, for the import of cowries continued to decrease, but were primarily the result of other monetary innovations, namely the demonetization of the dollar and the introduction of British silver coin, both of which had adverse effects on the value of the already depreciated cowry currency.[33]

Ekpo Eyo also reports on the impact of inflation on the value of cowry shells.[34] He provides Table 4, drawn from M.D.W. Jeffreys' study. Moreover, cowry currency played some significant role in the settlement of international disputes. King Dosumu in 1861 transferred the sovereignty over Lagos to the British for an annual payment of 1,200 bags of cowries valued by Ekpo Eyo in 1979 as 2,000 Naira.[35]

By the end of the nineteenth century, the value of cowry shells in Yorubaland had dropped to what became known as the "standard" of calculation in relation to British currency then being gradually introduced into the hinterland. According to Samuel Johnson, "the rate of exchange became practically fixed at 6d. for a "head"...that is 2,000 cowries; hence 3d. = 1,000 cowries."[36] However, because copper money was regarded as inferior in value, one penny (minted in copper, and called *kobo* in Yoruba) was taken at 300 cowries each. Thus, 3d. in copper money would be 900 cowries rather than 1,000. Bigger figures were based on the 2,000 cowries (*egbewa*) to 6d; thus, 5s. was 20,000 cowries (*oke kan*) and one British pound was 80,000 cowries (*oke merin*).

Cowry shells were in great use in the internal and international commerce of Yorubaland. Nevertheless, not all transactions reached the market as nonmonetary exchanges were as valid as buying and selling with cowry shells as the unit of account. It would seem that one "bag" of cowries was a lot of money. According to oral information, a farmer in the nineteenth century had to be quite industrious to earn as much as one "bag" of cowries (approximately 5s.) in a single harvest season. Also, a trader could begin a successful venture and participate in long-distance (caravan) trade with one "bag" of cowries.[37] Because of the bulk and weight of the shells,[38] and because the presence of tsetse fly in Yorubaland prevented the use of animals such as donkey and camel as beasts of burden, long-distance traders engaged head porters whose only duty was to carry money from one market to another. Because of the dangers of highwaymen, traders did not transport the money so conspicuously. According to oral information from those who were still engaged in the caravan trade early in this century, the cowries were usually put in a sack, and the sack placed in a wide-brimmed calabash for easy carrying on the head. In this way, too, no one could differentiate a load of cowries from a load of goods. In any case, protection was offered, even in periods of interethnic warfare, because many trading caravans were accompanied by armed guards.[39]

Other Uses of Cowries

Cowries and Rituals

The forgoing discussion not only demonstrates that cowries were widely accepted in Yorubaland as medium of exchange but indicates that the people had the ability to handle the counting, which went with their use. In Yorubaland, the use of cowries extended even into the religious realm. In the first few decades of missionary activity, cowries were used to pay pastoral wages.[40] When it appeared that the amount in local circulation was too small, the missionaries purchased cowries by the tons from as far as Sierra Leone. Naturally this kind of massive importation caused inflation and resulted in the depreciation of the local values of the cowries.[41]

The society itself used cowries in various ways. They were integrated into the various interpersonal communication strategies; used as gifts, and, in the form of *aroko,* served as a kind of diplomatic message. In entertainment and theater, cowries were a part of the musical instrument. To produce a rattle, the cowries were tied around an empty gourd so that when this was shaken, a musical sound was produced. The gourd and the cowries around it formed the *sekere.* The size of the *sekere* in the past mirrored the status of the personalities who employed the musical cast. A king with extensive power and territorial influence enjoyed the sound from a bigger and more decorated *sekere.*[42]

In sartorial matters, cowries also served to delineate status and professionalism, featuring in the apparel of such professionals as hunters, warriors, and priests. These were men of the upper strata of the Yoruba society. They enjoyed affluence, political *cum* religious power, and usually headed large family households. The symbolism that lies at the origin of this practice probably belongs to a deep level of thinking, "where the shells are attributed magical virtue, hence its association with those who need contact with the supernatural to maintain their elitist statuses."[43] In reality, the magical power of the cowry serves both

TABLE 1
Yoruba Ordinary and Numismatic Numerals (The First One Hundred)

Number	Simple Enumeration	Cowry Enumeration	Mathematics
1	Eni	Ookan	1
2	Eji	Eeji	2
3	Eta	Eeta	3
4	Erin	Eerin	4
5	Arun	Aarun	5
6	Efa	Eefa	6
7	Eje	Eeje	7
8	Ejo	Eejo	8
9	Esan	Eesan	9
10	Ewa	Eewa	10
11	Okanla	Ookanla	10+1
12	Ejila	Eejila	10+2
13	Etala	Eetala	10+3
14	Erinla	Eerinla	10+4
15	Edogun	Eedogun	20-5
16	Erindilogun	Eerindilogun	20-4
17	Etadilogun	Eetadilogun	20-3
18	Ejidilogun	Eejidilogun	20-2
19	Okandilogun	Ookandilogun	20-1
20	Ogun	Okowo	20
21	Okanlelogun	Ookanlelogun	20+1
22	Ejilelogun	Eejilelogun	20+2
23	Etalelogun	Eetalelogun	20+3
24	Erinlelogun	Eerinlelogun	20+4
25	Edogbon	Eedogbon	30-5
26	Erindilogbon	Eerindilogbon	30-4
27	Etadilogbon	Eetadilogbon	30-3
28	Ejidilogbon	Eejidilogbon	30-2
29	Okandilogbon	Ookandilogbon	30-1
30	Ogbon	Ogbowo	30
35	Arundilogoji	Aarundilogoji	40-5 or [(20 x2)-5]
40	Oji	Ogoji	20 x 2
45	Arundiladota	Aarundiladota	{[(20 x 3)-10]-5}
50	Adota	Aadota	[(20 x 3)-10]
55	Arundilogota	Aarundilogota	[(20 x 3)-5]
60	Ogota	Ogota	20 x 3
65	Arundiladorin	Aarundiladorin	{[(20 x 4)-10]-5}
70	Adorin	Aadorin	[(20 x 4)-10]
75	Arundilogorin	Aarundilogorin	[(20 x 4)-5]
80	Ogorin	Ogorin	20 x 4
85	Arundiladorun	Aarundiladoru	{[(20 x 5)-10]-5}
90	Adorun	Aadorun	[(20 x 5)-10]
95	Arundilogorun	Aarundilogorun	[(20 x 5)-5]
100	Ogorun	Ogorun	20 x 5

TABLE 2
Yoruba Numerals (Some Larger Figures)

Number	Yoruba Cowry Enumeration	Mathematics
110	Aadofa	[(20 x 6)-10]
120	Ogofa	20 x 6
130	Aadoje	[(20 x 7)-10]
140	Ogoje	20 x 7
150	Aadojo	[(20 x 8)-10]
160	Ogojo	20 x 8
170	Aadosan	[(20 x 9)-10]
180	Ogosan	20 x 9
190	Ewadinnigba	[(20 x 10)-10]
200	Igbiwo	20 x 10
210	Ewalerugba	(20 x 10)+10
220	Ogunlugba (or Okolugba)	(20 x 10)+20
230	Ogbonwolerugba	(20 x 10)+30
240	Ojilugba (or Ojilerugba)	(20 x 10) +40
250	Aadotalerugba	(20 x 10)+(20 x 3)-10
260	Otalerugba	(20 x 10)+(20 x 3)
270	Aadorinlerugba	(20 x 10)+(20 x 4)-10
280	Orinlugba	(20 x 10)+(20 x 4)
290	Aadorunlerugba	(20 x 10)+(20 x 5)-10
300	Odunrun	[20 x (20-5)]* or(20 x 20)-100**
400	Irinwo	20 x 20
500	Eedegbeta	(200 x 3)-100
600	Egbeta	200 x 3
700	Eedegberin	(200 x 4)-100
800	Egberin	200 x 4
900	Eedegberun	(200 x 5)-100
1000	Egberun	200 x 5
1100	Eedegbefa	(200 x 6)-100
1200	Egbefa	200 x 6
1300	Eedegbeje	(200 x 7)-100
1400	Egbeje	200 x 7
2000	Egbewa	200 x 10
2400	Egbejila	200 x 12
2500	Egbetala-din-ogorun	(200 x 13)-100
3500	Egbejidinlogun-din-ogorun	(200 x 18)-100
4000	Egbaji	2000 x 2
4500	Egbetalelogun-din-ogorun	(200 x 23)-100
5000	Egbedogbon	200 x 25
5500	Egbetalelogbon-din-ogorun	(200 x 33)-100
6000	Egbata	2000 x 3
7000	Edegbarin	(2000 x 4)-1000
8000	Egbarin	2000 x 4
9000	Edegbarun	(2000 x 5)-1000
10000	Egbarun	2000 x 5
20000	Egbaawa (or Oke kan)	2000 x 10
30000	Eedogun	2000 x 15
40000	Egbagun (or Oke meji)	20000 x 2
1000 000	Egbegberun	1000 x 1000

Notes: *Mathematical interpretation by Claudia Zaslavsky, "The Yoruba Number System," p. 122.
**More correct interpretation by Samuel Johnson, *The History of the Yorubas*, p. lv.

TABLE 3
Yoruba Cowry Currency

40 cowries =1 string	40 cowries
50 strings =1 head	2,000 cowries = 1 head
10 heads = 1 bag	20,000 cowries = 1 bag

Source: Samuel Johnson, *The History of the Yorubas*, pp. 118–19

TABLE 4
Instability of the Cowry Currency

Date	Number of Cowries to ¼oz of gold
11th century	1,150
16th century	3,000
1816	2,000
1853	3,000
1880	6,000
1912	12,000

Source: Ekpo Eyo, *Nigeria and the Evolution of Money*, p. 60.

men and the gods because in Yoruba religion, the cowries were offered as gifts to the gods, within an entire sacrificial package that might include animals and water. Large amounts of cowries, ranging from tens to several hundreds, could be offered as gifts to the gods. In this way the cowry served as a medium of appeal for better conditions of life for life supplicants. To men, it came back as wealth in that, as the god was made wealthy, the *orisa* was glorified and its reputation strengthened so that in turn it would bless the devotee through the supplicant. The relationship was reciprocal, for when the god was pleased with the offering, it answered prayers and the supplicant could then reward the priest handsomely.

Basically, the entire religious ritual was tinged with an economic tone. Most of the Yoruba gods to whom cowries were offered were linked to production or relations among people. The cowries, for instance, were offered to the farm god, *orisa oko*. This *orisa* was connected with harvests. Generally the deity was represented by an iron staff, thus associating it with hoe and cutlass, which were produced from iron. In addition, cowry shells were its characteristic emblems when sculptured.

Cowries were also associated with *Esu,* the Yoruba representation of the dynamism of the cosmos. *Esu* facilitated production or its destruction depending on its mood. It could destroy persons and any object toward whom its anger was directed, and therefore must be placated. The Yoruba made sure that it was not aroused to anger by sacrificing to it before attending to any other god. *Esu* was symbolized by any of the following: an ironstone rock roughly conical in shape, a laterite mound, a clay heap, and an inverted earthen ware pot with a hole at the bottom. Offerings to it consisted of sizeable portions of food prepared for other gods, palm oil, cowries, the blood of domestic animals and fowls and, in the past, human sacrifices.

Obatala was another god to whom cowries were offered as gifts. This god was known by various names among the various Yoruba subgroups. It was known in the Yoruba community of Ejigbo as *Ogiyan*, and as *Orisa ala* at Ibadan and Ado-Ekiti. It was *Orisanla* at Ife, and *Obatala* at Ikire, Ijaiye, Iwofin, and Egba districts of Yorubaland. In addition, different functions were ascribed to it in these different areas. For example, at Ife, it was associated with the creation of the landmass. At Ife the sacrificial package included sparkling sediment-free water drawn the first thing in the morning, kaolin, cowries, and white beads.

An examination of the specific situations in which the cowries were included in these arrangements suggests that they were being lifted out of their physical quality to symbolize the people's desire to enhance production and to protect persons or status. The productive representation was fullest in the *Aje* festival of the Ondo, which celebrated wealth and fertility. The festival was essentially for women, who in Yoruba society dominated the market economy. They did most of the buying and the selling. They also engaged in the various stages of farming and harvesting.[44] Usually men and women worked together because they were related to each other, or had other reciprocal social obligations. Yet the sexual division of labor impacted on the economic process in a way that the women who controlled the market economy were subordinated to male authority, and this is manifested in the *Aje* festival, which marked both the political inferiority of the women and their wealth. In Ondo the *Aje* bowl contained items such as cowry shells, coral beads, native cloth, white china plates, and white bird dolls.[45] The bird symbolized the power of transcendence over constraints. The china plates, cloth, coral beads, and cowry shells were symbols of wealth.

In a sense, the rights and obligations of Yoruba women were recognized in various myths, and their position and fears were institutionalized and expressed even in their own economic arrangements. We reproduce here in full an account of the myth of cowries' origins to testify to the role of cowry in social relation:

> After the first market of the Ondo had been established, the people were faced with the problem of which form of exchange to use. It was decided that Olodumare [the Supreme deity] should be met and the problem be presented to Him for solution. Olodumare was met and the matter was discussed. He, Olodumare, instructed that a ritual be done with a mother hen, a he-goat and a frog. Thereafter the contingent should meet with *Aje*. The ritual sacrifice was to protect the contingent from death or any danger on their way to *Aje*'s house. But then, in spite of the rituals, there were no human volunteers to meet with Aje. After a lot of persuasion and several days of waiting, the vulture bird agreed to go. Two women also volunteered. However, only the vulture eventually met with Aje, the women stood at a distance. On getting to Aje, the vulture narrated its mission. Aje knew so much already because she had been informed of the mission by Olodumare. She responded to the vulture's request by giving it some cowry shells which were to be used as medium of exchange. The vulture thanked her, swallowed the cowries to ensure that they were not lost, and traveled back to the waiting human crowd. She vomited the cowries in their presence. In appreciation of the role played by vulture, it was elevated to the level of sacredness. The Ondo were forbidden from killing the bird.[46]

There may be variants of this myth, but it is obvious that the myth is not about the scheme of reciprocity. Rather, it demonstrates how currency substantiated a particular form of social relation. God is a male; *Aje* is female, and the vulture, a symbol of death, mediates between the two. Because it was the vulture that championed the introduction of cowries into the market economy, it held the responsibility of ensuring the survival of the market and of the order of transactional relations that governed it. The basic orientation of the myth is the acceptance that the events which comprise the cowry exchange exhibit regularities whose forms are, as men and women, mutually interdependent. For this the Yoruba aphorism *aye l'oja orun ni ile,* ("the world is a market, heaven is home") is rather apt. The earth and heaven, much like market and home, define the totality of existence.

This myth also confirms our finding on the barter economy above that there was a market before the introduction of the cowry currency. The cowries in religion and in myths have value not only because of their practical usefulness through mythology—that is, a narrative form of symbolic classification[47]—but also because they function to establish information about widely different segments of society.

In linking cowries with the goddess of wealth and fertility (*Aje*) and with the gods of production (*Orisa Oko*), creativity (*Obatala*), and dynamism (*Esu*), the relations between messages become the grammar of interaction in the human group. It is both logical and fruitful to think that the cowry is essential to life-sustaining activities. After all, regardless of time and space, all people and societies share two basic economic needs: the biological one, which is met by fertility and food and the sociopsychological one, which requires repetitive provision of material goods and services. This latter aspect requires the services (roles and functions) of specialists such as priests, warriors, and hunters.[48] Incidentally, as the elites in the traditional society, they developed an elaborate use of cowries as a means of relaying information.

The Use of Cowries for Communication

Cowries had symbolic meanings in the use of *Aroko,* a system of communication evolved by the Yoruba to communicate with distant communities.[49] The communication was developed to link hunters, warriors, priests, kings, and chiefs within Yoruba society. When people of other status were used, they were tested for their ability to keep information and not to tamper with the *aroko,* by being initiated through elaborate rituals. Having gone through these rites, their person might not be violated even though they might bear unpleasant messages.

The effective use of *aroko* did not elude the attention of foreigners. For instance, Tucker described it as a "code of correspondence" used by the Ijesa and the Ekiti. He reported that three cowry shells strung together meant, "I shall have nothing more to do with you"; four cowry shells meant, "Your proposal is ridiculous"; five cowry shells meant, "The matter is plain;" six cowry shells meant, "I agree"; and a string of nine cowry shells meant, "It is preferably so."[50]

Aroko was also found among the Ijebu-Yoruba. Here the emphasis was on cowries of various designs, combinations, and arrangements. It would be misleading to reduce these to some kind of universal message both in form and in social function because even in a single tradition, *aroko* appeared in many different situations and were used for quite diverse social ends, including those of a most antisocial nature. Because the *aroko* was a complex code, the difficulty in breaking the code seemed to generate challenges to cultural rules about order. Consequently, because of its intricacy, some authors would rather think that the coding system was foreign to the Yoruba.[51]

Until the end of the nineteenth century, the *aroko* symbolisms were items of trade such as cowries, yams, banana, plantain, maize cobs, cloths, and agricultural tools. Each of these items had its own specific meaning and when combined with others, it created a relation between meanings.[52] For instance, the cowry shell ordinarily used in economic exchange would, strung in pairs back to back, indicate the intention of the sender to break relations with the recipient. When a similar number of cowries were strung facing each other, they conveyed ideas of solidarity. Furthermore, to the Ife-Yoruba, when two cowries were tied with black threads, the recipient was informed that something untoward was likely to happen to him. In a different vein, the Oyo-Yoruba would send two or three cowries tied in a leaf to request payment of an outstanding debt. Without the leaf, a parcel containing three cowries, whether strung together or not, symbolized rejection of an offer.

Among the Ekiti-Yoruba, a snail shell with a row of cowry shells glued around it and tied to a calabash lid and then hung around an object signified that the consequences of stealing that object or trespassing might be acute poverty and suffering. However, when a small gourd was filled with some medicinal stuff, its outer part covered with a row of rag and cowry shells, and the gourd attached to a calabash lid before being hung near an object, trespassers must beware of a dangerous charm capable of causing death. Finally, a broom with a single cowry shell fixed to its base and hung around an object meant that the trespasser might be induced to pluck the broom and sweep around the object/property until the owner arrived. The cowries obviously functioned in specialized settings of economic interest, yet its function as providing a sociopsychological assurance of status and of solidarity is also important.

The *Church Missionary Gleaner* for August of 1889 contained many expressions of *aroko*. In one of the quaint forms of communication, "a native general of the Ijebu force" sent an *aroko* of six cowries strung together face to face to a "native prince abroad." This was intended to carry with the message that "although the road between us both may be very long, yet I draw you to myself, and set my face towards you. So I desire you to set your face towards me, and draw to me."[53] In Yoruba cosmology an even number signified affinity, while an odd number implied danger of a kind. Six signified love, and the word "six" (*efa*) implied to draw near or close. Most *aroko* symbolizing social solidarity were likely to have an even number of cowries, preferably six. In addition, they might have a feather component that in birds not only protected against the harshness of the environment, but was also the equivalent for human mat. Consequently, in an *aroko* comprising eight cowries strung together and having a feather cap, the *Awujale,* or king of Ijebu-Ode, made it known to his nephew abroad that

> your words agree with mine very much. Your ways are pleasing to me, and I like them. Deceive me not because the spice would yield nothing else but a sweet and genuine odour unto God. I shall never deal doubly with you all my life long. The weight of your words to me is beyond all description. As it is on the same family mat we have been sitting and lying down together—I send to you. I am therefore anxiously waiting and hoping to hear from you.[54]

In the sociopsychological frame, the *aroko* referred to well-known social processes such as socialization, the performance of actors in a communication situation, and the homogeneity of experiences.

The various *aroko* were often used in day-to-day dealings, on episodic and diplomatic occasions, and during the infamous nineteenth-century interethnic warfare. There were two types of *aroko:* the verbal and the artifactual. Only the latter involved the use of cowries. The former existed as idiomatic expressions and did not require any diplomacy or initiation as did artifactual *aroko.* The artifactual *aroko* apparently functioned, to some extent, independently of the circulation of cowries in the market economy, since its code never changed in response to fluctuations in prices of goods or to the scarcity of cowries in the local economy. The popularity of the cowries in the *aroko* in the elite circles was ostensibly for practical reasons: they preserved the aura of importance considered essential to status. This aura would be violated if the coding system was not kept away from the lower class and if it was not consistent.

The Yoruba elites were careful to harness the mystical/magical power of the cowries for their own ends in a variety of ways. First, they stipulated just who could wear clothes ornamented with cowries. While the ornaments transformed the person, there were established limits to this alchemy: only members of a certain profession, of a specified age and status, with an attested esoteric specialty, might wear the cowry-ornamented cloths. A second function was that through the magical power of the cowry, debts were collected, property was protected, and the possibility of downward mobility resulting from theft and unrecoverable debts was minimized. The third function is that, by restricting the symbolic meaning of a specialized coding system to the elites, information about the unedifying behaviors of elites could not filter quickly and damagingly to the larger public.

In any system the elites know how to preserve their interest through exclusionary tactics, restriction, distortion, and manipulation of information; the creation of standards difficult to meet by many members of the society; and the institutionalization of coercive functions. In a society like that of the Yoruba, where the symbolism of prestige and status was very important, what was exchanged went beyond the exclusively nonmaterial things like military assistance and courtesies. They might exchange cowry both for goods and for information. These activities gave expression not only to relations among status groups but also to their obligatory character. The elites gave much to the *orisa* in the hope that the *orisa* would give much in return. They traded information in the hope that the parties would realize what they had at stake—reputation. The use of cowries in this society, therefore, was by no means limited to its function as a currency.

Summary

The foregoing discussion leads us to several conclusions. First, there was a transformation in Yorubaland from barter to money. It is probable that the transition was peaceful, but it was not complete. Exchanges by barter and money have persisted side by side into the present. Second, the Yoruba example has reinforced the point that African societies had currencies that performed the same functions as modern currency. Given the nature and size of the economy, the cowries provided a fairly satisfactory medium of exchange over a wide trade area. However, as the economy grew and became more global, cowries were replaced by modern (colonial and postcolonial) currencies that were more portable and had a greater convertibility.

Third, our findings in this chapter reinforce Simmel's position that "money has its origin in barter."[55] Money began to develop when "a single object is exchanged not for another single object but against several others." The exchange relations learned under barter became perfected or transformed with the introduction of cowries as medium of exchange.

Fourth, as they made the transition from barter to money, the Yoruba also began to develop idealistic and practical means of making money. In the next chapter we will examine the Yoruba view of money.

Notes

1. Marion Johnson, "The Cowry Currencies of West Africa," Part I, *Journal of African History*, xi, 1 1970, pp. 17–49; Part II, *JAH*, xi, 3, 1970, pp. 331–53; *idem* "The Nineteenth-Century Gold 'Mithqal' in West and North Africa," *JAH*, ix, 4, 1968, pp. 547–69; also Jan Hogendorn and Marion Johnson, *The Shell Money of the Slave Trade* (Cambridge: Cambridge University Press, 1986).
2. Among others, see Paul Lovejoy, "Interregional Monetary Flows in the Precolonial Trade of Nigeria," *JAH*, xv, 4, 1974, pp. 563–85; J. H. Latham, "Currency, Credit

and Capitalism on the Cross River in the Pre-colonial Era," *JAH*, xii, 4, 1971, pp. 599–605; A. G. Hopkins, "The Currency Revolution in South-West Nigeria in the Late Nineteenth Century," *Journal of the Historical Society of Nigeria*, iii, 3, 1966, pp. 471–83; M. Hiskett, "Materials Relating to the Cowry Currency of the Western Sudan," *Bulletin of the SOAS*, xxix, 1, 1966, pp. 122–42, and xxx, 3, 1967, pp. 340–66; G. I. Jones, "Native and Trade Currencies in Southern Nigeria During the Nineteenth Century," *Africa*, xxviii, 1, 1958, pp. 43–54; Stephen Baier, *An Economic History of Central Niger* (London: Clarendon, 1980), pp. 25–35, 105–15; Eugenia W. Herbert, "Aspects of the Use of Copper in Pre-Colonial West Africa," *JAH*, xiv, 1973, pp. 179–94.
3. Johnson, "Cowry Currencies," Part I, p. 17.
4. Toyin Falola and O. B. Lawuyi, "Not Just a Currency: The Cowrie in Nigerian Culture," in D. Henige and T. C. McCaskie, eds., *West African Economic and Social History: Studies in Memory of Marion Johnson* (Madison, WI: African Studies Program), p. 29.
5. *Ibid.*
6. Steve Wiliamson and Randall Wright, "Barter and Monetary Exchange under Private Information," *The American Economic Review*, vol. 84, March 1994, p. 104.
7. Falola and Lawuyi, "Not Just a Currency...," p. 29.
8. Herodotus and ibn Battuta have been known to have written about the silent trade in Mediterranean societies. A slight new twist is barter in the discussion of death and dying. See Joan Ryan, "Silent Barter," *Omega*, vol. 14, no. 2, 1983, pp. 145–54.
9. Bruce Fitzgerald, "Countertrade Reconsidered," *Finance and Development*, vol. 24, June 1987, p. 46.
10. For most recent writings on the subject, see Abhijit Banerjee and Eric S. Maskin, "A Walrasian Theory of Money and Barter," *Quarterly Journal of Economics*, vol. 111, Nov. 1996, pp. 955–1005; Steve Williamson and Randall Wright, "Barter and Monetary Exchange under Private Information," *The American Economic Review*, vol. 84, March 1994, pp. 104–23; Joseph A. Ritter, "The Transition from Barter to Fiat Money," *The American Economic Review*, vol. 85, March 1995, pp. 139–49; and Merwan Engineer and Dan Bernhardt, "Money, Barter, and the Optimality of Legal Restrictions," *Journal of Political Economy*, vol. 99, August 1991, pp. 743–73.
11. Falola and Lawuyi, p. 1.
12. *Encyclopedia Americana*, vol. 3, p. 275.
13. *Ibid.*
14. George Akerlof, "The Market for Lemons: Qualitative Uncertainty and Market Mechanism," *Quarterly Journal of Economics*, vol. LXXXIV, 1971, pp. 488–500.
15. Mary Rose Noberini and Rochel U. Berman, "Barter to Beat Inflation: Neighborhood network for swapping services on behalf of the aged," *The Gerontologist*, vol. 23, no. 5, 1983, p. 467.
16. The *Economist*, vol. 290, Feb. 4, 1984, p. 83.
17. Thomas Mayer, "Money," in *Grolier Multimedia Encyclopedia,* 1995.
18. In his 1987 article, Bruce Fitzgerald provides the following illuminating countertrade arrangements: "Coca Cola has traded its syrup for cheese from a factory it built in the Soviet Union, for oranges from the orchard it planted in Egypt, for tomato from a plant it installed in Turkey, for Polish beer, and for soft drink bottles from Hungary. A Swedish band was paid in coal for its concerts in Poland. Boeing exchanged ten 747s for 34 million barrels of Saudi Arabian oil.

Argentina awarded a fertilizer factory contract to Czechoslovakian firms with the stipulation that suppliers buy vegetables and other agricultural goods produced with the fertilizer." See "Countertrade Reconsidered," *Finance and Development*, June 1987, p. 46. In his review of Grant Hammond's book *Countertrade: Offsets and Barter in International Political Economy* (New York, St. Martin's Press, 1990), Nazir Bhagat claims that "estimates of countertrade activity varies from 5 to 40 percent of world trade..." See the review in *Journal of Economic Literature*, vol. 29, Dec. 1991, p. 1764.

19. Mary Rose Noberini and Rochel U. Berman, "Barter to Beat Inflation..." pp.467–68.
20. Arjun Appadurai, "Introduction: Commodities and the Politics of value," in Arjun Appadurai, ed., *The Social Life of Things: Commodities in Cultural Perspective* (Cambridge: CUP, 1986), p. 9, cited in R. H. Barnes and Ruth Barnes, "Barter and Money: In an Indonesian Village Economy," *Man*, vol. 24, Sept. 1989, p. 399.
21. In the case of southwestern Nigeria, colonial rule came early with the conquest of Lagos in 1851, and British coins were in use along the coastal cities particularly by the returnees, traders, and missionaries. Despite this, coins were not in wide circulation. In the hinterland, according to Johnson, they were "regarded more or less as a curiosity."
22. Johnson, "Cowry Currencies I," p. 18.
23. Johnson, "Cowry Currencies I," p. 41; also Claudia Zaslavsky, "The Yoruba Number System," in Ivan Van Sertima, ed., *Blacks in Science: Ancient and Modern* (New Brunswick: Transaction Publishers, 1983), pp. 125–26.
24. S. A. Akintoye, *Revolution and Power Politics in Yorubaland, 1840–1893* (London: Longman, 1971), pp. 25–26.
25. E. Adeniyi Oroge, "Iwofa: An Historical Survey of the Yoruba Institution of Indenture," *African Economic History*, 14, 1985, p. 75.
26. However, there is still some controversy over the level of dependence of the political economy of African states on the slave trade. See Robin Law, *The Oyo Empire, c. 1600–1836: A West African Imperialism in the Era of the Atlantic Slave Trade* (Oxford: Clarendon Press, 1977).
27. R.C.C. Law, "Contemporary Written Sources," in S. O. Biobaku, ed., *Sources of Yoruba History* (Oxford: Clarendon, 1973) pp. 9–11.
28. Mrs. Misitura Yusuf, 90+, personal interview, Iwo, 16 December, 1991.
29. Ekpo Eyo, *Nigeria and the Evolution of Money* (Lagos: Central Bank of Nigeria, 1979), p. 58.
30. Falola and Lawuyi, "Not Just a Currency...," p. 30.
31. Quoted in Van Sertima, *Blacks in Science*, p. 123.
32. Johnson, *The History*, pp. liv–lv.
33. A. G. Hopkins, "The Currency Revolution," pp. 474–75, 477.
34. Ekpo Eyo, p. 60.
35. *Ibid.*
36. Samuel Johnson, *The History*, p. 119. Other Nigerian communities counted their cowries differently. A good summary of this from Ekpo Eyo goes thus: "The Ibos, according to Jeffries, counted their cowries in units of six; a unit was called *ekpeti* and ten *ekpeti* made up one string or *ukwu*, twenty *ukwu* were equal to one *awka* and twenty *awka* made up one bag (*akpa*)...The value of the larger cowries was one third that of the smaller ones. Among the Fulani, the cowrie was known as *sedere* and twenty of these made up one *jalo*, five *jalo* were worth one *hemre* and ten *hemre* made one *zambarre* and one hundred *zambarre* (100,000 cowries) bought a slave..." See Ekpo Eyo, *Nigeria and the Evolution of Money*, p. 59.

37. Oral interviews at Iwo and Ilesa. Persons interviewed had been, in their prime, traders and farmers.
38. See Marion Johnson, "Cowry Currencies I," pp. 24–32, for a discussion of the relative weight of "big" and "small: cowries.
39. Toyin Falola, "The Yoruba Caravan System of the 19th Century," *International Journal of African Historical Studies*, 24, 1, 1991, pp. 111–32.
40. G. J. A. Ojo, *Yoruba Culture* (London, University of London Press, 1966), pp. 100–01.
41. Eyo, *Nigeria and the Evolution of Money*, p. 60.
42. Samuel Johnson, *History of the Yorubas*, 176.
43. Mircea Eliade, *Images and Symbols* (Kansas City, 1962), p. 126.
44. Toyin Falola, "The Place of Women in the Yoruba Pre-Colonial Domestic Economy," Seminar Paper, History Department, University of Ife, 1978.
45. O. B. Lawuyi and J. K. Olupona, "Making Sense of the *Aje* Festival: Wealth, Politics and the Status of Women Among the Ondo of Southwestern Nigeria," *Journal of Ritual Studies,* no. 1 (1987), 103.
46. Myths collected at Ondo by Jacob Olupona, 1988.
47. See Emile Durkheim and Marcel Mauss, *Primitive Classification* (Chicago: University of Chicago Press, 1963), p. 77.
48. George Dalton, *Traditional Tribal and Peasant Economies. An Introductory Survey of Economic Anthropology* (Reading, MA: Addison-Wesley, 1971), p. 4.
49. See I. Olomola, "Aroko: An Indigenous Yoruba Semiotic Device," *Odu*, no. 19 (1979), pp. 78–102; R. A. Olaniyan and A. G. Adebayo, "Yoruba intergroup relations and diplomacy," in Deji Ogunremi and Biodun Adediran, eds., *Culture and Society in Yorubaland* (Lagos: Rex Charles, 1998) pp. 103–07.
50. Reeve Tucker, *Abeokuta or Sunrise Within the Tropics: An Outline Of the Progress of the Yoruba Mission* (London, 1948, 2nd ed.), p. 409.
51. J. O. Lucas, *The Religion of the Yoruba* (Lagos: C.M.S. Bookshops, 1948), p. 409.
52. Many examples are cited from oral data collected by Falola and Lawuyi in 1985.
53. *The Church Missionary Gleaner* (August 1889), p. 117.
54. *Ibid.*
55. Georg Simmel, *The Philosophy of Money,* translated by Tom Bottomore and David Frisby (London: Routledge, 1990 [1900]), pp. 127–28.

3

The Ten Ideals: Money and Worldview

This chapter focuses on the Yoruba view of money. It proceeds from the premise that to understand a phenomenon, it is essential first to understand the *idea* on which it is based. An idea is given specific form in an invention, institutional development, or just an historical event. The *form* combines with other phenomena and experiences to reshape the idea. To put it concretely, the monetization of Yoruba economy in precolonial times promoted the development of the Yoruba *idea* of money. As monetization increased, new ideas were developed, which in turn influenced the further development of the financial institution. The reshaped institutions modified the idea, and so on *ad infinitum*. Therefore, it should be recognized from the onset that the Yoruba view of money is quite dynamic.

The Yoruba view money in many different ways. According to Toyin Falola, money is perceived as "*emi* (spirit), *osupa* (moon), *alejo* (visitor/stranger), or *aje* (witch)."[1] Karin Barber also explains that money in Yoruba culture is a vehicle for individual self-realization. "It is the medium in which human potential becomes fulfilled," she elaborates.[2] We propose in this chapter that nothing sums up the Yoruba view of money better than *kose-e-mani,* the idea that money is the "Indispensable One."

This chapter pursues the Yoruba view that money is the "Indispensable One." The first part explains the ten *ideals* of money. The second part examines the impact of rapid social change under colonialism on these ideals, particularly in reinforcing contradictions in the way money is conceptualized.

Kose-e-mani: The Yoruba Ideal of Money

Money can be viewed as an objective reality, and as a subjective ideal. An object is nothing until it is defined, or conceptualized. In this section, therefore, we will explain the Yoruba conception (or *ideals*) of money. The Yoruba have defined and redefined money several times. Perhaps the first time was when money in the form of cowry shells was introduced in precolonial times. Inflation, fluctuation in the value of the shells, commercial expansion, slave trade, state formation, and political instability all must have produced refinements in the view of money at various times and among different Yoruba groups before the nineteenth century. The revolutionary events of the nineteenth century—including the fall of the Oyo empire, the intraethnic warfare, the growth of new urbanized communities, renewed attempts at state formation, economic competition among the new states, and external forces such as the abolition of slave trade and expansion of British interests—all further contributed to the reconsideration of certain aspects of money. Then came the "currency revolution" promoted under colonial rule by the introduction of British currency. Having monetized their economies before colonialism, large sections of Yorubaland were at an advantage when the British introduced the new currency. In most cases they simply vested the new money with the ideals they had developed before colonialism. When these failed to apprehend new realities, they invented new ideals, or adapted European ideals that came with British currency.

A few words on the sources of these ideals will be appropriate here. Yorubaland is a complex society in several ways. This complexity arose partially from the composition of the society. As we indicated in chapter 1, Yorubaland is a collection of several ethnic groups who speak dialects of the Yoruba language.[3] The culture and worldview of the groups differ in several minor or major ways. We have, therefore, examined the common features or logic in their view of money. We seek the most widely used and accepted proverbs (*owe*), wise sayings, idiomatic expressions (*asayan oro*), stories (*alo*),[4] and Ifa verses (*ese Ifa*).[5] Our sources of these, apart from several published texts, are informal discussions and formal interviews conducted over many years in Iwo, Ile-Ife, Ado-Ekiti, Ondo, and Oyo.[6]

There can be no question about the validity of these texts as sources of deep philosophy and cognitive ideals. The texts (the proverbs, myths, family histories, and idiomatic expressions) are all taught to the Yoruba from childhood. They are considered important enough to constitute an integral part of the nonformal educational system. They are employed in settling minor and major disputes within or between families. They are the sources of Yoruba legal institutions, and form the basis of the colonial customary court system.[7] Kings, chiefs, and other people directly involved in the judicial system use these sources to determine who and what is right. The position of Ifa verse is slightly different. Ifa is the embodiment of collective wisdom and collective memory. The corpus is mostly sacred, and the verses are not openly recited. Nevertheless, Yoruba culture makes available to everyone several stories from Ifa verse, primarily to teach the young. In other words, the philosophy is not monopolized by Ifa and its priests, but is put in general wide circulation. Whereas Ifa priests may not tell tall tales, story tellers (*palo-palo*, or *awon apalo*) may adapt Ifa verses for their use.

The point, therefore, is that it is possible to identify Yoruba ideals, and to differentiate them from religious beliefs. Ideals are ethics, principles, or standards that strive at achieving perfection. Ideals are models, the ultimate goal a person or society seeks. In this section, we will discuss ten major ideals of money.

Kose-e-mani ni owo. The first ideal is that money is important. Money is the "Indispensable One."[8] This is one of several ways money has been personified by the Yoruba. It is this personification, this *idea*, that we shall explore extensively and intensively in this chapter. Conceived this way, money carries the capital M.

Money is important. The sign on the side panel of lorries owned by a rich Idofian transportation business owner, lorries that carried passengers between Ilorin and Lagos, and which passed through Iwo in the 1970s, read *Owo ni koko*, "money is the key." Money is truly indispensable in any market economy as a medium of exchange, and as a measure of value, transaction, and relationship. This indispensability is recognized in all societies, but not every society views money as a *being*. Jane Guyer thinks money is only an object. "Money is mundane," she says. It is a "mundane mystery" to most people. The object of which money is made in many cultures is certainly mundane—shell, paper, iron, cloth. Even where gold and silver and other precious metals are used, money is still an inanimate object. With the high rate of inflation, and the unequal exchange rates of many African "soft" currencies (vis-à-vis the "hard" currencies of capitalist West), money may indeed be seen as mundane.

In conceptual terms, however, the Yoruba think that money is the "indispensable one"—*kose-e-mani*. The Yoruba personify money, they give it a life form with such human attributes as movement, smile, and ability to do things. They think of money as a guest, as a friend (or an enemy), and even as a grandmother.[9] Money is capable of sitting (*aje o ku ijoko!*), of visiting and sleeping over (*owo ya ile sun*), of bearing witness for favorites (*owo jeri fun un*), of reproducing or hatching (*owo pa'mo*), and of working (*owo si'se*). The Yoruba imbue money with a great deal of power. To them, money is a being, a powerful being. To have power, therefore, one must have money (*ni owo*) or be close to someone who does (*f'ara m'olowo*).

Suru l'ere. The second ideal is that one must have patience to acquire money. Patience is profitable, *suru l'ere,* says the Yoruba. The ideal of patience pervades the morality, and this is taught from childhood. The following *alo* (myth or creative oral literature) bears this out:

He who has Patience has Everything

In the olden days there lived a man who was so poor that he had only one cloth and that was in rags. He had only a single wife, and she was childless. They had no other work to do except collecting firewood in the bush and had no reasonable hope of ever improving their condition. Nevertheless, they were content and believed that the future might bring them a better lot.

The poor man also had a friend called Abinuku—he is angry to death—who hated everybody in his heart, but did not show it in his face. The poor man thought he had a friend—but in reality he had nobody to love him, but himself.

The poor man prayed to God for many years, asking him to better his life; when at last the time came that the almighty God was ready to help him, He sent three heavenly creatures to visit the poor man, and they were called Money, Child, and Patience. He told the poor man that he would be allowed to keep one of these wonderful creatures, while the others must be allowed to return to their maker.

The three wonderful creatures accordingly set out on their long and troublesome road from Heaven to Earth. One day they arrived at a large river. The water was cold and deep, but Patience quietly walked through the flood. Then Child said to Money: "I am too weak to cross this river. You are big and strong. Please carry me across." But Money said angrily: "You impudent Child! Would you make your senior work for you? It is you who must carry me through the river—or there will be trouble." They were fighting for a long time, but in the end Patience returned and carried them both across.

The three wonderful creatures finally arrived at the poor man's house. They were well received by the poor man, who gave them all the food he could find in his home. The poor man felt pleased and honoured by the visit, but when he heard what they were coming about he got worried and confused. He felt quite unable to choose and so he asked the advice of his wife.

"You foolish man," the wife said. "Don't you realise that We need money most of all? If We have a child, what can We feed it on? And if We have patience—what use is that?"

The poor man was still not sure what to do and so he went to his friend Abinuku and asked his advice too. Abinuku was very jealous because the three wonderful creatures had not come to him. He did not want his friend to have either money or children and so he advised him to choose Patience. "If you choose Child—you will not have money to feed it. But if you choose Money and you have no child—your property will go to slaves after your death. So you had better have Patience."

The poor man did not know the answer to that and so he went and chose Patience. His wife was very annoyed when she saw Money and Child leaving the house and Patience settling down to live with them. But the poor man was content and Abinuku secretly triumphed.

Now Money and Child went on their way and they came back to the same river and they began to argue again, who should carry the other across. They quarrelled for a long time, and in the end they decided that, as they were unable to cross the river, they might just as well return to the poor man's house.

When they arrived at the poor man's house there was great happiness and the house became a house of song.

Thus Money and Child will in the end settle down where Patience has made its home. Patience is the father of every good thing in life.[10]

There are several versions of this story. The most popular, it seems, is the one that *juju* musician, Ebenezer Obey, made famous in the late 1970s. In this version, the poor man's name is Ogbon (meaning wisdom), and he has two wives. One wife has children, the other does not. Ogbon, the poor man, was also given a choice among Patience, Money, Child and Long-life. The childless wife insists on Child, the wife who already has children insists on Money, and his friends advised him to accept Long-life. Ogbon realizes that the wives were advising him from their self-interest. Probably to not appear partial, and possibly arising from his wisdom (after all, his name is Ogbon), and most certainly because he still listens to his parents, Ogbon chooses Patience. Money, Child, and Long-life leave, but they soon begin to miss Patience. At the end of the story, Money, Child, and Long-life seek Ogbon out in order to live with Patience.

The lesson of the story is that patience is profitable in the end, that money and all other good things of life will come if a person only has patience. The Yoruba frown at impatience. Indeed, impatience is considered the chief of all vices.[11] Patience is advocated for all occasions, except when one is in personal danger. Patience (*suru*) has several synonyms in Yoruba, including calmness (*pele pele*), endurance (*ifarada*), inner strength or reflection (*ogbon inu*), contentment (*ifokanbale*), and rest easy (*ifarabale*). Patience is never considered as total resignation. At the same time, the Yoruba frown at people who are opportunistic. The ideal patient person will not take undue advantage of other people. *Onisuru ni yio j'ogun aye*: "The patient person shall inherit the world." Certainly, the Yoruba say, every good thing, including money, will eventually come to the patient person.

Ibanuje ni ojo ori, owo l'agba.[12] Wealth and age need not correspond, and in any case *ojo ori* (age, or the state of being older than someone) only brings sadness if it is not accompanied by *owo* (money, or being rich). Yoruba society is gerontocratic, yet it gives positions of seniority (*ajulo*) to wealthy (rich) people. The new version of this third ideal is contained in the expression Karin Barber referred to in her essay thus: "*Olowo n soro, talika loun ni idea* (The rich person speaks [and is obeyed], the poor person says s/he has an idea)."[13] In other words, it does not matter how old the poor person is, he/she will be considered poor; and it does not matter how young the rich person is, he/she will be given respects deserving of an elder. According to Akinwumi Isola, no matter how old a laborer is (the proverb puts it beautifully as no matter how long and gray a laborer's beard is), his employer (that is the owner of the farm on which he is working) is his senior.[14]

Owo ko ni'ran. The fourth ideal is that money does not discriminate against lineages. This is the difference between *oro*, wealth or property, and *owo*, money. Money is acquired, but wealth is inherited.[15] It is true that money creates wealth, and that money can be used to acquire property; but wealth may have been established in a family for several generations. It is also true that the beginning of a lineage's wealth may have nothing to do with money. Before society became monetized, wealth or property was in several forms, including the size of farmland under cultivation, the number (and sometimes the color) of one's horses, the number of wives and children, the number of dependent clients and slaves, one's chieftaincy position or status (*ipo*), and certain attributes that one possesses such as knowledge, aptitude, skill, experience, character, and wisdom. The social stratification was not caste, but mobility was difficult. This problem of mobility began to ease with monetization, even when money was only cowry shells. Any individual or lineage could make money, acquire property, reinvest profit, be seen as wealthy, make more money, and use the money to buy popularity or acclaim (*f'owo ra'yi*). Money transformed the social structure, and the size of one's accumulation became a factor in the determination of one's position in the social ladder.

Age (*ojo ori*), wealth (*oro*), status (*ipo*), and money (*owo*) can be viewed as a series of spirals. One factor affects the other. Money stands out currently as a very significant factor. Let us consider age. Age used to be very important. Today, it is no match for money. A new Yoruba saying is *ajulo ko kan agba*, meaning seniority is not always according to age. Let us evaluate wealth. Money is used by the rich to purchase property and to accumulate wealth. As for status, money can now be used to purchase chieftaincy titles, even honorary doctorates. It is true that certain positions or statuses command respect, but they must be accompanied with money. A king or chief is as big as the size of his wallet. Moreover, with increased monetization and with the development of rabid materialism in society, people will accept certain positions only if these will guarantee continued access to money. Workers often do not look forward to promotion (which assures better status) in certain professions. A good example is the Nigerian Customs and Excise Department. Many customs officers make their money at border patrol posts, usually by accepting bribes from smugglers. Once promoted, the officers are expected to return to some headquarters office where, they say *ko si ije*, "there is nothing to eat." Promotion (that is, elevation to a higher status) is dreaded by many police officers, and is seen as a wicked act by the higher-ups to "take food from their mouth" (*gba ounje l'enu wa*). Promotion is viewed (and in some cases is used) as a punishment. This makes money a really powerful instrument in the determination of a person's worth.

Owo ni keke ihinrere. Money has established a prime place for itself in Yoruba religious expressions, be they traditional or foreign. Money is considered in all the religions as the vehicle (*keke*, literally bicycle) for missionary activity and as the surest medium for sending prayerful demands to God. We will deal with the role of money in each of the three religions separately but briefly.

In Yoruba traditional religion, money is offered in sacrifice to the *orisha*. Most Ifa priests receive cash payments for consultation, and they often prescribe sacrifices whose content also include money. It seems that the practice began very early, for most Ifa verses refer to the sacrifice of specific amounts of money. References to money in these verses are to cowry shells, but the Ifa priest could use his discretion to determine what kind of money he prefers. Many informants confirmed that cowry shells are used if cash is part of the sacrificial material; but they ask for *real* money if it is their own fee. Traditional healers and herbalists also demand money for their services. Sometimes they charge much more than they actually spent in preparing the medicine. Many of those interviewed explained that they do this in order that the charm (*oogun*) might appear to have value, because *oogun ti a o f'owo se, ehin aaro ni gbe*, meaning that a charm for which one has not paid good money is not highly valued. Thus, money plays a major role in the entire process of consultation, examination and the treatment.[16]

Money plays a major role in church ministry, too. Indeed, "*owo ni keke ihinrere,*" money is the engine for spreading the gospel, is a constant reminder to Christians to tithe and get involved in mission work. Money is employed in very ingenious ways by the various Africanized churches, such as the Cherubim and Seraphim, and the Celestial Church of Christ, where prayer sessions for the needy often involved the use of money in ways not unlike the traditional religion.

In Islam, especially at naming, wedding, and other ceremonies, money plays a significant role. Here especially, there is an emphasis on the ability of money to carry prayers to God. The more money one gives, the greater the chances of the prayer being answered. Several Islamic leaders said that there is no religious sanction for this practice. One of them called it "bold-faced robbery." Most say it is something done by corrupt Muslims to raise money for themselves. Nevertheless, anyone who has attended any of the so-called Muslim naming or wedding ceremonies conducted by members of certain Islamic denominations will come away with the impression that money really intercedes for people before Allah. Consider the following prayer session recorded at a function in Ile-Ife in February 1993:

Baba Isiaka mu owo wa	Isiaka's father offer money
Won ni kia fi se adura fun omo won	He asks us to offer prayer for his son
Ti o wa ni Kaduna	Who is living in Kaduna
Pe ki Oluwa so omo naa	That Allah may protect him
Pe ki Oluwa ba won mu oju ko oju	That Allah may bring them together again
L'ola Fatiha	[Let's pray by reciting the] Fatiha

Similar prayer sessions or cash-for-prayer transactions can be encountered easily in most Yoruba towns with a sizeable Muslim population. They can be heard in many mosques belonging to certain denominations, during the regularly scheduled prayers, or in private homes during a naming or some other ceremonies. Whenever this happens, money has become the enforcer, the facilitator, and the carrier of prayer to God. *Owo ni keke ihinrere* has, therefore, acquired a new meaning—that money is the fuel on which the vehicle that brings good news from God runs. So, the more money one gives, the faster the vehicle travels, and the sooner the good news (for example, a better paying job, a new car, healing, or protection for a loved one) is delivered.

Owo eru kii gb'oro. The sixth ideal is that money should be acquired in an honest, "clean" way. Money made any other way will not last. To the Yoruba, the end does not always justify the means. Money can attempt to justify itself, but it cannot legitimize itself. Although people may kowtow and show endless respect for the rich, it really matters to them not how much an individual is worth but how she/he came by the money. The culture advocates, even stipulates, that the means be clean.

The people want *owo tutu* (literally, "wet or cold money"), and could be seen at major social functions putting money (cowries, and later coins, but not paper currency) in cold water to cool and wet it for the recipient. Cold water, it is believed, symbolically offers the cooling and the regenerative processes, and protects the recipient from harm.

Owo eru (money acquired by mischief, treachery, or deceit) and *owo gbigbona* (literally hot money, indicating money acquired through satanic activities) are just a few examples of the types of money the Yoruba frown at. Lottery and football pool betting are also frowned upon. Any money made at the expense of another person is considered dishonest.

Hard work is recognized as a "clean" way to make money. *Ise l'oogun ise*, "[hard] work is the antidote for poverty." The Yoruba differentiate between hard work (*ise*) and stubborn, uncoordinated labor (*agbara*). The one who labors thoughtlessly and without focus is considered the biggest of fools and the laziest of people.[17] In that case, the Yoruba conclude, the path to riches is through hard work, not through purposeless labor (*owo nini o kan agbara*).

The ideal of earning money by the "clean" way does not imply that a person must only do white-collar jobs. Indeed, one must get one's hands dirty. *Isale oro l'egbin*, "at the bottom of most prosperity is some dirt." Moreover, *eni ti o le se bi alaaru l'Oyingbo, o le se bi Ajijoro l'Oja'ba*, "one who would not do the lowliest job at Oyingbo (a market in Lagos) cannot expect to wear the best attire like Ajojiro at Oja'ba (market also in Lagos)."

The ideal to make money in a clean way also allows the entrepreneur to keep the secret of his/her success from all. He is advised to *ba'nu so, ma b'eniyan so*, to "tell no one but himself" the secret of his business success. A strong capitalist ethic, this has the advantage of denying other people the opportunity for fair competition. The disadvantage is that the secret is often lost when it is not shared with anyone. All those who are not privy to the secret would then have to embark on a futile search.[18] Such people would also seek some short cuts.

Eni ya egbaa ti ko san o begi dina egbeje. The seventh ideal is to avoid debt generally, and bad debt (*gbese*) in particular. Owing to its history, especially the history of its perversion in the age of slave trade, credit (often called *debt*) has acquired a bad name among the Yoruba. In the era of slave trade, and in very difficult but not rare circumstances, a creditor could take away the freedom of the debtor and sell him into slavery; until the first half of this century, a debtor could pawn himself or his child to the creditor. To have good credit among the Yoruba is, therefore, to have money in your hand (*l'owo l'owo*) and not to have debt like a noose around your neck ready to choke you (*ni gbese l'orun*). It is to conclude a transaction by cash payment (*san'wo*) and not to do it on credit (*gb'awin*). The ideal of paying cash for goods or services is further advocated in the popular culture, especially music. Perhaps the best demonstration of this, albeit in a sexist manner, is in the following folk song in which a man asks a woman for a date:

Sisi t'o nlo w'eyin!	Lady, why don't you give me a chance!
Iwo l'anbawi ko w'eyin	I am asking you to respond (because)
Lowo lowo la wa	I operate strictly on cash-and-carry
Awa ki i se t'awin.	Not on credit

It must be clearly explained that this ideal allows the individual to borrow money for a pressing need or emergency. What it frowns at is to default in paying back (*aya-a-san*). The ideal situation is to promptly pay back the money borrowed so that one's credibility would be in good standing. The Yoruba say *eni ya egbaa ti ko san o begi dina egbeje*, admonishing that one should pay up small debts in order to qualify for big loans. To allow debt to accumulate, and to have no visible sign of ability to pay, is to invite the wrath of the creditor. Another thing to avoid is to die leaving a large debt for one's offspring. It is always an important prayerful wish that one manages to pay one's debts in one's lifetime (*emi ti o je gbese ni yio san-an*). This implies that one does not leave any debt for the children to pay. Bad debts are bad for the individual debtor, and drag his entire kin-group into disrepute.[19]

Owo fun ni ko to eniyan. The eighth ideal stipulates that (having) money is not everything but being a person (of good character) is of higher value. This is to caution the rich against being garrulous, and emphasize that good character is valued in society and preferred to money that is not put to good use. Power corrupts. Since money is power, then money corrupts as well. This ideal pulls the brake on reckless behavior by the rich, especially behaviors that might oppress the poor.[20]

Owo ree! Iku ree!! Behold Money! Behold Death!! The ninth ideal paints money in a negative light. It warns that money is death, or the reckless search for it could end in death. This lesson is clearly taught in the *ese ifa* (Ifa verse) called "Obara Kosun." Yemi Eleburuibon rendered the verse thus[21]:

Obatala and Money

The short palm tree in the savanna
It has numerous leaves.
Ifa divination was performed for Oosala
The day he traveled from Iranje-le to Iranje-oko.

There were two cities where Obatala was regarded as king
Iranje-Ile (Iranje-the-city) and Iranje-Oko (Iranje-the-farm).
Both Iranjes were big cities
And famous because of Obatala's reputation as a king and deity.
From time to time Obatala traveled from one [Iranje] to the other
There was a big temple at both cities for Orishaala.

Anytime Obatala left Iranje-Ile,
After paying homage to his ancestors at the shrine,
He was forbidden to turn back
Until he had reached Iranje-Oko.

Obatala was traveling with three brothers
Who always went with him as guides.
[One day as he was returning from Iranje-Ile]
Along the forest path there was light
The leaves from both sides [of the path] became white.
And they kept wondering what was before them.
As they proceeded further, there was the corpse of a rich woman
And Obatala identified her as Aje,
Money, the daughter of Olokun.

[Obatala's three brothers] wanted to know
Why this rich woman died along the path.
Obatala warned them never to stop, or even look at this woman.
According to him, that was the beginning of all evil.
He said, that is death. That is trouble.
That is the problem that all people have.
He warned them to desist from craving to see that woman.
And they departed.

A little while from the scene the three brothers asked Obatala to excuse them
Because they would like to relieve themselves.
Obatala told them it was forbidden for him
To stop his journey until he has reached Iranje-Oko.
Also it was forbidden to look back once he has left the shrine at Iranje-Ile.
He kept going, but warned these brothers never to go back to that woman
But to continue their journey and meet him at Iranje-Oko.
They promised to abide by his warning.

As soon as Obatala departed they quickly went back
To the scene where Aje was lying down.
In the olden days, exchange was by barter.
If someone had yams and needed clothes

He would give yams in exchange for clothes.
The hair of Aje was so beautiful, and they cut as much as they could
[Hoping it would be valuable enough] in exchange for something.
After they had enough, they became greedy and hated each other.

They sent the [youngest] one to go and buy them food
With a little piece of [adornments found on] Aje.
[The other two] conspired to kill him when he arrived.
When this boy went to buy pounded yam with okra stew
He also went to Asewo, those who make poison, and bought some.
He put poison in the food.

As soon as he arrived his brothers began to argue with him that he was late.
They took a cudgel and whip
And killed him.
They thought to share his part of Aje between them.
But before doing that, they thought to eat first.
As they finished the food, they both complained of stomach ache.
As there was no one around to come to their aid, they too died.

[Meanwhile] Obatala was expecting his brothers.
He could not find them.
After he finished all that he wanted to do at Iranje-Oko
He returned the next day [to Iranje-Ile].
Obatala was not surprised to see his three brothers [along the path], dead.
He said they had broken the taboo.

He pointed his staff at them and commanded them to arise.
One by one they revived and Obatala asked them what had happened.
They explained the whole story.
Obatala said, "Didn't I warn you not to go back to look at Aje?"
Money is death.
Money is trouble.
Money is all evil.

He said, "Since you have broken the taboo
And you all love money
Whoever is interested in these kinds of things
Will not live long."
And this is what will bring more problems upon human beings.
Your struggle will double, and you will keep wanting more.
You will become insatiable in search of money.

The key issue here is that Obatala's brothers had performed an abominable, reckless act and the repercussion was death. They had looked back, had deceived Obatala in order to go back to the scene of Aje, and had failed to exercise self-control on account of money. Such acts would lead to their death and the death of others. In this verse, Ifa was frowning at and warning against the situation in which brothers and sisters would kill each other for money. "Money is death. Money is trouble. Money is all evil," Obatala had proclaimed.

Ayanmo ko gb'oogun. The tenth ideal is that to be rich (to have money) is an act of fate or destiny. Perhaps it is important to state from the onset that most Yoruba strongly believe in destiny.[22] Destiny is that which is chosen in the mythical world inhabited by spirits before one was born. Destiny is that which also determines one's entire life activities and their result. It predetermines who will succeed and who will not. Certain persons are predestined to be rich or poor, to have or come by money, or to work hard and have nothing to show for it. Like money, destiny is personified. It is that all-powerful but invisible being which smiles on or torments people. The following *ese Ifa* explains the process by which individuals choose their destiny or fate in the spirit world:

Choosing a Fate

Mokewure, the priest of goats, and Mojewara, the priest of sheep, cast the Ifa oracle for three children:

Orisanku the son of Ogun
Oritemere the son of Ija
and for Afuwape the son of Orunmila.

It happened that these three children wanted to come into the world, and they must choose their own fate. None of them knew how to go about this and what to choose and what to avoid. But Afuwape's father, Orunmila, consulted the oracle. The priest told him that his son would be successful in the world. But before his son left heaven, Orunmila must make sacrifice for him.

Orunmila followed the instruction for sacrifice and gave his son a thousand cowrys, as advised by the *babalawo*. He told him that he must spend this money in the house of Ajalamo, "the one who moulds new children."

When Orisanku and Oritemere had been waiting for Afuwape for some time and did not see him they left for Ajalamo's house. When they arrived, they could not see Ajalamo. They saw many beautiful "heads" (*ori*), which they thought will be good for them, and they picked the ones they liked. Then they left for the world.

Later Afuwape arrived. He saw an old woman sitting on the floor, who seemed to be waiting for something. Afuwape asked her what was the matter? She replied that Ajalamo had bought some maize beer from her, but he had not paid her. Afuwape asked how much he owed her. She said "One thousand cowrys." Then Afuwape gave her the money.

The old woman asked him what he had come to do. He said he had come to pick his own "head" (*ori*). She told him that two other children had been there before him and they had chosen the heads they liked. Then she left, thanking him for the money.

Then Ajalamo came down from the rafters where he had been hiding. He thanked Afuwape for what he had done. Then he led him to the garden, where he kept all the heads. He showed him the beautiful heads that everyone liked to pick, but which might not let a man survive. He told him that some who picked beautiful heads do not succeed in the world and others will be surrounded by enemies. He warned him not to touch those beautiful heads.

Then Ajalamo showed him the right head to pick, and he told him that human beings bring trouble upon themselves, because they do not know what a good head is. Then he prayed for Afuwape and sent him to the world with his blessing.

Then Afuwape left for the world to become a successful and wealthy man. Orisanku the son of Ogun and Oritemere the son of Ija were surprised. They said, "Was it not the same place in which We picked our own heads?" That is why they sing:

I don't know where my friend picked his head
I would go and pick my own
It was the same place where We picked our own head
But fate is different
If I knew where Afuwape chose his head
I would go and choose my own again.[23]

It is significant that the Yoruba see destiny or fate as *ori* (head). To them, the head is the most important part of the body. Perhaps this can be proved scientifically. The head houses the brain, which biologically houses the central nervous system. A person is not pronounced dead today until he/she is brain dead. To the Yoruba, the head is the house of wisdom (*ile ogbon*). It is conceived in two ways: the metaphysical or inner (or hidden) head (*ori inu*) and the physical or outer head (*ori ode*). The physical head protects the metaphysical head, and the metaphysical head projects an individual's total personality and identity. Thus, one of the most powerful prayers offered by the Yoruba is *ki ori inu mi ma se ba t'ode je*, that is, for "God to protect my metaphysical head so as to not adversely affect people's perception of me." In short, a person's physical head (including the total physical appearance) is as important as his fate.

Although in theory destiny or fate always prevails, the Yoruba accepts that witches can change a person's good fortune for bad. The witches, it is believed, can turn the rich to poor by causing *agbana* to strike the former. According to Falola, "the problems attributed to *agbana* were probably no more than the inability of an individual to manage his resources, the failure to sustain an avenue for regular income, or ruination brought by a succession of misfortunes."[24] So strong is the myth of *agbana* that a rich person would offer sacrifices recommended by an Ifa priest (*babalawo*) to avoid it.

Destiny, therefore, determines the person or place to whom money goes. This notion is beautifully put in a song by Orlando Owoh: "that one should inquire from one's destiny before one goes into any relationship, start a business venture, or does virtually anything." Unfortunately, as the above *Ifa* verse indicates, one's destiny is an unknown, invisible element in the whole calculation. The rich and the poor choose their destiny in the same place. The poor are advised to resign to their fate, or to seek help from the *babalawo* in order to have their destiny changed.

The foregoing discussion of the ten ideals paints the picture of a perfect society, but Yoruba society was certainly not perfect. The discussion in this section shows that while the society had a monetized economy, it nonetheless insisted on high morality from its members. Members of its ruling class were expected to inhabit a high moral and ethical pedestal. The society developed several mechanisms and institutions to induce or coerce its members to comply and conform. It also had a reward system for compliance, and a punishment system for defiance. Despite these, Yoruba ideals have contradictions, many of them are as old as history; others are just emerging. We now turn attention to these contradictions.

Social Change and Contradiction in the Yoruba View of Money

Yoruba view of money has not been altogether consistent. Many of the ideals explained above have several contradictions. It also seems clear that the Yoruba maintain a double standard. There were, and still are, different sets of rules for the young and the old, for the rich and the poor, and for men and women. We will cite several examples of these, but in no particular order. Take the ideal that money is less important than good character. The Yoruba also posit that good character is itself a function of one's station on the cash scale. *Owo ko si, eniyan ko sunwon*, "without money there can be no good character."[25] Money, therefore, determines character rating. The standard for measuring good or bad character fluctuates according to the wallet of the person or persons involved. To put it mathematically, a poor person has to be twice or thrice as good as a rich person for his/her character to manifest and be recognized. There is clearly a deliberate perversion of the standard in order to elevate money (*owo*) over good conduct (*eniyan*).

Another contradiction can be seen in the ideal of patience. This probably emerged from Lagos and spread to other parts of Yorubaland, but it achieved the same result everywhere. It is not considered a virtue to be patient, because to wait patiently can mean to wait forever. The sarcastic saying intended to deride the opportunistic attitude of Lagos businessmen and street smartness of Lagos women proves this point: *Awon omoge iwoyi ko gbe Surulere mo, Olorunsogo ni won n gbe*, "women nowadays do not live in Surulere but take up residence in Olorunsogo."

The meaning is in the two names: Surulere and Olorunsogo, both in the suburbs of Lagos. Surulere, as revealed above, is "patience is profitable."[26] Well, patience is no longer a virtue, and people have moved away from it. They have now embraced (literally, "taken up residence at") Olorunsogo, meaning "God-has-provided," or God has given the opportunity. They have rejected the ideal of patience and embraced the gratification of opportunism. It is a contradiction that has spread from Lagos and to other urban centers and is filtering gradually into the rural areas.

The next contradiction is that which pertains to the development of the credit system. The ideal used to be to *have* (not to *owe*) money. The boundaries used to be clear: The *olowo* (rich person) own money, the *otosi* (poor person) does not have money, and the *onigbese* (debtor) owes money. As Western ideas of credit spread and became firmly rooted during colonialism and beyond, these boundaries became blurred. In today's Yorubaland, both the rich and the poor are in debt; and the chances are that the rich person's debt is proportionately higher than the poor person's. Yusuf Olatunji, the *sakara* musician, once put this in perspective in a song: *Ohun to se olowo to fi n roju, to ba se talika won a ti gbagbe e*, meaning "whatever would make a rich person sad (or complain) has the capacity to kill a poor person." To put it in context, if the rich and the poor were to owe the same amount in debt, chances are that the rich person would survive but the poor person would die of the debt burden.[27]

This point about money and debt does not need further elaboration, but it requires a little illustration. In the course of the research at Iwo, informants constantly referred to *owo atijo* (old-style money) and *owo igbalode* (new-style money). We always thought that they meant cowry shells and Naira, respectively, until one informant gave an illustration, using two chiefs to whom we will refer as Chief P and Chief Q.

> Chief P spends old-style money, but Chief Q is spending new-style money. They are both rich, but wait until you see Chief Q's name in the newspapers for owing National Bank or some other bank. Then you will know who is *really* rich. As for me, I pray to God to give me the Chief P type of money, because it comes with no strings attached, and it will not land me in prison.[28]

By some coincidence, Chief P was for a brief period Chief Q's father in-law. P was a prosperous farmer who had several people working for him. It cannot be ascertained that P did not borrow money to start his farming business, but, being illiterate, he probably didn't borrow from the bank. The impression people have is that he followed the ideal of avoiding debt. He was prosperous, many people were indebted to him, and he had several *iwofa* who worked for him. To be rich in the old style is to owe no debt. Rich people traditionally were lenders, not borrowers. They did not build their houses on credit, they did not purchase their property on credit. Their gross worth was also their net worth. To be rich in the new style is to be in huge debt, and our informants believed Chief Q is in big debt. He is also believed to have a net worth that is lower than the people's perception of the gross. It is clear why one informant, a farmer himself, would prefer the Chief P type of money. It did not matter to him that Chief P would qualify as an exploiter of the old school, with pawns and slaves working for him. However, the Q way is the new way, the capitalist way, and (we've been reminded) the only way.

Let us discuss one more example of contradiction at some length. The ideal is to make money in a honest, clean way. The perversion is to make money by all means necessary. With this notion, people found or devised various short cuts to riches. Several methods were used in precolonial times. These were carried over, but other devices were found in colonial and postcolonial eras. There were stealing (*ole jija*), and burglary (*ile kiko*), both old vices that probably began with property ownership and consequently expanded with the monetization of the economy. Stealing and burglary became so widespread in Ibadan early in its foundation in the nineteenth century that the *oriki* Ibadan proudly calls it the city of the boldest and meanest of thieves who carried out their activities on horse back (*Ibadan omo a g'esin ko'le*). Stealing, burglary, pick-pocketing, armed robbery, all are criminal short cuts to riches in today's modern cities.[29]

At the level of ritual, for which it is very hard to find concrete evidence, there are the various acclaimed magical acts to make money (*oogun owo*). There is a strong belief that money can be produced or conjured magically; that some people sell their soul to the devil (*gbe lukudi mi*) to arrive at riches; and that human beings can be sacrificed for the purpose of churning out crisp new currency notes. Furthermore, our informants believed that kidnapping (usually of children and pregnant women) becomes more frequent whenever there is a change of currency. The reason, they explained, is that the old ritual becomes invalid once the name, color, or design of the currency is changed, and a new ritual has to be prepared with the same materials. None of these can be proved. There is proof that ritual killing has continued, but there is no concrete evidence to connect the kidnapping to a ritualistic money minting venture. Nevertheless, this notion cannot be ignored.

And, there was (and still is) counterfeiting, the so-called *owo Ijebu*, "Ijebu's money."[30] Using government sources and bank reports, we show in chapter 10 the pervasive nature of this short cut to riches in colonial southwestern Nigeria from the 1920s to the 1950s. We compile several pages of tables on the frequency of reports on counterfeiting in Yorubaland, and we explain that counterfeiting offenses add to the list of old and new crimes with which the British had to deal. We also state that colonial rule created counterfeiting in two ways: first because the currency that it introduced was amenable to forgery; and second because the increased rate of monetization of society pressured individuals to seek opportunities to enrich themselves in both legal and nonlegal ways.[31] Simply put, the people found an additional means of contradicting the ideal of making money in a clean manner.

One must not forget deceit (*eru*) and cheating (*iyanje*), which find their peak in embezzlement, kickback, and other forms of graft. The perversion comes from the assertion that it is okay to spend other people's money without asking permission: *A t'owo olowo, a t'owo eni, Olorun ma jeki okankan won ni*, "whether it's mine or other people's, God please put money at my disposal." This prayer probably arose in late-colonial times, among the elite who had some access to state funds. The present day significance of the perversion is partially evident in the corruption that pervades local, state, and national politics. Spending "other people's money" is not ethical, but is not unusual. It is viewed positively in some quarters as "eating soup" (*ilabe*) or "eating money" (*ikowoje*).

Finally on this theme, there are the dirty tricks. The tricksters exploit the ideal that money is the "indispensable one," and also play on people's gullibility. Smartly dressed, sharp-eyed, and sweet-tongued, the tricksters promise their would-be victims that they will double or quadruple their money. Once a person has been sucked in, it is hard to get out. Often, there is a regional dimension to the tricks: the tricksters are believed to be from Lagos or some southern part of Yorubaland, while their victims are hinterland people who may in fact be residing in Lagos.[32]

In addition to the contradictions, the monetization of the economy has also challenged the concept of absolute truth. The Yoruba are no longer in consensus over certain values. One of these is the proposition that money is more important than children as a measure of individual worth: *owo l'egbon, omo l'aburo*. The Yoruba actually struggle with the question of ranking money and children. *Owo ju omo lo tabi omo ju owo lo?* Which is more important: money or child? There is no doubt that they value these two. Indeed, success is measured by thc simple process of ascertaining the amount of money or number of children a person has, or by a somewhat complex process of aggregating both money and children. The ideal picture of a successful person is one who has many children and a lot of money.

However, there is no consensus on the question of ranking money and child. It has provoked a debate that today is still being conducted in schools. Is money more important than children? Perhaps the issue is not importance but value: Is money more valuable than children? The proponent usually argues in favor of money thus: "You need money to have a wife or wives who will give you children." The opponent uses the following statement in favor of child: "Children cannot be bought." That is, you can only *have* a child of your own. And once you have children, you can make them earn money for you in a number of ways: by making them work for you or, as in those bygone days, by pawning them to raise a loan, or by selling them into slavery. Under present circumstances, most people will agree that money is more valuable than children. It is no longer mandatory for children to work *for* their parents and, thank goodness, the institutions of slavery and pawnship are dead. On the other hand one needs money, a huge quantity of it, to bring up children today. And, as Yoruba society becomes increasingly capitalist, the pursuit among the people (educated elite and peasantry alike) centers more on money than children. In today's circumstances, therefore, money is more important, more valuable, than children.

Summary

It is impossible to gloss over these contradictions; neither is it accurate to defend them. They can, however, be explained in four different ways. First, Yoruba culture is not homogeneous; it is a complex mixture in which the component parts never fully lost their individualities and uniqueness. What is considered fair game in one part of Yorubaland can be seen as a crime in another. Thus, it may be bad choice in Lagos (the most cosmopolitan city in Nigeria) to "live in Surulere," but in Ondo it may still be an extremely fine choice.

Furthermore, Yoruba philosophy or worldview is not always consistent. Perhaps we should state that no human society has offered a uniform, consistent body of thought. The Yoruba themselves recognize this in their philosophy. They frown at inconsistencies. Inconsistent people are called double-tongued (*elenu meji*), wishy-washy (*sehin-sohun*), and [bad] people (*araye!*).[33] Inconsistent people are compared to the devil in their mischief. At the same time, they recognize that people will create conditions to their own advantage. Thus, without really condoning inconsistency they allowed several, even contradictory, ideas to compete. If one idea locks a door, one must find another idea to open or break down the door.[34] A more recent notion of dealing with contradiction is *Oyinbo t'o se pencil lo se eraser*, "the same white people who make pencil also make the eraser." In essence, the goal is to make money and it should not matter how many ideals are broken, or erased, in the process.

Thirdly, the contradiction is a class issue. That is, the Yoruba call certain ideals or their contradictions into the service of social engineering depending on the status of the persons concerned. Thus, a poor man is expected to follow the ideal, for him the ideal is law. It used to be the rule for the rich person to be bound by the same principles, but it is becoming increasingly less so. Indeed, in some cases the rich, if they are not clearly above the law, are at least able to survive near the fringe. Bashorun Gaha of the Old Oyo Empire certainly lived above the law, and was a law unto himself. There are several contemporary examples among the rich Yoruba today.

Finally, the contradiction is historical. Every perversion of the ideal arose from increased pressure to meet new political and economic challenges. Patterns of livelihood and accumulation have undergone rapid changes. According to Sara Berry, "commercialization, political centralization, and the resulting patterns of production and investment have created an economy in western Nigeria in which prosperity is possible but uncertain."[35] The result is that this uncertainty compelled people to intensify their competition over "resources, profits and influence."

Indeed, Yoruba economy, like the economies of several coastal West African societies, has responded to pressure several times by reconceptualizing money. In the latter part of the eighteenth century, many parts of Yorubaland were participating in the slave trade. The Yoruba elite who acted as collaborators in the trade determined what qualified or did not qualify as good behavior. Some of them even opposed the abolition of the slave trade for their self-interest.

However, by the middle of the nineteenth century this slave trading elite and the trade itself were challenged head-on by the British. Legitimate trade was introduced, and a new elite was being produced. The change of power in Lagos from Kosoko to Akitoye clearly illustrates the British preference for a new set of collaborators, but this was within the same class. A more significant transformation was the emergence of the new mission-educated elite. These were the men and women who took Yorubaland into the mid-twentieth century. Their ideals and values were different. Owing to their mission education background, many of them were opposed to the traditional values and ideals. They expressed a preference for the Western ideals. A few of them wrote to extol the essence and value of Yoruba culture, history, and tradition, but most lived in westernized styles in such cities as Lagos, Badagry, and Abeokuta. For them, it was acceptable to charge usurious interest rates, and to help draft formal loan agreements that the borrower did not understand.[36] The transition to the educated elite is the subject of an extremely interesting novel whose fame is limited by the language in which it is written. Isaac Delano's *Aiye Daiye Oyinbo* (*It is a White Man's World*)[37] demonstrates vividly the demise of the old warrior aristocracy in Egbaland, and the emergence of a new elite of mission-educated clerks and petty traders.

Some members of the old slave trading elite took advantage of the new export trade in legitimate commodities, and fitted the old slave trading networks to the new palm oil trade, for instance. A majority did not. One reason for the inability of the old elite to transform itself to the new was the absence of capital formation in the era of the slave trade. Another factor was the nature of accumulation during the era of slave trade. The 'profit' from the trade, where that was money, usually went into supporting relationships or 'property' that were not only of non-financial nature but were also a drain on finances.[38] These forms of wealth included the accumulation of followers, clients, and servants. These clients were fondly and pejoratively called *b'esink'awo* meaning "[the one who] helps the horse to gallop." These were not the kinds of wealth that could easily be converted into cash and capital for engaging in the increasingly formal economy under growing British legitimate trade. Finally, the old cowries began to lose grounds to the new British currency.

The transformation continued, and by the end of colonial rule another generation of educated elite was emerging. Members of this elite were carefully and deliberately crafted by the departing British administration. They were the new capitalist and entrepreneurial class to whom the British intended to hand over some economic power. The British used money to create this class. The colonial government extended credit facilities and grants in aid to individuals and groups who met certain minimum criteria. Small-scale industrial projects in food processing and minor manufacturing were turned over to these men (and a few women). In other words, the colonial government used money—cash—to induce the birth of a small capitalist and entrepreneurial class. New virtues and ideals were created. To this class, borrowing was not of small sums, and default on loans was a mark of political connection and business smartness. Government money was *owo olowo* ("other people's money") that had been placed at their disposal to do with as they pleased. Moreover, government money was for the people, and could be used by the people. That is, the funds were theirs to use as they pleased. Do we need to mention names here?

We should stress that there was a discontinuity in Yoruba economic elite; every new elite has introduced one financial reform or another, and every reform has forced a revision of the existing ideals of money. The current contradiction in the Yoruba ideals of money mirrors the effort of a dynamic society to come to terms with a changing economic environment. It must also be viewed as an integral part of the contradiction in Nigeria's colonial and postcolonial society smarting under the influence of crass materialism.

The foregoing sections show that the Yoruba view of money has been dynamic. The ideals have been shaped and reshaped by local, national, and international environments of which Yorubaland is a part. As the economy develops in the future, further changes will be expected in the people's view of money and in the development of the financial system. One thing is clear: money is *kose-e-mani*, the "indispensable one." This ideal of money has been constant, and has remained strong, in the perception of the Yoruba people. It has also influenced the process of class formation and class mobilization among the people, a theme we explore in the next chapter.

Notes

1. Toyin Falola, "Money and Informal Credit Institutions in Colonial Western Nigeria," in Jane I. Guyer, ed., *Money Matters: Instability, Values and Social Payments in the Modern History of West African Communities* (Portsmouth, NH: Heinemann, 1995), p. 163.
2. Karin Barber, "Money, Self-Realization, and the Person in Yoruba Texts," in Guyer, ed., *Money Matters*, p. 207.
3. The classic text on this matter is the Reverend Samuel Johnson, *The History of the Yorubas* (Lagos: C.M.S. Bookshops, 1921, reprinted 1976).

4. Among others, see Bakare Gbadamosi and Ulli Beier, *Not even God is Ripe Enough: Yoruba Stories* (London: Heinemann, 1968); Ulli Beier, *Yoruba Myths* (Cambridge: Cambridge University Press, 1980); M. I. Ogumefu, *Yoruba Legends* (London: The Sheldon Press, 1929); Abayomi Fuja, *Fourteen Hundred Cowrys: Traditional Stories of the Yoruba* (London: Oxford University Press, 1962).
5. On Ifa, see William Bascom, *Ifa Divination: Communication between Gods and Men in West Africa* (Bloomington: Indiana University Press, 1969); Wande Abimbola, *Ifa: An Exposition of Ifa Literary Corpus* (Ibadan: Ibadan University Press, 1976); *idem, Ifa Divination Poetry* (New York: Nok Publishers, 1977); Afolabi A. Epega, *The Sacred Ifa Oracle* (San Francisco: Harper, 1995).
6. We do not use *oriki* in this essay partly because it is not very clear at what point an individual's praise name can be generalized for the community. *Orile* will be a much better text. However, for more information on *oriki*, see Ademola M. Adegbite, *Oriki: A Study in Yoruba Musical and Social Perception* (Ph.D. Thesis, University of Pittsburgh, 1978); also Karin Barber, *I Could Speak until Tomorrow: Oriki, Women and the Past in a Yoruba Town* (Edinburgh: Edinburgh University Press for I.A.I., 1991).
7. See G.B.A. Coker, *Family Property among the Yorubas* (London: Sweet and Maxwell, 1966), especially Part I: "The impact of English Law on Native Law and Custom."
8. We are grateful to Mr. A. A. Adediran, Vice-Principal of Iwo Grammar School, for the notion of money as *Kose-e-mani*, that money is the "Indispensable One." He expressed this idea in a private correspondence.
9. Concerning a rich person, the Yoruba often say "Money smiled on so and so." The statement *alejo l'owo* brings out the idea that money is a guest and whoever is the host should treat it well. The Yoruba pray that God should make money their friend. And whoever is extremely rich is said to have *iyalaya owo*, that is, "the grandmother of money." For more examples along this line, see Karin Barber, "Money, Self-Realization, and the Person."
10. Bakare Gbadamosi and Ulli Beier, *Not Even God is Ripe Enough: Yoruba Stories*, pp. 21–23.
11. *Ara ko bale ni oloori arun* ("Impatience is the worst of all diseases or vices").
12. The conclusion of this proverb varies. Sometimes it is *ipo lagba*, that is status is more important. However, status can also be based on money.
13. Karin Barber, "Money, Self-Realization and the Person," p. 219.
14. *Bi irungbon alagbaro ti gun to, eniti o gb'oko fun un ni oga re*. This proverb is based on the Yoruba ideal that grayness of hair and length of beard are marks of distinction and old age. See Akinwumi Isola, *Efunsetan Aniwura, Iyalode Ibadan* (Ibadan: Ibadan University Press, 1970).
15. Money can also be inherited. The Yoruba say *omo olowo j'ogun owo*, "a rich person's child inherits money."
16. For details, see Toyin Falola and Kathleen O'Connor, "Divination as an economic enterprise," *Paiduema*, forthcoming.
17. The Yoruba say *Alagbara ma m'ero ni baba ole*, "the one who labors senselessly is the laziest of all."
18. The way this is put is very interesting: *Eniti o mo ibi egbe oun ti la a sare ku*, meaning "the person who does not know the secret of his colleague's success will search till he dies."
19. For further information on this, see chapter 6 in this book.
20. For more information on this ideal, see Emmanuel D. Babatunde, *A Critical Study of Bini and Yoruba Value Systems of Nigeria in Change: Culture, Religion, and the Self* (Lewiston: The Edwin Mellen Press, 1992), pp. 87–119.

21. Ifayemi Eleburuibon, *The Adventures of Obatala: Ifa and Santeria God of Creativity* (Osogbo: API Production, 1989), pp. 67–69. The Odu was "Obara Kosun," one of the negative verses (*odu*) in the Ifa corpus.
22. They believe in fate and they are fatalistic to some extent.
23. Ulli Beier, *Yoruba Myths*, pp. 4–6.
24. Toyin Falola, "Money and Informal Credit Institutions," p. 166.
25. Note that the Yoruba call good conduct *eniyan*, that is person, or human being. This implies that a person of bad or questionable character is not a human being but an animal (*eranko*), or monkey (*obo*).
26. By the way, Surulere is a better place than Olorunsogo, which is a slum. But life in Olorunsogo is fast paced. It is possible for street-smart people to make money faster in Olorunsogo than in Surulere.
27. The validity of this statement can be demonstrated in international politics. Compare, for instance, the national debt of the United States with that of Nigeria. Nigeria's foreign debt is only a tiny proportion of the United States'. Yet, the United States only groans occasionally; Nigeria has virtually collapsed.
28. Interview with Adeyemo Ojo, Bale of Obamoro, February 1993.
29. See chapters 9, 10, and 11 in this book.
30. The Ijebu are known for their business skills. It is also probable that, unable to find the secret of Ijebu business success, other Yoruba groups accuse them of counterfeiting. The records, however, show counterfeiting in all Yoruba provinces under colonial rule.
31. See chapter 10 in this book.
32. Today, the phenomenon is widespread. It is more prevalent in Lagos than anywhere else, but Lagos is a cosmopolitan city. The "419" con business is not a monopoly of the Yoruba any more than it is local—American networks have carried stories of the international dimension of the business. One thing still stands out—the gullibility of the victims.
33. This is borne out by the saying *enu araye l'ebo: enu ti won fi pe Adegun ni won fi pe Adeogun*, meaning "people who double deal are bad: for they use their mouth to say 'Ade is straight' and also say 'Ade is crooked.'"
34. *Bi igba ko ba se si, a fo* ("if a calabash is impossible to open, then break it").
35. Sara Berry, *Fathers Work for their sons: Accumulation, Mobility, and Class Formation in an Extended Yoruba Community* (Berkeley: University of California Press, 1985), pp. 82–83.
36. See chapter 6 in this book.
37. Chief I. O. Delano's *Aiye Daiye Oyinbo* (London: Nelson, 1955) is similar to Achebe's *Things Fall Apart* (London: Heinemann, 1959), but the former is written in Yoruba and therefore has a smaller audience.
38. Jane Guyer's synthesis on this theme is very useful. See her "Wealth in People, Wealth in Things—Introduction," pp. 83–90.

4

Money and Social Stratification

This chapter examines the effects of the introduction of a widely circulating currency on the development of social classes. Our focus was during the cowry regime, up to the end of the nineteenth century. We deal with the interface between money and classes. There is some confusion in the literature on the notion of class in African societies. There is also an overemphasis on the supposedly "centerless" or "stateless" character of African societies. These prevent a rigorous discussion of class. It is asserted that traditional societies had no classes since there is a high degree of mechanical solidarity.[1] Therefore, because of the literature on the denial of classes in Africa and the excessive use of the concept of the "communal" we have devoted more space to the clarifications of class and stratification as they can be applied to the African situation.

Social Stratification in Africa

Perhaps it is appropriate to define social class and social stratification as they are employed in this chapter. By social class we refer, like McIver, to "any portion of community which is marked off from the rest," but unlike McIver such a distinction would not be "primarily by a sense of social distance."[2] Classes or strata have existed in Africa, and have been differentiated by such objective criteria as income levels, occupational distinctions, and the like, but members of the different classes have always been in social contact. We accept the rest of McIver's suggestion that class implies a sense of status, "sustained by economic, political, or ecclesiastical power," and that this sense of status "draws class apart from class, gives cohesion to each, and stratifies a whole society."[3] As a social stratum or class, therefore, we consider "a group of people occupying a similar position, distinguishing them from members of other groups in the process of earning a livelihood, in the administration of public affairs, and in the preservation of an ideology…"[4]

Social stratification, on the other hand, is the process that results in the arrangement of individuals within a society into hierarchically ranked groups. What are the determinants of stratification? Many scholars have spoken of subjective and objective factors that determine the process of stratification. Perhaps we can reduce all these factors into two: political and economic. Political determinants refer to the access that individuals and classes have to power; they also refer to the so-called conquest or ethnic stratification. This is the idea that different strata originate through the conquest of the territory of one ethnic group by another ethnic group, thus reducing the conquered group to the subordinate position. This is found in many African societies. Two examples will suffice. In Northern Nigeria, the Fulani conquered Hausaland and established their hegemony over the Hausa. The result was the emirate administration, which has continued to rule the area since the early nineteenth century. In the Central African states of Rwanda and Burundi, the minority Tutsi conquered and subdued the majority Hutu shortly before the establishment of colonial rule.

When considering social stratification in Africa,[5] however, most scholars use the economic determinants which derive from reading Marx[6] and Weber.[7] Marxism understands a class as a group of people with the same relations to the means of production, and the same rights and obligations resulting from them. Perhaps central to Marxist conception of class is the social division of labor. That is, people participating in a particular production process enter into certain production relations, it being understood that production relations among people always determine the character of every society.[8] Max Weber believes that this Marxist approach is oversimplified. The resulting Weberian approach divided society into *classes*, *estates*, and *parties*. Africanists, always eager to integrate approaches, have found some synthesis for the Marx-Weber approaches. The result has been a very sophisticated approach to understanding social stratification, its determinants, and its transformation.

The approach to stratification in Africa has been neither uniform nor static. This has made more difficult the task of generalization. The societies ranged from clan-based, noncentralized, village communities to vast empires and kingdoms; and there were several stations in-between. Surely, individuals were not ranked the same in these societies. It is probably valid to say that social stratification in each society in Africa features a mixed blend of ascription and achievement, and of political and economic determinants. Stratification in some societies was age based; in others it was based on kin-group's access to political authority. The point is that all these systems were transformed with the introduction of widely circulating currency.

One of the earliest forms of stratification was the age grade system. In many African societies, a person belonged to an age set. Members of an age set would graduate, as if in a school, from one stage to another. Each stage was known as an age grade. Vincent Khapoya described age grades as "almost a universal feature of traditional African societies."[9] He went on to describe the system among two communities: the Tiriki of Kenya[10] and the Afikpo Igbo of Nigeria. Among the Nuer of southern Sudan, it is reported that age sets are formed during ten-year intervals. The Nandi of Kenya are also reported to have seven male age sets: two of boys, one of warriors, and four of elders. Members of an age grade usually did many things together, fought together, and remained together for their entire lives, thus forming a very close nonkin group. Transition from one age grade to another was also marked by an initiation ceremony whose components varied from place to place.

Age grades and other systems of stratification would seem to cohere. African societies placed a great deal of emphasis on age as a means of access to political authority and obligation. The older generation, known collectively as "elders," performed judicial and advisory functions in most societies. It was assumed that prosperity, wisdom, and experiences all would come with advancement in age. Thus, the older one was, the greater the chances of political participation and economic accumulation. It was not by accident that those serving on the Council of Elders, which took the most critical decisions in segmentary societies, were men and women who had achieved a certain level of property ownership and accumulated much experience in addition to advancement in age.

As societies became more complex, and as political and economic structures changed, age grade systems became superceded in many societies by firm political groupings that seemed to separate the rulers from the ruled. In Africa's centralized societies, many of which have been wrongly likened to feudal arrangement, a ranked society emerged with the following hierarchies:

1. King and princes
2. Chiefs and nobles
3. Freeborn
4. Slaves

These hierarchies can be grouped into two. The first (3 and 4 above) is the group of individuals who had no independent access to power;

the second (1 and 2 above) is the group of individuals who exercised authority. According to Holy and Stuchlik, we can define the first group (3 and 4 above) thus:

> Individuals who have not acquired any authority and thus do not hold office. They are obliged to carry out non-economic services, but cannot command them from anyone else; they are persecuted for breaches against political norms, but are unable to prosecute another person; if they take any part at all in the formulation of political norms, then it is only anonymously and as a whole; offences against them are punished with milder sanctions than offences committed against the members of other categories...[11]

Holy also defines the second group (1 and 2 above) in the following way:

> Individuals who actually exercise authority and hold offices. In the activities connected with the exercising of authority they can command non-economic activities, pursue and punish deviations from political norms, and participate in the formulating of political norms. Their superordinate position over the members of the other categories, determined by their active part in the execution of political activities, is further fixed by their different norms of behavior and by the height of the sanctions for the offences against them.[12]

These immediately preceding discussions only differentiate between, to adopt very simple terms, the upper and lower classes. Several quick points remain to be made. There were significant differences between freeborn and slaves/strangers in the lower class category, and between kings/princes and chiefs/nobles in the upper class. These distinctions become much clearer in our examination of the Yoruba experience below. There was no middle class, no intervening class between the upper and the lower, between the ruler and the ruled. While in principle the upper and lower classes were rigid and apart, in practice a few members of the lower class were selectively inducted into the upper class. Although we cannot state with precision because of the absence of reliable census, the population in the lower class was (and still is) very large, much larger than that of the upper class.

Furthermore, membership in all the classes was by ascription. Some degree of upward mobility was allowed, but none could be king or prince except people of royal blood. Military adventurers might carry out a *coup d'etat* which, if successful, might result in the establishment of a new dynasty. Until that happened, an ambitious chief or nobleman could not be king. Before monetization the upper class collected taxes, tributes, fines, and market tolls—all in kind. For example, a farmer paid his annual tribute as a proportion of his produce, and this was paid during harvest time. Finally, kings could be absolute or they could be bounded by tradition or constitution but they were expected to exercise power. Thus autocratic African kings, like Shaka, made laws for the people. At public gatherings, these kings would promulgate new laws and abrogate old ones.

The above obtained in many centralized-state societies before the currency revolution. With the introduction of money, two simultaneous developments occurred. First, the upper class manipulated the emerging production relations in its favor; and second, groups of men and women among the lower class benefited from the new production relations by acquiring enough money and property to guarantee their upward mobility as *nouveaux riches*. Before turning attention to these developments, it is necessary to address the issue of gender and social stratification.

Gender and Class

The relationship between class and gender has been the subject of lively debate among Marxists and feminists. Sharon Stichter and Jane Parpart accept that the materialist mode of production analysis is applicable to the situation of women in Africa. However, they criticize Marxists for their slow response to the "Woman Question," and for overlooking the importance of the mode of human reproduction (MOHR) as distinct from the mode of production (MOP).[13] In their view, the woman's reproductive labor should be taken into account in any analysis of the MOP. Following on this position, Jeanne Koopman Henn states that under certain conditions, "gender relations actually become class relations."[14] Henn proposes the patriarchal MOP, and the argument that

> an articulation of modes of production framework, which includes the patriarchal mode of production, can produce a more rigorous and comprehensive understanding of the socio-economic effects of male dominated gender relations than can be gained by supplementing class analysis with a theoretically different form of gender analysis.

In essence, the foregoing analysis of social stratification in Africa is incomplete without the integration of gender relations. Perhaps it should be understood from the onset that most African societies were (and still are) patriarchal. Even where matriarchy was practiced, such as among the Akan of Ghana and the Herero of Namibia, males still held the most important political and economic positions. In Africa, therefore, men traditionally held positions superordinate to women. The question is: To what extent did this arrangement encourage or imply oppression or exploitation of women by men? There is no consensus yet, but it seems obvious from the several case studies that men have manipulated the gender classification to their advantage.[15]

Although few African societies subscribed to the aphorism that the place of women is in the home, women's productive and reproductive labors were still controlled by men in numerous ways. Many societies recognized women's right to property and would not deny them access to the means of acquiring such. Yet, their access to land, in many cases, depended on their acceptance of the reproductive roles traditionally associated with being a mother. In other words, women's access to land could be denied unless they were married and bore children. Even then, they did not have the same access to the labor of their children as the men. Whereas wives were required to work on their husband's farms, the reverse was not true and children were not compelled to work on their mothers' farms. Moreover, men had access to their wives' earnings from farming, food processing, or trade.

In addition to gender, however, women were also members of the different classes analyzed above. They were members of the royal family as Queens, Queen Mothers, and princesses.[16] They were also chiefs and occupied positions of great visibility and importance. Like the men, the majority of women were to be found in the lower class. Unlike the men, however, women's opportunity for advancement was further limited by gender issues. Thus, although there were women in high and low places, any analysis of African social stratification must recognize the superior position men held. Monetization affected this gender structure only very minimally.

The *Nouveaux Riches*: An Emerging Middle Class?

The preceding discussions demonstrate that to make money, an individual or group needed to have access to or participate in the monetized sectors of the economy, such as mining, manufacturing, food processing, and long-distance trade. There is no doubt that although they owned and controlled access to these businesses, members of the traditional political elite, that is the kings, princes, and chiefs, all depended on the services of members of the lower class. A patron-client relationship soon developed that the lower class could exploit in their efforts to improve their condition. In essence, unknown but large numbers of freeborn and manumitted slaves rose to important positions in the economic and political arrangement. This group of people we have chosen to call the *nouveau rich*.

A significant number of people in the lower classes became economically successful by several means, including having a large farm, operating mining and metallurgical industries, joining the army and being brave in battle, and participating in long-distance and international trade. Many of these activities were dependent on many variables, including natural/weather conditions, certain cultural practices, and political stability. For example, operating a large farm would require a large family since the family was the basic unit of labor, and having a conducive weather condition. A large family might imply polygamy, but the farmer had no control over weather conditions other than to hope that the king had performed all required sacrifices to the god of agriculture and fertility to ensure rainfall. In addition, to be successful in trade requires access to the initial capital, which was usually through family contribution and the rotating savings and credit associations (*roscas*). Since there were no formal educational institutions to teach business skills, an aspiring young person would have to be apprenticed for many years and learn the trade from someone already well established in the business. And since the business might involve traveling over long distances, some basic knowledge of direction, using every other thing but a map, might be required. Joining the army was even more risky, although it offered a greater chance for rapid success. The point to make here is that many things depended on the political and cultural conditions. It is not surprising that these same political and cultural situations often affected the outcome of a business venture, trade, or farming.

The most visible sign of "having arrived," of having made it, was to be vested with a chieftaincy title. This was induction, or rather the selective co-optation, of members of the lower class into the upper class. Co-optation did not come without a price. Having succeeded in farming, manufacturing, trade, or military, the lower class person must exhibit his wealth to attract the attention of the nobility and royalty. This usually involved the building of larger home, making large donations or contributions to some community projects, "lending" money to the royalty or nobility, and throwing a big party once in a while. Such a person would then be rewarded with a chieftaincy title. Unlike the traditional chiefs, however, the *nouveaux riches* were vested with titles that they could not transfer to their children.

Could the nouveaux riches be said to constitute a new class? Their character may suggest that they were; they were entrepreneurs, professionals in different trades, owners of capital, and so on. Nevertheless, they could not be equated with the middle class in the Weberian sense because they lacked independence. Their co-optation into the nobility also robbed them of the distinction and consciousness which Marxists look for in a class. The emergence of a real middle class in Africa had to await European colonialism. We now turn attention to the Yoruba experience in the next section.

Community, Political Power, and Class

Social stratification would seem to have started very early in Yorubaland, and to have passed through many phases at different times in the various states and kingdoms. In the early phases, classes were based on access to, and possession of, political power. There were distinctions based on economic pursuits as well. Although there was some variation from state to state, the general structure was similar. Class was better developed among the Yoruba of Oyo, who built the Old Oyo Empire, and Ile-Ife, the famed "cradle of mankind."

The earliest reference to social stratification among the Yoruba is William Bascom's study of social status in the Ife kingdom.[17] In this sociological study which, despite its importance, does not clearly differentiate between the pre- and post-monetization eras of Yoruba economic history, Bascom reaffirms that the Yoruba "have a complex and highly stratified social structure." Continuing in the same vein, he further asserts that

> rank depends upon a series of factors...including wealth, sex, his station as free or slave, his relative age or seniority, the rank of the clan into which he was born, the political or religious office which he achieves or inherits, and the social position of his relatives, friends or associates.[18]

In other words, the Yoruba today practice a complex system of social stratification in which ascription and achievement are intricately balanced. This is not the way it had always been: these were the results of changes and transformations, in turn resulting from the increasing variegation of society particularly since the introduction of money. Given the position of Ile-Ife in Yoruba history and social development, it is appropriate to begin this examination of precowry system of social stratification from that ancient city.

Bascom has identified nine strata of social structure in Ife society.[19] On further analysis we find that these can be collapsed into six main classes as follows:

1. The king (*Oni*) and the princely families;
2. The *Modewa* clans from which the palace chiefs are chosen; the *Ife* clans from which the town chiefs are chosen;
3. The priests and their families/clans;
4. The freeborn or Ife towns-people;
5. The palace officials, slaves, messengers and other functionaries;
6. Strangers: of two categories (i) Yoruba from other parts (*elu*); and (ii) non-Yoruba tribes-people (*kogbede*) such as Hausa, Edo, or Igbo.

In theory, vertical mobility was allowed among members of the lower classes; somehow even slaves, after manumission, could rise to important positions; but this was not expected among members of the first two classes. In practice, however, economic requirements for mobility were quite great, and often beyond the reach of the freeborn as well as slaves.[20] The Ife example is replicated in other parts of Yorubaland, for example, in Old Oyo. According to I. A. Akinjogbin, Oyo was a highly structured society, "with about five principal classes which were again internally divided into sub-classes."[21] These were, in descending order of power and influence in Oyo society:

Akeyo	The princes, from among whom the Alaafin was selected.
Ijoye	The chiefly families, of which the Oyomesi were the most powerful.
Omo ilu	The freeborn, "whose families owned land but were neither chiefly nor princely."
Eru	The slaves, among whom were the palace slaves who were even more powerful politically than the freeborn.
Ara oko	Literally "bush men," a category into which was lumped all those who lived outside of metropolitan Oyo.

The above was true for most parts of Yorubaland that had come under Oyo's influence. Perhaps we should start with the last category, the *ara oko*, which arose out of Oyo's economic prosperity, cultural arrogance, and political imperialism over many parts of Yorubaland. The *ara oko* phenomenon could be likened to the "stranger" category in Ife: the *elu* and the *kogbede* who were looked down upon and oppressed economically and politically. It could also be likened to the distinction in the ancient Roman Empire between the citizens and the barbarians. According to Akinjogbin, anyone who was not a resident of Old Oyo, or was not an Oyo Yoruba, was credited with less intelligence and civilization than, and certainly looked upon with disdain by, the lowliest slave in the metropolis. It did not matter if such an *ara oko* was a king, prince or chief in his own state: the bottom line was the ability to speak the Oyo dialect and imbibe Oyo culture. The Oyo had many statements that portrayed the contempt they had for the *ara oko*. Two examples will suffice here:

Aif'ini-p'eni, aif'eniyan-p'eniyan ni i mu ara oko san bante wolu.

> It is out of total disrespect for (Oyo) humanity and civilization that a "bush man" comes to town improperly clothed.

Ohun ti ara oko ba se ti o ba dara, eesi l'o se.

> The "bush man" cannot do anything right, except accidentally.

And as in imperial Rome, once the *ara oko* had imbibed the Oyo culture, and if he/she was not originally a slave, he/she was given Oyo citizenship, promoted to the class of the freeborn, and accorded all the benefits of an Oyo citizen.[22]

There were limits to the mobility allowed in the class system. Membership of the first two was by ascription. In Oyo, the princely class comprised the king, the *Alaafin*, his *Aremo* (first born or heir apparent, who, until the great changes of the nineteenth century, did not actually succeed his father), his other children, the children of previous *Alaafin*, and the king's wives. Although men (princes) performed most public functions, women were given important roles among the princely class. In particular, the *Olori*, the king's favorite wife, had immense political clout. In Ondo there was the office of the Queen Mother, which was a very important position. Slight variations occurred in other Yoruba states, but the princely class was basically the more important arm of the ruling elite. The other arm was the chiefly class, the *ijoye*, made up of civil and military chiefs. These were the kingmakers and advisers, and in their respective quarters and compounds they adjudicated in minor disputes. Among the Oyo, the most important chiefs were the *Oyomesi* made up of seven chiefs who, in full council, had the power to depose an *Alaafin* who, in their opinion, had violated the constitution. Again, although men occupied the most important chieftaincy titles, women members of the chiefly class were well respected. Indeed, depending on the personality of the occupant of the office, the title of *Iyalode* was a very powerful chieftaincy position. Membership of the chiefly and princely classes was determined by birth: children of chiefs could not aspire to be kings.

So much has been written about indigenous slavery in Africa.[23] It is, however, necessary to reiterate that there was a distinction in Yorubaland between the palace slaves (*eru oba*) and slaves owned by other members of the community. Whereas the former had enormous privileges and exercised greater political power than some chiefs, than most freeborn, and than all *ara oko*, the latter enjoyed little legal protection and, in the age of the Atlantic slave trade, could be sold at the slightest pretext. Despite the influence of the palace slaves, however, slave status was not cherished by the poorest freeborn. Indeed, the freeborn (*omo ilu*) was a large class to which the rich and the poor belonged. Most were engaged in agriculture, particularly in the production of food crops, but a large professional group was already developing by the sixteenth century of traders and manufacturers and craftsmen such as sculptors and other artists, weavers, dyers, tailors, smiths, and the like who pursued their businesses on a full-time basis. There was also a growing subclass of entertainers, including musicians (*onilu*, *olorin* or *akorin*), traveling theaters (*eegun alare*), magicians (*apidan* or *opidan*), and poets (*akewi* or *asunrara*) who gave public performances for all members of society, both rich and poor.

Despite its rigidity, the system allowed for some movement across the classes, especially between the two lower classes. Akinjogbin has offered the following description of the movement between the classes:

> A slave could purchase his freedom and become a freeman. But through the *orile* assigned to him his descendants would forever be remembered as offsprings of slaves. A female free citizen could marry into a princely family or chiefly class and her descendants would become centres of influence for their cousins of the lower classes. A princess could marry a free citizen, but her husband could not thereby control her. She was free to move out anytime she chose or have other lovers without moving out of her marital home. She might, however, choose to remain faithful to the husband and have children for him. Such issues, if they became successful later in life, could become princes and contest a vacancy on the throne.[24]

The relationship that existed between the classes was dynamic. For the most part, the different classes were dependent one on the other. However, as society became more complex and variegated, elements of intra- and interclass conflict, and the oppression of the lower by the upper classes, began to be introduced. Moreover, the solidarity that used to exist between the princely and the chiefly classes began to break down. Although most Yoruba kingdoms went through this transition, it was more severe and had more disastrous political consequences in the Old Oyo Empire.

Oyo's imperial expansion between the sixteenth and eighteenth centuries had been achieved by the co-operation of all the classes. Thereafter, members of the ruling classes (the princes and chiefs) sought not only to preside over the exploitation of the imperial economy but also to exclude members of the lower classes from the spoil. The sharing of the booty also drove a wedge into the solidarity that used to exist among the princes and chiefs. Among other issues, a long squabble arose over who was to control the economic advantages of imperial conquest. Generally regarded as the "Gaha's atrocities,"[25] this squabble is better appreciated as an intraclass struggle for the economic ascendancy of Oyo chiefs than as mere political trouble within metropolitan Oyo caused by *Basorun* Gaha. It was clear that Gaha was not simply pursuing a personal ambition, but that of his class. According to Samuel Johnson, "Gaha had a great influence with the people, and a great many followers who considered themselves safe under his protection."[26] It seemed at first that the *Alaafin* and the princes lacked the power to deal with the conspiracy; for, between 1735 and 1770 the *Basorun* (in conspiracy with the chiefs) deposed four *Alaafin* and forced them to commit suicide. In the same period, the *Basorun* sent his own agents to the provinces to collect the annual taxes and tributes. As the years wore on, cracks began to show in the ranks of the chiefs. Possibly because Gaha had become too greedy (he was said to have refused to share the booty and tributes equally among the *Oyomesi*), and partly because the military was tired of arbitrary orders from the *Basorun*, the *Are-ona-Kakanfo* (Field Marshall) Oyabi changed sides and gave *Alaafin* Abiodun military support to overcome the Gaha conspiracy in 1774. Abiodun's triumph was also victory for his class: in a bloodbath, he eliminated all pockets of opposition to the princes. However, since the conspirators were brave and experienced members of the armed force, the purge was counter-productive by rendering the Oyo army weak.[27]

Members of the lower classes bore the brunt of this intraclass struggle. The cruelty they suffered from the contesting parties could only be imagined. In such a troubled time when political autocracy was manifested, they no longer had access to justice or even "common decent treatment." Samuel Johnson provides a long list of abuses that the freeborn suffered from those who were supposed to be their protectors.[28] Two examples will suffice, one each representative of the cruelty of the *Alaafin* and Gaha's children, respectively:

> [*Alaafin* Ayibi] was one day in his bath, being attended by one of his favorite wives; and she, in a moment of self-forgetfulness (or rather of amorous regard) said jocularly to him, "And this is all of the man so much dreaded by all!" He took offence at this remark, but disguised his displeasure by a smile, but inwardly he was determined to convince her practically of the power which made him an object of dread to all. After leaving his bathroom, he gave an order to a Tetu (executioner) privately to fetch the heads of the wife's father and mother each in a calabash, and decently covered up. This order was promptly executed. The wife had by this time forgotten her remarks in the bathroom....The calabashes being brought and set before him, he sent for her from her apartment, and asked her to uncover those calabashes and tell the contents of them! "Do you know them?" asked he, "Yes I do," she replied trembling. "Then," rejoined he "that is the secret why I am so much dreaded by all, although to you I seem but commonplace and ordinary."[29]

> ...Gaha's sons were as ambitious and as cruel as their father....One of them once engaged a carrier to whom he gave a load too heavy for him to carry, but he dared not refuse to do so. He walked behind the man amusing himself with the sight of the man's sufferings from the weight of the load. He remarked in jest that the man's neck had become so thick that he doubted whether a sword could cut through. He suited his action to his words, drew his sword, and actually tried it! The man was decapitated, and his body was left wallowing in his blood, and another man was compelled to take up the load.[30]

The citizens were subjected to so much cruelty by a handful of authoritarian leaders. It was in this era that many slaves were sold into the Atlantic system. Commoners' wives and property were appropriated openly, and young women were debauched at puberty. A prince who decided to travel at night "could order whole villages on his path to be set on fire (the roofs were made of grass thatch) just so that he could see clearly."[31] Any member of the ruling elite could go to the countryside and impose himself on the people. It is important to recognize that this was an isolated circumstance in the history of Oyo empire and of Yorubaland.

Oyo at this time offered an extreme case of the coarseness of life in Yorubaland, but the crisis in the social stratification produced far-reaching consequences for a large part of the country. In particular, the oppressed classes of Oyo long remembered and resented any form of monarchical oppression when they had the opportunity to create a new society in the mid-nineteenth century. According to Akinjogbin,

> the Oyo survivors who seized political power in Ibadan around 1832 completely rejected any form of monarchical government or any kind of class division based on birth or families in their new settlement. Instead they opted for an open society where merit and ability would be the passport to leadership. That kind of decision coming from Oyo refugees must be striking for had they liked their former system, nothing would have been easier for them than to replicate it in their new home, as they had descendants of kings and chiefs among the settlers in Ibadan in the 1830's.[32]

Changes in Oyo social stratification had great and lasting impact on other parts of Yorubaland. As we have shown, the changes also affected the dispersal of Yoruba people to other parts of the world through the increase in the volume of victims of the wars sold into the Atlantic slave trade. At this stage, the question can be posed: What was the impact of money on this social structure? This is the focus of the next section.

Rich and Poor: Money and Changes in Social Stratification

Money, people say, is the root of all evils. The monetization of Yoruba economy brought its own evils. In this section, evidence will be presented to show that Yoruba society was moving away from the old stratification system into a strictly ordered system based on access to, and possession of, money and property before the coming of colonial rule. Owing largely to the increasing reliance on the market, there developed a clear distinction between those who had money and those who did not. In place of the earlier division based on birth, the new classes placed great emphasis on success and achievement. By the end of the nineteenth century, the society had become differentiated into two basic classes: the rich, *olowo*, and the poor, *otosi* or *talaka* (from the Hausa *talakawa*).

The next chapter is devoted to the various ways money was earned and the process of accumulation in Yorubaland. In the rest of this chapter, therefore, our attention will be focused on the impact of money and monetization on the pre-existing social structure. To begin with, who were the rich? From among which classes did they emerge? What were the social and political obligations imposed on them by the society? In general, the rich were of two categories: the "old" and the "new" elite. The old elite, that is, members of the ruling aristocratic class, including the kings, princes, town and quarter chiefs, and military leaders, employed their position (their access to land, labor and inheritance) to accumulate cowry currencies, the new source and measure of wealth. Whatever the merits of Yoruba land tenure, the fact remains that the members of the ruling elite, particularly the kings or village heads, derived a lot of wealth from their role as guardians of the family and communal lands. The statement *oba lo n'ile*, meaning "the land belongs to the king," is indeed very true. In theory, and as writings on Yoruba land law[33] have shown, land belongs to the entire community or lineage, and members of the lineage have no difficulty in obtaining land for agricultural and residential purposes. In theory, too, the land is held in trust for the people by the king, and, until the promulgation of the Nigerian Land Use and Allocation Decree of 1977,[34] he had the power to allocate parcels of the land, "including forests and thc plain," to outsiders for life. In practice, members of the lineage or community, as well as outsiders, were to pay a part of the annual yield on the farm as tribute, known in most parts of Yorubaland as *isakole*. This tribute was not exactly a land tax, but it subsequently formed the basis of accumulation by the ruling elite.[35] It was not unusual for some kings to fix the proportion of the yield payable as *isakole*. The food crops were consumed in the palace while the surplus was sold. For members of the ruling elite, therefore, the process of cowry accumulation rested on the tapping of the *isakole* system.

In addition to the collection of this internally generated *isakole*, the old elite also became rich from their exploitation of the vassal states. This was especially true of rulers of kingdoms with imperial status, such as Ife, Oyo, Ijesa, Ibadan, Ilorin, and Egba. The elite in these kingdoms collected annual tributes from the provinces and vassal states. This was in addition to the spoils of war at first conquest. It was also apart from punitive exactions that might be visited upon rebellious provinces. Originally, the tributes were paid in kind (in food crops as were the *isakole*) but surpluses were sold to generate cash. As the economy became increasingly monetized, kings and chiefs began to collect cowries in addition to food crops.

In essence, tributes constituted one of the main sources of wealth, and provided the initial capital which could be (and certainly was) invested to generate more wealth.[36] Thus, rather than displace members of the old aristocracy, cowries actually promoted the transformation of their economic status.[37] This, at least, was the case in Oyo empire in the age of *Alaafin* Abiodun, who was remembered in the traditions as a very rich trader. Before that, it was also the case during the era of *Basorun* Gaha, who received presents in cowries as well as building materials from vassals upon the occasion of the fire that razed down his compound.[38]

The Gaha example is very pertinent in this case, and the story is retold here the way it was narrated by Samuel Johnson. The story began with the ascension of *Alaafin* Abiodun to the throne of the Oyo Empire. The new king exercised caution, making sure to treat the powerful and much revered *Basorun* Gaha with respect. In an uncharacteristic move, Abiodun "went regularly every morning" to pay Gaha respects, but it was a plot to drain Gaha's resources. Customarily, a chief must give presents whenever the king visited. Every time Abiodun went to Gaha, he received "10 heads of cowries"[39] as presents. "This state of things continued for many years so much so that even the Basorun was becoming tired.... This man of blood was often heard to say "Who taught this king to be so wise? These daily presents are getting to be too heavy a charge on my exchequer now." Upon this he consulted the medicine men "to make him charms to get him plenty of cowries."

> One of his medicine men assured him that he can make him a soap to wash with, and before sunset, his wish will be realized. He made the soap, and [Gaha] used it according to directions, and strange to say, it took effect, but in a way no one anticipated. Whatever the cause was due to, nobody knew, but fire broke out in the Basorun's house that afternoon, and all efforts to extinguish it failed so [the house] was burnt to the ground. Owing to the Basorun's influence and power, and the dread all had of him, every rank and station, from the Alaafin downwards now vied to be the foremost in contributing to repair his losses, 10, 15, 20 bags of cowries came from all quarters. The heads of the different wards of the city, the Modade, Molaba, Nsise-ogun, Ntetu, T'onse-Awo, Aremu, Ita-Ologbo, Ajofa, and the Ogede quarters, all brought presents in cowries.
>
> Then the provincial kings and chiefs from the Onikoyi downwards brought building materials, and also their own contributions in cowries, which greatly augmented his store. The Basorun then asked the medicine man "Is this the way you promised to get me cowries?" He replied, "Yes...by what other means could you have amassed such an abundance in so short a time?"[40]

Moreover, the cowry currency boosted the economic importance of coastal states, such as the Popo, Egba, Egbado, and Ijebu, who became middlemen in the trade between the Europeans and the Yoruba, which trade brought cowry shells in exchange for slaves and legitimate goods. In other words, money promoted the advance of these coastal states and gave them greater capacity for competition with their counterparts in the hinterland. A major evidence in this regard was the Popo king, Elewi-odo, who visited Oyo in the days of *Basorun* Gaha. Elewi-odo was a friend of the *Alaafin* Agboluaje, and he was reputed to be very rich because he was nearer the coast and was trading with the Europeans.[41]

On the other hand, a new propertied class emerged among the free-born in the lower classes. As will be shown in the next chapter, opportunities existed in certain situations in precolonial Yorubaland for an individual in the lower classes (except the slaves) to have upward mobility. This could be achieved through excellence in farming, trading, or manufacturing. The Yoruba put everything to *ori* or *ayanmo*, luck or destiny; not necessarily *ogbon* or *agbara*, wisdom or hard work.[42] To be rich, a lower-class person might be asked to perform a number of sacrifices, to literally "wash his/her head," to bring him/her good luck. Riches might still elude him/her, despite the sacrifice, if his/her *ayanmo* (destiny) was to be poor. Of the different occupations or professions, trading and warfare provided the best avenue for upward mobility among members of the lower classes.

It is not possible to date the origin of the *nouveau riches* in Yorubaland. What is certain from the evidence available is the fact that the development was a gradual process that occurred at different times in the various kingdoms. And their emergence raised questions of the political role to be assigned to them. The most common approach to the issue, at least in the nineteenth century when we have better evidence, was their incorporation into the political process by their investment with honorary, sometimes traditional, but often nonhereditary, chieftaincy titles. There can be no doubt that this practice had begun quite earlier, its forerunner being the military practice of promoting brave soldiers into commanding positions and earning such titles as *Balogun* and *Jagun*. The most common of these nonhereditary, civilian titles conferred on the *nouveau riches* was usually in the area of military and trading, as head or assistant head of a detachment of the kingdom's army, or of a guild of traders. The latter would account for the proliferation of the title of *Parakoyi* (male head of traders) or *Iyalaje*[43] (female head of traders) in many parts of Yorubaland.

It was in the area of societal expectations that the differences between the old and new men and women of wealth became apparent. Money was important, but in the strict ordered society of the Yoruba it was never a substitute for being born into, or descended from, a titled class. At least, this was the way the old aristocracy sought to preserve its political status. Members of the new aristocracy or *nouveau riches* were incorporated into the political system, might be dining and wining with the kings and princes, but they had (and knew) their limits. No matter how wealthy, they were not to be insolent to members of the titled nobility even though the latter might not be as rich.

Beyond the above limitation, all members of the upper classes were obliged to perform certain duties for the benefit of their society. They were expected to provide good leadership at peace or war time, and upon them rested the patronage of the arts. They engaged the praise singers, poets and drummers; carvers and sculptors; tailors and embroiders; builders and palm-wine tappers. In all these, personal appearance was considered to be of great importance. Everyone expected the rich to dress well, and their king to be better dressed than any other individual. Thus, to return to the story of Elewi-odo on his state visit to

Oyo, the Oyo people expected the *Alaafin* to be better dressed than his friend. According to the narrative as recorded by Samuel Johnson, "as often as the King (*Alaafin*) changed his robes, he (Elewi-odo) changed his covering cloth to the one of the same material." At this,

> the citizens of Oyo grew jealous for the honour and glory of their King and wished him to appear superior to the Elewi-odo by robing himself with something the like of which even the Elewi had not.... The manufacturers were summoned and the case put before them, and they promised to rise to the occasion. A simple gown was thereupon woven, of common stuff indeed, but embossed all over with the silken wool of the large cotton tree; seen at a distance the nature of the cloth could not be made out by the crowd; when the sun shone upon it, it reflected a silken hue to the admiration of all; when the breeze blew, detached flosses of silk floated all around his majesty....The crowd went into an ecstatic frenzy about it, and shouted an applause.[44]

The import of the above is that, to a large extent, whereas the Yoruba people supported the idea that the rich should conform to certain standard of living, there was a certain restriction to how wealth should be flaunted.

The foregoing leads us to examine Bascom's division of the upper class into six different strata, as follows:

1. The wealthy man (*oloro*), who has the greatest amount of property;
2. The rich man (*olola*) or man of money (*olowo*);
3. The man of principle (*enia pataki*);
4. The gentleman (*gbajumo*);
5. The lucky man (*olori rere*);
6. The good hearted man (*oninu rere*).[45]

Although Bascom conceives the above classification within the context of Ife society, it is actually applicable to several Yoruba kingdoms and societies. The point to note is that monetization increased the membership of the upper classes, although the door was not thrown wide open for members of the lower classes. There were various restrictions consciously or unconsciously imposed on the common people. They had no access to vital information on the most lucrative economic activities. Where they did, their movement was restricted by the general insecurity resulting from slave trading by members of the upper classes.[46]

At the same time, money reinforced the inequality among members of the ruling class. The most important groups were the first two strata above—the *oloro* and *olowo*. It is also interesting to note that the positions are interchangeable. To be *olowo*, the *oloro* could sell some of his/her property, including slaves, clothes, farm crops, ornaments, and, more recently, land; to become *oloro* an *olowo* only has to invest his money on any or all items of property that appeal to him/her. Of the other four strata, the gentleman (*gbajumo*) deserves a brief mention. *Gbajumo* is from *igba oju mo*, meaning literally a person known by about two hundred eyes. Such a person was actually popular enough to have been well acquainted with people beyond his village or compound in the city. It was also assumed that the several "eyes" were not those of ordinary people but chiefs and princes. The *gbajumo* were men and women of ideas, and they promoted those ideas with their money: always on hand at important occasions, always ready to spend a few cowries on praise singers, always called upon to be spokesperson for the family or town, and so on. The possession of money (cowries) certainly made life worth living for members of the upper classes whether they belonged to the old aristocracy or the new.

On the other hand, the want of money made life difficult for members of the lower classes. The poor, *otosi* or *talaka* (from Hausa *talakawa*) were, to say the least, dependent on the rich either as slaves or as clients. As society became monetized and more complex, the exploitation of the slaves increased. Many Yoruba were sold into the Atlantic slave trade at different times, and members of the upper classes dominated this trade. Indeed, several *Alaafin* of Oyo participated in the trade. The ones who suffered most from incessant raids for captives were the members of the lower classes who resided in the villages or, as we have shown in the introduction, in the least-defended parts of the cities. It was also among the lower classes that the rank and file of the armies were conscripted. Although this might be an avenue for upward mobility for some, for a majority of them it was the route to capture and enslavement. When the slave trade came under attack in the latter part of the nineteenth century, the elites put the slaves already acquired to use in the farms and other occupations. The situation in Ibadan in the nineteenth century best proves this point. Toyin Falola has revealed that Ibadan chiefs and aristocrats established slave villages or plantations where the labor and the person of the slaves were exploited to the fullest degree possible.[47] Emancipation did not come to Yoruba slaves in the nineteenth century, nor in the period immediately after the establishment of colonial rule, for reasons of the dependence of production and capital accumulation on the exploitation of domestic slaves.

Next to the slaves in the lower class were the *iwofa,* whose emergence could be dated to the increased monetization of the economy and the development of the credit system. As will soon be demonstrated in chapter 6 the labor and services of the *iwofa* represented the interest on borrowed money. The value of this interest cannot be adequately quantified: it increased in direct proportion to the length of service, the sex and age of the person performing the service (the *iwofa*), and the conduct of the moneylender. There is no doubt, nevertheless, that it was exploitative and limited the chances of the debtor to repay the principal (which payment terminated the service or interest).

The dependence and poverty of the freeborn reached a greater proportion as a result of monetization. In theory, the poor members of a family had access to the wealth of other members through the extended family system. Their two basic needs—feeding and accommodation—were often assured in the big house of the wealthy member. On the other hand, this very facility imposed on them certain dependence on, and responsibilities to, the rich. This was one of the issues that nurtured the patron-client relationship between the freeborn and the rich. This point also becomes clearer in chapter 6. It should suffice here to note that the extended family system cushioned the degree of exploitation but did not remove it entirely. Indeed, the system worked in favor of the rich more than has been admitted in the literature. It kept down the poor and made them complacent, prevented them from identifying their patrons properly as their oppressors and rising against them, and preserved the class structure in favor of the dominant elites.

Summary

Two points, one old, the other revisionist, are worth emphasizing here. First, this chapter has demonstrated that cowry currency revolutionized the basis, pattern, and system of social classification in Yorubaland. New classes and new forms of exploitation were beginning to emerge before the imposition of colonial rule, and these took an active part in the subsequent programs of social and economic transformation. The second point is to emphasize that precolonial Africa was not the haven that some romantic scholars would have us believe: monetization, capital formation, and materialism, which had begun before European contact, had also produced a class society as variegated, as exploitative, and as dynamic as any other.

Notes

1. See S. N. Eisenstadt, *Social Differentiation and Stratification* (Glenview, IL: Scott, Foresman & Company, 1971), p. 76.
2. R. M. McIver, *Society: Its Structures and Changes* (New York: R. Long & R. R. Smith, 1931), pp. 78–79.
3. *Ibid.*
4. Ladislav Holy and Milan Stuchlik, eds., *Social Stratification in Tribal Africa* (Prague: Academy of Sciences, 1968), p. 10.
5. See Arthur Tuden and Leonard Plotnikov, eds., *Social Stratification in Africa* (New York: The Free Press, 1970); Ali Banuazizi, *Social Stratification in the Middle East and North Africa: A Bibliographical Survey* (London: Mansell, 1984).
6. The concept of class is discussed in many of Karl Marx's theoretical and empirical works, and in his joint work with Friedrich Engels. See especially *Capital, The Communist Manifesto, Theses on Feuerbach* and *The Class Struggles in France, 1848–1850,* all in Karl Marx and Friedrich Engels, *Collected Woks* (London: Lawrence & Wishart, 1976).
7. See H. Gerth and C. W. Mills, eds., *Max Weber: Essays in Sociology* (New York: J. B. Moler, 1922); and Max Weber, *The Theory of Social and Economic Organization* (New York: The Free Press, 1965).
8. For more information, see Allin Cottrell, *Social Classes in Marxist Theory* (London: Routledge & Kegan Paul, 1984); Peter Calvert, *The Concept of Class* (New York: St. Martin's Press, 1982).
9. Vincent B. Khapoya, *The African Experience: An Introduction* (Englewood Cliffs, NJ: Prentice Hall,1994), pp. 38–42.
10. See also Walter Sangree, "The Bantu Tiriki of Western Kenya," in James L. Gibbs, ed., *Peoples of Africa* (New York: Holt, Rinehart & Winston, 1965).
11. *Ibid,* p. 45.
12. *Ibid,* p. 46.
13. Sharon B. Stichter and Jane L. Parpart, "Introduction: Towards a Materialist Perspective on African Women," in Sharon B. Stichter and Jane L. Parpart, eds., *Patriarchy and Class: African Women in the Home and the Workforce* (Boulder: Westview Press, 1988), pp. 1–26.
14. Jeanne Koopman Henn, "The Material Basis of Sexism: A Mode of Production Analysis," in Sharon B. Stichter and Jane L. Parpart, eds., *Patriarchy and Class,* p. 27.
15. See C. Obbo, *African Women: Their Struggle for Economic Independence* (London: Zed, 1980); Claire Robertson and Iris Berger, eds., *Women and Class in Africa* (New York: Africana Publishing Company, 1986).
16. For a discussion of the career of some powerful women, see Filomina Chioma Steady, ed., *The Black Woman Cross-Culturally* (Cambridge: Schenkman Publishing, 1981).
17. William R. Bascom, "Social Status, Wealth and Individual Differences among the Yoruba," *American Anthropologist*, 53, 4, 1951, pp. 490–505.
18. *Ibid*, p. 491.
19. *Ibid*, p. 498.
20. See *Ibid*, pp. 499–501.
21. I. A. Akinjogbin, "The Causes of the 19th Century Yoruba Civil Wars," in I. A. Akinjogbin et al., eds., *War and Peace in Yorubaland* (Ibadan: Heineman, forthcoming), p. 274.

22. Perhaps it should be added, too, that economic prosperity, indicated by the access to and use of money by the *ara oko*, might be responsible for this treatment. According to Georg Simmel, "the money economy dominates the metropolis" (in this case, the Oyo metropolis) and the "metropolitan way of life is certainly the most fertile soil" for the discrimination against the *ara oko*. See Georg Simmel, *The Sociology of Georg Simmel* (London: The Free Press of Glencoe, 1950), p. 412.
23. See, among the more recent works, Paul Lovejoy, *Transformations in Slavery* (Cambridge: Cambridge University Press, 1982); *idem The Ideology of Slavery in Africa* (Beverly Hills, Sage, 1981); J. E. Inikori, *Forced Migration* (London: Hutchinson, 1982). With reference to slavery in Yorubaland, see E. A. Oroge, "The Institution of Slavery in Yorubaland with Particular Reference to the Nineteenth Century," Ph.D. Dissertation, University of Birmingham, 1971.
24. Akinjogbin, "The Causes of the 19th Century Yoruba Civil Wars," p. 276.
25. Samuel Johnson, *The History of the Yorubas*, pp. 178–87.
26. *Ibid*, p. 178.
27. This was not the end of the rivalry and contest between the princes and the chiefs. Later in the nineteenth century, Afonja, the *Are-ona-Kakanfo*, also rebelled against the imperial class and made a league with the new Fulani power at Ilorin. This rebellion actually precipitated the fall of the empire.
28. Johnson, *The History*, pp. 168–82. Because of Johnson's anti-Gaha's accounts and sources, some of these cases could have been exaggerated.
29. Johnson, *The History*, p. 172.
30. Johnson, *The History*, pp. 180–81.
31. Akinjogbin, "The Causes of the 19th Century Yoruba Civil Wars," p.279.
32. *Ibid*, p.281.
33. Among others, see P. C. Lloyd, *Yoruba Land Law* (London, Oxford University Press, 1962).
34. For a short but useful analysis of the impact of the Land Use Decree on traditional land tenure, see Y. L. Fabiyi, "Land Tenure Reform in Nigeria: Implications of the Land Use Decree for Africultural Development," *Ife Journal of Agriculture*, I, 2, 1979.
35. To this must be added the various other means of accumulation open to the kings of Yorubaland, such as outright appropriation of the property of the people. Kings sent their messengers to the market at any time to rake from the wares brought there for sale, and the unlucky trader could do nothing about it. Some instances existed of the *oba* appropriating even the common man's wife. Such appropriations did not constitute a real threat unless it became too frequent. In addition, town and palace chiefs could extract the free labor of the common people. For further information, see Samuel Johnson, *The History*; also William Bascom, "Social Status," pp. 502–03.
36. For more details on this theme, see Robin Law, "Slaves, Trade and Taxes: The Material Basis of Political Power in Precolonial West Africa," *Research in Economic Anthropology*, I, 1978.
37. This is not to deny that, in certain situations, some members of the old aristocracy who had insufficient money were unable to maintain a style of life befitting of an aristocrat. Many of them also went into debt, and this will be discussed in chapter 6.
38. Samuel Johnson, *The History*, pp. 182–83.
39. Apparently, the Basorun's messengers and attendants were also profiting in the deal. Whereas Gaha's account showed that ten heads of cowries had been withdrawn, Alaafin Abiodun only received about six heads, the difference having been embezzled by the Basorun's attendants. See Johnson, *The History*, p. 82.

40. Samuel Johnson, *The History*, pp. 182–3.
41. Samuel Johnson, *The History*, p. 179.
42. This philosophy served to console those who never made it rich, despite their striving; and to caution the rich from regarding the poor as lazy. The intention was not to make everyone complacent.
43. Note the root words here: *iya* (mother) *l'Aje* (of Aje). Aje is the Yoruba goddess of commerce, and apparently a woman who has made it rich is said to have related to Aje in a very cordial manner. For more information on this goddess of commerce, and on sociological interpretations of other Yoruba gods and goddesses, see Bernard I. Belasco, *The Entrepreneur as Culture Hero: Preadaptations in Nigerian Economic Development* (New York: Praeger, 1980), pp. 140–65.
44. Samuel Johnson, *The History*, p. 179.
45. William Bascom, "Social Status among the Yoruba," pp. 503–04.
46. Indeed, a huge proportion of the freeborn were made captives and sold into the Atlantic trade.
47. Toyin Falola, *The Political Economy of a Pre-Colonial African State: Ibadan, 1830–1900* (Ile-Ife: University of Ife Press, 1984), pp. 27–28.

5

Economic Basis of Power: Kings, Chiefs, and Tolls

Money changed the social stratification system in Yorubaland in a variety of ways. Members of the political elite transformed themselves into an economic elite through their access to the means of accumulation. Many members of the lower class, mostly among the freeborn, pursued the opportunity to move up into the class of nobility by engaging in money-making activities. Of course, many failed. Those who succeeded tried to engage in the politics of using their money for honor and privileges. Also, the gender division of labor was transformed in ways that made women more visible and more actively involved in the economic process, in the acquisition of property, and in the political system. In this chapter, we will examine the access that kings and chiefs had to making money, and how this strengthened their political power. We shall start by making some general statements on the nature of access to wealth, and then use the example of toll collection to illustrate the system during the pre-colonial and colonial period.

Access to Money and Opportunities

Kings and chiefs had the best access to the means to acquire money, although they were also the most notorious in its dissipation. The residence of the king, the palace, was the most imposing architectural building in the city, while he was generally reputed to be the wealthiest or at least the most visibly so. By and large, they amassed wealth because there was little or no distinction between personal and public revenues. The establishment of separate state and personal accounts was, in fact, inconceivable. This could mean one of two things: either the king's account was the kingdom's, or the kingdom's account was the king's. It would seem that Yoruba cities operated like a welfare state, and every member of the society had access to the king's coffers in times of scarcity or natural disaster. At such a time, the king's account was technically for the whole kingdom. Kings also spent a large amount of resources to entertain their friends, allies, and on occasions, members of the public. Ordinarily, however, kings had access to most of the resources of the kingdom, and the wealth of the king could be regarded as a measure of the kingdom's wealth.

The economic power of kings was also promoted by their access to the means of production, precisely land and surplus labor. In general, land ownership was vested in the community. As head, the king played a major role in the allocation and disposal of land. Kings had the power to accept newcomers (strangers or immigrants) whom they granted unoccupied land in the kingdom. In return for the security provided by the kings (they organized the expansion and protection of the kingdom's land through warfare), the people paid tax, tribute, or rent, subsequently shared by a king and his chiefs. Kings were also able to benefit from access to free labor, by using their power to requisition labor from their subjects, either for public good (as in the construction of bridges, roads and market stalls) or to work in private farms.

Chiefs and other members of the nobility were less powerful than kings, but they also had great access to the means of accumulating money. They were the king makers, a position that they often exploited whenever the throne was vacant. They were lobbied and bribed by rival princes. If they played their cards very well, they could receive further rewards if their candidate became a king. They had access to land and proceeds thereof. Like the kings, they could levy rents and taxes on land; they could requisition labor from the subjects to work on their large farms; as judges they collected fines from offenders; and they participated in long-distance trade. They did about anything the king did, within reasonable boundaries.

The avenues of making money and property were, among others, war booty, the establishment of royal monopolies over some key items of trade, profits from trade, both internal and long distance, and collection of market dues. To enhance their position, and remain on top of the social hierarchies, kings and chiefs endeavored to collect fines, tolls, tributes, and the like. They also monetized, collecting cash for a number of civil reasons. In addition to tolls that we discuss elaborately in this chapter, N. A. Fadipe has listed the following other important sources:

> *Cash levy from compounds...*collected annually from individual compounds. Its principal purpose was to defray the cost of the sacrifices offered annually to the

various *orisa* worshipped in the community. It was usually a flat rate levy of a head of cowries (2,000 cowries or sixpence). It was the duty of the *baale* of each compound to see that this amount was forthcoming from his compound. It was not considered an onerous obligation, and the amount was usually over-subscribed, the *baale* keeping the surplus as his perquisite for the work of administering the affairs of the compound....Only a small part of the *Owo Ode* (public money) collected from compounds was needed annually for defraying the cost of sacrifices. The rest was passed into the equivalent of the state treasury. This was sometimes the private treasury of the head of the state, which was undifferentiated from the public treasury. Any other calls upon the public funds during the year were met of this fund.

Non-recurrent Taxation. It was only extraordinary occasions that called for any extra levy beyond those given above. Such occasions were preparation for defraying the cost of meeting an invasion or conducting a campaign. This tax was also levied by the compound in the same way as that for meeting annually recurrent expenditures. Another extraordinary impost had to be borne by the inhabitants of a conquered town, a beleaguered town, or one threatened with war, in order to get the enemy to spare the town. Thereafter, such a town became a tributary town and had to make an annual collection from its inhabitants from which the amount required for tribute was deducted.

Court Fees, Fines and Damages. Another source of revenue derivable in cash came from litigation and the administration of justice....both plaintiff and defendant were required to pay before a case was inquired into, the plaintiff paying the summons fee while the defendant paid the hearing the fee. In all cases in which damages were awarded, the successful party had to pay to the court a portion of the damages he received while the defendant was also often fined in addition to the damages which he paid to his opponent. Lastly, in all criminal cases except those for which capital punishment was prescribed, fines were the invariable punishment.

...These fines and fees resulting from the administration of justice were usually divided up between the king and his chiefs.

Patronage. The king also received a fair income from patronage, as he had the final voice in the election of some of his big chiefs. Rival candidates sought his favour with payment of money. In some communities (among the Ijesa, for instance) when the choice had been finally made among the rivals, the money paid by unsuccessful candidates was returned to them. In other communities what unsuccessful candidates paid was cynically referred to as part of the burial expenses of their father.

Death Duties. In nearly every Yoruba community, there was a form of fines payable to the authorities on the death of a person. The death of practically every adult person who left children had to be notified to the authorities, and such notification had to be accompanied by a fee....Unless this was done, the relatives of the dead person might not wail over his body, much less bury it.

Revenue in kind. Among the revenues of the state which took other forms besides cash were:

(a) Slaves: either as a result of wars or as a form of fines from the estate of de ceased chiefs and others;
(b) Services of slaves from year to year both on the farm as well as in the palace;
(c) The products of the farm;
(d) Presents of farm produce by chiefs and others at the principal annual religious festivals of the king.[1]

In the rest of this chapter we will examine the theme of the economic basis of power by focusing on the toll system to illustrate one example in details.

The Yoruba toll system has not been studied extensively, in spite of its major role in the indigenous economy and politics. It is common knowledge that toll gates were prevalent in all Yoruba towns. What is less obvious is that the collection of duties from these gates was well integrated with the organization of trade and that proceeds from tolls were part of the revenues relied upon by the political elite in all Yoruba towns. Neither has the toll system received the attention it deserves in the analysis of the establishment of the colonial economy at the turn of this century. This neglect ignores the important fact that the attitude of British officials to the toll system became a major political issue in their relations with chiefs, and also generated widespread debate and responses not only among the Yoruba elite but also among European traders and officials in Nigeria and Britain. This chapter seeks to fill the gap in our knowledge of this significant aspect of commerce and politics. The Yoruba toll system is examined within the context of the precolonial and colonial state and economy. The discussion is restricted to two dominant but related themes: how the toll system operated in the nineteenth century, and how it was subsequently reformed and abolished by the British when they imposed colonial rule on Nigeria.

The Yoruba Toll System

The toll system was sustained by the nature of the Yoruba economy and Yoruba politics.[2] Commerce was well developed in the nineteenth century. There was large-scale production of agricultural and crafts products such that the markets were constantly supplied, despite the endemic warfare of the century.[3] Extensive commercial activities linked one Yoruba-speaking town with another, and the whole of the southwest with northern Nigeria and some other parts of Africa. The trade with the Europeans on the coast was similarly intense. This network of commerce involved both local exchange, long-distance trade between the Yoruba and others, and exchange with foreigners, Europeans and Arabs. It involved large-scale movements of people and goods, and called for transport, markets, currency, and other institutions. Commercial activities provided opportunities for individuals and the state to exploit and benefit from. While individuals produced for the market, sold to make profits, and offered their labor for different services, the state, through the political leaders, made use of commerce in varying ways to sustain itself. Traders not only offered gifts to rulers but paid dues in the markets, different types of levies, and tolls when they engaged in trade that transcended boundaries.

Such tolls were an integral part of the economic basis of power. They were a major source of revenue, together with taxation, levies, judicial fees and fines, and death duties. Tolls were more important than these other sources in a number of ways. For one thing, a large number of tolls was collected in cash, thus providing immediate and regular revenues. Secondly, revenues from tolls were more likely to be higher than those from other sources, such as patronage (limited to revenue from those who were seeking power or attachment to chiefs), death duties, and court fees and fines. While data for the amounts collected from these various sources during the nineteenth century is not available, evidence from the early years of the twentieth century showed that proceeds from tolls were huge: in 1902, Ibadan realized about £3,000 per annum while Abeokuta obtained £12,000.[4] Furthermore, the collection of tolls was a routine, not a convention whose interpretation varied from time to time. Unlike taxation and levies, the tolls themselves were only a temporary burden; the traders who paid knew how to pass on the bulk to consumers. Finally, therefore, toll collection called for the use of minimal coercion: collectors had little need to use arms to force travellers to pay.

All these advantages made tolls more reliable than tributes, an even bigger source of revenue. In the first place, not all states had access to tributes, since these were paid by colonies or dependent towns. Secondly, an uninterrupted collection of tributes required the regular use of the army to conquer, police and consolidate the colonies, as well as political stability in the metropolis, all of which consumed heavy resources in men and materials. Toll collection, on the other hand, entailed little or no risk.

The toll system was controlled by the chiefs, who also controlled access to power. The primary aim of collecting tolls was to have revenues. Public treasuries merged with the private purses of the chiefs: revenues were collected and spent to satisfy both private desires and public needs (e.g., road maintenance, payment of tributes if a community was under a metropolitan power, prosecution of war, etc.). The chiefs were not expected to spend the proceeds from tolls primarily to maintain the routes: they had access to free labor to do this. Nevertheless, the chiefs had to consider the political and economic consequences of ignoring trade routes for the strategy of consolidating and enhancing their status. Consequently, those who participated in road works had to be entertained with food, drinks and music, while the chiefs had to provide security on the roads. Since revenues would be lost if the routes were abandoned, deliberate efforts were made to give military protection to traders and to avoid, as much as possible, conflicts which would put the routes out of use. Conflicts were inevitable; but they were seldom allowed to degenerate into the permanent closure of routes. Traders were well aware of the danger; they knew that they paid for the maintenance of soldiers, but that they could not seek compensation from the state if there were trouble; they could only hope for the best and avoid dangerous routes.

The method employed by the chiefs to establish control of toll collection varied, but three main ones were widespread during the century. Each method depended largely on the pattern and nature of politics, the relationship between the king and all the other chiefs on the one hand and among the chiefs on the other, and the need to integrate new power elite into the political system.

First, in smaller states (for example, Ede, Ikirun, Osogbo), the proceeds from the gates were combined and divided among the chiefs and the kings, with the latter taking the largest share. In some others (e.g., Ikare, Ofa), the kings controlled the major toll gates and appropriated all proceeds from them while the remaining gates were divided among the chiefs.[5] The third and perhaps the most politically intricate was the distribution of all the gates among the leading chiefs. This was the practice in Oyo, Ilorin, Abeokuta, and Ibadan, where the gates were many and where it was very necessary, for the sake of political stability, to conciliate competing interests and chiefs. In these cases, a chief was identified with a gate.[6]

The old Oyo empire went a step further by actually controlling the toll gates in some of its provinces, as part of its policy of monitoring and controlling exchange. In the case of its Egbado province for instance, the *Alaafin* enjoyed the privilege of appointing toll collectors. An overseer of collectors, a political agent known as the *Onisare*, was an important figure early in the nineteenth century. Richard Lander reported that this overseer was based in the town of Ijanna, about seven kilometres from Ilaro, where he exercised power, up till the 1830s, as the "greatest man between Badagry and Katunga (that is, Oyo metropolis)."[7]

It was the responsibility of the chief(s) who controlled the gate to recruit and discipline the staff. A chief was not entitled to the entire takings, even when a gate had been allocated to him. He had to share them with collectors, the *oba*, and his colleagues. The failure to share was interpreted as selfishness and an abuse of privilege, and this could cause the chief to lose the gate. A chief lost the gate when he died, but also when he got into major political trouble, which led to his downfall. On the latter point, Samuel Johnson gave a good account of how an influential chief, Foko Aijenku of Ibadan, lost his gate in 1877. He also lost his life in the bitter struggle to challenge his colleagues who combined to oust him.[8]

Johnson's description of Foko's plight was in no way an exaggeration. As with the control of colonies, whoever had the opportunity to control a gate had to be cautious and diplomatic enough not to lose it. A chief was entitled to one at the height of his power and needed the takings as part of his resources to maintain a very expensive lifestyle, satisfy and add to his followers, and compete successfully with his peers.

The interests of the state and the individual chief were the prime considerations in the appointment of toll collectors.[9] The choice of collectors was influenced by a host of factors. They included the need to ensure loyalty to the chiefs; to deal with traders who were unwilling to part with their monies, or with spies who might pose as visitors; and to collect information on strategic matters. The toll collector had to be intelligent, smart, and strong enough to inspect baggage and to give warnings of impending attacks. Consequently, the preference was for strong and ruthless characters; and previous participation in war or familiarity with the use of weapons was an added advantage. All sources agree that gatekeepers were intolerable. The European travellers were generally upset by the behavior of most of them, and the traders certainly despised them. For their part, the toll collectors did not seek favorable reports. Indeed, most of them had no reasons to be proud of themselves: they were of very low social status, either as slaves, relations of slaves, exconvicts, or freeborn but worthless characters.[10]

To be a collector was a hard job. Once located in the gate of a town, he converted the place into his office and residence, and had to be there throughout the day and night.[11] Those on busy routes dealt with large caravans and engaged in arguments and bullying. When interstate relations broke down, collectors had to identify those from enemy territories and deal with them according to the guidelines provided by the state. The staff at Oru, for instance, prevented Ibadan traders from passing through Ijebuland during the Sixteen Years' War (1877–1893).[12]

The job had its rewards, however. In a century that placed emphasis on the use of force, on power and war, a collector had the privilege of exercising power; he could ill-treat or abuse people, or go to the extent of delaying or preventing them from entering the town.[13] The status of collectors was enhanced in several ways. To a slave, being a collector was an opportunity, since it brought freedom from the daily dealings with, and exploitation by, the master. It was also an opportunity to accumulate resources to obtain redemption. Any toll collector had avenues to make money: they used their spare time to farm or do other economic activities; they were entitled to small commissions from their collections; and they engaged in fraudulent practices. They were more associated with the latter: they vexed traders with exorbitant charges, colluded with them to receive bribes in lieu of tolls, and rendered false returns. From returns which Johnson said were made every eighteen or nineteen days,[14] what was expected was an average of the yields, and this allowed them to appropriate to themselves the surplus, especially the surplus made in brisk seasons.[15] Finally, they had access to farm products because they (and sometimes their masters) were entitled to tolls from farmers who passed through the gates. These small, non-monetary tolls (Johnson described them as trifles—"a head or two of corn, a handful of beans, a yam or two, a few dry sticks and so forth")[16] were generally consumed by toll collectors.[17] What Johnson called a trifle was sufficient, when all trifles were combined, for the collector to feed his family. During wars, farmers were required in addition to pay huge tolls in kind as their own contributions to the provisions for the military.[18]

Customs houses were located in the major gates of town walls through which the important routes passed. W. H. Clarke, the Baptist missionary who traveled in the Yoruba country in the middle of the century, reported on those of Ijaye, Ogbomoso, and Ilorin in 1855 and Ila-Orangun in 1857.[19] Large cities had more than four not only because of their size but also because they were economically significant, especially for their products and the network of trade routes that converged upon them. Documented examples of such cities include old and new Oyo, Ilorin, Abeokuta, Ilesa, and Ibadan.[20]

Toll houses or collectors were also found in other strategic places, where it was necessary to prevent traders who did not have to pass through the towns from escaping payment. Examples of such places included the banks of rivers and creeks,[21] water routes,[22] and highways. On the latter, there were two methods. Customs officers could stop a caravan and impose tolls on all the traders. This was always an unpopular thing to do, but the traders had to comply. It was certainly not too common, but the warfare of the century was used as the justification to impose more tolls in order to cater for the armed guards who accompanied the caravans.[23] Clarke again provided perhaps the most detailed eyewitness account of this in his 1855 report of his journey from Ijaye to Ogbomoso, a distance of about seventy miles.[24] The second method was to post customs men on the routes early in the morning because of smugglers, who found ways of evading the toll gates.[25] Other abnormal cases were reported by contemporary accounts. Lander for instance recorded that some traders and porters were detained on the Badagri-Oyo route by a chief who forced them to part with a levy of a bottle of rum.[26]

There were other notable features of the precolonial toll system. First, the customs houses shared the attributes of a market,[27] especially at the peak of their operations when traders in caravans had to pay. There was much noise, emanating from discussions by hundreds of people. W. H. Clarke was confused by one such incidence early in his journeys in 1854. He observed a large crowd in the customs house on the Ogun river and confessed to being frightened and confused by what he thought was a commotion.[28] Entertainment was provided by singers and drummers, who accompanied traders to the customs houses close to the towns. There were many others, mere spectators, who attended for social purposes. Part of the crowd also included food vendors and hawkers, who made use of the opportunity of the large crowd to make money.[29] This large crowd promoted extensive contacts between people from different states, the flow of information, and possibly of ideas. Agents of the state freely sought information on their neighbors and on other places. Strangers and travelers also used the gates to add to their information bank.

Second, some collection centers grew to become temporary settlements, as well as landmarks to demarcate boundaries or give directions. Clarke provides very good examples of these.[30] Because some centers had dwelling facilities, traders and strangers to the town were allowed to use them as temporary abodes. Some European travelers had to wait and sleep here to announce their arrival before they were received into the town.[31] It could, however, be inconvenient for visitors who had not joined caravans, because they might find the places desolate, especially in the evenings when the only available people were the customs staff.[32]

Thirdly, the multiplicity of toll houses as well as the large number of caravans involved in trade brought considerable delay in travelling. Several hours were lost in the line to pay.[33] Part of the consequence of

TABLE 1
Toll Rates on Major Items

Location and Item	Amount	Year	Sources
Oyo (old)			
Horse (described as a handsome one)	2,000 cowries[41]	1827	a
Egbado towns			
A load (goods unspecified)	5–10 cowries	1854	b
A slave	200 cowries	1854	b
Abeokuta		1866	c
1 lb. of shea (butter)	40 cowries		
1 gallon of palm oil and palm nut oil	40 cowries		
Cotton (quantity not indicated)	800 cowries		
1 lb. of ivory	120 cowries		
Between Ibadan and Oru		1890	d
Soap, per basket	2.4d.		
A sheep	2.4d.		
Pepper, per basket	2.4d.		
White beans, per load	4.8d.		
Yam flour, per load	4.8d.		
A goat	2.4d.		
A pig	7d.		
A fowl	2.4d.		
Yams, per load	2.4d.		
Sweet potatoes, per load	2.4d.		
Egusi (melon) 1s.			
Oyo (new)		Late 19th	
A big load (contents unspecified)	200 cowries	century	e
A small load (contents unspecified)	50 cowries		
One slave	2,000 cowries		f
Cattle	2,000 cowries		
Ilorin		1890s	g
A load (contents unspecified)	2d.		

Sources:
(a) Lander, *Records*, 223.
(b) NAI, C.M.S. CA2/031 (b), S. Crowther, Journals, 19 November 1845.
(c) C.M.S. CA2/07, Correspondence between the Colonial Government and Native Authorities, 1851–72; correspondence for 23 March 1866.
(d) C.O. 879/33: African (West) No. 399. Lagos Correspondence Native Affairs and Mr. Alvan Millson's Mission, 1889, p. 82.
(e) *Lagos Annual Report*, 1903.
(f) Fadipe, *Sociology*, 219
(g) NAI C.S.O. 16/5/49, tolls.

the time lost in the toll-collecting centers was the slow speed of transport, since traders had to wait for one another and travel in a single file. This slow speed and the tolls added to the cost of transportation, and resulted in increased price of articles.[34]

Finally, the tolls paid by traders were determined by the value, type, kind, quantity of goods, the status of the collecting center (e.g., whether located on a major highway or in small towns), the whims and caprices of toll collectors, and the rate imposed by the state. The amount paid varied not only from place to place but also from time to time (see Table 1). Most sources also indicate that duties could be fixed arbitrarily. Nevertheless, there was a sort of consistency in the tolls charged on certain commodities: a horse had a higher duty than other livestock; imports, especially luxury items, attracted higher duties than foodstuffs.

From Table 1 and other data, we can draw some other inferences from the duties imposed on goods. First, they were very high, when the overall total paid by a trader on an item is considered. The major reason for this was the number of toll gates a caravan had to pass through. For example, between Oru, one of the Ijebu's collecting centers, and Ibadan, a distance of only forty-five miles, there were four toll stations.[35] Since traders were always engaged in return trips, this meant that on this route they had to pay eight tolls. This was not a peculiarity of the Ibadan-Oru route. Clarke mentioned four between Ijaye and Ilorin. Since most sovereign towns had toll houses, traders had to pay as they moved from one town to another. Second, it follows that the total duties paid on a commodity might be close to its original purchasing cost. This was true of agricultural products and domestic livestock. Alvan Milson provided a good example drawn from his Oru-Ibadan experience where, as stated before, a trader paid four times along the way. A load of yams that cost 4d. to 6d. in Ibadan attracted a total of 2.4d. as toll, that is, two-fifths to three-fifths of its purchasing cost. The same applied to a load of maize, which cost between 2.5d. and 5d. but carried a duty of 2.4d. It was worse in the case of melons, where a load bought at Ibadan for 9d. was charged a total of one shilling.[36] Since these goods were taken further from Oru to Lagos more tolls would be paid, which had to be added to the prices that consumers would pay.

Prices, however, could not be driven up indefinitely. The heavy duties imposed on traders increased the price of commodities that entered into short- or long-distance trade. Because tolls had to be added to the transport cost, other inputs, and the trader's profit, it was uneconomical to trade in foodstuffs over long distances. Moreover, such commodities were unable to compete with similar or alternative local products. In these circumstances, there were at least two options open to traders. The first was to move basic foodstuffs over short distances only. The second was to trade in luxury and essential goods of foreign origin.

Certain categories of people were exempted from tolls. Traders and porters who worked for chiefs did not pay in the centers controlled by their chiefs and in their towns. The Landers observed in 1830 that the *Alaafin*'s trading wives[37] were exempted from tolls. These wives were identified because they used a special type of cloth to wrap their goods. Impersonators were punished by enslavement.[38] Ibadan chiefs enjoyed similar opportunities in their colonies. The *ajele* (governor) not only ensured the safety of these traders but also protected them against arbitrary and/or exorbitant levies, that is, if they paid at all.[39] Travelers who carried goods without the intention of selling them were not supposed to pay duties. But while they avoided payment in their communities, they were occasionally forced to pay in other centers. For instance, in Ilesa, Meffre observed that a traveller paid two cowries to pass through any of the seven gates.[40] This was probably uncommon because travellers were differentiated from traders both by the quantity and variety of goods they carried. Some states justified the minimal tolls paid by travellers by the need to raise revenues to maintain the army and security along the roads. Finally, diplomats and porters who carried tributes and gifts involved in interstate relations were exempted. These were known by the insignia of office and symbols which indicated that the agents were representing their states.

Above all, there were attempts, all involving smuggling tricks, by traders to evade payment. There were cases reported of those who seized the opportunity presented by European travellers to escape payment by pretending to be their attendants.[42] So also were the numerous cases of those who impersonated the agents of chiefs.[43] Since those who did not carry loads were generally exempted from payment, traders combined their articles in large loads in order to reduce the amount of duties. Some traders also developed strong friendships with collectors so that they could pay little or nothing. A small group of traders or a lone trader could take detours around toll-collection centers. These were made, but we have no evidence to conclude that the trick was widespread. The search for a detour not only involved familiarity with a region but entailed the risk of contacts with state agents, brigands, and soldiers.[44]

Reforms and Abolition of the Toll System, 1893–1906

The goals of the British colonial regime in Nigeria called for new and rapid changes to several aspects of the indigenous institutions. The new colonial economy could not depend on the indigenous infrastructure of commerce. Consequently, among the initial measures of the new administration were the construction of better roads and the first railway system, the introduction of a new currency, and the abolition of tolls and other obstacles to the free flow of trade to the ports.[45]

The new officials in Lagos and the hinterland were enthusiastic in introducing far-reaching changes. Top on the agenda of the colonial administration was to secure a free flow of trade from the hinterland to Lagos, a vital aspect of all the treaties signed with the Yoruba chiefs. Captain R. L. Bower, the first Resident and Travelling Commissioner, embodied this new era. He pursued his mission with energy. Not only did he assert political dominance, he was also in a hurry to lay the foundation of the new colonial economy. For this he used the chiefs to widen and clean the roads while he ordered the abolition of all tolls "throughout the country" (that is, lbadan, Oyo, Ilesa, Ekiti, Ife, Iseyin, and Ondo).[46] Also, the Royal Niger Company, which had established political influence in parts of eastern and northern Nigeria, attempted to prohibit the collection of tolls in Ilorin and its environs after 1897.[47]

These two initial attempts at abolition were unsuccessful. While it is true that the new administration resorted to the use of force to obtain compliance with some of its orders, it was difficult to do so in the case of tolls. It was in fact not part of the program of "pacification," and there were no complaints in the 1890s that toll collection was an obstacle to trade. The order for abolition remained only on paper.

Governor MacGregor was an advocate of gradual change. He did not appreciate why tolls should be abolished. Lagos had good reasons for allowing the chiefs to continue with toll collection. First, officials knew that it was a major source of revenue for the chiefs. For the states that had lost control of their colonies, tributes no longer constituted a regular source of income. Booty was also unavailable since there were no more wars. One result of these changes was that tolls became perhaps the most important and largest single source of revenue. The new colonial administration was yet to establish alternatives to compensate the chiefs, the major allies it relied upon for governing. The administration itself still depended on customs, and there was then no assurance that direct taxation could be successfully introduced. Indeed in the last decade of the century several of the towns rebuilt their toll gates, which they had abandoned because of the war.[48] In 1900, after observing that many towns and villages had toll gates, the Resident warned that any attempt to abolish these gates would meet with "greater obstacles now than ever before."[49] The chiefs were allowed to spend the revenue from tolls, while the nascent administration was sustained by meager funds from judicial fees and fines, market dues, and other petty sources.[50] A second reason for noninterference was to avoid an issue that could unite the different Yoruba towns in a possible confrontation with the British. MacGregor in fact feared that abolition was capable of degenerating into a military clash between these towns and the British.[51]

Thus, while the collection of tolls was allowed, the major concern of officials was how to organize and regulate it so that it would not impede commerce. Two major steps were taken to achieve this. First, the number of toll-collection centers was reduced. Many small communities lost the right to establish customs houses, while the towns which were allowed to retain theirs were prevented from duplicating them.[52] The closure of some customs houses reopened conflicts over political sovereignty and autonomy: those who lost theirs regarded it as a loss of power and a sign of subordination to their neighbors.[53] The reform raised the question of the interpretation of the treaties signed between the chiefs and the British, especially as to whether the new master had a wide-ranging power unilaterally to impose new rules.

The second step was to ensure uniformity in the duties charged on goods. The problem was with the system itself, which encouraged a. great deal of flexibility. While it was common to charge 200 cowries on a load, sometimes only half of this or even less might be collected, especially in the small towns that attracted few traders.[54] Not only was it difficult to force the towns to impose the same duties, it was impossible to control the toll collectors, who were in the service of chiefs. Nevertheless, success was achieved in Ibadan and Abeokuta, where it became possible to impose a printed tariff which related the amounts paid to specific quantities of goods, instead of referring simply to "a load."[55]

Nevertheless, there were pressure groups that wanted the abolition of the toll system. Among these were the traders and officials, who thought that abolition would enhance the flow of trade and the members of the Liverpool and Manchester Chambers of Commerce, who were in a hurry for change. In 1902 and 1903 the pressure groups employed two methods to achieve their aim: first, they criticized the Yoruba toll system with a view to bringing it into disrepute; and second, in

1903 the European merchants refused to pay tolls, and succeeded in precipitating a major crisis.

In 1902, many complaints were made about the toll system to officials in Lagos and the Colonial Office in London. The complaints not only indicted officials for their inability to supervise toll collection but warned that the toll system would continue to be a major obstacle to the expansion of trade.[56] In November the Colonial Office directed the Governor to "take an early opportunity of dealing with the matter of tolls so that trade would not be diverted to Dahomey."[57] It went on to suggest that chiefs might be compensated for any loss of revenue.[58] Lagos, however, still believed that the regulation of the indigenous system was the best policy, and promised London to avoid a situation that would lead to the diversion of trade to the neighboring country of Dahomey.

The second step culminated in a major crisis in 1903. This was the deliberate refusal of European traders in Ibadan to pay tolls. Since the establishment of British rule in 1893, traders had begun to move from Lagos to the hinterland, especially to Abeokuta and Ibadan, two leading commercial centers. Within a short period, these European traders had become the largest importers. But while the indigenous traders paid tolls at Ibadan, the Europeans were exempted. Early in the year, the chiefs, through the council, decided to ask Europeans to pay. As was to be expected, they refused, partly on the grounds that "the native tolls were collected in native fashion which was irregular and unsatisfactory."[59] The traders had the strong support of their counterparts in Lagos, who argued that they paid their duties on exports and imports passing through the ports. When the chiefs insisted on payment, Governor MacGregor urged the chiefs to appoint "proper customs staff to collect tolls in an approved manner."[60] The European traders objected to this proposal also. The Chambers of Commerce, which existed to serve their interests, petitioned the Colonial Office. John Holt seized the opportunity to criticize the governors in the colonies for taking measures to ruin trade.[61] The Liverpool and Manchester Chambers of Commerce raised several objections and made it clear that only abolition would satisfy them.[62] Joseph Chamberlain, the Secretary of State for the Colonies, intervened by ordering the suspension of the toll system with effect from in June.[63]

The decision, according to the Resident of Ibadan, "disturbed trade and embittered the relations between European traders and their public."[64] The Egba leaders were furious, and officials of the Egba United

Government felt that the decision was to deny them their independence.[65] They pointed out that they had been imposing levies on European traders since the middle of the nineteenth century,[66] and that these tolls were indirectly paid by the Egba consumers since the Europeans added the toll charges to their prices anyway.[67] The Egba decided to boycott the European merchants from 9 July to 4 August when the issue was temporarily resolved.[68]

Governor MacGregor was very diplomatic in his handling of the crisis. His goal was to come up with a policy that would satisfy European merchants, chiefs, indigenous traders, British officials, and the Colonial Office. For the first time, Lagos deliberately sought the views of all the pressure groups and "informed minds" on the toll system. Officials in the hinterland, indigenous traders, and "some informed minds" were of the opinion that abolition was unnecessary as long as it was possible to prevent the diversion of goods to Dahomey. The chiefs wanted tolls, understandably, because they needed the revenues. The merchants in Lagos were divided, though all objected to tolls in principle. On the one hand were those who believed, like the President of the Lagos Chambers of Commerce, that abolition would cause serious political and commercial disturbances. On the other hand there were merchants who thought that it would be unwise to increase import duties to find the means to run the administration and grant subsidies to the chiefs in place of tolls as well.[69]

MacGregor summarized all the information he had under two heads: the need for abolition and the need for reorganization. He drew this up in two proposals, which were to be presented before the chiefs of the Yoruba towns, especially Ibadan and Abeokuta where tolls had acquired a political significance. In drawing up these proposals, the Governor did not hide his intention to allow the collection of tolls. As Tamuno has explained in a related context, MacGregor could not afford a decision on an issue that would prevent the cultivation of more cotton, enable secret societies to challenge the colonial administration, and forestall the negotiations for more land and judicial agreements with Abeokuta and Ibadan.[70]

There were two sets of proposals, the first for Abeokuta and the second for Ibadan. The Abeokuta proposal contained the following issues.

1. To consider proposal of payment of subsidies with abolition of tolls. If that proposal is not entertained:
2. To propose that they publish Estimates of Revenue and Expenditure each year, with the Auditor's Reports submitted to the Abeokuta Council.

3. That they agree that no increase to present tolls be made without the sanctions of the Secretary of State either by extending the list of dutiable goods or by increasing existing dues.
4. That all goods not produce of the Abeokuta Province be free from dues in transit to the Railway Stations; also goods proceeding from Lagos by the Railway to places outside the Abeokuta Province.
5. That they allow drawback in full on all goods re-exported from the Abeokuta Province.[71]

The proposals to Ibadan were similar but differed in those aspects relating to the power to supervise; while Abeokuta had semiautonomous status, Ibadan was fully under the British. Thus, Ibadan's estimates had to be submitted to the Secretary of State for Colonies and not to Council; the Resident would audit the accounts monthly; and the Governor would appoint an Inspector of Tolls for them. As in the proposals to Abeokuta, the emphases were on the prevention of duties on goods in transit and arbitrary increases in tolls.

MacGregor first tested the reception to the proposals by requesting the comments of three "distinguished and informed Africans"—C. J. George, Sapara Williams, and Obadiah Johnson. All were opposed to abolition, and cautioned strongly that interference with its operation could bring the antagonism of chiefs.[72] These three responses enabled Lagos to anticipate criticisms of the two proposals. When they were in fact presented at Abeokuta, Ibadan, and Oyo the chiefs and the elites made similar remarks. At Ibadan, where the objections were loudest and well documented, the proposals were top of the list on the agenda in three meetings of Council. At an extraordinary meeting of Council on 28 July, the Balogun made it clear that they did not want a subsidy in lieu of tolls. They did not want the governor to appoint an Inspector, since they could do it themselves, and choose their own man, nor the Secretary of State to sanction their Estimates of Revenue and Expenditure.[73] Officials, however, threatened them with the consequences for tolls and revenue, and succeeded in persuading them to reconsider their objections.[74]

When the proposals were finally accepted, the Colonial Office authorized the collection of tolls with effect from 4 August 1903 in Abeokuta[75] and 18 August in Ibadan.[76] Henceforth in Ibadan tolls were to be collected under the supervision of the Resident and paid into the Ibadan Public Treasury. The government was to appoint the Inspector of Tolls, clerks of tolls, and other staff. They, like other civil servants, had their conditions of service,[77] and were all under the Resident. A

Customs Department, with its own financial estimates to cover expenditure on staff and stationery, was also established.[78] It became difficult, if not impossible, for the chiefs to influence the toll staff.

The chiefs lost control not only of the customs staff but also of revenues.[79] From 1903 onward, half of the revenues from tolls went to the chiefs while the other half was spent by the provincial administration.[80] In addition, the towns lost the power to impose levies on goods transported by the railway. This enabled the government to exercise the right to collect duties on liquor and exempt several other goods from taxation.[81] The towns were also prohibited from collecting tolls on transit goods, that is, goods not produced within a province or which passed through to other areas. Above all, it became the responsibility of government to determine duties. Table 2 shows the rate that had legal and official backing from 1904 till 1906, when tolls were abolished. Attempts by the chiefs to increase the duties were mostly turned down by the government, in order not to injure trade.[82]

The various reforms, however, neither satisfied those who were opposed to tolls nor put an end to the problems already associated with toll collection. Throughout 1904, the argument continued to rage around these issues. Abolitionists were particularly eager to emphasize the lapses in toll collection. They were right to a large extent because there were indeed genuine complaints. There was, for instance, the difficulty of controlling the toll staff. Senior staff did not enjoy much cooperation from the chiefs, European traders, or even from officials. Meanwhile there was the problem of corruption. Cases were reported of "petty pilfering," major stealing, and missing receipt books, perhaps to cover up fraudulent practices. Virtually all the major reports on the toll system conducted by officials sent from Lagos were critical. Even when there were no reported cases of fraud, staff were still suspected of being capable of forging receipts or destroying counterfoils to check vouchers.[83]

By mid-1904, many of the officials in Lagos and in the provinces had become convinced that abolition was necessary, mainly because of the lapses in collection. By then, they were in a position of strength to control the chiefs, while the several damaging reports on toll collection from traders and government departments were convincing enough to justify abolition. There was a proposal in August 1904 that there should not be more than six toll centers in the whole of the southwest. The Egba could collect in Abeokuta while Ibadan was to collect for all the principal towns in the hinterland, especially those like Iwo, Osogbo,

Ede, Ogbomoso, and Ikirun, which were to be affected by the railway extension.[84]

The Ekiti and Ijesa were not allowed to collect tolls, partly as one of the main measures to control the power of their chiefs.[85] In December, Oyo was ordered to abolish thirty-one toll gates in its dependent towns, and the chiefs in these places were compensated with sums ranging from £3 to 3s. per annum.[86] Almost immediately, the *Alaafin* was requested to abolish those at Oyo and elsewhere in the province effective 1 January 1905 for a compensation of £100 per annum. He complied.[87] In 1905, the *Ooni* was ordered to close down the toll gate at Ife. Ibadan's toll center at Adio in the southwest became less of a collecting center and more of a monitoring center for Lagos traders who alighted there from the trains to sell their liquor to petty traders who tried to smuggle this into Ibadan without paying duties. The Adio gate was thus retained to check smuggling and collect tolls on liquor.[88] But an unofficial traveller in eastern Yorubaland in mid-1905 reported that the Ibadan toll gate at Apomu was the only outlying station still in existence.[89]

In the north, those towns in the northeast were prevented from collecting tolls at all, while Ilorin, which had been the principal collector in the region, lost complete control of the operation. In 1904, the British established toll stations at the provincial frontier (far away from the Ilorin gates), where the Resident and his subordinates collected minimal tolls on behalf of the government. Even this came to an end, for after 1908 there were no further reports of toll collection in this region.[90]

Vigorous attempts were made meanwhile to abolish all customs houses in those areas close to the coast. Toll collection was not tolerated in Lagos, where the towns and villages were under the watchful eyes of officials. The Egbado and Ijebu were too weak to disobey instructions; the bombardment of the latter in 1892 had forced their chiefs to reconsider their earlier objections to receiving compensation equivalent to what they collected in tolls. The Egba were allowed to impose duties only in the Abeokuta township. This measure displeased the Awori towns, especially Otta, which claimed to be independent of Abeokuta and wanted subsidies,[91] but Lagos stood firm on the decision to prevent Otta and other "outlying districts" of Abeokuta from collecting tolls. A hint was even dropped to Egba chiefs that Abeokuta too would have to abolish its toll gate, since the other towns were no longer collecting. By the last quarter of 1905, almost all of the old toll gates, if they had not

TABLE 2
Toll Rates, 1904–1906

Article subject to rolls	Approximate value of article £	s.	d.	Rate of Duty	Unit
Aniseed	–	15	–	9d.	Gallon
Antimony	1	10	–	6d.	Key
Beads	6	15	–	1s.	Case
Beads	1	10	–	6d.	Bundle
Beer	1	10	–	1s.	Case
Birdshot	1	10	–	6d.	Cwt.
Biscuits	–	2	9	6d.	Cwt.
Blue	1	10	–	2d.	7 lb. tins
Brandy	1	10	–	9d.	Gallon
Buckets Galod	–	18	–	6d.	Dozen (large)
Buckets Galod	–	12	–	3d.	Dozen (small)
Camwood	–	5	–	3d.	Bag
Candles	–	10	–	6d.	Case
Cassava flakes	–	6	–	3d.	Flake
Champagne	3	10	–	2s.	Case
Velvet and domestics (cloth)	20	10	–	2s. 6d.	50 piece bales
Ajase bag	1	3	–	1s. 3d.	Bag
Large ordinary bag	15	–	–	9d.	Bag
Small ordinary bag	3	15	–	6d.	Bag
Crockery	–	8	–	3d.	Basket
Crockery	15	–	–	2s.	Puncheon
Crockery	20	–	–	2s. 6d.	Crate
Coconut	–	2	–	10d.	String bags
Crochet cotton	50	–	–	2s.	Bale
Cutlery	1	10	–	3d.	Case
Flint stones	1	–	–	3d.	Keg
Flour	2	10	–	6d.	Barrel
Gin	–	5	6	9d.	Gallon
Glassware	1	10	–	3d.	Basket
Glassware	15	–	–	2s.	Puncheon
Guinea-fowl	–	5	–	10d.	String
Gunpowder	–	2	6	2d.	8 lb. keg
Guns	12	–	–	2s. 6d.	Case
Hardware (excepting instrument of husbandry)	20	–	–	2s. 6d.	Case
Iron bars	–	–5	–	2d.	Bar
Iron	2	–	–	3d.	Bundle

TABLE 2 (continued)

Article subject to rolls	Approximate value of article £	s.	d.	Rate of Duty	Unit
Kerosene	–	10	–	6d.	Case
Kola nuts	1	10	–	6d.	Bag
Matches	4	10	–	1s. 6d.	Case
Matches	–	15	–	3d.	Tin
Packages	–	5	–	3d.	Package
Pipes, clay	–	8	6	3d.	Case
Pool wine	1	10	–	1s.	Case
Rice	–	15	–	6d.	Cwt.
Rum	–	6	–	9d.	Gallon
Sardines	1	1	–	3d.	Case
Salt	–	4	–	1d.	Cwt.
Soap	–	7	6	2d.	Case
Sewing machine	2	10	–	6d.	Each
Sprits (unspecified sweetened and unsweetened)	–	15	–	9d.	Gallon
Sherry	1	4	–	1s.	Case
Sugar	1	4	–	6d.	Cwt.
Sundries and haberdashery	1	–	–	6d.	Small case
Sundries and haberdashery	10	–	–	2s. 6d.	Large case
Tobacco	2	5	–	6d.	50 lbs.
Traps (large)	–	9	–	6d.	Dozen
Traps (small)	–	7	6	3d.	Dozen
Twine	–	7	6	3d.	Bundle
Twine	–	11	–	2s. 6d.	Bale
Whisky	–	15	–	9d.	Gallon
Wine (unspecified)	1	5	–	1s.	Case
Wine	20	–	–	10s.	Barrel
Jam	25	–	–	2s.	Bale

Source: NAI, C.S.O. 16/6/79-1561-1904, Requests that he may be supplied with 50 copies of "Ibadan Toll Regulations" as per attached copy.

ceased to exist, had become illegal, and collectors ran the risk of arrest by agents of the colonial administration. Moreover, it was reported for the first time that indigenous traders were refusing to pay at gates not authorized by the government.

By then, the argument for total abolition was coming to a head over the official Egba and Ibadan toll gates. The European merchants, now joined by the Railway Department, were unrelenting in their campaign, with two new arguments to support their case, both unanticipated by even the great supporters of tolls: smuggling and evasion. At Abeokuta, for example, European firms claimed that tolls made their goods uncompetitive, since smugglers were selling cheaper then they could.[92] While European traders could not escape payment, they further alleged that indigenous traders were able to bribe their way through, paying either little or nothing. The best documented example was liquor, for example, at Adio. Traders smuggled it into the towns to avoid the high duties, thus undercutting the European merchants.[93] Apart from such smuggling, there was evasion of a different kind: traders avoided places with toll gates when it was possible for them to sell elsewhere. This was reported, for example, in the case of those who dealt in palm oil and palm kernels. They avoided the Ibadan and Egba regions to sell in Ejinrin.[94]

Still more important, perhaps, was the difficulty of eradicating corruption in the matter of transit tolls. At Abeokuta, traders complained that they were often forced to pay tolls on goods in transit from the railway station to the Egbado town of Ilaro.[95] The case of Ibadan was worse, especially at the two out-stations established in Upper Ogun at Lanlate and Igboora in September 1904. Not only were clerks accused of dishonesty, but it was believed that tolls were systematically levied on all goods in transit. Both charges were confirmed by the devastating report of a Commercial Intelligence Officer who visited the district and uncovered several cases of illegal exaction of tolls and other corrupt practices.[96] The report caused Lagos to doubt previous favorable reports by the Resident, and to order him to explain why the two toll houses (and others) should be allowed to function at all.[97] The query forced Elgee, the Resident (author of *The Evolution of Ibadan*), to tour Upper Ogun in March 1905. He admitted that tolls were indeed collected on goods in transit, and that the clerks at both Lanlate and Igboora were corrupt, and ordered the immediate abolition of the two stations. Lagos was still not satisfied. It clarified the fact that Yoruba chiefs had no power to establish any collection center, and further requested that all the customs staff involved be punished, and if possible dismissed from the service.[98] By April 1905, therefore, Ibadan was left with only Apomu as an out-station, and that too was under threat. Acting on similar reports of irregular collection of transit tolls, Lagos ordered its closure in September, with an instruction that there must be no more such outlying toll stations in the province.[99]

The scene was thus set for the final abolition of the Yoruba toll system. A year later, in October 1906, the colonial administration abolished the payment of tolls on all goods except spirits.[100] The abolition struck at the major toll-collection center remaining in the hinterland, that of Ibadan, whose Council now reluctantly agreed to accept £2,500 per annum as compensation.[101] Traders were now free to traverse southwestern Nigeria without having to pay dues. By 1910, when six influential Yoruba scholars—including those who had argued in favor of tolls—submitted their Report on the Laws and Customs of the Yoruba Country,[102] there was not a single reference in it to tolls.

Abolition was possible not only because the colonial administration had the military and administrative power to enforce its laws, but also because it gave monetary compensations to the towns and, in the years ahead, succeeded in creating alternative and viable sources of revenue. This enabled the colonial government not only to maintain itself but also to pay the chiefs. The compensation enabled the chiefs, the major beneficiaries of tolls, to absorb the economic impact of abolition. As was to be expected, indigenous and European traders supported the measure. Although it is difficult to estimate the impact on the economy in general, or even on specific matters such as mobility and financial flow, it is certain that abolition contributed to the successful creation of a colonial economy.

Summary

This chapter fills the gap by examining toll collection among the Yoruba-speaking states of southwestern Nigeria. Two things have been emphasized. The first is that toll collection was practised before colonial rule. The second is that the colonial administration abandoned its earlier approach of reforming the toll system in favor of abolishing it. For the precolonial part, the chapter shows the dominant aspects of the system. These were the place of toll revenue in relation to other sources of income, the control of toll gates by chiefs in order to appropriate the revenues, and the character and privileges of collectors. Other issues were the features of collection at the toll gates, especially the duties imposed, and their implications for trade.

The second part explains the steps taken by the new colonial administration to regulate toll collection after 1893, notably by the reduction of customs houses and the printing of tariffs. These reforms failed to solve the problems of corruption by toll clerks and evasions and smuggling by traders, or allay the fear that the imposition of tolls constituted an obstacle to modern commerce. Consequently, the colonial administration decided to abolish the system, and was able to achieve this between 1904 and 1906. Both reforms and abolition were possible because of the gradual approach adopted, the administrative and military power available to the administration, and its ability to generate alternative sources of revenue to maintain itself and pay the chiefs. There can be no doubt that abolition was a major step towards the constitution of the colonial economy.

Notes

1. N. A. Fadipe, *The Sociology of the Yoruba*, edited and introduced by F. O. and O. O. Okediji (Ibadan: Ibadan University Press, 1970), pp. 221–22.
2. This chapter focuses on the nineteenth century because of the availability of reliable data on this period. There is evidence, however, that tolls were paid before the nineteenth century.
3. For a comprehensive study of this, see Toyin Falola, *The Political Economy of A Pre-colonial African State: Ibadan, 1830–1900* (Ile-Ife: University of Ife Press, 1984).
4. Public Record Office, London (hereafter P.R.O.), Colonial Office (hereafter C.O.) 147/166, MacGregor to Colonial Office, Conf. 7 July 1903, enclosure, appendix 8.
5. Fieldnotes: interviews with chiefs and local historians in these towns.
6. See Samuel Johnson, *The History of the Yorubas*, (Lagos: C.M.S. Bookshops, 1921, reprinted 1976), pp. 9I, 366–81, 407–10; Records of the Church Missionary Society, Birmingham University Library (hereafter C.M.S.) CA2/049 (b), Journal Extracts of David Hinderer for the quarter ending March 25, 1851; P.R.O. Foreign Office (hereafter FO) 2132, Glover to Baikie, 20 July 1895, enclosure in Baikie to Malmesbury, 6 August 1895; S. Tucker, *Abeokuta: or Sunrise Within The Tropics. An Outline of the Origin and Progress of The Yoruba Mission* (London, 1853), p. 231; and N. A. Fadipe, *The Sociology of the Yoruba*, edited by F. O. and O. O. Okediji (Ibadan, 1970; the manuscript was completed as a Ph.D. thesis in 1939), p. 219.
7. R. Lander, *Record of Captain Clapperton's Last Expedition To Africa,* I (London, 1830), p. 65. See also P. Morton-Williams, "The Oyo Yoruba and the Atlantic Trade, 1670-1830," *Journal of the Historical Society of Nigeria*, III, 1 (1964), p. 41.
8. Johnson, *History,* pp. 408–18.
9. The common Yoruba name for the toll collector was the *Onibode*. There were two other less popular variants: the *Lagbogbo* in Ondo, and the *Olutoro* among the Owo. See National Archives Ibadan (NAI), Chief Secretary's Office (hereafter C.S.O.) 26/4/30172, Intelligence Report Of Ondo District (by A. F. B. Bridges), p. 18.
10. Fieldnotes: interviews conducted in different towns, 1987; Johnson, *History*, 62; A. K. Ajisafe, *A History of Abeokuta* (self-published by author, Fola Bookshop, Abeokuta, revised edition, 1964; first published in 1916), 46; Fadipe, *Sociology of the Yoruba,* p. 219.

11. See T. J. Bowen, *Adventures and Missionary Labours in Several Countries in the Interior of Africa From 1849–1956* (New York, 1969 reprint; originally published in 1857 by the Southern Baptist Publication Society), p. 295.
12. C.O. 879/333, Alvan Millson to the Colonial Secretary, enclosure I in No. 23 of 14 February 1890.
13. See Bowen, *Adventures*, pp. 168, 191.
14. Johnson, *History*, p. 92.
15. See C.O. 879/33; C.M.S. CA2/056, Letters and Journals of James Johnson, Native Pastor, 21 March 1877; CA2/056, Report from J. Johnson, August 1877; and CA2/085 (a), Townsend to Venn, 30 August 1852.
16. Johnson, *History*, p. 92.
17. Johnson, *History*, pp. 91–92; Fadipe, *Sociology*, p. 219–20; Bowen, *Adventures*, p. 318.
18. Fieldnotes: interviews in different towns, 1987; R. Campbell, *A Pilgrimage To My Motherland* (New York, 1861), pp. 78–79.
19. W. H. Clarke, *Travels and Explorations In Yorubaland, 1854–1858*, ed. J. A. Atanda (Ibadan, 1972), pp. 23, 33, 81–86, and 157.
20. See C.M.S. CA2/049, Hinderer to Venn, 4 January 1861; NAI, C.M.S. "Y" Series, 1/7/5, Meffre, "A note on towns destroyed in the Ijesha country by the Ibadan," January 1882; C.M.S. CA2/068, J. A. Maser, *Letters and Journals, 1853–1879*; Clarke, *Travels*, p. 186; Johnson, *History*, 91; H. Clapperton, *Journal of a Second Expedition into the Interior of Africa* (London, 1829), p. 58; Bowen, *Adventures*, p. 106.
21. See Clarke, *Travels*, pp. 11, 15, and 25.
22. See C.M.S. CA2/07, Correspondence between the Colonial Government and Native Authorities, 1851–1872; Correspondence for 23 March 1866.
23. The use of armed guards to accompany traders was very common during the century. See for instance, Bowen, *Adventures*, 76; Clarke, *Travels*; H. Clapperton, *Journal*, pp. 1–59, 310–11; A. Hinderer, *Seventeen Years in Yoruba Country* (London, 1872), p. 229; C.M.S. CA2/083, Journal of J. Smith, 27 June 1865; C.M.S. CA2/049, Journal of David Hinderer: Journey to the interior, 2 August to 1 September, 1858; ibid., Account of David Hinderer's journey to Ijebu, December 1854 to January 1855; C.M.S. CA1/087, S. Crowther to Major Straith, 22 February 1837. See also P. D. Curtin (ed.), *Africa Remembered: Narratives by West Africans from the Era of the Slave Trade* (Madison, WI, 1967), Part III.
24. Clarke, *Travels*, pp. 26–29.
25. See *ibid.*, p. 256.
26. Lander, *Record*, I, 57, p. 60.
27. On this, see B. W. Hodder and U. I. Ukwu, *Markets in West Africa: Studies of markets and trade among the Yoruba and Ibo* (Ibadan, 1969), chap. 4.
28. Clarke, *Travels*, p. 11.
29. *Ibid.*, pp. 23, 25, 33, 34, 94, and 95; C.M.S. CA1/089, S. Crowther to Major Straith, 22 February 1837; C.M.S. CA2/066, Journal of Rev. A. Mann, 1852–80.
30. Clarke, *Travels*, pp. 15, 25.
31. Clarke (*ibid.*) gave many examples: at Ilorin (p. 94), Erinle (p. 112), Okebode (p. 125), and Ilesa (p. 129), all in his travels of 1857.
32. See *ibid.*, p. 95.
33. This was a common experience described by most of the European travelers. See among others, D. J. May, "Journey in the Yoruba and Nupe Countries in 1858," *Journal of the Royal Geographical Society*, xxx (1860), p. 212–33; C.M.S. CA2/049, Hinderer to Straith, 20 July 1855; C.M.S. CA2/0I9, W. S. Allen's

Journal Extracts for half-year ending June 1879;Clarke, *Travels*, pp. 25, 26–27, 33–34.
34. G. O. Ogunremi, *Counting the Camels: The Economics of Transportation in Pre-Industrial Nigeria* (New York, 1982), p. 59.
35. C.O. 879/33 (reference as for Table 1, note (d)).
36. *Ibid.*
37. See Robin Law, *The Oyo Empire c. 1600 – c. 1836* (Oxford, 1977), p. 232.
38. R. and J. Lander, *Journal of an Expedition to explore the Course and Termination of the Niger*, 3 vols. (London, 1832), I, 110. See p.196 for a similar observation.
39. D. J. May, "Journey…1858," pp. 212–33; Clarke, *Travels*, pp. 160–72.
40. Meffre, "A Note on Towns."
41. The value of the cowry fluctuated in the second half of the nineteenth century when English coins were in circulation, especially in Lagos. The rate of exchange was fixed at 6d. per head (2,000 cowries). For copper coins, the exchange rate was 1d. to 300 cowries. See Johnson, *History*, p. 119. On problems of calculation and other aspects of the cowry, See M. Johnson, "The Cowrie Currencies of West Africa," *Journal of African History*, xi 1970, pp. 17–49 and 331–53.
42. See Clapperton, *Second Expedition*, pp. 73, 115; Journal extracts of Hinderer and Mann (notes 5, 28).
43. For instance, the Landers noted (*Journal*, p. 110) that there were "strong inducements" for people to impersonate the wives of the *Alaafin* not only to escape duties but also to receive lavish entertainment from the chiefs of the towns they passed through.
44. See Toyin Falola, "Brigandage and Piracy In 19th Century Yorubaland," *Journal of the Historical Society of Nigeria*, forthcoming.
45. On the colonial policy, see two recent collections by Toyin Falola and S. A. Olanrewaju (eds.), *Transport Systems in Nigeria* (Syracuse, NY, 1986) and Toyin Falola (ed.), *Nigeria and Britain: Exploitation or Development?* (London, 1987).
46. NAI, C.S.O. 16/5/49 Conf. 115/1903 Tolls, enclosure, extract letter from Major R. L. Bower, C.M.G., to Captain Roupell, D.S.O., dated 3 November 1902.
47. *Ibid.* enclosure, Memorandum relative to the Customs on imports to Northern Nigeria collected in Lagos.
48. See Johnson, *History*, p.608; *Lagos Standard*, 9 August 1905 (article by Atundaolu); Rhodes House Mss Afr. 5958, Report on Ilorin, July 1902; and J.D.Y. Peel, *Ijesha and Nigerians: The Incorporation of a Yoruba Kingdom 1890s–1970s* (Cambridge, 1983), pp. 94 and 96.
49. NAI, C.S.O. 12/19/11–2441/1900, Resident Ibadan, supplying information about tolls.
50. See the early estimates for the provinces, for example,. NAI, C.S.O. 16/3/47, Confidential 97, 1901, Ibadan Estimates.
51. C.O. 147/149. MacGregor to Colonial Office Conf. 17 June 1900.
52. NAI, Iba Prof. 3/6, The Resident's Travel Journal, 1897–1899, entries relating to tolls; Ibadan City Council, Letter Book No. 92 of 31 March 1903, enclosure, Elgee to the Alaafin of Oyo.
53. NAI, C.S.O. 16/7/39, Egba Tolls; NAI, C.S.O. 12/24/25–3038/1905, Letter from the Oni of Ife on the question of the boundary between Ibadan and Ife, and the establishment of a toll house at Apomu—submitted.
54. NAI, C.S.O. 12/10/11–2441/100.
55. NAI, C.S.O. 12/21/15–C1011/1902, Forwards Tariff of Proposed Tolls of the Railway (Iddo) gate.

56. NAI, C.S.O. 16/5/49 Conf. 115/1903, enclosure, an appendix to the letter of 29 November 1902 and memorandum relative to the customs on imports to Northern Nigeria collected in Lagos.
57. *Ibid.*, enclosure titled "Letter to Sir W. MacGregor on 2 November 1902 at Downing Street."
58. *Ibid.*, enclosure titled "Letter to the officer administering the Government of Lagos on 29th November, 1902 at Downing Street."
59. C. H. Elgee, *The Evolution of Ibadan*, entry for 1903 (Lagos: Government Printer, 1914). The author was the Resident of Ibadan from 1903 to 1913.
60. *Ibid.*, entry for 1903.
61. T. N. Tamuno, *The Evolution of the Nigerian State: the Southern Phase, 1898–1914* (London, 1972), pp. 271–72.
62. C.O. 147/186, Colonial Office to MacGregor, telegram 18 June 1903.
63. NAI, C.S.O. 16/5/35–c.80/1903, suspension of arrangements for collecting tolls at Ibadan.
64. Elgee, *Ibadan*, entry for 1903.
65. On the autonomy that the Egba enjoyed during this period, see A. Pallinder-Law, "Government in Abeokuta 1830–1914, with special reference to the Egba United Government 1898–94" (Ph.D. thesis, University of Goteborg, 1973).
66. C.O. 147/166, MacGregor to Colonial Office Conf. 22 July I903, enclosure.
67. Ajisafe, *History of Abeokuta*, p. 162.
68. *Ibid.*
69. NAI, C.S.O. 16/5/34 c.80/1903.
70. Tamuno, *Nigerian State*, pp. 273–74.
71. NAI, C.S.O. 16/5/60.
72. NAI, C.S.O. 18/3/14, Correspondence on the levying of tolls, 1903.
73. NAI, C.S.O. 14/2/5–A4170/10, Preparation requested of Short Precis of the Ibadan Financial Arrangements Showing the Development and the like from 1903.
74. NAI, C.S.O. 16/5/60 enclosure, Minutes of meeting; NAI, C.S.O. 16/5/34 c. 80/1903.
75. Ajisafe, *History of Abeokuta*, p. 162.
76. Elgee, *Ibadan*, entry for 1903; NAI, C.S.O. 16/5/61 c. 37/1903. Request instructions on the date upon which the collection of tolls should commence.
77. NAI, C.S.O. 16/6/4: NAI, C.S.O. 16/6/6. Application for appointment of Collector of Customs; NAI, C.S.O. 16/5/61 c–37/1903; NAI, C.S.O. 16/5/77–c. 166/ 1903, Minutes of the Ibadan Council held at the Bale's House on 7 September 1903 onward.
78. *Ibid.* See also the estimates of the provinces; and NAI, C.S.O. 16/6/1905 279–1904, Bills of J. P. Jackson for Stationery for Ibadan Tolls Service—disputed by Ag. Resident Ibadan.
79. NAI, C.S.O. 16/5/60. Proposals as to tolls, Bale and Chiefs of Ibadans Objections to, enclosure, MacGregor to the Resident, August 1903.
80. See NAI, C.S.O. 16/5/74 c. 160/1903, Estimates of Revenues and Expenditure, Ibadan, for period from 1 September 1903 to 31 March 1904 onward; NAI, C.S.O. 16/6/,76–241/1904, Estimates for financial year 1905–1906; NAI, C.S.O. 12/22/ 34–3172/1903, Estimates, Province of Ibadan December 1903–March 1904–April 1904–March 1905: NAI, C.S.O. 16/7/95–142/1905, Estimates Ibadan Station 1905–06—submitted.
81. NAI, C.S.O. 147/161, MacGregor to Colonial Office, Conf. 7 July 1903.
82. All these changes were incorporated into the Toll Regulations enacted for the provinces and passed into law early in 1904. See NAI, C.S.O. 16/6/79; NAI, C.S.O. 16/6/57 Customs Tariff; and NAI, C.S.O. 14/2/5–A4170/10.

83. NAI, C.S.O. 16/6/64, Report by Mr. Lambert, Assistant Auditor, on the accounts of Mr. Henwood, Late Inspector of Tolls, Ibadan; NAI, C.S.O. 16/5/94, Infringing the toll regulations charge against Mr. Chersworth agents of PZ; and NAI, C.S.O. 16/5/95, Fine imposed on a clerk of Messrs PZ for false declaration of the contents of certain packages imported into Ibadan.
84. NAI, C.S.O. 147/166, MacGregor to the Colonial Office.
85. NAI, C.S.O. 147/,75 Conf., *Lagos Weekly Record*, 16 January 1904.
86. NAI, C.S.O. 16/6/2, Tolls at Oyo (1904).
87. Ibid, enclosure, Letter from Government House, Lagos to the *Alaafin* at Oyo on 23 December 1903. See also NAI, C.S.O. 16/7/52, Report on Tour.
88. NAI, C.S.O. 16/7/52, enclosure, Letter from C. H. Elgee, Resident, Ibadan to the Honourable Colonial Secretary, Lagos on 7 April 1905.
89. NAI, C.S.O. 16/7/72–104/1905, The Collection of Transit Tolls in the Interior.
90. NAI, C.S.O. 446/46 Reg. No. 38925, Wallace to Secretary of State 7 October 1905, enclosing Resident's responses to questionnaire on collection of tolls.
91. NAI, C.S.O. 16/7/39, Egba Tolls at Otta.
92. *Ibid.*
93. NAI, C.S.O. 16/7/28 42/05, Report of Commercial Intelligence Office on Illicit Transit Tolls at Lanlate.
94. NAI, C.S.O. 16/7/22/630/05, Report on Ibadan and Egba Tolls.
95. NAI, C.S.O. 16/7/22/630/05.
96. NAI, C.S.O. 16/728–42/05, enclosure, C.I.O. to Colonial Secretary, 7 June 1905.
97. NAI, C.S.O. 16/7/28–42/05.
98. *Ibid.*
99. NAI, C.S.O. 16/7/23–42/05, enclosure, telegram of 26/9/1905.
100. Elgee, *Ibadan*, entry for 1906. The toll on liquor, subsequently lifted a few years later, was allowed as part of the colonial fiscal measures for generating revenues to run the provinces.
101. Elgee, *Ibadan*, entry for 1906. As Elgee explained, this sum was arrived at by taking "the mean of the net sum realised upon such articles" between 1903 and 1906. See also NAI, C.S.O. 14/2/5–A4170/10.
102. See A. G. Hopkins, "A Report on the Yoruba, 1910," *Journal of the Historical Society of Nigeria,* V, 1, (December 1969), pp. 67–100.

6

Savings, Credit, and Banking

Traditional savings, credit, and banking institutions in Africa have not received the kind of attention they deserve; indeed, were it not for the interest of sociologists and economic anthropologists, the subject could be described as neglected. Writings on rural or traditional economy often lament the poverty of preindustrial credit systems in Africa, but no effort has been made to assess the degree of this poverty. Writings on banking and finance in colonial and postcolonial Africa avoid dealing with traditional financial institutions under the pretext that they were, strictly speaking, not *banks*. Indeed, these studies popularized the myth that Africans actually did not produce surplus wealth worth saving, and the little that was produced by quite a handful of the people was *kept* (as distinct from *saved*) in pots and buried in the ground, thus putting the money away from any possibility of its being put to immediate economic use by others. The more sympathetic general works on African economic history often treat traditional savings and credit institutions as mere footnotes. Sociologists have done more work on the field than historians, but they have left us with the impression of institutions as mere social rather than economic organizations. For example, N. A. Fadipe describes rotating savings and credit associations (henceforth referred to as ROSCAs), the *ajo* and *esusu* among the Yoruba, as "mutual help associations."[1] This misleading definition has been further slandered by A. G. Hopkins, who states that ROSCAs are "devoted mainly to social purposes, such as raising money for funerals."[2] It is necessary to correct such misconceptions and place ROSCAs in proper perspective as economic institutions which the level of societal sophistication and needs in preindustrial times could possibly devise.

More recently, especially since the 1980s, traditional savings and credit markets have come under sharp focus partly because of the new emphasis on rural development and partly because of the need for creditor nations and international organizations to understand the problems of screening and enforcement in debtor countries. Conducted almost exclusively by economists, these studies have advanced the frontiers of our knowledge of traditional credit markets—albeit from the narrow economic angle. These studies, while interested in "the application of economic behaviour" to underdeveloped rural economies, are still grappling with the problem of definition. Thus, there is some controversy on the proper characterization of traditional credit markets: are they competitive or monopolistic? Even when it is admitted that they are imperfect or incomplete markets, it has been difficult to come up with a theoretical paradigm that holds for most societies with a variety of savings and credit institutions. Moreover, there are not enough empirical studies upon which to build an enduring theory. The kind of study that Joseph Stiglitz has done, which enables him to propose the model of "peer monitoring" in traditional credit markets,[3] can only be tentative, based as it were on four empirical studies of Northern Nigeria, Thailand, India, and Pakistan.

The necessity for this chapter is, therefore, established: the existing studies are insufficient to guide longer-term policy measures, and they leave too many gaps. In essence, the main objective of this chapter is to examine the origin, development, features, modes of operation, problems, challenges and impact of traditional (or informal) savings and credit institutions.

Definition of Terms

For clarity, it is necessary to define a number of terms employed in the chapter. First, what is "saving"? J.M. Keynes defined saving as the "excess of income over expenditure on consumption."[4] This definition has been employed by government agencies in western societies to estimate consumer savings. However, Robert Ferber has identified four senses in which saving is used. These are: the process of accumulating money or material goods for future use; the flow of money or resources that is accumulated during a particular period; the process of economizing or conserving on resources; and those resources which are kept in being by such economizing.[5] There can be no doubt that Ferber's characterization is very elastic, but only upon such a wide conception of saving can a meaningful discussion of precolonial Yoruba saving institutions be understood. Utilizing these four usages, it is obvious that saving as an economic habit was not alien to the precolonial Yoruba people. According to T. A. Oyejide, "in general, most people save a part of the increase in their income."[6] Furthermore, Oyejide has identified six main ways by which a saver disposes of his saving:

> He can add to his cash balances, i.e. hold more cash; he can directly purchase capital (investment) goods as an entrepreneur; he can repay outstanding loans or make fresh ones; he can purchase securities from business organizations, financial institutions or government agencies; he can place his excess cash in some savings instruments; or he can make grants or gifts.[7]

It is instructive to note that many of these avenues for saving were available in precolonial societies, but modern (or western) saving instruments or institutions, especially banks (in the narrow way in which banks are now known), were lacking. This necessarily leads to the question: What are banks, and what is banking? A bank deals in money and money substitutes, and provides a wide range of financial services. In a strictly formal sense, it borrows or receives deposits from firms, individuals or governments, and makes loans to customers. It covers its expenses and earns profits by borrowing at one (lower) rate of interest and lending at a higher rate. In a general sense, however, a bank is an establishment for keeping money and valuables safely.[8] This general definition is employed in our treatment of banking in traditional societies, and it does not necessarily contrast with the formal sense of the term.

The type of institutions for saving money which were developed among the Yoruba and which are still in operation in many places today, were those that suited the economic pursuits, social organization, and cultural setting. These institutions are examined historically here. It should suffice to say at this stage that the increasing westernization of society since the colonial era, and the economic changes that have taken place in Africa since World War II, have affected both the rural and urban areas and the traditional institutions available in them. As the changes became increasingly severe, particularly as the rate of rural-urban migration rose, the contrast between the rural areas—which are still sustained largely by traditional institutions—and the urban areas—which are served by western institutions—became sharp. Policymakers, with little justification, have concluded that the rural sector has remained backward because of low saving and reliance on inefficient economic institutions. In Nigeria, for instance, it was felt in 1977 that rural wealth had to be mobilized, pooled, and made available for national development. This reasoning ultimately led to the introduction of the Rural Banking Program,[9] which extended western saving instruments (banks) to the rural areas hitherto predominantly served by the traditional system. The point that was missed (and which soon became clear when these Rural Banks could not generate enough revenue to cover their operational cost, not to mention making profit) was that the rural areas were poor not because they had no banks but because they were poor.[10]

This disappointing result has been noted in other parts of the world where the assumption has been that traditional societies lacked dynamic institutions. Although we disagree with Clifford Geertz's view that non-Western economies are necessarily static,[11] his explanations for the failure of government-sponsored intervention in the traditional sector are valid:

> [T]he first because deep-rooted customs yield very little to official sponsored exhortations to discard them in the interest of progress; and the second because the impersonality, complexity, and foreignness of the mode of operation of such "capitalist" institutions tends to make the traditionalistic peasants, small traders, and civil servants suspicious of them.[12]

What are ROSCAs? ROSCAs are numerous and varied, and any definition, to be acceptable, must allow the inclusion of those various properties. It is difficult to accept Geertz's position that "the basic principle upon which the rotating credit association is founded is everywhere the same," and that that principle is "a lump sum fund composed of fixed contributions from each member of the association is distributed, at fixed intervals and as a whole, to each member in turn."[13] As Shirley Ardener has pointed out, this description is too restrictive. "Contributions are not always fixed...and the whole of the lump sum is not always received by a member."[14] Against Geertz's definition, Ardener has proposed another that ROSCAs be taken as "an association formed upon a core of participants who agree to make regular contributions to a fund which is given, in whole or in part, to each contributor in rotation."[15] This definition is much more appropriate, for it includes the two elements of regularity and rotation which Ardener regards as the "essential criteria" that differentiates ROSCAs from "the whole range of mutual benefit clubs and co-operative undertakings."

The existing literature has documented the existence of ROSCAs in virtually all parts of the Third World. Shirley Ardener has recorded its existence in Asia (in several parts of China, India, Malaya, Vietnam), Africa (among the Yoruba, Igbo, Ibibio, Tiv, Nupe, Hausa of Nigeria; the Creole of Sierra Leone; several ethnic groups in the Cameroons, Ghana, Zambia, Malawi, South Africa, Egypt, Sudan), and the Americas (Barbados, Trinidad, Guiana).[16] A series of articles that she recently edited focuses on these various areas.[17] Unlike most anthropologists, Ardener made some efforts at explaining the origins of ROSCAs; however, the attempt fails partly because the available evidence was (and still is) scanty, and partly because of the eagerness to employ the diffusion theory.[18] Therefore, our discussion of the Yoruba experience has proceeded against the background of these known features and operations of ROSCAs in other parts of the world. The advantage of such a comparison[19] is apparent: it builds trends into the somewhat static treatment that anthropologists have adopted.

Ajo: A Yoruba Savings Institution

The Yoruba have two basic institutions for saving and credit. The first, *esusu*, was more developed and served the people in most senses of the term "savings." The second is *ajo*, which was probably devised simply to satisfy the first sense in which savings has been used by economists, that is, the process of accumulating money. Thus, it is believed to have originated to replace the practice of burying money in the ground for safekeeping. *Esusu* and *ajo* did not replace each other; rather, the two institutions continued to exist side by side, and individuals freely chose to patronize one or/and the other. This has led to some speculation on the relationship between the two institutions. It is not clear which of them first emerged; and we are willing to speculate that both developed separately in different parts of Yorubaland, and later spread evenly.

Unlike *esusu*, the *ajo* institution has not received attention in scholarly writings. This is probably because of the series of abuses that its operation had witnessed in precolonial Yorubaland (and continues to witness in modern times). *Ajo* is probably a short word for *akojo* (pool together). Thus, under the *ajo* institution, an individual entered into an agreement with a savings collector, paid a fixed sum of money at regular intervals to this collector, and drew all his contribution at the end of an agreed period or anytime it was needed. The frequency of payment might be daily, weekly, fortnightly, monthly, or simply "every market day," but it must be regular. The main attraction of this system, therefore, is the element of promptness, that is, the contributor could draw his/her money at short notice, unlike in the *esusu* where he/she had to wait his/her turn. The pivot of this system was the *alajo* (the savings collector or treasurer). This man or woman was a mobile bank *par excellence*. Depending upon the size of his/her customers and the extent of their geographical spread, the *alajo* pursued this vocation either as a full- or part-time work, walking from one client to another to collect their savings.

Information collected from *alajo*[20] and their clients reveal a lot of interesting facts on the operation of the *ajo* institution. First, as the society was nonliterate, both the *alajo* and the contributors relied on the power of the human memory. Since this was (and still is) limited, mistake or cheating was not uncommon. Some contributors tried to keep record by drawing lines on the wall of their room with charcoal, but this was not foolproof as the *alajo* often insisted on the accuracy of their own "records." Like *esusu*, a round of the contribution was meant for the *alajo*, but they usually appropriated more than one round. Secondly, the *alajo* had been known to disappear with their contributors' money. Contributors had no way of identifying such charlatans before entrusting to them their hard-earned savings. This was probably why *ajo* contributors were usually lower than *esusu* contributions.

Another main disadvantage of *ajo* as it was practiced in precolonial Yorubaland was the fact that the fund that accumulated in the hands of the *alajo* was not made available for investment. Rather, because the depositor might require his fund at short notice, the *alajo* did not often make such funds available for borrowers. There were instances, however, where he had been known to make big loans to the state, particularly when the community was at war and there were promises of booty to be had. As society became more complex, the *alajo* also developed more complicated approaches to their operation. They began to extend credit to their clients and other needy members of the community. The *alajo* formed the nucleus of the money-lending business which we will address in chapters 6 and 7.

Esusu: ROSCAS among the Yoruba

The pioneering, and so far the most detailed and comprehensive, study of *esusu* among the Yoruba is William Bascom's article that appeared in the *Journal of the Royal Anthropological Institute* in 1952.[21] Subsequent writers have consciously and unconsciously recycled the ideas (and speculations) in this essay. Indeed, for quite a long time the Yoruba name (*esusu*) was adopted for similar institutions found in other parts of the world.[22]

The root name for this Yoruba name is "*su*," which means literally "pooling together or contributing." *Esusu* could, therefore, refer to that fund which has been pooled or is being contributed into a pool. As

Bascom has correctly observed, *esusu* rarely refers to the contributors.[23] Samuel Johnson has defined the operation of *esusu* thus:

> A fixed sum agreed upon is given by each at a fixed time (usually every week) and place, under a president; the total amount is paid to each member in rotation.[24]

Bascom, using the current currency, further illustrates the operation of esusu thus:

> [W]e may imagine a simple case where twenty members contribute one shilling each, monthly. At the end of twenty months, which completes the cycle in this case, each member will have contributed twenty shillings or one pound, and will, on one occasion, have received the amount of one pound in return.[25]

All evidence points in the direction that ROSCAs was an ancient institution among the Yoruba. However, it has not been possible to date its origin. Its emergence probably predated the introduction of cowry currencies, as the similarity between *esusu* and other mutual help associations (such as *aro* and *owe* in the supply of agricultural labor force[26]) would seem to suggest. Nevertheless, its development was assisted by the monetization of the economy, which made more accurate the measurement of value as well as the quantification of *esusu* found. There is little validity in the suggestion that *esusu* diffused from some other parts of West Africa into Yorubaland,[27] although it could have spread throughout Yorubaland by diffusion. On the contrary, there is greater evidence in support of crediting the Yoruba with the invention of their own brand of ROSCAs.

Among the features of *esusu*, Geertz (via Bascom) has recorded three. First, membership was larger, and the length of a cycle was longer—"as many as 200 members, with cycles of four or five years."[28] This had the advantage of pooling a sizeable sum fund that the receiver, if a businessman or woman, was able to put to good use. On the other hand, those who had yet to collect their fund were forced to save and tie down their money. The situation could be more pathetic if the *esusu* died "on the road,"[29] as sometimes happened. Secondly, the larger *esusu* groups formed something akin to a bureaucracy: "the head of the *esusu* may not even be personally acquainted with all its members; his relations are mainly with the subgroup heads."[30] On this point, Bascom has been more elaborate. According to him, "the larger esusu groups are divided into four or more subgroups or 'roads' (*ona*), which are numbered (first, second, third, fourth) according to the order in which they receive the fund, which is rotated among the subgroups in turn."[31] Furthermore, the "members pay in and take out through the agency of the subgroup head, and it is he who determines the order of the distribution of the fund among members of the subgroup.... If a member defaults after he has received the fund every effort is made to force him to pay. The overall head attempts to coerce the subgroup head, and the subgroup head the member."[32] The advantage of this was that the *esusu* head had a core of trusted assistants who ensured the smooth running of the association. These subgroup heads were also understudying the overall head in an informal manner with a view to acquiring the relevant skills and experience to organize their own *esusu* independently later.

This implies that there is some economic benefit to be had in being the head of an *esusu*. There was, otherwise the head would not have had the full commitment and devotion. On the other hand, these benefits may actually be derived illegally. This was more prevalent in the larger *esusu* where the individual had no knowledge of how many members there were, or how long the cycle was. In theory, the head was allowed to keep one round of the fund in order to cushion the effect of default by one member or more at a point in time. However, it was regarded as the norm for the head to keep more than one round to himself,[33] even though respected members of the community (such as chiefs, princes or princesses, successful merchants, or farmers) were selected to head *esusu*.

The third unique feature is that the number of members does not always coincide with the number of memberships. "A single individual may hold more 'membership' in a given *esusu* group by regularly making more than one contribution and receiving the fund more than once during a single cycle. Conversely, a single 'membership' may be shared by two or more individuals who are not able to afford the entire contribution separately."[34] Our recent investigation reveals that what Bascom calls "membership" is, in Yoruba economic terms, known as *owo* (hand).[35] A membership was one *owo*: One affluent member could contribute two or more *owo* (and receive the fund more than once); while two or more less affluent members could jointly contribute one *owo*. This had the advantage of encouraging the rich as well the poor to save according to their individual capacity; also, it pooled resources together from every strata of society and placed them at one time or another at the disposal of the needy contributor, businessman, or farmer.

If we speculate that *esusu* is "native" to Yorubaland, we still have to deal with the date of its origin. Shirley Ardener (via Biobaku) seems to support a nineteenth-century introduction.[36] Our investigations indicate a much earlier origin. *Esusu* is known to have been practiced by Oyo traders in the era of *Alaafin* Abiodun in the late eighteenth century (which was also associated with the empire's expanded economic activity through participation in the Atlantic trade).[37] We suggest that the institution could have been exported to the West Indies at about this time, where it has survived in Trinidad under its Yoruba name. In addition, it is possible that the institution had developed much earlier than this time, if we accept to generalize Ardener's finding with respect to the Mba-Ise Igbo that ROSCAs constituted one of the causative factors in the "transition from a mainly agricultural to a predominantly trading economy."[38]

The foregoing discussion can be summarized. First, ROSCAs (*esusu*) among the Yoruba was similar to other mutual help organizations in the society (such as *aro* in agricultural labor supply). It could be rightly taken as a social organization to assist members in very stringent financial problems, such as the need to meet obligations arising from ordinary marriage, funeral, and religious functions. It also functioned to meet economically pressing needs to expand business or farm, or even to prosecute a war or pay a debt. Second, ROSCAs—along with other institutions in precolonial Yoruba society—helped in bridging the gap between the rich and the poor, for they brought both classes together in the same organization.[39] This was an advantage when one considers the role of *esusu* in the process of capital formation among the Yoruba. Third, ROSCAs among the Yoruba were neither "curious economic institutions," an "adaptation to a condition of poverty or relative deprivation" (as Donald Kurtz would have us believe),[40] nor were they a "middle rung" in development (as Clifford Geertz has asserted).[41] Rather, they were rational economic institutions developed to meet the needs of members of society. These derogatory terminologies arise from the effort of scholars to use foreign standards to judge the development of other people and their institutions. It cannot be over emphasized that scholars should endeavor to evaluate a people's economic and other institutions within the context of their historical experiences. However, many historians have not paid attention to this. For instance, Geertz has argued that ROSCAs bridge the gap "between agrarian and commercial economic patterns and between the peasant and trader attitudes toward money and its uses."[42] On the other hand, we know that the gap between the peasant and trader was not so wide. Although there was occupational specialization, variegation in African precolonial economies did not quite resemble the western notion of dichotomy between agriculture, industry, and commerce. Rather, through the extended family and other networks, all members of different occupational groups were in close touch with each other; within the same compound farmers, craftsmen, and traders often belonged to the same *esusu* society. In addition, there was little differentiation between the urban and rural settlements, as dwellers of the latter regarded the former as "home" with which they maintained perfect and constant contact and to which they returned during every major festival. Thus, even though the major market centers were located in the cities and towns, the traders were both from outlying villages and distant towns. *Esusu*, therefore, did not bridge a gap (there was none to bridge); rather, it reinforced the integrated rural-urban interactions and pooled resources across the board.

ROSCAs and Capital Formation

This leads inevitably to a consideration of the role of ROSCAs in precolonial banking and finance. ROSCAs did not have the same structure as modern banks; however, they performed in precolonial Africa many of the functions that banks now perform in these societies. Because they were also culturally rooted, and the people had faith in them, these institutions were able to perform those banking functions more efficiently. As can be recalled from chapter 4 (on money and social stratification), the size of capital required for business was large but within manageable limits, and the expectations of the different classes were high but easy to meet. We do not agree with those who have argued that ROSCAs were incapable of pooling together a huge capital fund for the development of private business. We seek to differ, too, from the assumption that precolonial societies lacked a capital market.

Indeed, the primary function of ROSCAs has been to "assist in small-scale (sic) capital formation," or to stimulate saving. Here, we find ourselves agreeing more and more with Shirley Ardener's point that

> Members (of ROSCAs) could save their contributions themselves at home and accumulate their own 'funds', but this would withdraw money from circulation: in rotating credit associations capital need never be idle. If, instead of being used at home, money were given to a treasurer to keep, he could (not) put it into circulation until it was transferred back to the subscribers...an advantage of the rotating credit institution is that each fund (or part of it) is immediately possessed by one of the contributors and cannot be embezzled.[43]

Unlike *ajo* where, as we have shown, the chances of embezzlement were high, *esusu* was a great innovation in that it provided sufficient security for the fund. This security was reinforced by religious (including ritualistic) sanctions. In Oyo, for example, cases of cheating and misappropriation were prevented or settled through appeal to Sango (god of thunder, known to strike cheats, thieves, and wrongdoers with thunderstorm) and Ogun (god of iron, known to harm those who have committed acts of injustice). Moreover, in the determination of how members were to receive *esusu* funds in turns, a *babalawo* (Ifa priest) was often invited and his word was accepted as final.[44]

Just like banks, ROSCAs extended a line of credit to members. Such loans were, however, restricted to members adjudged to be creditworthy by the *esusu* head or group leader. Unlike modern banking practice, no security was required to qualify for these loans, a factor that continues today to recommend ROSCAs against modern banks. Indeed, except for the last member or two to take the fund, all members of ROSCAs received the total fund in the form of a credit and continue to repay the debt till the end of the cycle. The advantage of Yoruba *esusu* credit over modern bank credit was principally in the absence of an interest.[45] This is certainly "unbusinesslike" when considered in the context of modern banking practice.[46] However, the points to stress are the communal spirit involved in this particular institution (*esusu*), the manner in which business was expected to serve the people rather than vice versa, and the existence of another institution for money lending and interest charging (the *s'ogund'ogoji*, literally "turn twenty to forty"). In other words, the "unbusinesslike" feature of *esusu* was also its appeal to the poor and the rich: interest charging was frowned upon, and those who did such a business (money lenders) were not well liked nor respected in Yoruba society.

ROSCAs, therefore, performed capital formation functions in precolonial societies. Such savings were made available as credit to those who needed them to expand their businesses or farms, or to meet an urgent financial need. Traders were known to have taken advantage of the funds more than any other groups of professionals possibly because, unlike craftsmen (weavers, dyers, smiths, and the like), traders required a great deal of capital.

The Nineteenth Century

It is instructive to document here the changes that had taken place in the *ajo* and *esusu* institutions among the Yoruba in the late nineteenth century. The entire century was a period of turbulence and interstate conflict in Yorubaland. War, as we well know, brings rapid and sometimes irreversible changes to society and its institutions. The situation was not different in Yorubaland: wars, slavery and abolition, migration and resettlement of refugees, famine, and the general insecurity that characterized the century produced remarkable changes in the structure, cohesion, and function of the family, community, and interpersonal relationships. These changes were bound to affect ROSCAs in many different ways.

For instance, as wars and slave raids ravaged the countryside, it became exceedingly difficult to guarantee the successful completion of the entire cycle of an *esusu* group. Some members might have to flee after or before taking their funds, or the entire village or city might be attacked and destroyed. As ROSCAs were not designed to serve a population on the move, many associations collapsed with the marked shifts in population from the north to the south. Among the major cities that were lost in the course of the nineteenth century were Oyo, Owu, Ikoyi, Iresa, Iwere, and Onko. This list does not include several minor towns and countless villages. Their displaced populations (that is, those not sold into slavery outright) were never able to regroup in sufficient numbers to reactivate their *esusu,* which had prematurely collapsed. Moreover, religious and other social sanctions were breaking down, traditional practices were being challenged, and the ruling elites in many communities were being replaced. In many instances, therefore, the insecurity to life and property was responsible for the development of the wrong attitude to savings in Yorubaland on the eve of the colonial conquest. Conversely, the insecurity encouraged the practice of hoarding money and other valuables (that is, burying them in the ground with the hope of coming back to recover them when normalcy was restored).[47]

Wars have been known as well to bring out the ingenuity in people, and for the Yoruba, the century-long wars produced positive and negative changes. In the first instance, not all Yoruba states participated in the wars all the time. In such nonbelligerent states, (or between wars in the belligerent ones) Yoruba institutions and traditions were preserved. But, even here, ROSCAs underwent changes particularly in the length of a cycle. *Esusu* cycles became shorter, and membership became smaller, with the possibility that participants would have taken their turns before the next series of cataclysmic changes. Although long-distance trade had become more perilous, the incentive to organize ROSCAs had not declined. Trade in legitimate commodities (which had been opened in the mid-nineteenth century) required much capital and brought immediate profit. An *esusu* of a few big traders was found to be even more effective than one composed of all and sundry. This increased the role of guilds in the generation of investment capital for members. Thus, membership of *esusu* became increasingly coterminous with membership of traders or crafts guilds. In other words, in place of the homogeneous lineage, ROSCAs began to take a cosmopolitan, heterogeneous complexion.

An important change that ROSCAs witnessed among the Yoruba in the nineteenth century was the introduction of record keeping. This arose partly from the activities of Christian missions in the development of western education, and partly from the role of the returnees (Yoruba freed slaves educated in Sierra Leone who chose to return "home" from 1839)[48] in the social, political, and economic development of Lagos, Abeokuta, Ibadan, and other parts of the Yoruba hinterland. This development clearly revolutionized ROSCAs in that accurate records began to be kept.

Modern Banking Institutions and the Resilience of ROSCAs

Colonial rule everywhere served as agent for change and modernization. It is a different question entirely if such changes were desired, positive, or far reaching. Inevitably, the change in the structure and operation of the economy, the desire to extract as much of the resources of the colony as possible, the reliance of business and credit on a larger volume of credit, and the provision that each colony should pay its way, all paved the way for the introduction of modern banking and insurance systems. It is interesting to note, nevertheless, that the modern did not replace the traditional banking institutions.

Modern banking began in Nigeria in 1872, when the African Banking Corporation (ABC) was established in Lagos.[49] In addition to performing normal commercial bank functions, the ABC was also charged with the distribution of Bank of England notes in the Colony of Lagos. In 1894, however, the ABC was taken over by the newly established Bank of British West Africa (BBWA), which was also charged with the importation of British currency into the colony. BBWA (now renamed First Bank) maintained a monopoly of banking in Lagos Colony (and in Nigeria) throughout the nineteenth century. Early in this century, however, the Barclays Bank (now called Union Bank) and the United Bank for Africa were established. These banks were established primarily to provide banking services to British companies and other arms of the colonial enterprise in Nigeria. By extension, therefore, the banks provided credit facilities to favored expatriate businesses in Nigeria to the detriment of indigenous entrepreneurs. The excuse was that African business men and women lacked the expertise to manage modern business, and that they could not provide the type of collateral being demanded against large loans. The situation encouraged the continuation of all precolonial credit institutions by Nigerian entrepreneurs throughout the colonial era.

Nigerian entrepreneurs also established commercial banks; but the banks often collapsed owing to a myriad of reasons including lack of expertise and experience, discrimination by expatriate banks, and discriminatory laws by the colonial state. The first indigenous bank to survive under this unfavorable colonial climate was the National Bank of Nigeria (NBN), established in 1933. Two earlier banks—Industrial and Commercial Bank and the Nigerian Mercantile Bank—had failed. Also, between May 1945 and January 1947, four additional banks were established of which only two—the African Continental Bank and the Agbonmagbe (now Wema) Bank—survived. The survival of these indigenous banks (NBN, ACB, and Wema) owed largely to the injection of Regional Government funds in the 1950s. Those other indigenous banks that lacked state banking, and which also lacked the requisite expertise and management, collapsed in the wake of the Banking Ordinance of 1952. Such banks had emerged during the "banking boom" of 1950–51, when eighteen indigenous banks were hurriedly established. The collapse of banks under colonial rule weakened public confidence in modern banking institutions and, according to Ajayi and Ojo, banks have not recovered from this "crisis of confidence."[50] Thus, a large number of people continued to save their money with the *alajo* and derive the initial capital for their business from *esusu* funds.

The fact that a building is set aside in a community and called a bank, in Yoruba *ile ifowopamo*, was novel. The fact that the money put (saved) in this "building" would not be within reach was also novel. As we have consistently maintained in this chapter, saving money in one form or another was not an unfamiliar notion, and banking was not an altogether strange idea. Modern banking was not (initially) a popular institution among the Yoruba, but not simply for those reasons of the conflict between African and Western traditions. In our thinking, the main reason banking was an unpopular ideal was historical.

From its inception in 1872, modern commercial banking in Nigeria was a monopoly of British conglomerates, which derived a large proportion of its patronage from the colonial administration. The few indigenous commercial banks were weak, and all but three—the National Bank, Agbonmagbe (Wema) Bank, and the African Continental Bank—had collapsed before the end of colonial rule. The collapse of indigenous commercial banks was due to two inter-related factors: the discriminatory colonial regulation and the inability of indigenous banks to compete. Before their collapse, these banks had succeeded in doing two things. They had made commercial banks unpopular among the people and they had taught those that survived the lesson that success lay in establishing structural linkages with government revenue. This was not novel. The powerful British banks had benefited from the patronage of the colonial government. The result was that the African elite used the revenue of the new regional governments to bail out the surviving banks.

Indigenous commercial banks found regional government revenues indispensable for their operation. A great and enduring relationship emerged by which the banks became an instrument of financial transfer from the taxpayers to the political leadership elite. It was quite a simple process: the banks held state revenue and they made out loans to state officials to further their business interest. The banks had to compromise on their lending policies in order to continue to enjoy the patronage of the state; and state officials had to compromise state regulations in order to be in the good books of the banks. The banks and the politicians, like Siamese twins joined at the throat, needed each other to eat and survive. That was the main problem: they were too interdependent for one to survive without the other. The National Bank and the ACB survived a series of political and economic crises. They survived the devastating effects of the fall of the First Republic, the Civil War, collapse of the Second Republic, decline in oil prices, economic crisis of the early 1980s, political instability since the military coup of December 1993, and the deregulation of foreign exchange market induced by IMF and World Bank demands. They eventually collapsed in 1995.

One main problem was that the commercial banks focused on the formal sectors of the Nigerian economy. They also exploited the structural linkages with government and major import-export businesses. The formal sector of the economy has come under intense pressure from the decline of government revenue, the corruption in what remains of it, the devaluation of the currency, and the inflationary trend in the economy. The banking boom that occurred in the late 1980s and early 1990s, resulting largely from currency exchange manipulations, lacked any real base to have been sustained. In any case, the boom only trickled down to the commercial banks from the merchant banks that mushroomed in the wake of SFEM and FEM.

This brief review of the travail of commercial banks in Western (and Eastern) Nigeria also reveals a little bit of the effect that the Yoruba view of money has had on the development of modern financial institutions. The importance of access to money for investment purposes was recognized. For the ordinary (usually illiterate) person, this was difficult, even near impossible, during the first few decades of colonial rule. As a result, almost all the ideals of money came under pressure. When the opportunity arose for a small group of the educated elite, the political elite, at the very end of colonial rule, at least in Western Nigeria, the notion of "other people's money" began to prevail over other more subtle and much saner voices. The evidence for this can be found partially in the sumptuous salaries and allowances the political elite received[51]; and in the diversion of public funds into private businesses, as the report of the Coker Commission shows.[52]

While the elite knew something about how banks operate and they aspired to use these formal institutions, the rest of the population—the farmers, the petty traders, artisans, and the like—turned to the informal financial institutions like the *ajo*, *esusu*, *paaro*, *s'ogun-d'ogoji*, and other avenues. They were responsible largely for the resilience of these precolonial institutions. There were other options, too.

For one thing, the farmers concentrated on the production of cash crops in order to participate in the cash economy. Cocoa and palm oil were the most attractive among the Yoruba, but kolanuts, rubber, coffee, tobacco, groundnuts, and cotton were cultivated in limited quantities. Cocoa and oil palm were the principal cash crops, known in many parts of Yorubaland as *igi owo*, money-producing trees. Focusing on *igi owo*, many were able to meet their financial obligations to the state and to each other. The most obvious ones were the payment of taxes and levies to the colonial government; payment of tuition if one had a child or two in school; and the payment of tribute to the chiefs, who now seemed to have more powers. The less obvious ones were equally important. Social payments that used to be made in kind, such as bride price, gifts from one friend to another in times of celebration or calamities, and gifts to artists and performers in appreciation of their talents, all were now monetized. Little wonder many people had to seek several short cuts to making money, even at this level. There was, indeed, a currency revolution. These multiplicity of monetized social payments also resulted in labor migration from one part of Yorubaland to another, generally into areas that could support the cultivation of *igi owo*. This phenomenon had major consequences for kinship relations and on social stability, but its financial implications were clear: they were driven by the need to accumulate money, and they would not rest until the need was achieved.

Some farmers were clearly successful, but most were on the fringe. It is true that the volume of agricultural production rose, but the proceeds from agricultural export trade did not reach the producers directly. Prices were low and the profit that could have filtered down to the farmers was creamed off by the raw materials exporting companies and by the colonial (and subsequently the regional) government through the erstwhile marketing boards. Money made from rural agriculture was concentrated in the government and, through the perversions discussed above, was put at the disposal of the elite as "other people's money." Agricultural credit schemes were introduced which did not go far enough to address the problems of investment that farmers faced. Consequently, when they received money from the government they were more inclined to divert it to the most pressing needs at the moment—which may be to pay bridewealth or to perform burial ritual.

As for the traders and craftsmen, who really needed more substantial investment capital than the farmers, they not only relied on the traditional financial institutions but they were also very creative. Partnerships were formed, cooperative societies and occupational guilds were organized, and their training and apprenticeship programs were reviewed. Unable to qualify for loans, many of them pooled their family resources and those of friends together to start the business, or they organized *esusu* societies for the same purpose. The formation of partnerships predated colonialism, but it became more widespread. Studies of Yoruba business organization has not reported of the existence of corporate behavior, or the formation of joint stock companies. Even then, most partnerships probably failed. The reason is that money made and broke relationships. Friendship became the victim of shattered business partnerships. The Yoruba had strongly advised against permitting money to come between friends. They know that money has the ability to split friendship (*owo ni i b'oju ore je*),[53] principally because of such vices as greed and accumulative drive, and also because the conflict between the virtues of friendship and modern business. *Odaju lo b'owo, itiju lo bi gbese*, that is, "assertiveness begats money but passivity begats debt." Although to be successful a businessman has to be shrewd, unfortunately shrewdness is bad between friends. Access to investment capital was (and still is) certainly a problem for these tradespeople.

This is why, for these small-scale merchants and business operators, the establishment of community banks in 1990 was truly a shot in the arm. Community banks combined the traditional and modern financial systems in an ingenious way. Although the initial seed money came from the government, these banks could theoretically succeed where the commercial banks had failed. Akin Mabogunje has expressed great optimism about the community banks.[54] For one thing the banks are growing both in their number and in the size of business. More significantly, the banks are established by the local community for their specific needs. They do business where they are most needed: at the grassroots. They lend money to people who could use credit but who would not qualify for commercial bank loans in a million years. They stimulate economic growth at the lower levels, at the level of tradespeople, small farmers, petty traders, butchers, food processing operators, and the like. Finally, community banks have begun to significantly affect the Yoruba ideal that debt, *gbese*, is to be avoided. According to Mabogunje, the banks are helping to show that credit is "the oil that keeps the wheel of production turning smoothly" and this has begun to alter the "lingering tendency or attitude that regards borrowing, even for business purposes, in a somewhat negative light."[55]

Why have *ajo* and *esusu* been resilient? Earlier answers to this question have emphasized the "foreignness" of modern, commercial banking traditional economies. We seek to show here that the reasons could be found not merely in this "foreignness." More specifically, they could be found in the manner in which they (the new banks) were introduced, the financial demands of colonial administration on the indigenous people, and the amenability of ROSCAs to the new needs for loans and small-scale capital. Thus, while the formal sector has relied on modern banking for investment capital, the informal sector derives a large percentage of the initial capital from the traditional institutions.

Taxation under colonial rule indirectly encouraged the patronage of ROSCAs. The British introduced direct taxation to Yorubaland in 1918. Although the British currency had not been widely circulated, the colonial administration insisted that the tax be paid not in cowry shells. Writers have shown that to obtain the required amount, many farmers had to seek unskilled, poorly paid wage employment as porters and railway workers in the expanding colonial enterprise. In addition to this, many had to organize *esusu* and use the proceeds to pay their tax (rather than invest them). Any examination of the underdevelopment of Africa is incomplete without the inclusion of the use of taxation to uproot the people, suck away their resources, and remove from them not just a part of their income but the actual investment capital they had managed to save. The point to note here, however, is that the traditional savings and credit associations were organized in the period partly in order to raise enough cash to pay tax to the colonial and postcolonial state.

Three features of modern (commercial) banking in Nigeria also deserve mention here to account for the resilience of ROSCAs. For one, the banks were, from the beginning, of the branch-banking type, that is, each of them maintained branches in different locations in the country. Second, the banking industry, like most modern investments in the country, has been dominated by foreign, transnational banks. For instance, the three expatriate banks (Union Bank, First Bank, and UBA) share between them 50.4 percent of the total assets of banks in Nigeria in 1990. These banks operate as capitalist institutions with the making and repatriation of profit being their main goals. Finally, the siting of banks has been concentrated in the urban areas. For illustration, as of 1990, out of the 1665 branches, only 602 (37 percent) were located in the rural areas.[56] What this has meant is that the rural areas, where the majority of the people reside, have had to rely on ROSCAs for savings and credit facilities, while banking loan policies in the urban areas have continued to discriminate against the small scale industrialists who have also resorted to ROSCAs.

Government intervention in the banking and financial system has also lent a helping hand to the continued popularity of ROSCAs among the people. The colonial and postcolonial state attempted to organize cooperatives without success. The postcolonial state has gone a step further by establishing state-owned commercial banks and insurance companies. The state built an institutional framework for pooling rural savings (through the Rural Banking Program introduced in 1977); of making loans to agricultural operators (through the Nigerian Agricultural and Cooperative Bank, NACB); of advancing credit to industrialists (through the Nigerian Industrial Development Bank, NDB); and of making small loans to the poor in general (through the People's Bank introduced in 1990).[57] For several reasons, these programs have not met with great success. Their failures have, therefore, encouraged the reliance of the people on the time-tested institution, ROSCAs.

Summary

Traditional savings, credit, and banking have come a long way in

Yorubaland. There is no doubt that in the precolonial era, when traditional norms and laws were still intact, and when the requirements of the economy were within manageable proportions, *ajo* and *esusu* were sufficient tools for pooling savings and sustaining a small but viable capital market. Traditional values and norms came under pressure in the period of British colonial domination, the economy also witnessed fundamental structural changes. That *ajo* and *esusu* survived these challenges is remarkable enough; but they cannot be expected to perform the very functions they used to perform before the coming of the great changes. Thus, whereas nowadays ROSCAs are seen as mere mutual help associations able to grant small credits to members, they had been banks in their time.

Notes

1. N. A. Fadipe, *The Sociology of the Yoruba,* F.O. and O.O. Okediji, eds. (Ibadan: Ibadan University Press, 1970), p. 256.
2. A. G. Hopkins, *An Economic History of West Africa* (London: Longman, 1973), pp. 70–71.
3. Joseph Stiglitz, "Peer Monitoring and Credit Markets," *The World Bank Economic Review*, iv, 3, 1990, pp. 351–66.
4. John M. Keynes, *The General Theory of Employment, Interest and Money* (London, 1936), p. 61.
5. Robert Ferber, "Saving," in Julius Gould and William Kolb, eds., *A Dictionary of the Social Sciences* (Paris: UNESCO, 1964), pp. 611–12.
6. T. A. Oyejide, "A Structural Analysis of Some Institutionalised Saving Patterns in Nigeria, 1961–73," *Journal of Business and Social Studies*, 1, 1, 1977, p.1. In spite of this wide conception of savings, however, Oyejide still betrays the preference of his discipline by criticizing traditional approaches to saving.
7. *Ibid*, p.1.
8. Goldsmiths in Africa did not play the same role in the development of money and banking as their counterparts in Western Europe. Indeed, African banking institutions did not rely on smiths possibly because coinage was not very widespread.
9. O. Ojo, "Rural Banking Scheme as a Strategy for Bank Location," *Ife Social Sciences Review*, vi, 1&2, 1983, pp. 84–90.
10. This may sound tautological, but the point will be proved later in the chapter. It should suffice to say here that the rural areas are not the only places where the traditional banking institutions have survived.
11. Clifford Geertz, "The Rotating Credit Association: A 'Middle Rung' in Development," *Economic Development and Cultural Change*, x, 1962, p. 242.
12. *Ibid*.
13. Clifford Geertz, "The Rotating Credit Association," p. 243.
14. Shirley Ardener, "The Comparative Study of Rotating Credit Associations," *Journal of the Royal Anthropological Institute*, xciv, 1964, p. 201.
15. *Ibid*.
16. *Ibid*, pp. 202–09.
17. Her recent writing on the subject does not focus very much on the Yoruba experience. See Shirley Ardener and Sandra Burman, *Money-Go-Rounds: The Impor-*

tance of Rotating Savings and Credit Associations for Women (Oxford: Berg, 1995).

18. *Ibid.*, pp. 208–10.
19. In this regard, we have found these essays very useful: Clifford Geertz, "The Rotating Credit Associations," pp. 241–63; Shirley Ardener, "The Comparative Study of Rotating Credit Associations," pp. 201–28.
20. In Yoruba language, the same expression is used for singular and plural. In this specific instance, *alajo* expresses both singular and plural of the term.
21. William Bascom, "The Esusu: A Credit Institution of the Yoruba," *Journal of the Royal Anthropological Institute*, lxxxii, 1, 1952, pp. 63–69.
22. This was before Clifford Geertz came up with the name "rotating credit association."
23. Bascom, "The *Esusu,*" p. 63.
24. The Reverend Samuel Johnson, *The History of the Yorubas* (Lagos: C.M.S. Bookshops, 1921, reprinted 1976), p. 119.
25. Bascom, "The *Esusu,*" p. 63.
26. In *aro*, a small group of friends or relations (between three and seven) form a club, all members of that club go to work in one member's farm in turn. This is usually organized during the rains when weeds grow fast and need to be cleared even faster.
27. This suggestion is contained in a passage in Ardener's otherwise balanced essay thus: "Mention was made earlier of connections between Trinidad, Sierra Leone and Yoruba country through the various forms of *esusu*."
28. Geertz, "The Rotating Credit Association," p. 256.
29. For *esusu* to "die on the road" is for it to die prematurely. Bascom has applied this in a narrow sense to mean the inability of one member to keep up his/her contribution. This is actually the beginning of the "death."
30. Geertz, "The Rotating Credit Association," p. 256.
31. Bascom, "The *Esusu,*" p. 64.
32. Geertz, "The Rotating Credit Association," p. 256.
33. According to Bascom ("The *Esusu,*" p. 68), "it is thought to be unlikely that the *esusu* head could take a third round for himself during the cycle without being caught."
34. Bascom, "The *Esusu,*" p. 64.
35. Bascom's interpretation of *owo* is slightly different from our finding. Oral tradition collected in Iwo indicates that *owo* is amount of money "handed in," which could mean the contribution made by or given to an individual.
36. Ardener, "The Comparative Study," p. 209; S.O. Biobaku, *The Egba and Their Neighbours, 1842–1872*, (London: OUP, 1957), p. 26.
37. Robin Law, *The Oyo Empire*, pp.
38. Ardener, "The Comparative Study," p. 221.
39. It can, however, be argued that the togetherness benefited the rich more than the poor, because it afforded the former access to the little resources that the former could muster, and in the organization the poor had little voice.
40. Donald V. Kurtz, "The Rotating Credit Association: An Adaptation to Poverty," *Human Organization*, 32, 1973, pp. 49–58.
41. Geertz, "The Rotating Credit Association," pp. 266–63.
42. This is Kurtz's ("The Rotating Credit Association," p. 50) summary of Geertz's position ("The Rotating Credit Association," pp. 261–63).
43. Ardener, "The Comparative Study," p. 217.
44. It is necessary to point out here, although the point will be made again later, that all the cultural and religious backing for ROSCAs began to weaken shortly before the establishment of British colonial rule over Yorubaland.

45. This is to differentiate the Yoruba practice from other ROSCAs elsewhere. For instance, Ardener has noticed the charging of interest on ROSCAs credit in India (see "Comparative Study").
46. Geertz ("The Rotating Credit Association," p. 254) makes the distinction between "businesslike" and "unbusinesslike" associations.
47. As so many never returned to their original places of abode, and as those who did could not accurately identify the hiding places, so much money and valuables were lost. For instance, a large pot containing thousands of cowry shells was accidentally found in one of the authors' father's farm in 1967 when they were making yam ridges.
48. For more details on the history and activities of the *Saro* immigrants (as "Sierra Leoneans" were called), see J. H. Kopytoff, *Preface to Modern Nigeria: The 'Sierra Leoneans' in Yoruba* (Madison: University of Wisconsin Press, 1965).
49. The discussion on modern banking in Nigeria is based is based on the following source: S. I. Ajayi and O. O. Ojo, *Money and Banking Analysis and Policy in the Nigerian Context* (London: George Allen and Unwin, 1981).
50. Ajayi and Ojo, *Money and Banking Analysis*, p. 16.
51. Adebayo showed that under the 1951 Constitution, the Western Region was paying its legislators £420 per annum. This was higher that the allowances paid by the Northern and Eastern Regional Governments by £20. This difference alone is substantial for, at the time, many workers in Nigeria did not earn so much as £20 per annum. For more detail, see A. G. Adebayo, *Embattled Federalism: A History of Revenue allocation in Nigeria, 1946–79* (New York: Peter Lang, 1993), pp. 192–94.
52. The report finds, among other things, that between 1954 and 1961 the Western Regional Government invested a large part of the surplus funds of the Western Regional Marketing Board as loan to the Nigerian Investment and Properties Company and the National Bank. The Commission described these loans as "imprudent…and constituted a most flagrant breach of trust and an infamous design by which the peoples of Western Region have been robbed of the financial benefits to which they are entitled from the Western Regional Marketing Board."
53. The Yoruba classify friendships into several categories, including *ore imule*, *ore kori-kosun*, *ore bi ajobi*, *ore dabe-n-yanko*, *ore odale*. Even the best of friendships can collapse due to disagreement on or misunderstanding about money.
54. Akin L. Mabogunje, "The Capitalization of Money and Credit in the Development Process: The Case of Community Banking in Nigeria," in Jane Guyer, *Money Matters*, pp. 277–95.
55. *Ibid*, p. 292.
56. A. G. Adebayo, *Nigerian Economic Development Since Independence* (Lagos, forthcoming).
57. Among many writings, see Ukandi G. Damachi and Hans Dieter Seibel, eds. *Social Change and Economic Development in Nigeria* (New York: Praeger, 1973); H. A. Oluwasanmi and J. A. Alao, "The Role of Credit in the Transformation of Traditional Agriculture: The Nigerian Experience," *Nigerian Journal of Economic and Social Studies*, vii, 1, 1965, pp. 31–50; Ade T. Ojo and W. Adewunmi, *Cooperative Banking in Nigeria: Evolution, Structure and Operations* (Lagos: University of Lagos Press, 1980); O. A. Lewis, "Economic Performance Orientation and Problems of Small Scale Industries in Nigeria's Former Western State," *Quarterly Journal of Administration*, xii, 1, 1977.

Part 2

Money and Its Problems

7

Forms of Credit and Loan Repayment

Access to credit was, and still is, one of the major impediments to economic development in Africa. The problem was no more serious in the period before colonial rule than it is now. Where the fund provided through the rotating savings and credit associations (ROSCAs) was not sufficient, as was often the case, the Yoruba in need of money had to seek additional funds from moneylenders.

The existence of traditional markets has long been recognized by scholars. In general, the policymakers' response has focused on replacing these traditional mechanisms with the modern or western. These efforts have been unsuccessful. According to Karla Hoff and Joseph Stiglitz, "the past forty years of experience of government intervention in rural credit markets suggest that the creation of institutional alternatives has failed to drive the traditional moneylender out of the market."[1] It is remarkable that it is this very failure that has increased scholars' interest in understanding the traditional institutional frameworks for moneylending.

The credit market dominated by moneylenders[2] has also begun to attract attention as part of the increased interest in the study of the slave trade, rural development, or of Africa's current indebtedness. Needless to say, these studies have been extremely critical of African traditional credit markets, viewing them as usurious and outmoded. Our perspective here is not to dispute the exploitative nature of traditional moneylending. Rather, we seek to show that modern credit systems are no less usurious, to explain the basis for the high interest rate charged, and to account for the following that these credit markets still enjoy among the people.

As has been explicitly stated in earlier writings on the subject, this credit system operated (and still operates, with slight modification) on a very high interest rate paid by the borrower in cash or in kind. Among the Yoruba, there were several institutional mechanisms for money lending and interest collection in precolonial times. Of these, three will be given extensive discussion here. The first is the system of pledging crops as collaterals and as interest. The second is the *iwofa* system, where the borrower paid the interest in labor supply on the creditor's farm or industry. The third is the *s'ogund'ogoji* system, under which the interest was paid in cash which was, at the very least, an amount equal to the principal. The manner in which these three systems operated, and the institutional mechanism that protected the creditor from default, are examined in this chapter.

Several features of Yoruba social and political systems supported the credit institutions. One was the centralized political and administrative system in each kingdom, where major policy decisions were taken by the *oba* (king) in council and which, with a few exceptions, positively affected the conduct of economic programmes. Another was the stratified society which, nevertheless, celebrated and rewarded success and hard work, particularly success in farming, trade, and industry. Yet another was the urbanized social life, which encouraged industrial production and promoted division of labor. Others included a devoted religious life, characterized by the worshipping of the Supreme God (*Olodumare*) through a pantheon of highly feared and respected gods and goddesses; and, closely associated with this, an ordered society with laws assumed to be binding on every member irrespective of his/her position, and with punishment for every misdemeanor believed to be handed down for the common good directly or indirectly by the gods. Before their collapse and restructuring in the nineteenth century, these features of the social and political systems worked effectively to promote and protect investments and played a crucial role in the development of credit institutions.

It is important to briefly explain the main motives for credit among the Yoruba. Very often, it has been said that people in traditional societies do not need credit, and that when they do it is usually for frivolous and noneconomic uses. With specific reference to the Yoruba, it has been suggested that they used the loans to marry more wives or finance expensive burial ceremonies. When considered in its context, there was nothing really uneconomical in having many wives, given the dependence of the occupations at the time on manual labor; the high mortality rate among children; the insecurity, kidnapping, and child stealing in the era of the slave trade; and the fact that most wives and children constituted the labor force. The addition of a woman into the family was the injection of an actual human power and, subsequently, if the marriage was fruitful, additional (potential) human power from the children. Big burial was a waste of scarce resources, but the social embarrassment and humiliation that attended a substandard burial ceremony among the Yoruba was as great as the economic cost of an expensive one.[3] In any case, on a large number of occasions, loans were sought more for clear economic purposes than for burial and other ceremonies. Small or big loans were taken by farmers to expand their farmlands (usually by buying more slaves and agricultural implements), by traders to embark on a trading mission, and tradesmen/craftsmen (blacksmiths, goldsmiths, weavers, and so on) to purchase raw materials and finance different stages of the production.

It is also important to point out that credit among the Yoruba involved more than the lender and the borrower. In almost all cases, there was also a guarantor, an *onigbowo*, familiar to both parties, capable of speaking for the borrower and assuming the responsibility for the repayment if the borrower defaulted, and respected and trusted enough by the lender to accept whatever condition he suggested for the transaction. As was to be expected, this was the ideal condition. In many cases, the *onigbowo* was not very familiar to the borrower but was only doing the duty for a fee, which was deducted from the principal received by the borrower up front. Moreover, the lenders knew that the responsibility for the recovery of the money was theirs, and not that of the *onigbowo* if he was unwilling to help. This third party made sense only as a witness to the loan having been made out. In some instances, it was deemed necessary to make the borrower's family aware of the loan.[4] This was found to be helpful at the moment of enforcing repayment, as the entire family might have to contribute the principal if the borrower declared bankruptcy. Before the colonial era, all this comprehensive contract was often unwritten but binding on all parties concerned.

Most moneylenders were men, although the business was not closed to women; there was also no conscious division among borrowers along gender lines, although most were men. In addition, most moneylenders were urban dwellers and had businesses there. Most were members of the urban aristocracy or absentee landlords who had made their money through farming and trading. Traditional Yoruba society, as we have pointed out in the general introduction, was urban based. Even though farmers might spend a greater part of their lives in the villages, they saw themselves primarily as members of particular compounds in the cities. Thus, even the borrowers could be said to be urban dwellers. In any case, the contract for the loan was often finalized in the house of the lender wherever it was located. Where the lender was also resident in the village, the task became easier, for he was able to scrutinize the credentials of the borrower for the loan, evaluate his progress toward repayment, and judge fairly correctly the profitability of the interest. On the other hand, draconian measures might be difficult to enforce where the relationship between the lender and the borrower was close. The point to emphasize here is that the risk to lending under the traditional credit market system was different from lending under the modern system in one significant respect: there was a perfect information flow.

Pledging Farm Crops as Collateral and Interest on Loan

One of the earliest forms of credit available in most traditional societies is the granting of usufruct loans. This credit system has been noted in many parts of India and Africa.[5] Under the system, the borrower pledges to the lender, both as security and as interest, the whole or part of the proceeds from his farm. The size of the interest derived from such loans by the lender, therefore, depended on the size and current market prices of the crop upon harvest. According to Christopher Udry, this type of credit system has several advantages to the creditor and virtually none to the debtor. In his view,

> collateral pledged in exchange for the receipt of a loan directly reduces the cost to the lender of a default on a loan; it can reduce the moral hazard associated with lending by providing an added incentive for the borrower to repay; and it can alleviate the problem of adverse selection by screening out those borrowers most likely to default.[6]

The Yoruba had knowledge of this type of credit system, although information available is still too scanty on the origin of the system. What is clear is that they had two variants of usufruct loans. In one form (we call this Type A), a lender acquired the right to occupy the borrower's farm and harvest the crops until the principal was paid. In this instance, the collateral was the farm while the harvest was the interest. Probably of late nineteenth century origin, this system became widespread in the colonial era, and was a common practice among cocoa, kolanut, rubber and palm oil farmers in Yorubaland. The connection between this type of usufruct loan and *iwofa* (see below) has been noted and this would seem to suggest that the former was an offshoot of the latter.

In the second form (Type B), the borrower insured the loan against a particular crop and pledged to *sell* whatever was harvested to the lender. This was known in Yoruba as *agbasile* (or *agbaale*) meaning simply "advance collection" (of payment by a farmer for crops yet to be harvested). It was most beneficial to the creditor if he/she was also a trader in that particular commodity, and where the market for the commodity was competitive. Melon and locust bean seeds are often mentioned as crops with such a high degree of commercial value probably because their cultivation was restricted to the savanna. Under this system, the profit made by the creditor-trader in the sale of the crops was the interest while the *guarantee* of first choice as buyer was the collateral. Needless to say, the creditor-trader paid an noncompetitive price for the crop, a price that was usually too low for the debtor to be able to repay the principal, thus ensuring that the loan spilled over to the following harvest season.[7]

As could be expected, Type A was much preferred by the lender, while the borrower preferred Type B. The choice of borrowing and lending options were therefore contingent upon many factors, including the size of loan sought, the good reputation or credit worthiness of borrower, the shrewdness or compassion of lender, the condition of the market in the commodities, and how urgently the borrower needed the money. A big loan, for instance, constituted a major risk to the lender, and all measures were taken against the possibility of default as well as to ensure maximum interest yield. The guarantee of crop sale to the lender would not be sufficient collateral or interest against such loans; the free harvest of the entire farm would be much preferred, although this also limited the borrower's ability to repay the principal. Moreover, a hard-pressed borrower would accept any and all conditionalities, even if it was only a small loan being sought.

In clear economic terms, the costs to the borrower of pledging crops as security for and interest on loans are enormous. In Type A what the borrower lost (and the creditor gained) included the initial labor expended in making the farm and subsequent labor used in maintaining it in good condition for the creditor, the entire crop at harvest time, the anticipated profit from the sale of the crops, and the possibility of reusing his farmland during another planting season. In Type B, the borrower lost the freedom to choose the best market, that is, the ability to sell to a buyer willing to pay a better price, and the capacity of making maximum profit from the sale of the crops.

In other words, the pledging of crops as collateral against loans (of either Type A or B) was counter-productive to the borrower. It limited the ability of the borrower to repay, increased the exploitation of the borrower by the lender, deepened the gulf between the rich and the poor in the society, and exposed the latter to various forms of abuse.

Pledging Service as Interest: The *Iwofa* System

Another very exploitative lending condition was the system of pledging service to the creditor until the principal is fully paid. This was known as the *iwofa* system. Although so much has been written about the *iwofa* system among the Yoruba,[8] especially in making a differentiation between it and slavery on the one hand,[9] and pawnship on the other,[10] so much is still unknown about it as a credit system.

As has been correctly pointed out by Samuel Johnson, the term *iwofa* is not equivalent to the English "pawn" for, "to pawn in Yoruba is *fi d'ogo* which term is never applied to human being," whereas *iwofa* derives from *iwo* (the entering into) and *efa* (six) meaning a person's voluntary entry into "a recurrent sixth day service" agreement. *Iwofa* is also distinct from slave (*eru*) in the sense that while the latter was bought (*ra*) the former was engaged (*ya*).[11]

These points of distinction are salient, for the *iwofa* system was a mechanism for paying interest on borrowed money. According to Johnson, "the service rendered goes for the interest, and only the principal is paid back whenever payment is made whether after a few days or after several years."[12] *Iwofa*, the person rendering the service, might be the borrower himself or his/her child (boy or girl).

The type of service rendered varied according to the sex and occupation of the lender, and the sex, skill, and age of the *iwofa*. The general practice was to engage the male *iwofa* in agricultural service. He was "required to clear a piece of land equal to 100 yam heaps or an equivalent in his master's farm once a week." Since ordinarily an able-bodied man would clear up to 300 heaps daily on his own farm, "a strong man often found it possible to work in three different farms on the same day, for different masters, or to do three week's work at a time in one farm, and have 14 off days at a stretch, in which he is free to follow his own trade without interrruption."[13]

This was the practice before the period of large-scale insecurity in the nineteenth century, when the moneylenders changed the rules in the bid to make maximum profit from their operations that had suddenly become very precarious. In that period, it was not uncommon for lenders to demand more than a day's work from their adult *iwofa*. Also, it was possible for them to abuse the labor of other *iwofa*, particularly the young boys and girls.

Most borrowers preferred to send their female children to be the *iwofa*, the situation being that male children were needed more in their parents' farms, and the advantage being that they (the borrowers) would continue to have access to their male children's labor in the farms. On the other hand, the law that protected the female *iwofa* from abuse also worked in favor of the borrower parents. Creditors were not to have sexual intimacy with their female *iwofa*, but if this happened the creditor would be bound to marry her and the original loan was regarded as forming a part of the bride wealth payable to the parents-in-law. From the point of view of the borrower, this was a very good way of avoiding payment, and a very profitable way of marrying off the daughter to a rich man. The borrower won more in this event than the lender. In order to avoid such accidental marriages and loss of principal as well as interest, most male creditors preferred to have male *iwofa*.

Female *iwofa* were engaged in domestic duties. However, a good number of them assisted their masters in trading activities. In this instance, a young girl was preferred who would be staying in the compound of the creditor and taken into the household. The boys were known to tend their master's horses and run errands for him. If a boy or girl *iwofa* died during service, the master had to explain the cause of death and prove beyond doubts that he had provided adequate medical services and that death was not as a result of overwork. This legal protection worked to make life bearable in the minimum for the *iwofa*, but it was more than many creditors could take. This group of creditors either broke the laws with impunity, or preferred that service be provided by the borrower himself.

Several cases of abuse have been recorded by Adeniyi Oroge.[14] One was the *Baba-ni-nma-sa* system in Ibadan in the period of Ijaye and Kiriji wars (1860s to 1880s). Two leading Ibadan war chiefs, Ibikunle and Ogunmola, initiated this system. Oroge attributes the origin of the system to the scarcity of cowries in Ibadan during these great wars and the consequent increase in the number of children sent into *iwofa* service. As could be expected, many of these children were "pawned" to military leaders who then sought to militarize the iwofa system by taking the young boys to the battle front. *Baba-ni-nma-sa*, meaning literally "father has told me not to run away," was designed, according to Oroge, "as a means of training the youths in military tactics at first hand."[15] According to Johnson, these unfortunate children were all dressed in red uniforms, "and were to sit around their master whatever may be the condition of the fight."[16] An abuse of the service provided under the *iwofa* system, and a disregard for the protection of the *iwofa* in practice, the *Baba-ni-nma-sa* system was also an example of child abuse. The evil system lasted until about 1880, and was discontinued after a major catastrophe. According to Oroge,

> lucky parents managed to raise loans from traders and missionaries but the less fortunate had to receive loans from war chiefs who might decide to take their pawns to the battle-front as *baba-ni-nma-sa*. It is on record that Babalola, the son and heir to Balogun Ajayi Ogboriefon, who took 400 *baba-ni-nma-sa* to Kiriji in c. 1880, lost 140 killed and wounded in his first fight, while by the end of the third fight the remnants had been wiped out. It was apparently after this catastrophe that the custom was discontinued in favour of the genuine *iwofa* system.[17]

The important point to note in this discussion is the economic advantage of lending under the *iwofa* system. The borrower had sufficient encouragement to work and repay the principal, the lender also made good profit from the labor of the *iwofa*. Also, unlike the condition that obtained under the system of pledging crops as interest on loan, the lender did not have to worry too much about the security of his investment. Again, in the positive light, many *iwofa*, particularly the young boys and girls, learned different skills (such as war tactics, traditional medicinal practices, manufacturing, and trading) from their masters that paid off later in their lives. One must not fail to mention the impact of all these on the size of Yoruba family. The idea of obtaining credit by sending children to be *iwofa* gave an incentive to many men to have large families even when it was obvious that their resources were too low to provide adequately for them. This was a social question that came under sharp focus in the colonial era. As Toyin Falola has shown, however, the popularity of lending under the *iwofa* system had not diminished in the period and the British authorities found it difficult to combat because it was neither slavery nor was it excessively oppressive on the borrower—*iwofa*. Moreover, the institution provided, under colonial rule as in the previous era, a great source of cheap labor.

Osomalo: Hire Purchase among the Yoruba

Hire-purchase, or the *osomalo* system, was another credit arrangement that developed among the Ijesa and spread to many parts of Yorubaland, especially the Oyo empire, through interregional trade. *Osomalo* is a term derived from the conflictive end of the transaction, and has been considered in the pejorative. *Osomalo* is the short term for *oso ni maa lo gb'owo mi*, which in Ijesa dialect means "I will remain in this crouching position till I am paid." The term is also a constant reminder that the person that overreaches himself gets into debt and trouble.

This transaction usually began on a very good note. The *osomalo* was a trader in expensive clothes, which he sold on credit. People bought from the *osomalo*, promising to pay in installments. The *osomalo* thus provided the goods on a hire-purchase basis, and would have built his interest into the price. Most transactions probably ended in a conflict, which could arise from several sources: disagreement over prices (especially since the transaction was unwritten), *osomalo*'s impatience or fear of bankruptcy, buyer's inability to pay owing to crop failure, and *osomalo*'s unilateral revision of price owing to rising costs.

Whenever there was a default, the *osomalo* resorted to crude and tough means to recover the money. As most of the goods involved were perishable items like cloths, the *osomalo* could not recover the goods but could only insist on full payment. This was when the *osomalo* could be heard shouting *oso ni maa lo gb'owo mi*. Crouching is an extremely uncomfortable position and, in Yoruba ethics, one should not subject one's benefactor to such a pain. Moreover, the *osomalo* might, from that crouching position, make any irreverent demands on the buyer or buyer's household, which must be met. The strategy would seem to be effective, but it gave the business a very bad name. Another important point to note is that the *osomalo* was an Ijesa trader and the creditor-buyers were often the Oyo Yoruba well known for their conspicuous consumption (*afefeyeye*) and fashion.

S'ogund'ogoji: Lending under Usurious Interest Rate

A group of traditional moneylenders operated like modern credit institutions by demanding that interest on loan be paid in cash. The rate of such interest, however, marked them out from the modern institutions. Generally, it was a callous and usurious rate. Among the Yoruba, such moneylenders were, and still are, known as *s'ogund'ogoji*, literally meaning "convert twenty to forty." The minimum interest rate charged on their loans was 100 percent[18]; hence, the name *s'ogund'ogoji*. The available information is too scanty on its origin, but given its emphasis on cash transactions there could be no doubt that it evolved consequent to the monetization of the economy.

Borrowing from this group of moneylenders was usually the least attractive option considered by people in the business profession. This is because of the callous and oppressive interest rate. To take the option, a scrupulous investor had to be sure that he would make as profit an amount much greater than the interest on the loan. Because this was very unlikely, it was only those in great difficulties, or strangers in cities who could not be plugged to established credit institutions, that turned to *s'ogund'ogoji*. Among other "problems" that required urgent financial assistance, and that drove people to the bear hug of *s'ogund'ogoji* because they could not be postponed indefinitely, were funeral and marriage ceremonies, religious festivals, and the repayment of earlier debts that had fallen due.

Before going any further, two issues require some clarification. For one, the interest rate might be quantifiable, but it could not be said to have been significantly higher than the pledging of crops (assuming that it was possible to accurately estimate this). We can imagine here the situation of harvesting all the crops in a particularly large farm (for several years, if tree crops and if the borrower failed to repay the principal within the year) as interest on a loan. If there was a good harvest, and a good price for the crops, the interest could actually treble (or at least, more than double) the principal. In the absence of an inflation, however, cash interest payment protected the lender from the vagaries of the weather and fluctuations in price. Second, *s'ogund'ogoji* credit market was not altogether uneconomic for the enterprising borrower/trader. Some traders interviewed in various parts of Yorubaland admitted to taking *s'ogund'ogoji* loans at different stages in the development of their enterprises.[19]

What type of person was the *s'ogund'ogoji* (moneylender)? Although not by a conscious differentiation according to sex, the moneylender was generally a man. Also, although he could originally have been a successful farmer or trader, the moneylender was a professional because money lending was a serious, full-time business. He was usually a resident in the city, but had many agents working for him in the villages. Furthermore, as the society was not then literate, transactions were conducted in the presence of a surety and/or witnesses. Finally, although a member of the dominant elite, he was not usually regarded as a part of the ruling class and he was feared rather than respected or loved. Although benefiting from the political support of the *oba* (king) of the community, for economic reasons, particularly because of the chances of default, he generally avoided giving big loans to members of the political elite. Politically, therefore, the *s'ogund'ogoji* creditor was an outcast among the ruling class and the masses of the people.

What actually gave the *s'ogund'ogoji* credit system a bad name was its cumbersome organization. The moneylenders had unlimited leeway to cheat the borrower. In addition to a high interest rate, the lender could coerce the borrower into indicating that he had collected more money as principal. This problem of lending with a high interest rate is discussed further in the next chapter.

How did moneylenders reduce or limit the margin of loss? The first method was to screen borrowers. This was very easy to do where the lender and the borrower were familiar with one another, and where they both resided in the same locality. The second was to engage as surety a fairly well-to-do man capable of repaying the loan in case the borrower defaulted and ran away. The third was to be in close and constant touch with the borrower, assess the progress of his/her farm or business, watch over his/her health and offer medical assistance if necessary (God forbid the sickness or death of a debtor!), remind him/her of the due date for repayment, and encourage him/her to take the option of installmental repayment. Also, the lender often resorted to the employment of supernatural means to take the borrower's interest off all considerations of default, but rather have great interest in repaying the loan.[20] Finally, the lender could use force. However, because force was a double-edged sword, it had to be applied with care so as not to scare away the debtor, but win support for the lender among members of the borrower's family.

In certain instances, particularly where the moneylender had the support of the traditional ruler or local authority, these avenues protected the lender from risk. However, default was not totally eliminated. Present-day moneylenders are not able to estimate with precision the proportion of this default, but their testimonies indicate that "several people" owe them money.

Enforcing Repayment I: The Licensed Distrainer

Moneylending, as we have shown, was a risky business for the lender. Generally, there was every incentive for the borrower to repay the loan (to reclaim his property from the lender, to liberate himself or his child from pawnship, and so on); unfortunately, these very "incentives" or conditionalities of lending often made him unable to repay promptly. Indeed, given the high and exploitative interest rates, it was a wonder that many still turned to moneylenders for assistance, and it is not surprising that most borrowers became incorrigible debtors. In some of the Yoruba sayings that portray the attitude of debtors to their creditors under extreme conditions, the debtor is said to resign himself to the worst.[21]

As members of the ruling elite, moneylenders employed existing traditional institutions and values of the society (and introduced new ones) to ensure the profitability and security of their business and to make the borrower or his family repay the principal. This was irrespective of what the lender might have derived from the exploitation of agricultural and/or human resources of the borrower. Samuel Johnson does not write about the practice of moneylending in the nineteenth century. However, he has left a vivid description of debt collection mechanism among the Yoruba in the period. According to him,

> the Yorubas have a peculiar method of forcing payment out of an incorrigible debtor. When a creditor who has obtained judgment for debt finds it impossible to recover any thing out of the debtor, he applies to the town authorities for a licensed distrainor. This individual is called Ogo, he is said to *d'ogo ti* i. e. to sit on the debtor (as it were). For that purpose, he enters the premises, seeks out the debtor, or ensconces himself in his apartment until he makes his appearance, and then he makes himself an intolerable nuisance to him and to members of the house generally until the money is paid.
>
> The distrainor is a man of imperturbable temper, but of a foul tongue, a veritable Thersites. He adopts any measure he likes, sometimes by inflicting his presence and attention on the debtor everywhere and anywhere he may go, denying him privacy of any kind, and in the meantime using his tongue most foully upon him, his own person being inviolable, for touching him implies doing violence to the person of the authorities who appoint him the task. He demands and obtains whatever diet he may require, however sumptuous and may help himself if not quickly served. If he thinks fit, he may hold on any poultry or cattle he finds in the premises, and prepare himself food, and all at the expense of the debtor. He must not take anything away but he may enjoy the use of anything he finds in the house.[22]

The distrainer was usually a man of bad and contemptuous manners. He could be a leper, chosen so that he would spread the disease. The appointment of a distrainer was usually the last resort that both the lender and the borrower detested. To the borrower, it damaged his standing in the household. But the risk was still that of the lender. This is because, by the activities of the distrainer, the lender got a bad name, and the method might even backfire. The mechanism was based on the belief in the homogeneity of the compound and the readiness of its members jointly to rescue another member in trouble. According to Johnson,

> loud in his abuses, intolerable in his manners to all in the house whilst going in and out with the debtor, he goes on in this way all day, and from day to day if needs be, until even the inmates of the compound get tired of this, and then means will quickly be found of getting rid of the distrainor by paying off the debt.[23]

N.A. Fadipe, writing during the colonial period, added to the information supplied by Johnson. The distrainer could prevent the members of the debtor's household from entering or leaving the house, kill their livestock, and could do other things to force the debtor's relations to assist in paying. The debtor was also forced to pay for the services of the distrainer. According to Fadipe there were other draconian methods. When slave trade was possible, such a debtor could be sold. Relations of debtors were forced to seek the means to pay in three other ways:

> An alternative method...was to seize anyone belonging to his (i.e., debtor's) extended family of his kindred and hold him or her prisoner until the debt was paid. Still a third method of recovering debts was to go to the market and start to buy goods right and left, but without paying. After the goods were safe in the creditor's possession he informed the sellers that such and such would be liable.[24]

If, however, the borrower was not a well-respected member of the compound, or had brought disrepute upon the family several times, the entire compound might not be interested in assisting him to repay his creditor, for he (the borrower) was not strictly speaking expected to refund the family for such help. Having been cast out by the compound, the distrainer's duty became more difficult, and the creditor's chances of recovering his money became very slim.

Enforcing Repayment II: Denial of a Decent Burial

To further protect the lender from total forfeiture of his money upon the death of the borrower, the Yoruba had an institutional mechanism that forced members of the deceased debtor's family, who had the responsibility of burying him, to also pay his debts. This has been known to work effectively where the deceased was well loved by other members of the extended family and where there was much solidarity with the deceased's own children in the final rite of their father/mother. It has also been known to be ineffective where there was no interest to restore the reputation of the deceased. In fact, N. A. Fadipe has provided evidence to show the greater risk that the lender bore in his effort to recover his money by force after the death of the borrower. According to him, although it was usual to deny a deceased debtor the right to decent burial,

> but this was as much a measure of protection for the creditor as for the relatives of the debtor, the underlying idea being that his relatives would be horrified at the thought of his soul being left in a state of suspense, and that they would , therefore, find means of paying his creditors. On the other hand, those who took the responsibility of burying a person were supposed by that action to accept the responsibility for his debts. Accordingly, before health regulations were made and enforced, when an habitual debtor or one for whose debts his relatives would not make them-

> selves responsible died, his body was placed in a stretcher and left in the bush so that any of his creditors could be directed to it should the need arise.[25]

In other words, despite the draconian methods adopted by creditors for ensuring repayment, many loans were still passed off as bad debts either during the lifetime of the borrower or upon his death. This both explains the high and exploitative interest rates as well as the lack of popularity of moneylenders as members of the ruling elite.

Prelude to Colonialism: Moneylending in the Nineteenth Century

Yoruba society underwent significant changes in the nineteenth century. Many existing institutions came under pressure as a result of dramatic conditions of warfare and insecurity to life, property, and investments. Moneylending and loan repayment were affected in many ways. Initially, moneylenders abhorred wars, especially if their communities or those of their clients were under attack. As warfare became endemic, however, some avenues were open for bold entrepreneurs to invest in the production and/or distribution of arms and ammunitions. The experiences of moneylenders differed according to the political situation and the role of the state or kingdom in the ongoing interethnic wars. Generally, there were four types of states in Yorubaland in the course of the century (see Table 1). Business and investment opportunities varied according to the level of participation of each state in the wars. For states in category B, for instance, all economic activities ceased when they were routed and utterly destroyed. States in category A1 were the most favored because the involvement of the elite in the war promoted business; and since they were also wise to ensure that their own state was never seriously under attack, there was every incentive for the immigration of enterprising young men and women. States in Category C were perhaps not well favored by those interested in taking a quick and short road to riches. Life in such states was dull simply because many of their young men had emigrated to active settlements like Ibadan and Modakeke, and business enterprise was limited to the provision of food and some basic necessities. As many investments were in the munitions industry, moneylenders probably did good business in such belligerent states as in Category A (1 and 2).

Men and women in the coastal cities were engaged in a variety of business in the period. Generally, many traders from the hinterland probably turned to moneylenders for investment funds, organized trading links with the coastal states for the supply of firearms, and sold them at

TABLE 1
Categories of States in Nineteenth-Century Yorubaland

Categories	Description	Examples
Type A: Belligerent States	Type A1 States constantly in the attack	Ibadan, Ilorin, Ijebu, Modakeke
	Type A2 States constantly attacked or in the defensive	Ekiti, Ijesa, Ife, Egba villages, Egbado, Igbomina
Type B	States, communities or cities utterly destroyed by war	Old Oyo, Ijaye, Owu, Ikoyi, Iresa, Egba villages, etc.
Type C	Partially Belligerent States	New Oyo, Iwo, Ondo
Type D	Coastal States	Lagos, Epe, Badagry, etc.

high prices that also left them a margin of handsome profit in the interior. As far as the business of moneylenders was concerned, therefore, the immediate impact of the general insecurity was that it made moneylending a more risky venture and raised the interest rate.

In addition, nineteenth-century political economy brought about greater ethnic admixture. As contacts between the various ethnic groups increased, and as the new settlements became more cosmopolitan (with the immigration of people from other Yoruba subethnic groups), variations in the credit systems became harmonized. Thus, the Ijesa *osomalo* system was spread to many parts of Oyo-speaking Yorubaland.

As the century progressed, and as western education continued to spread from the coast to the hinterland, moneylending was revolutionized by the art of writing. This was not a straightforward positive effect. The interest rate was not lowered, and the exploitation of the borrower by the lender did not abate.[26] However, writing reduced the area of dispute between the lender and the borrower. The anchor for this revolution was the public letter writer whose role in the judicial arena in southern Nigeria under colonial rule has been examined by O. Adewoye.[27] The letter writer drafted the loan contract, known simply as "Agreement," gave it some legal authority, gave both parties a copy and kept one for future reference, and acted as witness in some instances. The cost of this was borne by the borrower, thus increasing his burden. This paper (*iwe*) or "Agreement" was the legal document binding the borrower to the lender. The crucial clause was the fraudulent practice by which the borrower was coerced into admitting that he/she took an interest-free loan (or one with low interest). Of course, the 100 percent or more interest had been cleverly added on to the principal for which the borrower signed. The *iwe* was, therefore, one big fraud; and shows that one of the first activities of educated elites in the economy of southwestern Nigeria was to take the exploitation of the old *nouveaux riches* and the poor to new levels.

Increased monetization of the economy; the opening up of trade in legitimate commodities; the introduction of tree crops like cocoa, coffee, rubber, and kolanuts; and other changes in the political economy of southern Nigeria shortly before and during the era of colonial rule all gave an increased role for the moneylender in the economy. The introduction of taxation later in the twentieth century, and the social implication of tax evasion,[28] all promoted the business of moneylenders. It also added to the use to which loans were put: loans were sought for social engagements, to pay tax, children's school fees, and other levies of the colonial state in addition to business and economic uses.

Summary

A number of important conclusions emanate from this chapter. By the time of British conquest and colonial rule Yorubaland had developed a variety of credit institutions ranging from the interest-free funds from ROSCAs, to loan markets based on kinship, but which were also guided by the "capitalist" goals of profit making and accumulation.

Also, the institutional frameworks for moneylending (particularly the pledging of service by the borrower to the lender) promoted the development of clietelism in Yorubaland. Through this, the moneylender (who was often a rich but nontitled private man) was patron to his clients (the debtors). This patron-client relationship imposed duties on the clients that were at once beneficial to the moneylender and burdensome to the borrower. In its most exploitative form, the labor of the client-borrower (and the fruits of that labor in the form of crops pledged as interest) was made available to the patron-moneylender, but the latter sometimes paid dearly for the followership of his/her clients, particularly when he/she had to forfeit large sums of money as bad debts. To the nontitled rich man or woman moneylending offered one good opportunity to win clients and "followers," in addition to the ultimate economic goals and possibilities of making more money.

Finally, moneylending and loan repayment strategies were dynamic. By the end of the nineteenth century, the institutional frameworks for charging interest in cash had been established. Western banking institutions emerged that did business among the educated elite and foreign firms. Another important component was the attempt made under colonial rule to abolish the controversial *iwofa* system. Among the majority of the people, however, access to credit was still through the *s'ogund'ogoji*. The problems of this indigenous lending practice are examined in the next chapter.

Notes

1. Karla Hoff and Joseph E. Stiglitz, "Introduction: Imperfect Information and Rural Credit Markets—Puzzles and Policy Perspectives," *The World Bank Economic Review*, iv, 3, 1990, p. 235.
2. It should be pointed out here that moneylenders control a credit market that is different from the preserve of ROSCAs. Whereas ROSCAs served as banks in which members—except under certain circumstances—had to wait their turns, moneylenders provided credit of the emergency type. They could be approached at any time, at short notice, and for any size of loan.
3. A man was required to pay befitting last respects to his forebears. It was believed that failure to do so was to invite the wrath of the ancestors in the spirit world. Many people were believed to be haunted by the spirit of their ancestors whose funerary rites they had not yet performed. Such haunted people were of little economic use to themselves and society. Contemporary conditions in society, especially the cash crunch, do not support the performance of expensive burials. However, many are still caught up in the mire of traditional beliefs, and this would seem to account for the debt that many people incurred in the process of doing the rite right.
4. Some of the classical Yoruba sayings bear this out. An example is *"Bi ara ile eni ba n je kokoro buburu, o ye k'a tete so fun un; bi bee ko, here-huru-here re ko ni jeki a sun loru,"* meaning "If a member of one's family is eating a poisonous food, it is better to warn him/her; otherwise, the repercussion might be sleepless nights for everyone." See the section on "Enforcing Repayment" in this chapter for the actual "sleepless nights" for the household in case the borrower defaulted. For a short account of the importance attached to burial ceremonies among the Yoruba, see E. Dada Adelowo, "A Comparative Look at the Phenomena of Death (*Iku*), Burial and Funeral Rites (*Isinku*) in Yorubaland," *Odu: A Journal of West African Studies*, 33, 1988, pp. 163–88.
5. Ammar Siamwalla *et al.*, "The Thai Rural Credit System: Public Subsidies, Private Information and Segmented Markets," *The World Bank Economic Review*, iv, 3, 1990, pp. 271–96; R. O. Adegboye, "Procuring Loans by Pledging Cocoa Trees," in J. D. von Piscke *et al.*, eds. *Rural Financial Markets in Developing Countries* (Baltimore, MD: Johns Hopkins University Press, 1983).
6. Christopher Udry, "Credit Markets in Northern Nigeria: Credit as Insurance in a Rural Economy," *World Bank Economic Review*, iv, 3, 1990, p. 252.
7. A contemporary practice simply modified this system and adapted it for the modern economy. This refers to the activities of the licensed buying agents purchasing cocoa and other cash crops from farmers. They would "advance" cash crop farmers some credit, which ensures that the latter would sell their farm produce to the company or individual who extended the credit, no matter the better prices

available via the competitors. For the disadvantages of this system in relation to the maintenance of high quality in the hides and skins production and export, see A. G. Adebayo, "The Production and Export of Hides and Skins in Colonial Northern Nigeria, 1900–45," *Journal of African History*, 33, 1992, pp. 273–300.

8. E. A. Oroge, "*Iwofa*: An Historical Survey of the Yoruba Institution of Indenture," *African Economic History*, 14, 1985, pp. 75–106.
9. The Reverend Samuel Johnson, *The History of the Yorubas* (Lagos: C.M.S. Bookshops, 1921, reprinted 1976), pp. 126–30.
10. Toyin Falola, "Pawnship in Colonial Southwestern Nigeria," paper presented at the CAAS Meeting, York University, May 1991
11. Samuel Johnson, *The History*, pp. 126–27.
12. *Ibid*, p. 127.
13. *Ibid*. It is necessary to point out here that a typical Yoruba week is five days. Three weeks are equal to fifteen days.
14. E. Adeniyi Oroge, "Iwofa," pp. 79–83.
15. *Ibid*, p. 80.
16. Johnson, *The History*, pp. 443–44.
17. E. Adeniyi Oroge, "Iwofa," p. 80.
18. The interest rate could be as high as 300 percent. See the next chapter.
19. In any case, in the colonial era and beyond, many people took loans to pay tax and to settle children's school fees.
20. In Yoruba folk medical thought, the supernatural is believed to intervene in the thoughts and deeds of people. However, as the lender employed the method to promote his business, the borrower was also known to seek supernatural assistance to ensure that the lender forgets about the loan and concentrates on other debtors. In the people's belief, the stronger *juju* overcomes the weaker.
21. One of these is the statement that "*Bi o ba le tan, onigbese a so ara re di iyawo, a ni ki won wa gbe oun*," meaning "Pushed to the wall, the debtor turns himself to the bride, asking his creditors to arrest him." Note the use of "bride" (in place of "criminal") in a euphemistic manner for which the Yoruba are famous.
22. Samuel Johnson, *The History*, pp. 130–31.
23. *Ibid*, p. 131.
24. N. A. Fadipe, *The Sociology of the Yoruba*, pp. 164–65.
25. *Ibid*.
26. Where the lender was literate, it increased his opportunity to cheat the borrower, since he could originate a different agreement. Where both were illiterate, the public letter writer was approached, but the letter writer's fee was another burden borne by the borrower.
27. O. Adewoye, "The Legal Profession in Southern Nigeria, 1863–1943," Ph.D. dissertation, Columbia University, 1970.
28. A popular Yoruba saying is "*dandan ni owo ori*," meaning tax payment is compulsory.

8

The Agony of Credit: High Interest Loans

> I do not guarantee the house of my father as a security to the unlicensed moneylender. The house of my father is a family property.[1]
>
> The thief and the moneylender are kinsmen.[2]
>
> Mr. Okeowo my friend, is a Shylock: for a loan of £5 he wants to have everything that I have acquired in life.[3]

In the preceding chapter we examined the institutional frameworks for moneylending and loan repayment in the precolonial era. We also explained the transition to colonialism as well as the transformation that this promised in the Yoruba financial system. In particular, the opportunities and deprivations of the colonial era led to major changes in the organization of credit and loans. At least three processes were at work at the same time: the introduction of modern banking and insurance; the continuation of older indigenous institutions; and the synthesis of the indigenous and alien credit systems. At the end of the colonial period, the third process, that of a synthesis, had become the most dominant. Modern and alien institutions were forced to respond to many aspects of indigenous culture and values.[4] At the same time some indigenous institutions that survived did so because they were able to "modernize" themselves by borrowing from alien ideas and practices and by responding to the demands of a "new" colonial society.[5] This chapter concentrates on one such product of synthesis of old and new: moneylending.

Continuity and Transition

The demands of the family; the pressure to fulfill social obligations; and the desire to be successful, prominent, and healthy fuelled borrowing in precolonial and colonial Yorubaland. There were several types of credit institutions. For most of the precolonial period, *ajo* and *esusu* provided credit on generous terms to members of rotating savings and credit associations, so generous that neither collateral nor interest was required. A more costly arrangement, and usually the only alternative for raising large sums, was the *iwofa* system (pawnship), which demanded the use of labor for interest on loan until it was fully repaid.[6]

Esusu, *ajo,* and *iwofa* were carried to the colonial period. The *esusu* involved a number of people who agreed to save money for a limited time period. In some arrangements, one participant was a "banker" for the duration of savings. At the end of the period, the "banker" would return each participant's savings. In other arrangements, participants agreed to contribute the same amount of money at the end of a week or a month. The total sum collected was given to each person in rotation. There was neither interest nor deduction of fees in *esusu*. It was a moral obligation to complete the agreed upon contribution to the *esusu.* When a contributor died his/her savings were returned to a relation.

The *ajo* resembled the *esusu* in that contributors had to know one another well. The organization of *ajo* also varied. Sometimes contributors decided on the amount and the duration of savings to be collected by a chosen leader. At the end of the designated time each participant's contributions were returned. In other arrangements each member contributed what he or she could afford and could collect his/her savings at any time when money was needed. Members contributing to an *ajo* never receive interest for so doing.

It was difficult for the three forms to have survived the colonial period without transformation. In the case of *iwofa* we have explained its decline and demise. *Esusu* and *ajo* had to be substantially reformed to meet the demands of a new age. Both relied on a great deal of trust to function. To ensure that everybody paid and was repaid, participants in the *esusu* and *ajo* were limited to residents of the same area who were relations or friends. The immediate political authority served as mediator of disputes and the members swore on oath not to betray one another.

As new cities grew and older ones became more and more heterogeneous, it became difficult to organize *esusu* and *ajo* in the old ways. Religious sanctions were weakening, indigenous authorities were losing their grip, society was changing in a direction that many contemporaries would regard as degenerate. Assumptions of trust and cordiality, which were at the roots of the success of *esusu* and *ajo,* could no longer be taken for granted. Contributors defaulted and people ran away with collections. Both *ajo* and *esusu* were also best suited to those who had the time to save for a lump sum to spend on "worthwhile" project.[7] One could use the savings in *esusu* and *ajo* as collateral to raise loans or a member could privately negotiate to borrow from the savings of others. However, unlike *iwofa* neither *esusu* nor *ajo* was an efficient means of meeting emergency requirements or of raising large sums. Both were equally located in the context of *iranlowo* ("help"), which was for participants to club together to assist one another. Unlike the *iwofa*, both *esusu* and *ajo* were not designed for raising loans but were more for savings.

As in the case of *iwofa*, both *esusu* and *ajo* could survive the change of the colonial era only by undergoing reform. Both were modernized to involve many more people and to ensure collection and repayment. There emerged the new occupation of the *alajo*, money collector. The *alajo* operated as a mobile bank: he chose the most convenient time for his clients, usually after 5 P.M., to collect and return savings. Savings were usually collected daily and returned monthly. The customer would save a specific amount everyday and would collect the entire savings, minus a day's, the *alajo*'s commission. The major clients of the *alajo* were market women, petty traders, craftsmen, and others who realized small income on a daily basis. As in the past, the clients never received interest on their savings; their only reward was that they had a bulk sum to spend.

The reformed *ajo* and *esusu* were inadequate to cope with the demands for capital for big projects such as building and trade. They were too slow to cater to city dwellers who needed immediate cash to settle domestic problems or to invest in a quick, risky ventures. Their operations were limited in space: the *alajo* had to be well known to his clients while those who still organized *esusu* had to have preexisting ties.

More efficient new institutions were emerging: cooperative societies, modern banking, and hire purchase. Most of these alien practices were gradually introduced to different parts of the country. All eventually became successful, and acquired distinct characters of their own. Except for cooperative societies after the 1940s, the new institutions were not accessible to most members of the society. They were urban based, and were primarily established for a new elite who had the education to understand their operations, and with regular and secured jobs to benefit from them. Some of the new banks even engaged in discrimination against the lower ranks of the civil servants and indigenous small-scale entrepreneurs.[8]

To those who lacked the credentials to benefit from the modern institutions or those who suffered discrimination, they had to seek alternative ways to raise money. The elite and wage earners among them could not fall back on the ancient *esusu* and *ajo*. The indigenous system was adapted to meet new demands. Three major credit arrangements developed, combining both indigenous and modern practices. The first was the reform of *ajo* and *esusu* via the operation of the *alajo* mentioned above. The second was the emergence of a class of traders known as the *osomalo,* who sold on credit.[9] The third was the *sogundogoji* ("convert twenty to forty"), a class of moneylenders who organized their lending businesses with a great deal of ruthlessness and callousness. Some of the *alajo* mentioned above belonged to the *sogundogoji*, although these occupations were different. The concern of this chapter is with the *sogundogoji*, one of the most creative indigenous responses to change.

Indigenous pawnship and lending provided the basis for the emergence of professional moneylenders during this century. In whatever form it took, moneylending was based on the charging of huge interest rates, either in cash or in labor. In the case of pawnship the interest in labor was often converted to cash by selling the products of labor. Although it was not a good option, many people borrowed at high interest rate when there was no other alternative. In general, it was those in great difficulties who turned to moneylenders. As noted in chapter 7, strangers in cities who could not be plugged to established credit institutions also relied on lending to solve their problems. The borrower would not use any labor to pay for interest as in pawnship. Neither would he be forced to provide collateral, although he would be required to procure a surety. The burden was a very high interest, from a 100 percent to 300 percent, depending on the principal and the length of repayment. Both the interest and the principal had to be paid on the agreed date, although some lenders could collect the interest either before or after the payment of the principal.

High interest rates and forcible collection of debts were the notorious features of moneylending throughout the colonial period. In spite of the fact that everybody knew that it was unwise to do business with the moneylender, the decline of indigenous alternative methods, notably pawnship, and the inaccessibility of new alien institutions encouraged moneylending to flourish. Borrowing from the "callous" moneylenders became the alternative for people in the cities who could not go to banks for lack of security and regular employment and who had no gold or items to sell to pawnbrokers.[10]

Moneylenders borrowed ideas from modern banking. Transactions involving large sums had to be documented. Public Letter Writers prepared the lease to be signed by the borrower and his surety, lease which was accepted in court as evidence. Secured loans attracted lower interest than the unsecured. A borrower must have a surety who would be forced to pay the debt in case of default. Unlike in pawnship, moneylenders were not interested in using labor as interest but in cash. They encouraged borrowers to use as security their property such as land, houses, and crops, which were then confiscated if there was a default. Collection of debt was prompt and brutal. When the borrower defaulted, the moneylender could take the matter to court or resort to the indigenous methods. Evidence from the second decade of this century shows that a number of people still believed in *dogo* (use of a distrainer), as a witness tried to assert before the West African Lands Committee.[11] The witness told the Committee that the moneylender could use force to collect his money, by sending an elderly person to live in the borrower's house and have the borrower assumed responsibility for feeding and funeral expenses should the person die.

Whereas there were sympathetic considerations in the case of *iwofa*, as when a pawn died for instance, and in the case of *ajo* and *esusu* if a member found it hard to contribute, there was no such consideration in *sogundogoji*. A borrower must not fall sick or die when repayment was due, as none would constitute a reason why the lender should wait. The lender would pounce on the borrower or the surety.

Tension and Conflicts

Moneylending was a frustrating business. No borrower was ever happy. First, it was usually a desperate option. Those who were forced to the *sogundogoji* did so because they had nowhere to turn. If the credit was used for consumption (e.g., festivals, funerals, and marriages), the end of the ceremony was the beginning of sorrow, as the borrower was left alone to face the agony of loan repayment.

Second, the moneylender might cheat in a variety of ways. Apart from the high interest rate—which we will discuss in a moment—a moneylender could force the borrower to indicate in the lease that he had taken more money as principal. The addition was a bonus, to thank the lender for the assistance. If the moneylender insisted on a surety, as they often did when they suggested the use of wage earners, the borrower was also forced to give the surety some money, again in appreciation for the assistance.

A third problem was the high interest rate. A common practice was to collect a minimum of 100 percent. The rate on mortgages was 6d.

per pound per month. Big lenders could reduce the mortgage rate to 3d on good titles located in cities. Farmlands, undeveloped land in the city, and mud houses were not considered good enough security to reduce the interest rate. The following two cases illustrate the gargantuan problem of the borrower:

> .A borrowed £5 but he signed a lease for £7 because the moneylender insisted. Of the £5 he collected, he gave the surety on the spot a gift of £1, leaving with £4. His interest at the end of a year was £7, forcing him to look for £14 within twelve months all because of £4... B approached a moneylender the second day that he lost his father and he had to bury him immediately and entertain his guest. Mr.— who introduced him to the moneylender collected £1 for his services. Mr.— who agreed to serve as surety collected £3 and the moneylender gave him £15 with the understanding that he would collect £35 after ten months.[12]

A lot of investigations by the senior staff of the government and the European firms and banks revealed staggering interest rates. In a 1936 investigation conducted in Lagos by a British staff of the John Holt, he encountered "five amazing cases":

> (a) For a loan of £10 used only for 3 months a repayment of £15 is claimed
> (b) In one case £2 was borrowed in 1932 and despite various payments the business has been managed in such a manner that the debtor still owes £2 to-day
> (c) For a loan of £20 for 12 months a Promissory Note for £32 has to be given
> (d) Interest at the rate of 1/6d. per £1 per month is common whilst interest at the rate of 1s. per £1 per month is general
> (e) there are "receipt" irregularities due to fear on the part of the borrower to Court proceedings.[13]

This agent concluded that "the borrower once involved is unable to free himself. The usurous demands of the one money lender forces the borrower on to another to meet the claims of the first one."[14]

A.C. Smith, a Police Magistrate, also recorded his experience:

> Loans secured by first mortgages on real estate bear interest at rates of 15 percent to 50 percent, the usual rate charged for unsecured loans is 60 percent and sometimes it is as high as 200 percent. These high rates are doubtless attributable partly to the all too prevalent combination of cupidity of lenders and the stupidity and thriftiness of borrowers, and partly to general economic and social conditions, which it would doubtless be inadvisable to attempt to influence too rapidly by legislation.[15]

For the moneylenders to maximize profit, they needed not only high interest but as many borrowers as possible. Indiscriminate lending became common.[16] Moneylenders advertised their trade, approached wage earners in government offices and firms, left leaflets in key places, and used so many informal means to woo borrowers. The chase for borrowers is not an indication of liberal credit conditions or of competition among the lenders. Irrespective of how the borrower and the lender discovered one another, the latter was still a sucker.

Why did moneylenders collect huge interest? The first answer was the profit motive. The second and most important, as far as the lenders were concerned, is that their business was a very risky one.[17] A borrower could run away, leaving the lender to do battle with the surety. Many did not have collateral. They did not trust most of the items used as security and they spent a lot of time and efforts collecting the loan: "titles are insecure, the type of buildings are poor and subject to heavy depreciation, proper maintenance of buildings amongst Africans is almost unknown. In addition, the whole tradition of the country is to avoid payment of sums due until the last possible moment, so that heavy expense is always incurred in the collection of interest."[18] To those who secured loans with farmlands, houses, and clothes, selling these items was never easy. The borrower would fight to prevent the sales of his property. In cases of land and houses, the borrower's escape was to ask other members of the family to lay claim to them. Rather than part with valuable property, the borrower often preferred a court settlement that would mandate that the debt be paid in installments. A third reason was that the cost of debt collection, in time and money, was high. The lender had to chase the borrower and the surety, an endless chase if the borrower was hard up.

A fourth reason for high interest was poor and fraudulent documentation. Some moneylenders and their clients could not read or write. They either relied on memory or on a promissory note prepared by Public Letter Writers. Either to pay less (borrower) or to take more (lender) there were conflicts over the original principal and the interest. In the case of literate moneylenders, there was always a possibility of tricking illiterate borrowers into paying more principal and interest.

Finally, the surety—the intermediary between the lender and the debtor—was another source of trouble. A moneylender had to be satisfied with the choice of a surety. People with responsibility and who had some connections with the borrower were ideal. Compound heads, relations who worked for the government, school teachers, religious leaders, and traders were preferred. The surety had to make a commitment to the lender to liquidate the debt should the borrower not pay for whatever reason. As long as the borrower was alive and met the repayment conditions (even with occasional delays), the surety had no problem.

Problems arose if the borrower had no means to pay, fell sick, died, or ran off. Then the surety and the borrower had to sit down to discuss recovery. The surety, always eager to avoid any such payment, would fight with the moneylender, and suggest that the matter be referred to the court. If the moneylender was afraid of the court, he might resort to force by seeking the means to force the relations of the debtor to pay. As in the case of the *Onigbowo* in pawnship, a number of sureties collected service charge from the borrower, partly as compensation for services but not certainly for taking risk.

The Intervention of the Colonial State

All the aforementioned problems generated many conflicts. Hundreds of cases were reported to administrators and the police, not a few of which involved street fights, illegal confiscation, assault, deliberate damage of properties, all in the attempt to recover debts. The courts became a final arbiter in many others. By the late 1920s, some Ijebu towns were fed up with the conflicts arising from moneylending.[19]

By the early 1930s, governments at all levels were becoming worried about the "evil" of the system. Complaints about moneylending were numerous and disturbing. In a number of instances, officials intervened to recover money. This was not easy as each case had to be investigated. As sympathy was always for the borrower (because of the high interest rate and the high handedness of the lender), the lender usually felt dissatisfied by the settlement terms.

Government establishments were mired in the conflicts and problems of moneylending because civil servants, especially the junior ones, were often involved in borrowing, lending, or serving as sureties. The government and the big foreign firms were worried about the involvement of their staff and its effects on job performance.

Wage earners were drawn to moneylending for a variety of reasons. Moneylenders preferred them both as surety and lender because they enjoyed regular salaries, had permanent jobs and addresses, could not risk public embarrassment, and they enjoyed the image of responsible people. Civil servants themselves, when in need of money, used their salaries as collateral. Those who needed money to engage in trade, speculate on business, build a house, or meet social expenses took loans from moneylenders. One loan could lead to another:

> It is a fact that domestic troubles compel an official to "raise the wind" but under present conditions that wind becomes a gale which engulfs an honest official until

> he is swamped.... It is an established fact the efficiency of many employees is impaired through privation and starvation because the major portion of their salary goes in meeting usurious claims.... An even worse feature is the threat of legal action held over a man knowing full well that such action would reveal the man's position to his employers. In order to evade this, the man borrows afresh at further usurious rates and the "snow-ball" rolls on.[20]

The average civil servant was in a weak position in rescheduling loan payment. The borrower facing court action and/or public disclosure was often coerced by the moneylender into taking a new loan that included previous arrears and interest. The threat to go to court or report the matter to the government would compel many debtors to find money to pay, usually by taking more loan. The aim was to have a receipt to show that previous debts had been paid, especially when evidence of this was required at the place of work; but in actual fact the debtor was in more trouble. When the debt of a staff member became known by his superiors, he would be warned to pay off the loan or face the consequences. His salary could be stopped (a further complication to a person in crisis), he could be suspended, or even dismissed from service.

A number of rare cases were reported of male civil servants being forced to liquidate loans acquired by their wives. For instance in Lagos in the 1920s, a District Clerk was forced to pay the debt of his wife. When the man was slow in paying, the wife was bold enough to petition the Administrator of the Colony:

> [O]wing to financial stringency caused by lack of support from my husband I was compelled to borrow money from Moneylenders in Lagos of an account of £10 nett (sic) to liquidate my petty debts and asked the Resident kindly to assist me in getting my husband to pay this amount with whatever interest shall accrue thereon. The Resident...was then kind enough to forward my complaint...for investigation which resulted in a promise from Mr. Hamilton that he will pay. This promise I regret to observe has not been wholeley (sic) fulfilled as only £4 was paid with further promise to pay the balance at the end of that month which up to date he has not done. As interest is still accruing on the principal and repeated letter from me to him have vought (sic) no reply, I should be greatly obliged if you would be good enough to assist me further in this matter which is causing great unrest in my mind.[21]

Hamilton was forced to pay the money.

Repeated warnings were made to civil servants, especially junior ones, to avoid moneylending. In the 1930s, teachers were threatened with punishment should they become victims of or serve as moneylenders.[22] In the 1938 Ordinance on moneylending, any person in government employ who acted as a moneylender or an agent to one was subject to instant dismissal.

In a 1938 report in the influential *West Africa*, an observer commented on the "evil" of moneylending as it affected the staff of government:

> Pressure, it is added, is continually brought to bear upon subordinate officials to stand surety for relatives, which pressure, owing to the strength of family ties, is difficult to resist. As a result, arrests of junior public officers for debt are so frequent as seriously to impair the efficiency of the Public Service...the amount of indebtedness among African Government officials, especially junior men, is "appalling,"...and imprisonment for debt being commonplace incidents.[23]

In Lagos and Ibadan "discoveries" were made in the 1920s and 1930s that a high number of government staff were engaged part time as moneylenders, operating during office hours in the premises of their departments. In July 1935 in Lagos, 106 clerks and an equal number of employees of European firms appeared in court for unpaid loans to moneylenders. Many of these debtors were described as "hopelessly insolvent."[24] A senior police officer dismissed the 1935 figure as a gross understatement:

> Only a modicum of officials who became entangled in the web of the money lender appear in Court; and of these less number are eventually reported to their respective heads of Department, as many cases are withdrawn on the defendant making desperate last minute settlements to avoid subsequent departmental action.[25]

Suggestions were made by high-ranking officials to protect the junior staff. Some thought that the debts they owed should not be recovered and that they should be prevented from serving as surety. Officials of firms also joined in urging the government to check moneylending to make it less attractive and lucrative. The John Holt complained in March 1936:

> Without official supervision of their transactions, without legislation legalizing a rate of interest and without the business being controlled as Money Lending and Pawn Broking is done at home constitutes a menace and tends to incite the continuance of a practice which must eventually corrupt all official services.[26]

By the mid-1930s all the people in the colonial administration had reached the conclusion that moneylending was a "stinking fish," and that in order to help the poor and protect civil servants, moneylending had to be reformed. When discussions on reforms were initiated in the late 1930s, it was realised that the Moneylenders Ordinance of 1917 was ineffective.[27] This first ordinance was designed to provide a minimum control on moneylenders and had limited application in the country. It was generally not popularized or enforced with any seriousness, while there were little or no provision on interest rate and book keeping.

In May 1937 the office of the Chief Secretary to the Government in Lagos set up a committee on moneylending, comprising indigenes like lawyer A. Latunde Johnson, Jibowu of the Police Magistrate Court, K. M. Kinnison, the Manager of Barclays Bank (D.C. & O.) who represented the Chamber of Commerce, and C. W. W. Greenidge, the Acting Attorney General of the country. The Committee held its first meeting on 28 June 1937. The terms of reference provided by the Governor were:

> To inquire into, and report on moneylending in Nigeria and to recommend any legislative measures considered necessary to:
>
> limit the rate of interest charged in the case of
>
> (a) mortgages;
>
> (b) loans secured by sureties or otherwise; and
>
> (c) unsecured loans
>
> and to protect borrowers from harsh terms attached to loans;
>
> and to protect lenders as far as possible from the dishonesty of borrowers.

At its meeting the Committee was guided by the Moneylender's Ordinance of Trinidad,[28] which it read clause by clause for suggestions, modifications, and approval. The Committee made only five modifications and adopted the Trinidad Ordinance for Nigeria.[29] Before giving its final approval the government also borrowed ideas from the Trinidad and Tobago Ordinance of 1932 and the Straits Settlements Ordinance of 1935, both of which drew from the British Imperial Acts of 1900 and 1927.

The Moneylender's Ordinance of 1938 set out many conditions on moneylending with a view to tightening up the law, regulating and defining the role of lenders and borrowers in particular circumstances. Its provisions were "better calculated to protect unsophisticated persons from the evils of borrowing."[30] It defined a moneylender as someone who lent money at interest, either as a habit or an occupation (excluding Cooperative Societies, banking and insurance businesses):

> any person who lends money at interest or who lends a sum of money in consideration of a larger sum being repaid shall be presumed to be a moneylender until the contrary be proved.

Moneylenders were required to take a license, renewable every year, or pay a penalty of a £100 or/and imprisonment for three years. The license specified the name and address of the business and stated that the moneylender must not operate as a modern bank. A business could not be transferred to locations not specified in the license without the permission of a Magistrate and the police and moneylenders were prohibited from engaging in excessive advertisements, both additional ways of limiting their operations.

Application for a license had to be directed to the police and the Magistrate with the jurisdiction over the area where the lender would operate. The police and the judiciary were involved to ensure that lenders were people of integrity and good character.

Next the ordinance tried to abolish the role of middlemen. Any person who acted as an agent to a moneylender or who accepted a commission for introducing business was liable to a fine of £20. Moreover the contracts so procured would be null and void.

Much concern was given to both documentation and rates of interest. No debt to a moneylender was recoverable at law unless both parties had had a written contract that stated the date the money was lent, the principal and the rate of interest of the loan. The moneylender must issue receipts for payment and keep books of all his transactions. Failure to keep books and issue receipts would deny him the opportunity of recovering his debts. At the request of the borrower the moneylender was required to issue a statement of accounts detailing how much had been paid.

A battery of clauses dealt with the interest on loans, with stiff penalties if they were flouted. To solve the problems on what constituted interest, the ordinance defined it as including "all discounts, commissions, bonuses, fines, expenses, and any amount by whatsoever name called, in excess of the principal, paid or payable to the moneylender in consideration of or otherwise in respect of a loan."[31] The rates for secured and unsecured loan varied,[32] but none were allowed to exceed 30 percent per annum:

> (a) on loans secured by a charge on any freehold property or Government bonds or insurance policy or the debentures or shares of any company or by a bill of sale in respect of any goods or by the assignment of any personal rights legally enforceable, or by the indemnity or personal guarantee of a third party, simple interest at the rate of 12½ percent per centum per annum for the first £500 or part thereof and at the rate of 10 per centum per annum on any amount in excess of £500
>
> (b) on loans secured by a second charge on any of the real or personal property or rights refered to [above] simple interest at the rate of 15 per centum per annum for the first £500 or part thereof and at the rate of 12½ per centum per annum on any amount in excess of £500
>
> (c) on unsecured loans simple interest at the rate of 25 percent per centum per annum.

Compound interest was prohibited. Any contract providing for the payment of interest in advance by deduction of an amount from the sum lent was illegal. Neither was the lender authorized to collect compound interest or to increase the interest rate because the borrower defaulted in payment.[33]

The government expected debtors and members of the public to report moneylenders to the police or administrators:

> Any person, not the borrower in the transaction at issue, who informs the authorities of a contravention of this Ordinance which leads to a conviction, may be rewarded, at the discretion of the Court, an amount not exceeding half the fine.

Lenders were prohibited from inducing people to borrowing, falsely increasing the principal on the contract, and intimidating borrowers to pay their debts. The court had the last say on many issues in the ordinance: a judge could require all evidence of transactions and insist on the adoption of the ordinance, determine contract and force borrowers to pay, pronounce that interest rate was high, and reopen "harsh and unconscionable" transactions.

Public Reactions to the Ordinance

A number of officials, private individuals, and the association of moneylenders responded to the 1938 Ordinance. The views of borrowers are generally undocumented so that what we have are those of the elite. Perhaps the most profound response by an individual was that of R. M. Williams, a senior Nigerian staff of the United Africa Company Ltd. Williams agreed that moneylending was evil and the ordinance was necessary to protect "unsophisticated persons from the evils of borrowing." He thought that the stringent provisions of the ordinance were unlikely to correct the ills because

> moneylending is so wide-spread in Nigeria that it is probably impossible to prescribe any measure which compels even a small fraction of the money lenders to become registered or to comply with the provisions of the bill if they were. Most of them are quite illiterate and could not be expected to understand the provisions of the bill. A very large amount of the petty trade of the country is financed by loans from such money lenders. To attempt to stop this type of lending would, if it could be done, materially injure the petty trader.[34]

Williams suggested alternatives to moneylending: the education of Africans; the establishment of many cooperative thrift societies; and the introduction of private European capital to take up mortgages at reasonable rates on security.

Several officials found faults with the ordinance, especially the high interest rate. According to a staff member in the office of the Governor:

> I consider the rates of interest on both secured and unsecured loans too high. I repeat my statement that no loan at a rate of interest such as 45 percent can lead to anything but the further impoverishment and degradation of the borrower. No one should lend to a man whose creditworthiness is so low that 45 percent is a logical rate of interest except for a charitable gift from a friend disguised as a loan. I particularly object to the proposal that interest on a judgement should be at the same rate as the original loan. I recommend the following rates: properly secured loans…12½ percent if the loan is not more than £1000-10 percent or larger loans. Unsecured loans 25 percent on loans not exceeding £50, 20 percent on loans of over £50.[35]

Another officer suggested 12½ percent on secured loans up to £500, 10 percent on secured loans above £500, 15 percent on secured second charges loans of sums over £500, 25 percent on all unsecured loans, and the maximum rates of interest chargeable on occasional loans by persons other than moneylenders should be limited by law to 2½ percent more than may be charged by registered lenders in the case of secured loans and 5 percent more in the case of unsecured loans.

The Secretary to the Government, too, agreed that high interest rates would injure borrowers:

> The plain fact is that there is no legitimate object for which money can be used which can yield a rate of interest of anything like 48 percent, and anyone who borrows at such a rate inevitably loses and goes steadily deeper and deeper into debt. Especially in backward countries where money is borrowed without any thought of the difficulty of repayment usurious moneylending should be in every way discouraged.[36]

Other senior officials commented that the government should supervise the signing of contracts to protect illiterates, fictitious promissory notes should not be enforced,[37] and the license fee of moneylenders should be raised to limit their numbers.[38]

The Nigerian Moneylenders Association submitted a petition, after reading the ordinance with "consternation and uneasiness." In the Association's view, several sections of the ordinance characterized the moneylender "as a felon, a heartless fraud or a Shylock and not as an ordinary respectable member of society carrying on a legitimate business, a business of finance on which the foundation of all national wealth and welfare are built."[39] The Association thought that the government should make it easier to obtain a license, allow a lender to function in many branches in a town, extend the life of a license to three years, reduce the fines for violating the provisions of the ordinance, and increase the interest rates because

> of the peculiar circumstances surrounding the lending of money in this country, the present general state of civilization, the need for finance in a country just in a state of early development, the finances necessary for commercial development, the insecurity of titles to lands and properties; the lack of organizations with mobilized capital, all these go towards proving the need for a higher rate of remuneration for the lenders...most borrowers had no "sense of responsibility," no secure employment, fixed home, no insurance.[40]

The Association demanded 6d. per pound for mortgages, and 60 percent per annum or 1s. on a pound per month simple interest on unsecured loans. The high rates were justified on the basis of the risk involved in lending, and the expenses of collecting debts, "which invariably end in a Court Order for payment extending over a period of 2 to 4 years at the same time no more interest being chargeable after judgment."[41]

The Ordinance in Practice

After 1 January 1939, a moneylender was required to carry license. Applicants who fulfilled the conditions in the ordinance were licensed. In the 1940s and 1950s when the number of licensed lenders was high the government rejected many applications just to keep the number down.[42] An annual list of registered lenders was prepared, and every approved license was published in the gazette. Most of the lenders were Ijebu, Ijesa, and Lebanese. The majority were located in the cities, although this did not prevent them from servicing the surrounding villages. Because of the rules on record keeping, a licensed money lender was expected to be literate. The majority of the illiterates who applied were rejected. However, many illiterates continued to operate illegally with absolute disregard for the ordinance. Applicants who were thought to be employees of the government were also denied.[43]

Many moneylenders subverted the requirement that they operate as a business concern by inventing hundreds of business names (e.g., Orukope Money Lending Association, Stephen George Loan Bureau, Public Service Bureau, Moderate Loan Syndicate).[44] Most moneylenders, however, continued to operate as a one-man businesses. Even in cases where they supplied names and addresses of partners, it turned out that such partners were their relations and dependants who had no role whatsoever to play in the business. A few societies and guilds registered as moneylenders in order to assist their members and give loans at lower interest than the individual lender.[45]

Whether a person applied as a company or in his name, the police or an administrator would investigate the character of the moneylender. Cited below is one such report on Yusufu Apewaje:

> I was detailed to investigate on one Yusufu Apewaje (m) of Yoruba who applied for a money lender's license in Agbor. Enquiries made from various persons in the town as regard to his character and his financial ability enquiry revealed that he had been here since 1914, he is a trader and lorry owner he had about three lorries and a car, he is honest, and a well to do gentleman, though an illiterate person. He had never been to prison before, he is a man of good conduct. Steady in business of his, his financial standing is about £1000 and he never use to make noise by giving troubles in the town. I therefore recommend his application for the licence.[46]

Most moneylenders had cash (roughly estimated at between £20 and £150), and other investments. In general, moneylending was combined with other activities like trading. Many already had lorries and houses, big cocoa and kolanut farms, and had acquired some fame in the town as investors or *alajo*. The women among them were traders or wives to husbands with money and connections.

It was important to start the business with a lot of cash to lend. A Police report on an applicant made this clear:

> There is nothing known against this applicant from a Police point of view, and his general character can be assessed as good. His financial resources, however appear to be lean. He keeps a small banking account at the Post Office (balance less than £10, date) but states that he has merchandise warth (sic) £200 in the hands of his petty traders which he proposes to sell off in order to acquire the necessary cash to start the money-lending business.[47]

Yet another report:

> The applicant is a wealthy farmer with a sum of over £1000 cash on hand. He has cocoa, kolanut and palm plantations which yield annual income of about £600. Nothing is known against him from Police point of view.[48]

The Ordinance introduced many reforms. One major change concerned documentation. Moneylenders carried receipts, record books, and loan forms. The loan form was the most complicated of all. It detailed the names of a borrower, the loan, the monthly interest, the date of final payment, and an oath that the document was translated and explained in the "simplest Yoruba Language" to the borrower. Moneylenders insisted on security (land, crops, house, car, and the like) on the understanding that in case of failure to refund same at the expiration of the above specified time, the said firm should take action against me/us in any appropriate Court for whatever is due to them and failing to satisfy any judgement debt and costs that may be reasonably given against me/us immediately, the said Firm should legally proceed against thc said properties and take proceeds of same to liquidate any judgement debt and costs arising from this Memorial.

The samc form contained the signature of a surety and a commitment

> if the said Borrower/Borrowers fails/fail to refund the said and every part thereof at the expiration of the time specified, the said Firm should proceed legally against me/us jointly and severally with the said Borrower/Borrowers in any appropriate Court and in case the legal proceeds of the Borrower's/Borrowers' Security is insufficient to liquidate the judgement debt and costs finally, the said firm should proceed further jointly and severally against me/us with the said Borrower/Borrowers for receiver of whatever is due.[49]

The majority of the licensed moneylenders kept records of their transactions. Some of the books were printed as Register of Moneylender's Transaction,[50] Register of Moneylender,[51] and so on.

There were numerous disputes on the value of properties used as security for a loan. Borrowers always thought that the value of security was much higher than the loan, and that the moneylenders had no right to confiscate these even when the entire loan had not been paid. In one celebrated dispute, a woman reported an Ijebu-Ode lender, described as unlicensed, to the District Officer, in June 1941:

> That Mdm. Jane Efutage of Okojagun-Isonyin jurisdiction Ijebu-Ode, an unlicensed moneylender loan me a sum of (30s.) thirty shillings sterling @ 1/6d. interest monthly. The attach (sic) agreement dated 4th November 1936 prepared by the then letter-writer Mr J.B. Okubote of Odolowun-Isonyin district Ijebu Ode approved: that I have paid interests amounted to £4.18s. to Mdm Jane Efutege-Okejagun since I loan the 30s. @ 1/6d. int.monthly.(sic) That the unlicensed moneylender Jane Efutege-Okojagun-Isonyin obtained 2 securities of one Irobirin velvet and one Jojo Agba which cost me £2.10s. to purchase. That the 2 securities are in possession of the unlicenced moneylender Jane Efutege-Okejagun who proceeded and attached my father's house at Idona-Imusin yesterday vide action taken by the Debts Collector Mr Godwin Orebanjo-Okejaun-Isoyin now at Epe N.O. Suit 33/41. That both of us are residentials in the Ijebu Ode area in the land of Awujale. I pray for necessary action viz: to ask her license for money lending upon interest ii to release my father's house attached because she obtained 2 securities cost me £2.10s. to purchase. I do not guarantee the house of my father as a security to the unlicensed moneylender. The house of my father is a family property.[52]

The D.O. was sympathetic to the debtor, in spite of the fact that the Native Court had allowed the moneylender to take the house. To the D.O., "the rate of interest is excessive and illegal." The D.O. gave a fresh judgment that gave £1/10 to the moneylender.

The confiscation of property by the moneylender was always a source of trouble. As the collateral was usually the most valued item of the borrower (a house, land) or a necessity for work (tools, farmland), any move by the moneylender to seize it was always resisted. In initial contracts moneylenders simplified the procedure to adopt to confiscate property. When seizure became necessary borrowers sought the means to prevent this by appealing to administrators, a step which irritated moneylenders. One lender, was so annoyed by his inability to move quickly against a defaulting borrower that he wrote to the Ijebu-Ode Magistrate in July 1942 to seek clarification:

> I have the honour to inform Your Worship that there are some Borrowers who secured themselves with certain properties, moveable and immovable, on the stipulations in the documents respectively concerned that if they fail to refund the amount borrowed, without taking legal process against them in any Court, such pledged property/properties should be disposed of through a recognized Public Auction Mart after an interval of grace of certain time and to be followed by a previous Public Auction Notice being placarded. I beg to request Your Worship kindly to advise me as to what should be done, although provision has been widely made to sell the property/properties without going to Court in the documents.[53]

Moneylenders who fell foul of the ordinance had their license withdrawn and several were convicted.

Problems of Intervention

The major problem was the widespread disregard of the Ordinance. Not all moneylenders obtained a license. There were cases when administrators reported an absence of moneylenders in their areas (because none applied for license) later to realize that there had been a lot of loan transactions and conflicts arising from them. Many moneylenders did not register to avoid payment of income tax.[54] A number of part-time lenders, too, did not care to register.

As long as there was no conflict referred to courts or the administrators, an unlicensed moneylender could get away with many illegalities. In some cases unlicensed lenders even took their debtors to the native courts to recover their money. In the Ijebu Remo division during the 1930s cases of unlicensed moneylenders were many, and the district administration and the native courts assisted these lenders in debt recovery. In 1943 a son of a moneylender inquired of the Resident whether he could collect the money lent by his unlicensed parents in the 1930s. According to him, his parents and hundreds of others were not aware of rules that insisted on registration. The Assistant District Officer's handwritten minutes on this letter provides useful information:

> The position is governed by Ordinance No 45 of 1938, but of course hundreds of people continue to lend money at interest and to reclaim it in the Native Courts though they are not licensed money-lenders. I have no sympathy with unlicensed money lenders, but to refuse suddenly to recognize their claims would probably ruin the trade of the country! In a recent case I reviewed in Ijebu Igbo a debtor pleaded that his creditor was not a licensed money lender...I agreed that he could only be ordered to refund the principal debt, but said that should be enforced at once, and that the public should see that no one lent him money again!

The Resident made a final decision on this matter:

> [T]he legal position is that only a licensed money-lender can charge interest and that only the principal loan can be recovered in court by anyone. I am not in favour of issuing any such instruction to Native Courts, however.[55]

The reply to the query was negative: his parents had acted illegally and he should not do anything to recover the debt.

Unlicensed moneylenders tried to avoid the law by lending as if they were private individuals. Whether the transaction was documented or not, it carried with it a number of lies on the amount of principal and the interest rate. To minimize risk, unlicensed lenders gave small loans and mainly to those that they knew well. Recovery could be difficult: an intransigent borrower would attempt to hide behind the courts and the administrators.[56] A ruthless moneylender, too, would ignore the "modern steps" and resorted to *dogo*.

Unlike the precolonial period, family members were becoming less involved in the loan settlements. Relations of a debtor would contest a loan contract if it was realized that family collective property had been used as security and could be confiscated. A lot of tension was generated by those who used land and houses as security, having succeeded in deceiving lenders that the property was theirs. There were instances when borrowers themselves admitted to having made an error in using family rather than individual properties as collateral. In Ijebu Ode in the 1940s, many of the attempts by moneylenders to confiscate the houses of loan defaulters ran into trouble.[57] The courts and the government were sensitive to the issue, and took a common stand that a family should not forfeit its assets because of the loan of a member.

Debtors often escaped payment by relocating elsewhere. When they pledged immovable properties, it was not easy for the moneylender to recover those without authorization from the court. A number of moneylenders sought the assistance of Debt Collectors to hunt defaulters. Debt Collectors doubled as Public Letter Writers: they were, in general, semieducated but with a great understanding of laws and legal technicalities. The D.O. often received letters from Debt Collectors who sought assistance to locate debtors. Should the debtor be discovered and sufficiently harassed, he would pay in addition for the services of the Debt Collector.

The reforms did not suppress the role of indigenous culture in this institution. The lender was still superior to the borrower. To the unlicensed lenders, the ordinance was not a regulator of behavior. To the licensed, the document was a mere guide not to conduct business or respect debtors but to anticipate the actions of government and the court. The philosophy that guided the action of lenders was underlined by the most common preliminary remark to lenders: "if you want money on government rate go to the bank or the D.O."

To the lender, a borrower was looked upon with derision as *onigbese* who was at the mercy of a careful, concerned and industrious person. In arrogant tone and manner, the lenders believed that they were performing an essential service by giving favor and gratification to those in trouble. That a debt must be repaid was not negotiable.

To the debtor, the lender was a ruthless and callous operator. It was a career for the wicked. Should the lender be at the same time politically powerful or wealthy, the dread of him increased. The lender could reach the police before the debtor and bribe indigenous authorities. The lender could also hire the services of *agbowopa* (people who could use force) to collect money. Above all, many people believed that lenders could kill to recover their money.

In debt recovery, most lenders disregarded the provisions of the Ordinance which were too slow for them. Instead they employed crude means.[58] When payment was due, the lender would issue the final reminder. If the money was not paid, the lender made a public exposure of the debtor, through a careful broadcasting of the terms and failure to pay to important relations and contacts. The intention of the moneylender was to ostracize the debtor by characterizing him as unreliable and useless. Those with regular employment would panic at this stage, not wanting their employers to know. Finally, physical means could be used to collect money.

The interest rates in the ordinance were ignored with impunity. A perceptive observer commented that there appears to be too many loopholes for evading them. It is true that certain practices are prohibited in the bill, under penalty, but can proof be obtained when these prohibitions are contravened? Clause 16 of the bill , for instance, prohibits the payment of interest in advance. Clause 27 makes it an offence to take security for a loan on a promissory note in which the principal is not truly stated. Money lenders may insert higher sums in mortgage deeds than are actually lent. In all these cases there is nothing to prove an offence but a bare denial on the part of the borrower who has affixed his signature to an original document.[59]

Moneylenders forced borrowers to conspire with them to falsify records in a way favorable to them:

> [P]romissory notes falling due at regular intervals of time in repayment of principal and interest completely disguise the actual rate of interest which is being paid...it is already quite a common form of security to make the borrower sign two sets of promissory notes, one representing the actual amounts due, and the other double these amounts, which are held to be used should the borrower default on the payment of the first series. There is, legally, apparently, no protection for the borrower if the money lender presents both, but I am told in practice this is not done, and they are used as security only..A further way in which the provisions of the bill can be evaded would seem to be by the execution of mortgages as security for an existing debt. Once the amount of the debt was inserted in the mortgage it would be very difficult for the debtor to claim that the amount is not truly stated and it would also seem that such a debt can provide for the repayment of the debt and interest by instalments which would in fact be the repayment of the smaller debt plus a usurious rate of interest. For instance, a man who borrowed £100 might execute a mortgage to cover the repayment of the debt £200 repayable at equal intervals over the period of a year, plus a small interest in the deed to comply with the terms of the ordinance.[60]

Summary

Moneylenders provided an efficient and ruthless alternative to modern banking. With or without security anyone in search of money, especially in the cities, had a place to turn. It was, however, a very risky, costly, and frustrating path to take. Debtors must pay in a hard and expensive way. The frustration that the practice brought to borrowers, the ruthlessness of moneylenders, and the involvement of government officials as lenders and borrowers all forced the state to intervene. The intervention of the state was corrective, by passing an ordinance to protect borrowers. The effectiveness of the ordinance depended on the extent to which both the lenders and the borrowers respected the laws. But lenders subverted the law and desperate borrowers accepted whatever terms were laid down by lenders. Although many cases went to court, the role of culture and ancient practices tended to slow down the modernization process. As in the precolonial times, the lender was superior to the borrower, and could use force to recover loans in total disregard of the ordinance.

Older values and ideals examined in chapter three were at the same time breaking down. Whereas in the precolonial times relations would rally round to help the borrowers this was not always the case during the colonial period. Values of affection were being replaced with values of capitalism, a development underscored by the popular saying:

> Odaju lo bi owo, itiju lo bi gbese ("shrewdness is the mother of riches shame is the mother of indebtedness").

Both the lender and the borrower were taking risks and each was concerned with the benefits that money could confer. An appeal to blood or extended relationship, kinship, and *ajogbe* (residency in the same community) diminished in importance. Consequently, moneylenders ensured that there were sureties who could be called upon to pay. In view of the lender, sureties provided more security than relations of the borrower, as the relations were not obliged to assist. In the thinking of moneylenders, anything that could yield profit, minimize losses and ensure payment was the ideal measures to pursue.

Violence, both in the use of language and physical force, became more widespread as a means of recovery. A debtor reported that his first son was seized by a moneylender because he failed to meet his commitments. Another had his farm confiscated. Houses were auctioned. Debtors became objects of public ridicule.

Finally, the reasons for acquiring debts in spite of the great troubles that it brought explain both continuity and change in social payments and values. As in the precolonial times funeral, marriage, and naming ceremonies continued to demand high expenses. Meeting social expectations imposed a lot of pressure on individuals. On the other hand new demand for loans arose among many salary earners who desired credit to invest, acquire foreign products like radios, clothes, jewellery, and spend on entertainment, were major reasons. On the whole most people borrowed money for purposes of consumption.

Moneylenders' businesses encouraged accumulation and investment, however, for moneylenders had to save in order to have enough money to lend. A good number of them were engaged in other occupations in order to generate more capital.[61] The gains from lending were invested, a wise strategy of building fortunes out of the misfortunes of others.

Notes

1. National Archives, Ibadan [hereafter N.A.I]., Ije Prof 4/956 Vol. I, Money Lenders' Ordinance Cap 147 Corresp. in re 1929/44. [Petition of Mrs Gbolade Dele to the District Officer, June 29, 1941].
2. *Ibid.*
3. N.A.I. Oyo Prof 1/1477 Vol. II, Money Lenders Amendment Ordinance 1935 [Petition by A Sanni].
4. The impact of African culture on alien institutions like banking and insurance is yet to be fully investigated. These new institutions were forced to adapt to the local milieu and to take into consideration values on death, debts, and the role of the extended family.
5. This process of adaptation is one of the issues pursued in this paper, although the space does not permit its full elaboration.
6. The *iwofa* system has been discussed in chapter 7. Also, see Toyin Falola, "Pawnship in colonial southwestern Nigeria," in Toyin Falola and Paul Lovejoy, eds., *Pawnship in Africa* (Boulder, CO: Westview, 1994).
7. The Reverend Samuel Johnson, *The History of the Yorubas* (Lagos: C.M.S. Bookshops, 1921, reprinted 1976), p. 119.
8. A. Ale, *The Underdevelopment of Indigenous Entrepreneurship in Nigeria* (Ibadan: Ibadan University Press, 1984).
9. For more information on the *osomalo*, see chapter 7 in this book.
10. Pawnbroking (different from pawnship) was yet another trade that developed during the colonial period. This trade is yet to be investigated.
11. N.A.I., West African Lands Committee, *Papers and Correspondence* (London, Colonial Office, 1916), Questions 7, 538–63.
12. N.A.I., C.S.O. 30315 Vol. II.
13. N.A.I. C.S.O. 30315 Vol. I, Money Lenders Amendment Ordinance 1935 [District Agent of John Holt to the Chief Secretary to the Government, 4 March 1936].
14. N. A.I. C.S.O. 30315 Vol. I; District Agent of John Holt to the Chief Secretary to the Government, 4 March 1936.
15. C.S.O. 26/30315 Vol. I.
16. N.A.I. Okiti Div 1/1/O.K. 1238, Money Lenders' Ordinance Cap 136 [Application letter of M. Emmanuel to the District Officer, 28 August 1953].
17. N.A.I., C.S.O. 26/30315 Vol. II; Oral Interviews: M. Ajitoni, (Age, 70+) Moneylender at Ibadan in the 1950s; A. Adeoti (80+) Moneylender in Lagos in the 1940s.
18. N.A.I., C.S.O. 26/ 30315 Vol. III.
19. N.A.I. Ije Prof 4/7.679 Money Lenders Ordinance CAP. 147 Corresp. Re.
20. *Ibid.*, John Holt to the Lagos Town Council 4 March 1936.
21. N.A.I., Com Col 1/553, Indebtedness of Mrs. Hilda Hamilton to Lagos Money Lender.
22. N.A.I. Agbo Dist. 1/ AG 530, Money Lenders Ordinance.
23. *West Africa*, Saturday August 20, 1938, p. 1122.
24. C.S.O. 26/30315 Vol. I, Police Magistrate to Chief Registrar of Supreme Court, 26 August 1935.
25. C.S.O. 26/30315 Vol. I, Acting Police Magistrate to the Chief Registrar, Supreme Court, Lagos, 30 November 1936.
26. C.S.O. 26/30315 Vol. I, John Holt to the Lagos Town Council.
27. See for instance N.A.I., Ije Prof 4/J.679 Money Lenders Ordinance Cap 147 Corresp in re. 1929/44 and Ijaw W. 4/W.1 167 Vol. I Money Lenders' License-Matters Re 1937/48.; and Kuku Div.2 KD 928, Money Lenders Re.

28. The ordinance for Trinidad borrowed extensively from the English Moneylenders Act of 1927.
29. For the Trinidad Ordinance see C.S.O. 26/30315 Vol. II, Money Lenders Amendment Ordinance 1935. [The five modifications were that: moneylending and pawnbroking transactions carried out by the same person should be differentiated; "signatures" by marks made by illiterate parties to moneylending contracts should be authenticated by suitable officials; maximum rates of interest should vary from 10 percent to 4.5 percent according to the security and the period of the loan; interest on amounts awarded to moneylenders by judgement of courts should be at the same rates as those on the original loan.]
30. C.S.O. 26/ 30315 Vol. II [Memo by the Governor General].
31. Borrowers were exempted from paying as part of interest the expenses on stamp duties, registration of documents, preparation of documents by legal practitioners, and other costs that should be incurred by the lender.
32. Interest was calculated as rates in the body of the ordinance but an appendix to it provided guidelines for other methods not based on percentages.
33. However, if a lender defaulted the moneylender could charge a simple interest from the date of default until the sum was paid.
34. N.A.I. C.S.O. 26/ 30315 Vol. III, Money Lenders Amendment Ordinances 1935 [Williams to The Acting Chief Secretary to the Government, 26 August 1938].
35. C.S.O. 26/ 30315 Vol. II.
36. C.S.O. 26/30315 Vol. I.
37. C.S.O. 26/30315 Vol. II, [Clerk, Executive Council to the Ex. Co.].
38. N.A.I. C.S.O. 26/ 30315 Vol. 1.
39. C.S.O. 26/30315 Vol. III, [Nigerian Moneylenders Association to the Governor of Nigeria].
40. *Ibid.*
41. CSO 26/30315 Vol. III.
42. *Ibid.*
43. N.A.I., Ben Prof 1/BP 1423, Money Lenders' Ordinance.
44. N.A.I. Oyo Prof 1/1477 Vol. 1., Money Lenders Ordinance: Corresp. Re. and Vol. 2., Money Lenders' Ordinance Corresp. Re.
45. N.A.I., Iba Div 1/.1331, Vol. IV Money Lenders' Licenses.
46. 4 Agbor Dist 1/Ag 530; [Police report of 26/6/52].
47. N.A.I. Iba Div 1/ 1331 Vol. IV.
48. N.A.I. Iba Div. 1/ 1331 Vol. IV.
49. N.A.I., Ije Prof 4/956 Vol. I.
50. This contained information on the name of moneylender, name of borrower, amount of loan, security, if any, purpose for which loan was required, length of period for which loan was required, amount of interest charged, names and addresses of witnesses, and the date of transaction.
51. This contained information on names and address, the class of business and the date license approved.
52. *Ibid.*
53. N.A.I. Ije Prof 4/956 Vol.I; letter of 10 July, 1942.
54. N.A.I. Ak Div Co 9/450. Money Lenders 1961.
55. N.A.I. Ije Prof 4/956 Vol.I.
56. See for instance the case of Afolabi Fadugba, who struggled to recover a loan of £80 in N.A.I. AK Div Co. 1/166.
57. N.A.I. Ak Div. Co 9/450.
58. See for instance N.A.I. Ondo Prof 1/1/570 Money Lenders' Ordinance Corresp. Re.

59. N.A.I. C.S.O. 26/30315 Vol. II.
60. *Ibid.*
61. *Ibid*; Oral interviews with informants previously cited.

9

Money and Criminality: Theft

A short cut to making money is through stealing. The Yoruba have always witnessed cases of theft, leading to rampant rate of armed robbery, since the 1970s. The abundant data and archival resources on crime in southwestern Nigeria[1] have hardly been used, not even for straightforward administrative history, not to mention the more complicated social issues. In an elite conception of history like the one that has dominated Yoruba studies, an investigation into crime is relegated to the background except in cases when the elite intervened to restore order, as in the judiciary or the police which have received significant scholarly attention. Crime should, however, be understood because it is partly a reaction and a response to the state, the economy, and the law. Either for protest or any other motive, crime enables a better understanding of social order, the nature of conflicts, and the norms of legal and cultural behavior. An understanding of crime enriches popular history, one in which the elite enters the picture from the perspective of the masses.

The present contribution is limited to thieves who operated in the category of 'professional underworld' and excludes those who used their wits to steal from the government or gullible individuals.[2] The chapter provides additional data on motives of theft and discusses the methods employed by thieves and the attempts by the state and public to curtail theft. By drawing on a large number of documented cases spanning the entire period of colonial rule, the chapter highlights the dominant and most enduring characteristics of theft in southwestern Nigeria.

Inspired by the excellent studies on the social history of England in the eighteenth century,[3] the theoretical works by Friedrich Engels,[4] Karl Marx,[5] and Eric Hobsbawm,[6] a collection has attempted a linkage between criminality and social protest in Africa.[7] In his competent introduction to this volume, Professor Crummey laments the failure of scholars to draw from the insights of Engels, Marx, and Hobsbawm to see theft as a form of protest. To correct this error, the first section of the volume is devoted to exploring "crime as a dimension of social protest."[8] Whilst this volume succeeds in its goal, it is clear from some of the contributions and the present essay that not all of the insights of Hobsbawm and the other writers that have been mentioned are of direct application or relevance to Africa. For instance, in the first chapter by Larry Yarak on the Gold Coast in the early nineteenth century, the author finds no evidence of social banditry. In the only theoretical essay in the collection Professor Ralph Austen cautions on the applicability of the concepts of social bandit to Africa and offers, as an alternative, the idioms of magic and witchcraft to the understanding of deviance.

In the present study, we found no data to relate theft to any significant resistance to the colonial state or to any sustained social protest. Instead of the "heroic criminals" that Hobsbawm talks about, there is more evidence to support his category of "professional underworld"; no thief in our data became a hero, none was a "populist-re-distributor," the Robin Hood who robbed the rich to help the poor. Because it violated the law, theft is generally characterized as protest, especially in situations where laws were made by one social group in the society to protect itself and its interest. Such a protest might contribute to the development of class consciousness or "class-conscious" criminality, as in the case of theft among the tin miners of Jos studied by Professor William Freund.[9] However, the data for the present study reveals little on "class-conscious deviance." The sources are silent on the social backgrounds of most of the thieves, focusing instead on their ethnic origins. Most of them were poor, a strong indication that theft was one means of survival. The thieves attacked the rich, not because they were opposed to accumulation but because they targeted those who had the goods they wanted to steal. The thieves raided the poor as well, especially in cases where they stole livestock, farm crops, and low-value commodities.

There is, however, limited data that point to theft as two forms of protest to the state, one as a reaction to its taxation policy and the other to unemployment. The only and very rare data of theft as protest against the taxation policy of the state was the sporadic outbreak of theft in the Egbado cluster of villages of Maun in 1954 following the introduction and collection of capitation tax.[10] The members of the Ayepeju Society organized and led an antitax protest. This Society was proscribed in order for the government to break the rank of the protesters and collect tax. Policemen were dispatched to the area to collect tax by force. Following the departure of the police, the members of the proscribed

Ayepeju Society took to stealing to recoup the money they had paid as tax. The thieves, however, left the poor and the innocent, by attacking only the rich and the members of the Tax Assessment Committee and those who had supported the government in its call for the capitation taxation.[11] The investigation by the government confirmed the cases of theft, and concluded that the area had become "the centre of organised criminal activity."[12] In a very rare suggestion to curb crime the Divisional Officer did not emphasize the use of more police but advocated a general economic improvement of the area:

> There is no doubt that the area round Maun needs opening up.... Yesterday the Agricultural Superintendent said that he was planning a Group Farming Scheme at or near Ipokia itself. I have asked him to investigate the possibility of centring it either near Maun or in the Egun villages beyond Maun and he has readily agreed to do so. With some scheme of this nature, a motorable road and regular visits, any concentration of criminal activity in future in this area can probably be prevented.[13]

There is more evidence of the relationship between theft and unemployment. A good number of the reasons given by the thieves for their action was the need for survival, that is, stealing was "an alternative economy" to derive an income. A major report on thieves in Egbado in 1930 sought an answer to the question of why young Nigerians joined the gang of thieves formed by the migrants from Dahomey. It concluded that they did so "for love of adventure, love of gain and owing to scarcity of money, etc., due to land hunger."[14] An earlier report on Lagos in 1921 attributed the increase in stealing in 1920 to "unemployment caused by the present trade depression."[15]

Not too many officers or judges were impressed or convinced whenever the thieves mentioned the lack of money or of good jobs as their reasons for crime, but we want to suggest here that some people probably took to theft in reaction to the pressure by the society.[16] Colonial southwestern Nigeria was stratified, such that it was possible to identify the rich and the poor. This stratification was partly a function of the continuation of older precolonial structures and institutions and of the economy and politics in which rewards and profits that accrued to an individual depended very much on one's access to production, commerce, and power. Agriculture was very successful, with a massive production of cocoa and timber. The bureaucracy expanded; so too were the other social and political sectors. Population growth and the rate of migration and urbanization were all high. Compared with many other African societies during the same period, southwestern Nigeria was prosperous, a prosperity that found expression in extensive material acquisitions, construction of thousands of new modern buildings, and participation in politics. The wealth was, however, unevenly distributed.

Values and culture were affected by these rapid changes.[17] The poor, the unemployed, and the marginalized immigrants responded to the changes in different ways, including theft. This argument is not to suggest that theft had its origins in colonialism. The history of theft is much more ancient, although there is no extant literature to support a comparative analysis. What is clear is that the colonial state expanded the definition of crime (including theft) to include such new offences as counterfeiting, distillation of gin, trespasses into forest reserves, and the like.

There is likely to be less controversy on the suggestion that established thieves recruited new ones through contacts and the impact they established on them. David Oloyede told the Ijebu Provincial Court in 1934 how he became a thief:

> Kamiu Mustafa and I became acquainted while serving sentences in Epe prison. Before my discharge, Kamiu told me to go to his mother Kafawu and stay with her at Shagamu till he was discharged also. He told me that...if I waited for him at Shagamu he would teach me a more profitable trade, viz. Stealing.... I went at once and stayed with him. He introduced me to one J. A. Disalu. After a little while they suggested that we should go and rob the house of a washman. We did so in the night with two others...and took a lot of clothing giving him to wash. The same five of us then burgled Beji's house at Shagamu.... We continued on burglaries mostly in Shagamu but sometimes in Ikorodu.[18]

Oloyede's case was not peculiar; it brings out two aspects common in most of the accounts that emanated from thieves. First, a good number of them were exconvicts, either having gone to jail because of petty stealing or for other matters. Most admitted that they took to stealing (as a full-time occupation) because they had nothing else to do. Second, there was always a contact person who introduced them to the trade.

A few cases of theft suggest that the thieves were also concerned with revenge to score a point in addition to whatever gains that might accrue to them. Cases of revenge were not directed at the state but at the individuals who cheated them. Two thieves said that they burgled the houses of two women who failed to reciprocate love and friendship, in spite of everything they did to satisfy these women with all sorts of goods and money. In both cases the women admitted that they knew the thieves and regretted their association with them.[19] Several thieves confessed that they raided some people to use force to collect the goods which they kept with them and which these people refused to return. Some thieves returned from jail to discover that their former associates or friends had spent the money they kept with them or were unwilling to return the goods they were supposed to keep for them. To recover their "property, they had to steal, and some of them got into problems once again. On the latter, the evidence of Lasisi, a thief who appeared in court, which discredited a witness and put her in trouble, is important to cite in spite of the bad language:

> I am a native of Ishara. The first witness is my confidential friend. I am a thief and the first witness used to keep stolen property for me. When I was sent to prison sometime ago the first witness kept five pounds and a gold ring for me. When I discharged I asked her for it and she refused to give it to me and said that if I came to her house asking for it again, she would shout out and tell everybody what I was. That is why I went to her house and took her property. When I was discharged from prison I had no money, so as she refused to give me back my money, I planned to take her property and sell.... I wanted to recover the stolen property.[20]

Methods of Operation

The primary goal of a thief was to rob his victim of his valuables. Items lost to thieves included: money, clothes, bicycles, petrol, household goods (mattresses, net, beds, utensils, chairs, etc.), foodstuffs, and livestock (for example, cows, goats, and pigs). Most victims complained of great losses, which would be true since the thieves were interested in their most valuable possessions. Victims were not restricted to the poor; government officials (including Europeans), missionaries, and highly placed citizens were among the list of those who were robbed.

Losses were not limited to goods but also to lives. Two lives were lost and many were wounded when a gang of robbers attacked a village at Ipokia (Egbado area) in 1933.[21] Other cases were reported,[22] although a colonial administrator, Captain Scot, concluded in his very thoughtful report on robbery in 1930 that thieves did not set out to kill their victims:

> I have no record of the robbers ever using guns except for making a noise before attacking, but anyone who resisted them they mercilessly hacked with cutlasses or beat insensible. It is alleged one or two women have been raped and some inhabitants have died from wounds either at the once or later. Whenever possible the robbers resist arrest and one constable and the Bale of Ijofin have been cut or stabbed and also one or two of the Bale's followers, when making arrests.[23]

The most organized robbery was always by a gang, like the one reported for Egbado in the 1930s in which the number of the thieves in the gang was high.[24] Some other gangs in the same area were described as having about fifty thieves who operated at once.[25]

Many cases were reported in which a gang comprised thieves of the same ethnic group. In Egbado, most of the dangerous thieves in the 1920s and 1930s were from Dahomey or Nigerians with relations in Dahomey.[26] These thieves were described in 1930 as "French ex-convicts or people whose activities in Dahomey have made that country unhealthy for them."[27] The linkage provided them with the opportunity to seek refuge whenever there was trouble.

The most documented cases on ethnicity were on Hausa thieves, perhaps because they were the most prominent and notorious. Virtually all the districts in the region had cause to complain about Hausa thieves during the colonial era. The earliest complaint was made at Ibadan in 1906 and 1907. In this complaint, the chiefs put pressure on the colonial administrators to recognize a Hausa leader who would be held responsible for the crime of fellow Hausa, to restrict them to a separate quarter and to imprison any one of them who left this quarter in the evening for whatever reason.[28] The colonial government did not give its approval to this suggestion. Because Hausa thieves continued to steal, Ibadan chiefs, too, became more relentless in seeking solution to their menace until 1916 when a separate community was founded for them. In the 1950s a gang of Hausa thieves, based at Agenebode, raided many communities in the area, sometimes crossing the River Niger to steal at Idah.[29] In 1934 when Osogbo experienced large-scale burglaries, many were attributed to the Hausa, and the *Oba* of Osogbo had to appeal to the government to force all the Hausa to live in a separate quarter (Sabongari) so that their activities could be curbed.[30] In cases where the Sabongeri were searched by the police or administrators, large quantities of stolen goods were recovered and many of the people who were interrogated confessed that they were thieves.[31] It became a rule in the Oyo Province that whenever a major case of theft was reported, the first place to search was the Hausa community.[32] The colonial administrators in Abeokuta made similar discoveries.[33]

Abner Cohen has pointed out that thieves were part of the legitimate inhabitants of Hausa quarters. His conclusion derives from a study of the Hausa in Ibadan where thieves joined a large body of migrants who had to provide services to established cattle traders. He argues that the competition for trade between the Yoruba and the Hausa and the extortion of Hausa traders by their Yoruba hosts compelled the Hausa to demand a separate quarter, a demand which they justified on cultural grounds and on the needs to check the thieves among themselves.[34] The prevalence of Hausa thieves was not, however, limited to the need to justify segregation. As Cohen points out, thieves "constituted a significant structural factor in both the internal and the external politics of the Quarter."[35] The number of Hausa thieves multiplied at an alarming rate, to the extent that four-fifths of the recorded cases of arrest in Ibadan in the 1940s were Hausa while two Chiefs of the Hausa quarter were found guilty of theft in the 1920s and 1940s. Hausa thieves became highly specialized and skilled, in the different departments of selling stolen goods, housebreaking, shoplifting, and pocket picking. The thieves were allowed to stay and interact with the others in the quarter as long as they did not steal from fellow Hausa citizens and provided they did not escalate the tension between the Hausa community and the indigenous authorities and the government to an unmanageable proportion.

The prominence of aliens from Dahomey (now Benin) and northern Nigeria should not create a misleading impression that there were no Yoruba thieves. Yoruba thieves went elsewhere as well, while the majority of the thieves chose to locate themselves outside of their towns. The best recorded cases of theft in Ijebu mentioned the places of origin of the thieves as Ilorin, Lagos, and eastern Nigeria. Thieves of Ijebu origins were arrested and jailed at Ibadan. Many of the thieves found in Ilorin were from northern Nigeria, Ibadan, and Osogbo. Edo thieves were mentioned in Owo and Auchi. It is difficult to know the precise towns of many of the thieves because they could lie about these (and also about names). There was also the problem of using imprecise geographical and ethnic categories to describe people. For instance, most people from northern Nigeria were called Hausa and Nupe, even when they were not. Most people from central Nigeria could simply be called Igbirra; while light skinned people from the east could be described as Igbo, even if they were Ijo or Itsekiri.

Most of the gangs investigated by the police had a leader. Thus, the Divisional Officer (D.O.) of Abeokuta could describe the leader of the gang that raided ten Imala villages on eight separate occasions as a "light skinned Hausa living at Igaun village in the same District."[36] In 1930 when the government had to take drastic measures to curb the activities of thieves in Egbado, one of the methods it emphasized was the arrest of the gang leaders. After an intensive investigation, it was discovered that

> Tofisade, alias Hegbere, is the acknowledged Commander-in-Chief. He is a Native of Dahomey....His second in command was Yawmede. The other gang-leaders,

> living in different villages throughout the areas, obeyed the general directions of Tofisade, although individually with their gangs they frequently undertook enterprises of their own.[37]

The same report provides a rare piece of information on an aspect of the relationship between the leader and his men:

> At the conclusion of the undertaking, the successful gang had to report to Tofisade and the booty, if sufficient, was shared with him and the other gang leaders. The individual members of the gangs lived in their own villages either in their own houses or, if recent migrants, in lodgings and would assemble at the order of Tofisade or one gang would go to the help of another. After the enterprise was carried out the disposal of the booty, etc., would be arranged and the members would disperse to their respective villages.[38]

A gang had the capabilities and the resources to operate far and wide. The one led by Tofisade was discovered to have raided places in Ijebu Ode in the east, Iwoye in the north, lagoon villages in the south, and Dahomey villages in the west. Some groups based at Agenebode and Benin in the 1940s covered a much wider territory, encompassing the Ondo and Benin provinces, and across the Niger.

In 1954, the Senior D.O. of Egbado, assisted by the chiefs of Maun, also prepared a list (see Table 1 below) which provides many hints on leadership and the towns of origin of the thieves in this area.

In the case of Hausa thieves studied by Cohen, he found that they were also organized by a leader whom he described as a forceful character with a network of connections to influential elite within and outside the quarter. His major role was to protect the thieves from arrest, and he received due commission for this. Other data reveal similar tendencies: The gang leader procured arms and ammunition, linked up with dealers in stolen properties, and sought the protection of corrupt security agents.

Cases of thieves who operated on their own and who carried out operations all by themselves were equally common and very well reported. White collar criminality of stealing government property was one example, although this requires a separate study of its own. Schools, offices, hospitals, and such experienced minor and major cases of theft in which the staff of these places were either the suspects or the thieves.[39] Many of the pickpockets and shopbreakers arrested in Lagos between 1919 and 1921 and in Ijebu in the 1930s operated individually.[40]

Thieves relied on dangerous weapons, including bows and arrows, machetes, guns, knives, and cutlasses. Like the warriors of the nineteenth century, thieves believed in the efficacy of charms to succeed in

TABLE 1
Thieves in Egbado, 1954

Name of Thief	Place of Origin	Place of Residence (in Egbado Division)	Comments
Hun Kokue	Ajara (in Dahomey)	Itamosa	Gang leader of the thieves in the Ijofin area.
Jean	Aorranku (in Dahomey)	Itamosa	
Asogba	Itamosa	Itamosa	
Alufa	Isie (in Agbado)	Isie	
Ojo Adeniyi and his brother Ashiru Adeniyi Tijani	Ijofin	Ijofin	
Durowoju	Ijofin	Ijofin	
Posu	Baho (in Dahomey)	Ijofin	
Whesu	Age (in Dahomey)	Maun	Gang leader in Maun.
Posu	Age	Maun	
Louis	Unknown	Maun	
Agosu	Bawe Hundo	Bawe Hundo	
Dansu	Maun	Maun	
Hungeru	Maun Seji	Maun Seji	
Wheo	Ipinle	Ipinle	
Ogunbiyi	Maun	Maun	He was alleged to have been responsible for introducing all the thieves to Maun.
Hunkokue	Atunto (in Dahomey)	Tube	Gang leader for Tube area.
Gbagba	Aragoji	Tube	
Sochouedo	Tube	Tube	
Korananu	Tube	Tube	
Amosu	Bogi	Tube	
Fasina	Bogi	Bogi	
Adunpe	Bogi	Bogi	
Ajase	Ilufe	Ilufe	

Sources: N.A.I. Ab Prof 2/ABP 342; Senior D.O. Egbado Division to the Senior Superintendent of Police, the Nigerian Police, Abeokuta, 4 September 1954.

their operations. Cases of successful robberies are narrated with stories of how the thieves used charms to make their victims sleep, dumb, or weak to resist. Thieves used charms to turn invisible when detected, resist gun shot and machete cut, and to even escape from police cell.[41] Some thieves specialized in stealing certain commodities. Hausa thieves in Egbado in the 1930s preferred to steal clothes and fowls.

The methods employed in stealing were similar, the common ones were to break into houses, shops, and offices. Most cases of theft occurred at night: many people would be asleep and it was easier for thieves to escape should there be trouble. Cases of theft on farms, in the markets, and along roads and bush paths were also recorded, although most of these were limited in scale. In the cities, pickpockets moved in organized groups, and they became part of the features of the big markets and motor parks. Worse cases of armed robbery, in which people were brutally attacked, were also reported.

The 1930 report by Captain Scot provides very useful and reliable evidence on some of the tactics adopted by thieves. The more confident groups moved in large number and in the night; for instance, he described how Ifonyin was attacked by a prominent gang that woke up the people with drums. According to Scot, the most common method

> adopted by the robbers was to arrive at the village, farm settlement or house intended to be looted at night and let off Dane guns and create an uproar. The inhabitants invariably then ran into the bush and the robbers were free to help themselves.[42]

One case was more daring than this. On 25 October 1953, the citizens of Uhomora in Ora, woke up to discover a notice:

> Nigerian Burglary Society have been hearing about the Ritches(sic) of your town Uhomora-Ora, concerning your cocoa and Rubber. This year will be the beginning of our visit to this town from henceforth and rob (steal) all your riches. Prepare all your medicines, cutlass, Guns and Charms ready for us; we only fear two men in this town because they are bolder than us in all things. We shall be killed and we also shall kill some of you too. Stand by now Uhomora Cocoa owner. Ogboni men are our leader in all things. No case we can not win in Nigeria.[43]

As the use of lorry became popular as a faster means of transportation, some well-organized thieves turned this to advantage to loot shops and carry large quantities of goods. Modern materials for construction (like the hammer and chisel) became objects that facilitated house breaking by force and very quickly, too.[44]

The police, the public, and administrators agreed that the most dangerous thieves were those alien to the community because of the opportunity that they had to escape to other towns, to recruit new thieves, and to shift their locations with ease. In Lagos and Egbado, thieves were drawn from Dahomey, across the border, and they disappeared with their loots, never to be found. The great bicycle theft relied on the trade connections between Nigeria and Dahomey: stolen bicycles were immediately sent across the border,[45] the great beyond where the owners could never dream of recovering them even if the thieves were arrested.

The State, the Public, and the Thief

Colonial administrators regarded the prevention of theft as part of their primary goal of maintaining law and order. Not only were they responsible for the formulation and revision of laws to curb crime, they made use of both the judiciary and the police to fight the thieves. Cases of theft were often reported both to the police and administrative officers. Administrators always instructed the police on what to do, and occasionally went behind them to make their own investigations and take decisions. Stringent laws were made and implemented to deal with established cases; those who were arrested and found guilty were sent to jail.

Administrators often initiated measures to cope with cases of theft, and this could require taking decisions on behalf of the police. A common measure was to request additional policemen, as was done in 1930 when armed robbers operated in the southern part of Ilaro division. Such were the atrocities of thieves that the Resident thought that a European officer had to accompany an additional number of twenty-five policemen.[46] Administrators conducted an investigation that helped the police to make arrest. By making use of chiefs, spies, and members of the public, they collected information on thieves. They were also keen on making suggestions to minimize cases of theft. For most of the time, suggestions focused on increasing police activities, restricting immigrants from Dahomey, cooperating with the French authorities, and closer supervision of the borders. Most of the security measures devolved on the police. When thefts were committed, especially when lives or injuries were involved, more constables were usually deployed to such an area. However, these constables were only on temporary duties, and were withdrawn to their locations after some days.[47] The thieves and the members of the public were aware of this arrangement, which did not prevent robbery in the first place, lead to the arrest of the thieves, or prevent the thieves from striking again once the police were withdrawn. The area from where the police were withdrawn became exposed, leading to fears that the thieves might know and attack. In the example just mentioned, the constables that went to Ipokia were all taken from the neighbouring town of Ilaro, thus depleting the number of policemen to three. Although the gang of robbers that was being hunted by the police did not attack Ilaro, it nevertheless shifted its operation to the small village of Igo, which had not a single policeman.[48]

The pattern of police investigation and methods was clear. It involved the arrest of a large number of suspects, selected for reasons best known to the police. In a very successful investigation, the stolen goods were recovered. Most of the people arrested were men, although women were implicated, because those found with stolen goods were also arrested and punished.[49] The police occasionally rewarded those who assisted them to arrest thieves.[50] In difficult cases, when the operations of thieves had assumed a large scale, the police concentrated their efforts on the gang leaders, hoping that their arrest would disperse the thieves.

The police were not always successful in arresting thieves or curbing their activities. Indeed, the police failed to be useful to the public on many occasions. The reasons for their failure were many. For one, the force never had adequate men to police the region. Requests for additional policemen to cope with urgent crisis were either not met at all, or had to wait till the time that a unit could redistribute its men or until it could obtain a loan of men from other units. Delays to deploy men to vulnerable areas were also caused by arguments between the administrators as to who should shoulder the financial responsibility, especially when the policemen would work in divisions outside their normal locations. One request was delayed in 1930 over an argument as to who would provide the tent where the police would live or whether they should occupy any house of their choice without paying rent.

There was yet another delay, which owed to the argument on how a high number of policemen, with 1,220 rounds of ammunition, would suddenly appear in an area without causing panic. A Divisional Officer based at the thief-infested town of Ilaro in the 1930s argued that thieves disappeared as soon as the police appeared, later to return when they departed. He advocated the use of a smaller number of policemen and an officer who would work quietly to obtain information, gather witnesses, and make their arrests at a time when the thieves least expected.[51] The arguments on logistics only helped the thieves to have more time and to plan their activities very well and with a level of coordination that always amazed the administrative officers. The thieves knew the movements of the police and could therefore operate where there were either no policemen or where the number of the available police was small. The thieves knew as well that the government policed an area that had recently been attacked, and that the police would be withdrawn as soon as there was evidence of security. The thieves struck, following such withdrawal. The case of Egbado in the 1930s is very well documented. When the thieves invaded the area in 1930, the government policed the area. By the end of the year, administrators were jubilating over the success of the police in curbing thieves, and urged Lagos to withdraw them because peace had returned. In 1931, the number of the police was reduced. As soon as the thieves knew this, they resumed their activities once again and by 1932, the rate of robberies had become high.[52]

Second, the language barrier occasionally impeded investigation, as was the case in Egbado in 1933 when Igbo-speaking policemen were posted to Ipokia to investigate robbery. These policemen could not speak to the villagers because they did not understand Yoruba.[53]

Third, identifying and tracking down thieves was difficult. Some of them were said to "live in shacks in the farms, while others live in towns and appear to be respectable citizens in the day time."[54] Nobody knew when a new thief was born or when one made his first appearance in a place. There was as well the big problem of making false accusations about innocent people. A Police Officer confessed in 1930 that many innocent people were arrested on the basis of false allegations: "It is one of the habits of these pleasant people to give information about anybody they don't like regardless of whether it is true or not."[55] The same officer reported the wrongful arrest of many innocent hunters, simply because their enemies accused them of robbery.

Fourth, the police complained that some of their attempts to minimise thefts were frustrated by the demands by the courts for concrete evidence of crime. Those who should give evidence were either not available or had taken to the bush when the thieves struck, making whatever evidence they had unreliable.

Fifth, the police complained of inadequate facilities and the means to combat the thieves. The complaint was either about transportation difficulties, when they thought that they needed more bicycles to travel to send patrols to many villages, or about guns or money.

Sixth, the police complained that members of the public did not cooperate enough to simplify their work. When the people of Ilaro complained of a wave of burglaries in 1945 and demanded an effective police action, it was made clear to the *Oba* of the town that there was nothing the police could do "if the public is not going to cooperate by at least reporting when a burglary has occurred."[56]

The allegation that the members of the public did not cooperate with the police is difficult to sustain. There is abundant evidence that the public, through the chiefs and in private capacities, reported theft to the police and colonial administrators, sometimes receiving replies and immediate actions, and sometimes without any reply. The Maun chiefs were depressed to report in 1954 that

> as elders of the village we made every effort to check these (i.e., wave of stealing) but in vain. We wrote letters to the Police Station or to the nearest High Authorities but no step has ever been taken as aid or prevention. Things are getting worse from time to time. We listed down the names of the members of this Evil Society and handed it over to the Police at Ipokia our nearest Police Station, but to this there was no outcome.[57]

They made a fresh plea for the police to be stationed in their villages, and they promised to cooperate in revealing the identities of the thieves.

Contrary to the allegation of noncooperation by the public, the people would appear to have done a lot to clear their areas of thieves. True, there were problems that could create a false impression of nonchalance on the part of the members of the public. A common problem reported in the sources was the refusal of many people to testify in courts. Victims had no choice but to go to the court or the police station, but witnesses complained that repeated journeys to the court and police station wasted time and money, while many could not understand the reasons for rigorous questioning and cross examinations by the police and judges.[58] A few complained that the thieves or members of their gang could seek revenge by attacking them. A few cynics mentioned the uselessness of their evidence when the police or the court would in the end conclude that they had no solid evidence to prosecute the thieves.[59] In spite of the problems encountered by the public, they were more useful in investigating cases and arresting thieves than the police were willing to admit. Victims assisted the police to locate thieves and their stolen goods. Perhaps more than the police, victims of theft worked hard in investigation and they served as the primary and most reliable witnesses when a case ended in court.

Indigenous authorities were equally interested in peace, security, and prosperity. To the majority of them, their town would acquire a bad name if they could not rid it of criminals. In a number of cases, the chiefs were held responsible for security and the arrest of thieves, especially in the early years of the colonial administration. As late as the 1920s the *Ataoja* of Osogbo was reminded on two occasions of his responsibility to keep order, arrest, and deal with thieves, and was warned to remind all his chiefs that they must ensure that their quarters were free of "suspicious strangers."[60] The *Timi* of Ede received a similar letter in 1926, with a specific instruction to arrest one particular thief.[61] Four years later, when the town of Ede became a refuge to thieves, plain clothes police went to the town and made many arrests, including the staff of the *Timi's* palace. When the *Timi* complained to the Resident at Ibadan, the D.O. of Osogbo justified the action of the police thus: "The state of the town and the absolute and complete indifference of the chiefs necessitated drastic action, and the sheep could not be separated from the goats until the cases came up for hearing."[62] Consequently, the chiefs cooperated with the administrators and the police to arrest suspected thieves.

In the early 1930s, the *Baale* of the Egbado town of Ijofin became famous for arresting over fifty thieves, in spite of the great risk that this involved to his life. The *Oba* of Ipokia was praised for making a similar contribution to the arrest of prominent criminals, while the *Baale* of Tube was credited with the arrest of four robbers in 1930.[63] During the same period the palace of the *Akarigbo* of Ijebu Remo was turned into a court to prosecute thieves.[64] Many towns and wards within towns complemented police work by establishing vigilante groups, mainly of hunters and other brave men. It is certain that thieves feared the vigilante groups more than the police. When thieves anticipated that they would confront night guards, they prepared harder for a fight and would not hesitate to injure or kill. Thieves were afraid because if they were unlucky enough to be caught, the night guards would alert the public, who could then resort to mob action. The consequences of a mob action were better imagined than experienced; humiliation and severe beatings could lead to complicated injuries or death. Police records report cases in which thieves were forced to drink poison or nailed on the head and then set free, since it was certain that the thief would die some hours later. Thieves (and the public, too) believed that night guards had magical powers (which the police did not have) to arrest with minimal difficulty.

Hundreds of "laws and regulations" were made in many villages, towns, and establishments to protect lives and property. Some of these "laws and regulations" enjoyed the support of government, while many were lacking in authority and unenforceable in any court of law.[65] The laws varied greatly, each depending on how a community or an organization thought it could defend itself. For instance, some areas required residents to carry lamps at night; some controlled the entries of strangers and monitored the movements and activities of those who were allowed to stay. Some improved on their fences and vaults, many employed night guards, and many also summoned their charm makers and diviners to protect their communities. When cases of theft reached an alarming proportion, communities resorted to all sorts of draconian measures, many of which were illegal. For instance, in the 1950s, many communities between Owo and Auchi went to the extent of authorizing their night guards to kill thieves whenever they were cut, while cases of mob actions against suspected thieves increased, in spite of constant reminders by the authorities that these were illegal.

Some communities were more legal minded, and they informed colonial administrators on the steps they wanted to take or they requested the government for assistance. In many cases, calls were made to resort to ancient practices to deal with thieves. For instance, suggestions were made that the hands and legs of thieves be amputated, that they should be paraded naked in public, that they should be expelled from the town, and that their wives be told to divorce them. Suggestions were always made to redeploy policemen and to curb the activities of strangers.[66]

The case of Benin in 1953 is better documented than many others, and it is used here to illustrate an example of a desperate reaction by one society. For most of 1952, Benin and its district were invaded by thieves, to the extent of rendering "life and property most unsafe."[67] Benin became so notorious that passengers in transit were put under perpetual fear. The members of the public complained to all available authorities, traditional and modern. In mid-January 1953, the Benin Divisional Council devoted a session to the issue, concluding that the police should work harder to deal with the problem. Shortly after this meeting, the Resident was frightened by fresh reports of burglaries (he had to alert his boss at Ibadan) to the extent that the police force could no longer restore public confidence in its ability to control the situation. The Resident requested an extra Inspector and twenty-five policemen to strengthen the Native Authority Police night patrols.[68]

Dealing with thieves became a political issue between the Resident, the Native Authority Police (NAPF), the Nigeria Police Force (NPF), the indigenous chiefs, and the Native Authority. While each was interested in curbing the menace, they differed on methods and the extent to which they wanted to take responsibility. On the part of the Resident and some administrators, the police had failed to check the menace while their promise to reinforce the available local police forces was not met. In the last week of January, the NPF promised to transfer more men to assist the NAPF This promise was fulfilled; on 29 January, thirty-one men led by a Sergeant and a Corporal reported in Benin. On the part of the N.A., reliance was placed on its police force, which unfortunately had little public image. To meet the demands of the public, the N.A. decided to recruit Night Watchmen to patrol different wards. The police and administrators were against the use of the Night Watchmen, and both pressed for their withdrawal. Administrators described them as "gangs of hooligans" who disturbed people's peace in the night and created inconveniences on the roads by stopping motor traffic at their illegal road blocks.[69] The N.A. refused to withdraw the Night Watchmen; the public showed more confidence in them, in spite of their excesses, and the police continued to attack their presence.

Increasing cases of theft, and the politics of control, led to a meeting between the Resident and the *Oba* of Benin in the last day of January. A long discussion ensued. The *Oba* and his chiefs objected to the withdrawal of the Night Watchmen because this would give the impression that the government was assisting the thieves. Finally, a compromise was reached. It was agreed that the Night Watchmen be withdrawn but every ward should use "responsible individuals" for patrol in cooperation with the police whose number would be increased.[70]

By February, the public had lost patience with the government and police. Some wards began to organize the purchase of guns and gunpowder. One ward was bold enough to write to the government requesting machetes, guns, lamps, kerosene, cudgels, and whistles to defend itself, while it went further to ask three embarrassing questions:

> Should in case a man is seen outside the street as from 12 p.m. [sic] midnight and should be arrested what assistance will the N.A. perform? If one of the watchmen thereby shot to death by the thieves what help will the N.A. render to the family? Are there no policemen in the town?[71]

An organization that cuts across wards wrote a petition along the same line, and made nine suggestions:

1. Each ward to appoint honest and reliable men to watch in turns at night;
2. The use of torch lights should be abolished, and hurricane lanterns be used instead;
3. After 10 p.m. any one going from one part of the town to another without the approved light to be arrested;
4. The police force to be re-organised and re-shuffled with a view to improving its efficiency even up to or above the standard attained when Ben Edo was the head of the force;
5. The police man in charge of the quarter when theft is committed to be called to question;

6. Lorries or cars coming into or leaving the town after 12 midnight to be detained and searched;
7. Thieves caught to be severely dealt with;
8. Government should allow citizens to wound any thief that is caught.
9. All non-native robbers who have been jailed twice or thrice to be repatriated while the native robbers who have been jailed a similar number of times to be bound over.[72]

None of these suggestions was considered by the government because it believed that the police could control robberies. Indeed, cases of theft were not recorded for four nights in February, but these were days when the thieves operated in the districts. Daylight robberies also subsided, and the government attributed this to the efficiency of the men of the NPF. In the last week of February, acting on the assumption that effective policing by the NAPF would stamp out theft, the Resident allowed the additional contingent of the NPF to leave the city. He, however, anticipated problems, and he warned that the NAPF would be held responsible for any further escalation of robberies. He asked the *Oba* of Benin to address the NAPF, to warn them that "inefficiency, neglect of duty, or bribe taking would result in instant dismissal" and that the police would be judged by its ability to protect lives and property.[73] The *Oba* carried out this instruction where he insinuated that the police had bad eggs among its men and threatened that many of them would be dismissed.

The *Oba*'s threat was of no consequence. By the end of the year, cases of theft had again become rampant. In January 1954, a union of Benin indigenes based at Ibadan expressed concern that their town would acquire a "national disgrace" because of the activities of the thieves who had become so bold that they sometimes confronted their targets to demand money or risk an attack. Many suggestions, some old and some new, were made by members of the public. For instance, they wanted the payment of small wages to Night Guards, the detention of thieves and people without regular jobs, and the provision of jobs for all. They also made the plea for the police to be "reshuffled since there is much corruption among the ranks and file of its members," and longer prison terms for convicted thieves. Many gave up on the expectation that the police could help and they found ways to protect their lives and property, mainly by hiring guards who carried dangerous weapons (in violation of the law) or by relying on supernatural means.

Responses by Thieves to Security Measures

When under pressure by the police or the public, thieves sought the means to escape. Those in places near the borders ran to the neighboring country of Dahomey[74]; Hausa thieves disappeared into Sabongeri or returned to northern Nigeria. Dealing with aliens was always a problem. To those from outside of the country, the easiest measure of control was to prevent their entry. To those already within, Section 59 of the Local Government Laws of the 1950s authorized a Council to invite any stranger to prove his means of subsistence. If the means were found inadequate, a Council had the power to expel such a person from its district and to report him to the Police. A few attempts were made to contact the French authorities in the case of those from Dahomey. The suggestions made by administrators in the field—that the Nigerian government should cooperate with the police in Dahomey, that the extradition laws which provided the thieves with a sanctuary in Nigeria be relaxed, and that power should be entrusted to a Police Officer who would cross boundaries without reference to the jurisdiction of the local Magistrates—fell through. In the case of Nigerians, it was difficult to deal with aliens because a proof of theft must first of all be established before any measure could be taken to expel anybody from the community. This was a complicated and lengthy procedure.

Organized gangs sought the means to collaborate with the police and chiefs in order to escape arrest. In the case of Hausa thieves, an established practice was to hide behind powerful landlords, who were themselves Hausa but who were engaged in the lucrative trade of selling cattle or kolanuts.[75] In other cases, thieves sought the support of corrupt chiefs. In 1930, the *Baale* of Ago Sasa was suspected of offering assistance to thieves and he was recommended for suspension.[76] In 1931, a senior chief of Ede, the *Jagun,* was suspended for trying to hide information on thieves.[77] In 1952, the Head Chief of Lampese, a village in the Auchi Division, was accused of protecting thieves and of receiving stolen goods from them.[78] In 1954, an Egbado chief was accused of making peace with the thieves.[79] Some of the informants that the police relied upon to investigate cases of theft often turned out to have been thieves themselves.[80] There were also cases of serving and retired policemen who were implicated in some cases,[81] while there were always rumors that some night guards aided and abetted robberies.[82] In 1954, a widespread complaint was that the police and some chiefs gave assistance to the chiefs, and a prominent club had to call for an inquiry to understand why this cooperation was possible:

> There are some high ranking officers in the Police Force who support the culprit it is alleged each time they are caught or brought to the Police Station. For instance, a thief may be caught taken to the Police Station, the Police would act as if the thief will be executed, sent to the cell at once and ask the complainant to go. Immediately afterwards, the thief will be released and at times would be given a lift home by another known member. There are some of the prominent chiefs too who appear to be honest but they instigate the thieves and some of the evil doers by encouraging them. The queer task of these chiefs is to bail the thief or act as advisers to any criminal by backing the thief with monetary help. They do this because they get a share from the booty.[83]

When caught, a thief did everything possible to discredit the evidence and the witnesses to convict him. Cases of the destruction of evidence and bribing witnesses not to appear in court were common. When this failed, he struggled further to escape from police cell. There were successful cases of escape, one of which was described as follows:

> I was unfortunate enough to lose 17 prisoners, including 3 or 4 gang-leaders on 28/1/30 from Idiroko N.C. Lock-up. The wife of one of the gang-leaders passed a handcuff key in a loaf of bread into him. He released himself and then the others and overpowered the Police Constable on Guard.[84]

When everything failed, and it became certain that a heavy punishment would be imposed, some thieves showed remorse and promised the world to reform themselves. Some showed courage, suggesting that the prison was nothing to fear. One thief, before he was sentenced, admitted to committing theft but wondered why it was necessary to tell lies against him: "What the witness says is all correct except for the money. We stole no money, because we found none."[85]

Summary

Cases of theft were common throughout the colonial period, and were reported every where, although the urban centers recorded higher rates. Villages close to the Nigerian-Dahomey borders also had a higher rate because they sheltered alien thieves and the volume of trade was high. Most thieves operated outside their own towns, to use anonymity as one source of protection.

The goods that were stolen provide some comments on the taste and aspirations of thieves or their ambition for money, and their understanding of commerce. On aspirations, the primary consideration was to have money or to have goods that gave the impression of wealth. On taste, fine clothes, and jewelry were stolen either for use by the thieves or to exchange for money. On trade, thieves stole the goods that had ready markets. By the 1950s, items like motor parts, radios, and most modern objects had become the most highly prized. They had traders who purchased stolen items from them, explaining why the police arrested traders as suspects and as criminals. The best article to steal was money, as it involved no problem of disposal and evidence of theft was difficult to establish, unless the money was marked. Other goods had to be sold, if the thieves wanted money, and some of them were arrested either when they were about to sell, usually at lower prices, or thereafter when the buyers led the police to their hideouts.[86]

Notes

1. The variety and problems of defining crime are taken into consideration in making this statement on this lacunae.
2. See chapter 11 in this book.
3. Douglas Hay, Peter Linebaugh, John G. Rule, E. P. Thompson, and Cal Winslow, *Albion's Fatal Tree: Crime and Society in Eighteenth Century England* (London: Allen Lane, 1975 rep.)
4. See, for instance, *The Conditions of the Working Class in England* (London: Panther Books, 1969 rep.)
5. Karl Marx, *Capital,* vol. 1 (London, 1967).
6. E. J. Hobsbawm, *Primitive Rebels: Studies in Archaic Forms of Social Movement in the 19th and 20th Centuries* (Manchester: Manchester University Press, 1959); and *idem*, *Bandits* (Harmondsworth: Penguin, 1972; 2nd ed., 1981).
7. D. Crummey, ed., *Banditry, Rebellion and Social Protest in Africa* (London and New Hampshire: James Currey and Heinemann, 1986).
8. *Ibid.* p. 4.
9. "Theft and Social Protest Among the Tin Miners of Northern Nigeria" in Crummey, *Banditry and Rebellion*, chap. 2.
10. "Tax Collection in the Western Region, 1953–54," Paper laid on the Table of the Western House of Assembly by the Chief Secretary, February 1954. Lagos: Gov ernment Printer, 1954.
11. National Archives, Ibadan [N.A.I.] Abe Prof2/342, Bale of Maun village and thirty others to the D.O. Ilaro, 29 August, 1954.
12. *Ibid.* Senior D.O., Egbado Division to Resident, Abeokuta, 9 May 1954.
13. *Ibid.*
14. *Ibid.* Captain Scot's Report On Robbers, 1930.
15. N.A.I., C.S.O. 19/9–N3027/1921, Cases of robberies and burglaries in Lagos-Return of-asks for.
16. The linkage between socioeconomic conditions (such an inequality, values that sustain inequality, poverty, unemployment, etc.) and crime has generated a lively debate. Among others, see R.K. Merton, *Social Theory And Social Structure* (New York: The Free Press, 1969); E. Durkheim, *The Division of Labour in Society* (New York: The Free Press, 1973 repr.); and F. Alexander and W. Healey, *Roots of Crime* (New Jersey: Patterson Smith, 1969).

17. The theme of culture change is under researched, and my conclusion here is tentative.
18. N.A.I. Ije Prof 4/J.458, Rex vs. David Oloyede of Abeokuta: Charged with robbery.
19. N.A.I. Ije Prof 4/J626 Rex vs. Lasisi Oyebanjo: Charged with burglary.
20. N.A.I. Ije Prof 4/458, Rex vs. David Oloyede of Abeokuta: Charged with burglary.
21. N.A.I. Abe Prof /ABP 342 Robberies in the Ilaro Division; Jackson to Resident, Abeokuta, 12 June 1933.
22. See for instance, N.A.I. Ije. Prof.4/J.1225, Highway Robbery and Murder at Ode Oko.
23. Captain Scot's report on robbers.
24. N.A.I. Abe Prof 2/ABP 342, Jackson to Resident, Abeokuta, 22 June 1933.
25. N.A.I. Abe Prof 2/ABP 342/1; Resident, Abeokuta Province to the Senior Commissioner of Police, Western Area, Lagos 7 March 1930.
26. N.A.I. Kuku Div 2/K.D.1401, Burglary; Chief P.O. Izwukai to the D.O., Auchi, 23 April, 1954.
27. N.A.I. Abe Prof. 2/ABP 342/1 Captain Scot's report on robbers, 1930.
28. Ibadan Municipal Papers, Minutes of Council Meetings, 13 and 30 October, 1906 and 23 May 1907.
29. N.A.I. Kuku Div. 2/K.D. 1401, Burglary.
30. N.A.I. Oshun Div. 1/1/196 Vol. l; Ataoja to the D.O., 29 March 1934.
31. See examples of cases in Oshun Div.1/1/196 Vol. 1, Burglaries, Oshogbo District.
32. N.A.I. Oyo Prof 1/1175, Burglaries in Oyo Province: Reports on.
33. N.A.I. Abe Prof 1/ 2nd. Acc. Rex vs. Yaya Sokoto & Seven Others Charge: Armed Robbery contra.
34. Abner Cohen, *Custom and Politics in Urban Africa: A Study of Hausa Migrants in Yoruba Towns* (London: Routledge and Kegan Paul, 1969) pp. 103–07.
35. *Ibid*, p. 107.
36. N.A.I. Ab Prof /342 D. O. Egba Div. to Resident, Abeokuta, 4 December 1933.
37. N.A.I. Ab Prof 2/ABO 342/1 Captain Scot's report on robbery, 1930.
38. Cpt. Scot's report on robbery, 1930.
39. See, for instance: N.A.I., C.S.O. 26–21351/S.88 Burglary at the Onitsha Forestry Office; C.S.0.26–21351/S.167, Ikot Ekan Government School Store-Burglary At; C.S.O. 26/21351/S.169 Umuahia Government College-Burglary At; and War Prof 3/10/130/28 Burglary at Ase.
40. N.A.I. C.S.O. 26/19/9/N.3027/1921; and Ije Prof. 1/925, Pick Pockets Raiding Markets.
41. N.A.I. Ije Prof 4/J.458.
42. Captain Scott's report on robbery.
43. N.A.I. Kuku Div./K.D.1401, Burglary.
44. N.A.I. Oyo Prof 1/1175, Burglaries in Oyo Province: Reports on; see reports for the 1930s and 1940s.
45. See, for instance, Abe Prof/342 Chief of Maun and others to the D.O. Ilaro.
46. N.A.I. Abe Prof 2/ABP 342/1; Senior Commissioner of Police, Western Area, Lagos to the Resident, Abeokuta Province, 1 March 1930.
47. See, for instance, N.A.I. Abe Prof/342, Jackson to Resident Abeokuta, 22 June 1933.
48. N.A.I. Abe Prof /342; D.O. Ilaro to Resident, Abeokuta, 19 June 1930.
49. In the case of Egbado in the 1930s, a woman was caught for receiving stolen cloth and was fined for 5 pounds.
50. N.A.I. Ab Prof/ 342 D.O. Ilaro to Resident Abeokuta, 15 Jan 1936.
51. N.A.I. Abe Prof/2/ABP 342/1,D.O.Ilaro to Resident, Abeokuta, 15 March 1930.
52. For similar cases see N.A.I. C.S.0.26–21351/S.173 Government School, Owerri, Burglary At.

53. N.A.I., Abe Prof /342 D.O. to Resident, 19 June 1933.
54. N.A.I., Abe Prof 2/ABP 342/1; Senior Commissioner of Police, 17 March 1930.
55. N.A.I. Abe Prof 2/ABP 342/1; Assistant Commissioner of Police, Ilaro to the Resident, Abeokuta Province, 24 March 1930.
56. Abe Prof /342 Ag. D.O. to the Olu of Ilaro, 8 January 1945.
57. N.A.I Ab Prof/342; Bale of Maun and thirty others to D.O. Ilaro 29 August 1954.
58. See, for instance, N.A.I. Ugheli Dist. 1/322, Rex vs. Ogunade and two others involved in burglary.
59. See for instance, N.A.I. Ije Prof 4/J.459.
60. N.A.I. Oshun Div. 1/1/196 Vol. l; A.D.O. Oshogbo to the Ataoja, 12 May 1926.
61. *Ibid*, D.O. Oshogbo to the Timi of Ede, 31 Dec. 1926.
62. *Ibid*, D.O. Oshogbo to Resident, Oyo Prov. 22 July 1930.
63. N.A.I. Abe Prof 2/ABP 342/1; Captain Scot's report on robbers in Ilaro, 1930.
64. N.A.I. Ije Prof 4/J.459 Rex vs. Imoru of Ilorin charged with burglary.
65. For examples, among others, see N.A.I. C.S.O. 19/7–N/871/1919 and War Prof. 3/10 Burglary at Ase.
66. See, for instance, N.A.I. Iba. Div.l/l, Robbers-Ibadan Div. in re.
67. N.A.I. Ben Prof.l/B.P. 2982, Armed Burglars in Benin; From the Admin. Secretary, Benin Native Administration to the Resident, Benin Prov., the Senior D.O. Benin, the Senior Supt. of Police, Benin, 15 Jan. 1953.
68. *Ibid*, Ag. Resident to Secretary, Western Region, Ibadan, 18 Jan. 1953.
69. *Ibid*.
70. *Ibid*, report of the meeting with chiefs.
71. *Ibid*, From Upper Oghene Osa street Ward to the N.A. Feb. 1953.
72. *Ibid*, From Otu-Emwanta to the Resident, Benin February 1953.
73. *Ibid*, Resident to the Senior D.O. February 1953.
74. Abe. Prof/342, D.O. to Resident 19 June 1933.
75. See, for instance, Abner Cohen, Custom and Politics, p. 112.
76. N.A.I. Ab Prof 2/ABP 342222/1; D.O. Ilaro Division to the Resident, Abeokuta, April 1930.
77. N.A.I. Oyo Prof. 1/1175; D.O. Oshogbo to Senior Resident, Ibadan 24 January 1931.
78. N.A.I. Kuku Div./K.D. 1401, Burglary.
79. N.A.I. Ab Prof 342; Senior D.O. Egbado to the Resident, 9 May 1954.
80. See the interesting case of one Ilari, regarded by the Ado police as an informant until he was discovered to be a thief himself; N.A.I. Abe Prof 2/ABP 342/1;D.O.Ilaro to the Senior Resident, Abeokuta, 4 May 1932.
81. N.A.I. Ije Prof 4/J.458.See also Oyo Prof. 1/2971 Arrest of four Native Admin. Constables at Ilesa.
82. N.A.I. Kuku Div. 2/K.D.1401 Burglary; From N.C.O. i/c Police to D.O. Kukuruku, 15 January 1951.
83. N.A.I. Ben Prof. l/B.P.2982, Armed Burglars in Benin; From Otu-Emwanta to the Resident, 1 March 1954.
84. Cpt Scot's report on robbers, 1930. See also N.A.I., Oyo Div. 1/1, Escaped Prisoners.
85. N.A.I. Ije Prof 4/J.458 Rex vs. David Oloyede.
86. See, for instance, the case of Ata, arrested at Ogbomoso in 1926 in N.A.I. Osun Div. 1/1/196 Vol. 1.; and Ije Prof.4/J.474, Rex vs. Folabi, Olayemi charged with receiving stolen goods.

10

Money and Criminality: Counterfeiting

Yet another short-cut to making money is to engage in its private manufacturing. In 1937, the British colonial government became alarmed over the high rate of currency counterfeiting and the ease with which such illegal money circulated all over Nigeria. In that year, over two thousand counterfeit coins were discovered in the Oyo province alone.[1] Not only was counterfeit money spent in the local markets, it was also used for many official transactions in the payment of taxes, licenses, market levies, court fees, fines, and so on. Several major banks made monthly reports and returns that indicated that they frequently received forged coins and notes in error. So serious was the situation that the District Officers (D.O.) and many local chiefs began to call for greater punishment for offenders.

Before this alarm, many cases had previously been reported in different parts of the country and a number of people were actually serving prison terms for currency forgery.[2] Early in the 1920s, the colonial secretariat in Lagos instructed all its political officers in the districts and provinces to cooperate with the police in the apprehension of counterfeiters and to punish those arrested in a most severe manner.[3] In 1935, the Secretary of the Southern Provinces based at Enugu had to write to all the Residents to find the means to stamp out counterfeiting. As if anticipating the trouble of 1937, he reported that

> the quantity of counterfeit coins in circulation has increased of late to an extent and with a rapidity which is producing a difficult situation.... Evilly disposed persons have discovered simple means of making passable representations of current legal coins and are circulating large sums of counterfeit coin and now selling the secret of its manufacture to people in other parts of the country.[4]

Almost everywhere, political officers began to consider measures to prevent the circulation of forged money. After the 1937 panic, many more reports were made, and fresh arrests were reported, but forgers continued to thrive, perfecting their illegal businesses. The Regional Treasurer based at Ibadan complained in 1950 that the paper money was too easy to forge and he recommended a change.[5] The secretariat in Lagos agreed with this complaint:

> Forgeries of existing notes are improving in design and some very realistic specimen have recently come into possession of the police and the currency officer. Furthermore, they are increasing in numbers and it is not unlikely that something like 10,000 a year are being put into circulation of forged notes which will tend to find their way into backward areas.[6]

Currency counterfeiting was one crime that the colonial authorities could not stamp out, although they were probably able to control its negative impact on the monetary system as a whole. After colonial rule, currency forgery became even more endemic, partly necessitating the change of the Nigerian currency once in the 1960s, twice in the 1970s, and once in the 1980s when no one knew the amount of money in circulation.[7] With the high inflation rates of the 1980s, coin money lost its monetary value altogether, and became more useful for making decorative ornaments.[8] This was also a period of rapid changes, mainly associated with the colonial impact: new currency, transport system, an influx of aliens from Europe and Asia, establishment of a modern bureaucracy, judiciary, police, army, prisons, and so on.[9]

This chapter sets out to explore currency forgery—hitherto a neglected topic—as yet another aspect of the problems of new money in colonial Nigeria. The data is drawn from the southwest, comprising eight provinces, namely, the Colony, Abeokuta, Benin, Ibadan, Oyo, Ijebu, Ondo, and Warri, all areas noted for their intense agricultural production, commercial exchange, high rate of urbanization, and rural-urban migration.

While there can be no doubt that the introduction of British currency and the monetization of society were part of the profound colonial changes,[10] studies on money remain weak on the implications of the transition from an indigenous currency to a colonial one. Some of the problems of transition and adjustments can only be outlined here. At every turn in the introduction of any new currency, there was always the trouble of reception and conversion so that the people would not feel cheated; at the same time confidence grew in the new system.[11] There was never an equitable way of converting the precolonial currency of the cowry to the new money or of rewarding those who suffered from the depreciation of the new currency.[12] Paying and renegotiating debts arranged during the nineteenth century with the cowry became a source of tension, as many fought over exchange rates while some others insisted that they would repay with the old money whose value was being quickly eroded. When nickel coinage (one-tenth of a penny) reached many areas in the 1920s, rather than keeping to the rate of twelve nickel pence for one alloy shilling, many received ten in the open markets.[13] The new money could be scarce, as was the case of nickel in the late 1920s, pressuring people to withhold their goods or to sell at lower prices.[14] It could be too large to service the majority of routine domestic transactions, as in the case of large denomination coins and paper money that were less useful in buying smaller items. Even as late as the 1950s, nickel tenths were still in high demand to facilitate purchases of smaller household items.[15]

The new currency of paper money and metal coins (silver, bronze) made counterfeiting possible.[16] No one could forge the cowry, the precolonial currency.[17] Although several means were used to acquire money in precolonial societies—rituals and charms to "invent" money, stealing, the use of power by chiefs to exact tributes, fines, war booty, and the like[18]—counterfeiting was not a possible option. With coins and paper money, the possibility of forgery was opened. From the point of view of many indigenous people, there was little respect for the new colonial currency in the early years. Many were to deride the paper money as *takada*, an Hausa word for paper, turned around to mean worthlessness, and the coins, as *owo pelebe* ("flat money") or *owo were* ("small change").[19] They eventually succeeded in becoming legal tender partly because the colonial government was able to devise the means to circulate the new currencies through the established channels of the cowries[20] and partly because economic factors favored such a circulation.[21] Another reason for their acceptance, which owed to the indigenous population, was the transfer of values and characteristics previously associated with cowries.[22]

There was, however, one problem. To many people, it would appear that it was easier to obtain the new money than the cowry. Chroniclers and oral sources talk of young people with access to money, spending it with ease on clothes, drinks, and women.[23] These sources are right on one point: the introduction of wage labor enabled those with jobs to have access to the new money and to cultivate a taste for western products. Usually young and/or educated, they were noticeable. Their new lifestyles and tastes also added to their high visibility. While many understood how they acquired the money, there were also those who believed that they too could have access through other means. Older techniques of "making money" were resorted to, but we have no way of knowing whether these were successful or not. Newer techniques were sought, and counterfeiting became one method. After all, the new money was "just paper or small metals"[24] that looked as if they could be duplicated. Indeed, they were duplicated, initially as toys, with any available object.[25] Perhaps beginning as a joke, rumors, too, began to spread that blacksmiths and goldsmiths could make the money,[26] and it was no coincidence that many of the initial suspects in forgery were smiths. The jokes pointed either to the possibility of making money or early attempts by some to duplicate the new currency.

There was another source of information on forgery. In trying to prevent counterfeiting, the colonial government included information on it as part of its propaganda to advertise the new currency and encourage its use. Specimens were distributed, and people warned were to be on the look out for fakes. This propaganda was like providing ideas to crooks. The press and some educated people talked about forgery, too, with a few references to similar occurrences in Britain.[27] The point is that some people knew that the new money could be forged.

There was a third source, derived from oral documentation. Most informants were quick to allege that counterfeiting was brought to Nigeria by the Lebanese and Indians.[28] As to the validity of this, we can never be certain. The British administrators, however, exonerated this group of aliens from the crime, attributing everything to "Africans of criminal disposition."[29] However, it was difficult to find any informant who did not believe that Asian traders were counterfeiters. Perhaps this belief was just part of the general one which associated Asians with sharp practices, or it could be a reflection of their resentment by their Nigerian rivals.[30]

Currency forgery was not an isolated case. Nor was it restricted to one corner of the southwest, without the bad money reaching other places. From 1918 when the first report was made up till the end of colonial rule currency forgery persisted. What is difficult to determine is the amount of forged money in circulation. Nor is its impact on the economy possible to measure. Tables 1 to 4 provide data on places where counterfeits were found and some cases of prosecution. However, these tables must be read with some caution. They are incomplete: they only report cases that were discovered and do not indicate the total amount or people involved. As the D.O. of Ife/Ilesa explained in 1935, every arrest and conviction depended more on good fortune,

TABLE 1
Counterfeit Reports by some Banks

Province/Date	Sum reported £. s. d.
Ijebu Province, 1926	£78. 6s.
Lagos Colony, 1929	£111. 2s.
Ibadan	
July-September, 1937 (3 banks)	£141. 11s.
Barclays Bank in:	
October, 1937	£6. 18s. 6d.
November, 1937	£27. 8s. 9d
December, 1937	£35. 14s. 7d.
	(2881 pieces)
January, 1938	£31. 6s. 6d.
February, 1938	£102. 15s. 7d.
March, 1938	£23. 1s. 6d.
Bank of British West Africa in:	(1405 pieces)
October, 1937	£11. 1s. 6d.
November, 1937	£12. 5s. 6d.
December, 1937	£11. 9s. 9d.
	1862 pieces
January, 1938	£16. 8s. 9d.
February, 1938	£14. 0s. 5d.
March, 1938	£212
Banks, Oyo Province, 1941	(699 pieces)
Banks, Ibadan, 1948	£300. 1s. 2d.
Banks, Lagos, 1954	£287. 11s
Banks, Ijebu-Ode, 1959	£87

Source: Ije Prof 4/J 433, Vol. 1; Oyo Prof 1/1592, Vol. II, Counterfeit Coinage: Correspondence Re.; *Annual Reports*, various years.

than on excellent police detective work, and it should therefore be presumed that for every case discovered by accident, there were many others which would never come to light. The Assistant Superintendent of Police in Lagos made a similar statement in 1937, saying that the "percentage of cases detected must be small when compared to those actually committed."[31] As limited as the tables are, they do offer useful data for analysis, for they reveal the extent to which forged money was used in transactions: they were found in courts, banks, markets, and the like. The use of forged money was not particularly an urban problem. As the tables show, small towns and villages also reported the existence

TABLE 2
Counterfeit Reports in Towns and Divisions

Towns/Divisions	Amount involved
Ijebu-Igbo, 1923	"too many, serious proportion"
Osogbo, 1925	£17. 17/–
Ibadan, 1926	£2. 7
Ilegbo, 1926	11 pieces of counterfeit silvers
Iseyin, 1926	£8. 18. 6/–
Ijebu-Ode, 1933	Many three pence coins
Ijebu Province, 1933	100 shillings
Ijebu Ode, 1933	£5
Ijebu-Ode, 1934	69 shillings
Ijebu-Ode, 1934	£4. 10/–
Ijebu-Ode, 1934	£27. 12. 1
Ijebu-Ode, 1934	40/–
Ijebu-Ode, 1935	£2. 17. 6
Itele, 1934	258/–
Ile-Ife, 1935	£5
Okitipupa, 1935	"prevalent"
Ibadan, 1935	1/– in every £100 bank deposit "very considerable amount"
Osogbo, 1935	30/– per £1000 of tax collection
Ilesa, 1936	£7
Osogbo, 1936	8 pieces of 14/–
Osogbo-Ilesa road	39 pieces worth 33/–
Ibadan, 1936	6d in every £100
Iwo, 1936	1/– per every £100
Oyo, 1936	"considerable quantity"
Ijebu-Ode, 1937	21/–
Ijebu-Ode	£1. 1/–
Bere Court 1, December, 1937	41 shillings
Ilesa township, 1937	£2
Ile-Ife township, 1937	£7. 17/–
Ede, 1937	£5. 6/–
Iwo, 1937	"several shillings"
Ibadan, 1937	£135
Iseyin 1937	£2. 7. 6 and "a complete counterfeit apparatus"
Saki, 1937	£13. 7. 0
Ibadan Division, June 1937	31 florins, 758 shillings, 59 sixpence and 2 three pence
Oyo province	"more than 2,000 coins of different denominations"
Ijaye, 1937	2 pieces

TABLE 2 (continued)

Towns/Divisions	Amount involved
Iresa 1937	13 pieces
Gbongan, 1937	20 pieces
Odeomu, 1937	21 pieces
Ogbomoso, 1937	32 pieces
Iwo, 1937	76 pieces
Igboora, 1937	4 pieces
Tribute, Ibadan, 1937	277 pieces
Tribute, Ibadan, 1938	66 pieces
Ogbomoso, 1938	15 pieces
Odeomu, 1938	10 pieces
Gbongan, 1938	5 pieces
Iresa, 1938	5 pieces
Ibadan Division, March 1938:	
Ago-Owu	11 pieces
Ikire	16 pieces
Okuku	19 pieces
Inisha	23 pieces
Iwo	14 pieces
Oyan	15 pieces
Barclays Bank	3145 pieces
B.B.W.A.	974 pieces
Ibadan	£2.15.0
Warri Province, 1940	"too many"
Ondo Division, 1940	17 pieces
Ijebu	74 pieces
Oyo Division, 1945	19 pieces
Ibadan, 1947	65 pieces
Ijebu-Ode, 1947	27 pieces
Lagos, 1951	£34
Ijebu, 1951	128 pieces
Oyo Province, 1953	389 pieces
Ondo, 1954	7 pieces
Lagos, 1954	188 pieces
Benin Province, 1954	"a lot"
Ife-Ijesa, 1955	23 pieces
Ekiti, 1956	88 pieces
Lagos Colony, 1957	"just too many"
Oyo Province, 1958	"thousands of pieces"

Source: Ije Prof 4/J 433, Vol. 1; and Oyo Prof 1/1592, Vol. II, Counterfeit Coinage: Correspondence Re.; *Annual Reports*, various years.

TABLE 3
Reports Filed by Native Courts, Ibadan Division, 1937 and 1938

Name of Court	Number of counterfeit coins tendered	
	1937*	1938**
Bere I	35	–
Bere II	30	–
Licensing Clerk	6	–
Ojaba	37	12
N.A. Treasury	28	8
Okuku	23	11
Inisha	8	4
Igbajo	6	–
Iressi	9	5
Ada	18	10
Iragbiji	34	17
Ede	20	–
Lanlate	8	–
Eruwa	10	7
Oyan	13	–
Ejigbo	4	10
Lalupon	17	–
Lagun	4	–
Ago-Owu	–	–
Ikire	–	–
Ire	–	–
Otan	–	–
Apomu	–	–
Erin	–	–
Ifon	–	–
Ilobu	–	–
Iroko	–	–
Igangan	–	–

Source: Iba Div 1/1/1557; Oyo Prof 1/1592, Vol. II.

Notes: * July-December, 1937
** January-March, 1938

TABLE 4
Prosecution Statistics in Six Provinces

Province/Date	Number of cases
Ijebu Province:	
1921	17
1935	23
1941	37
1946	26
1950	27
1956	31
Warri Province:	
1937	19
1956	38
Abeokuta Province:	
1928	12
1944	21
Oyo Province:	
1925	42
1926	51
1936	67
1937	34
1938	39
1942	64
1954	21
1956	43
1958	67
Benin Province:	
1932	20
1946	12
Ondo Province:	
1937	11
1952	23

Source: Oyo Prof 2/3/C.23; *Annual Reports*, various years and provinces.

of counterfeits. Coins were forged more than notes because they were more common in local transactions. Notes were not introduced until 1928, and they circulated more in high level transactions.[32] The government released more coins than notes. Paper money increased in circulation in the 1940s, and became more common in the 1950s. Of the £66 million in circulation in 1950, paper money was less than half of this. The tables indicate the difficulty of detection. More than two-thirds of forged money that was discovered had already been used in one transaction or another. For instance, most of the reports made were after transactions had been concluded, and without being able to pin down the person who was responsible for manufacturing the money or putting it into circulation. One last point: there is no correlation between the performance of the economy (e.g., growth, depression, expansion, etc.) and counterfeiting.

"Making Money Without Sweat": Motivations and Methods

If colonial currencies were amenable to forgery, certain aspects of indigenous attitudes about money enabled the practice to flourish.[33] There had always been a belief that one could cut corners to make money through the use and abuse of power, corruption, war booty, or the possession of powerful charms to conjure money. At the root of counterfeiting was this belief that work, especially hard work, could be circumvented in the search for money. "If hard work brings money," goes a popular proverb, "all the Hausa in Sabo would have become rich." Sabo (or Sabongeri) is the strangers' quarters in southwestern towns and cities where the Hausa from northern Nigeria resided. The Hausa were famed for their industriousness, energy, and perseverance. They were relied upon to supply labor for all sorts of purposes, sell water in large buckets and firewood in large quantity, and work as night guards. Yet they remained poor, as evidenced by their untidy appearances in many urban centers and a lifestyle that showed little appreciation for material acquisition. Hard work and poverty need not be companions, although the Hausa of Sabo would appear to have combined them, in the thinking of many Yoruba urban dwellers. How best could one avoid this combination? That is, how could one avoid becoming like one of the "poor Hausa of Sabo"? The answer was *ise kekere, owo nla*, that is, "little work, big money." In other words, a possible route to wealth was to work smart. Minimal, smart work could be rewarded in one of two ways. The first would be to receive the blessing of God or the gods, a view that has persisted to this very day, and is now deeply ingrained in both Islamic and Christian perceptions of wealth. Waiting for God's blessings could take time, thus opening the window to the second way: "work smart, not hard!"

Counterfeiters were engaged in such smart work. Money production was not described as idle. One suspect told the police in 1935: "*Ise ni mo nse, mi ki se ole. Ise lile ni ise wa*" (translation: "I work for a living, I am not a thief. This is hard work.")

Contrasting counterfeiting with theft is both interesting and revealing. Counterfeiters never saw themselves as thieves. The public, too, did not see them as such. The most common thing was to reject counterfeits and the very worst was to call the authority to arrest the couriers. As to whether it was a crime, many of course were aware of the position of the government. Suspects tried to avoid arrest, and one jumped out of a moving lorry in 1937 in order to escape.[34] However, it was a different matter as to whether counterfeiters believed that their work should be criminalized. Their activities and "work" were described as "*fi ogbon ori jeun,*" that is, "using one's brain (or cleverness) to survive," and far better than approaching money lenders for loans on high interest or even of pawning oneself. Being clever was not the same thing as being a criminal, went a common rationalization. Once counterfeiters rationalized their activities in such a positive way, they were able to decriminalize it, at least to themselves. Of course, they were aware that the business was risky because they would be jailed when arrested. Consequently, counterfeiting was described by many members of the public as "*ise oran,*" that is, "the occupation of trouble," and its practitioners as "*odaran,*" that is, criminals or "trouble makers." As one informant elegantly put it: "*roworowo aro ijongbon*"—"counterfeiters, the manufacturers of trouble."

The state and counterfeiters did not agree upon the interpretation of the counterfeit business. To the state, counterfeiters were criminals who should be put away in prison. As explained below, the state wanted to protect the economy and the integrity of its currency. To the counterfeiters, they needed not be portrayed as criminals. They disguised their operations not because they were criminals, some would argue, but because they did not want the secret of their operations to leak so that others would flood into it and thus reduce its profitability. "Those who make iron ore at Isundunrin never tell people how they make it"[35] was one remark of a suspect to explain why he made money on his farm instead of in the open, if he knew that he was doing the right thing.

Most counterfeiters did not understand monetary policies. They did not know how their activities could injure the economy or the currency, those issues that worried the government. This ignorance made them critical of the state for criminalizing them. While the public did not support counterfeiters, their view was different from that of the state. To the public, counterfeiters were able to understand the "source" of money, denying others this knowledge, living a better life, and climbing rapidly the social stratification ladder.[36] This position was consistent with the value placed on work and money. Counterfeiters knew how to "work little and make big money," whereas others had to work hard and make little money, like the Hausa of Sabo. Counterfeiters should be arrested and put away, not for the reasons advanced by the state, but to end the career of "lazy, smart people" making money the easy way and thus dampening the morale of hard workers. Many colonial officers were quick to understand how the public was thinking—in their campaign against counterfeiters, they emphasized the same moral point instead of the technical one of the danger of illegal money on the economy.

To turn to the methods employed in making money, documentary evidence is rather poor. The reasons are obvious. The majority of arrests were of those who carried or attempted to spend counterfeits and not those who made them. A good number of leads to homes of suspected currency forgers yielded limited information on how money was manufactured. Few confessed to any knowledge of forgery. From a small reliable pool of data a few points can be made. With respect to paper currency, the most common method was described by the Lagos Secretariat in 1950: "All forgeries so far discovered in Nigeria have been produced by photographic methods and not by engraving."[37]

A few cases of hand-printed notes were discovered in 1924, described as "bad imitations yet not bad enough to deceive the native eye."[38] With respect to coins, arrests were made as early as 1918 in Ijebu Ode. Three years later, it was reported that money was being manufactured in the various small towns and villages of the Ijebu-Ode province.[39] In 1928 at Ilesa, "two moulds were discovered, 1 for the manufacture of 2s. piece; 3 for 1s. pieces and two for 6d. pieces."[40] The arrest of two forgers at Ibadan in 1937 yielded "moulds, unfinished coins, etc." but full descriptions were not provided.[41] Similarly, an arrest was made of three people at Ede in the same year, found with £5. 6s. and "slate fragments, frames, files, bottles, liquid and brass screws," all objects for making money. How these objects were combined was not explained. In 1936, four people were arrested at Ilesa: "various tools and materials used in connection with the making of the coins were hidden in Awe's farm... [and] the actual moulds were also found."[42] A man was also prosecuted in 1936 on the basis of a letter he wrote to a German firm to order "a machine for making money."[43] At Osogbo in the same year, four people were arrested with forged coins, and equipment for making money which comprised wooden moulds, bellows, and cement.[44] A very thin report was made at Ibadan in 1935:

> Most counterfeit coins now in circulation appear to have been milled after they have been cast...a number of goldsmiths in Ibadan used to reproduce the mills which are capable of being used to reproduce the milled edges of coins.[45]

One inference that can be drawn from this is that the equipment for forgery could be made locally, and possibly refined with time and practice, thus increasing the opportunity available to counterfeiters. The best evidence was reported at Ile-Ife in 1936 when four men arrested for counterfeiting led the police and political officers to their "factory." The D.O. reported the use of a "new" mould to make money and he described the methods in the following words:

> It consists of two wood frames, hinged so that they open or close on to each other like an open and shut book, these frames are then filled with fine cement and genuine coins are laid in row on one side and joined by a "gutter," the frame is then closed and when the cement hardens it is opened and the coins removed leaving a double impression on each side of the frame, the frame is filling the various impressions, when cool it is opened and produces a string of quite good counterfeit coins joined by the metal strip which remains in the gutter, the coins are then separated and finished by hand.[46]

To the D.O., this "new" method was so simple that anyone with the knowledge and equipment could manufacture money:

> This "new" mould undoubtedly adds to the prevalence of coining as anyone with a rudimentary knowledge of carpentry and a bag of cement can make them.[47]

Before this discovery, the D.O. had thought that the usual method was to "obtain special impressions in metal," which was more difficult than the cement one. True to his thinking, similar new cement moulds were found later in the same year at Efon in the Ekiti country.

Another method, that of melting, was discovered in 1925. French francs were melted to produce English shillings. In areas close to Dahomey, French coins were accepted as legal tender, and were exchanged in local markets, even in places like Ilaro and Abeokuta. The British administration fought against this,[48] but its importation never ceased, because of their value as currency and for counterfeiting. In the 1920s, the price of alloy francs in Porto Novo was five for an English shilling. The alloy for franc and shilling was identical. A "handsome profit" was made by melting down the French coins and recasting them as shillings, a craft that had developed to perfection among many Ijebu smiths.[49] The demand for francs became so high that Lagos had to consider measures to prohibit its trafficking.

Melting has continued to this day as one way of "legally" profiting from coin money. Whenever the value of earrings, bracelets, and other ornaments are worth more than the coins, coin money became objects to create alternative uses and wealth. For instance in the 1940s, nickel coins were used to replace the more expensive galvanized washers for roofing.[50]

It would appear as if Lagos, Ibadan, and Ijebu towns were the major homes of money manufacturers. Bad money was usually called "Owo Ijebu" ("Ijebu money") to indicate an association of counterfeiting with the Ijebu Yoruba subgroup. The origin of this association is unknown. There are also stereotypes that see the Ijebu as "greedy money makers." The origin of the stereotypes and their relevance to counterfeiting are difficult to interpret, although there is one plausible explanation which links all negative stereotypes to the entrepreneurship of the Ijebu.[51] However, it might be suggested that proximity to the coast and perhaps the sources of money making moulds placed Ijebu counterfeiters at an advantage over those in the hinterland. A good number of those arrested in the hinterland were of Ijebu origin. In 1935, the D.O. of Ife/Ilesa attributed the discovery of equipment for making money in the division to the proximity with the Ijebu who were, according to him, addicted to money making.[52] In the same year, the Resident of Oyo province said that most of the machines and mills for making money belonged to the Ijebu.[53]

However, from official records, centers of money production were many, including all provinces, urban and rural areas. Many of the leads on sources were done in Ibadan and Lagos. Six people confessed in 1937 at Ibadan to making money within the town,[54] while arrests were made at Efon, Ilesa, Oyo, Ile-Ife, Ede, and Iwo, to mention a few prominent places.[55]

For the public, there were additional sources of counterfeit money. Those in eastern Yorubaland credited the Igbo traders from eastern Nigeria with trafficking in forged money.[56] There must have been an East-West traffic in counterfeits. Similar reports were made of counterfeits in the Eastern provinces.[57] However, there must also have been a West-East trafficking, which is to imply that counterfeits circulated over a wider region. The negative attachment of the Igbo to counterfeits can be dismissed as a stereotype. When asked to explain the association, the best the informants could say was that the Igbo people were aggressive, loved money to excess, and too ambitious. Even if these qualities were true (and there is no way to prove them), it does not mean that they were attributes required of counterfeiters. It might well be that counterfeiters and their agents in this part of southwestern Nigeria put the blame on others to divert attention away from themselves.

Official sources indicated strongly that there was probably a traffic in illegal notes in the British colonies of Nigeria, Sierra Leone, and the Gold Coast. In 1927 and 1932, forged West African Currency Board 20s. notes were discovered in the Gold Coast and Sierra Leone respectively. Following upon this, the Board altered the design of the note.[58] Similarly in 1934, forged 100-franc notes were reported in Dahomey, and the Colonial Secretariat in Lagos was worried that this currency would reach Badagri, Ojo, Saki, and other markets frequented by traders from Dahomey.[59] While officials did not discover these forged notes in Nigeria, this is no confirmation that they did not reach the country. There were also rumors in the mid-1930s in the Oyo province that counterfeit coins were being imported from abroad, notably from the United States, but the government was unable to confirm this.[60]

Counterfeit money varied in quality. Some were so perfect that discovering them as bad money was very difficult. The three-penny pieces that were faked in the Ijebu province in the early 1930s were so good that many just accepted them as good money. The Barclays Bank in Ijebu-Ode had to use a microscope on a number of occasions to reach the opinion that some coins were counterfeits. In 1937, the Resident described the three-penny pieces as "marvelously fine"[61] and confessed that it was difficult for the Europeans to detect spurious coins and forged notes, which may be yet another indication of excellent forgery. In 1937 at Osogbo, the G. B. Ollivant Ltd., a private European firm, received "a large amount of counterfeit," all "well made" that it was so difficult to discover them.[62] There were also cases in which good money was taken for counterfeits, suggesting the very difficulty of distinguishing between fake and genuine money.[63] If counterfeits could be perfect imitations, one implication is that the official data on the amount of bad money in circulation was a gross undercounting.

Many counterfeits were bad, just because they were easily discovered: they either could weigh more than the good ones, or something could be wrong with their size, color, or look. "Some counterfeits were so bad that a blind man would know," asserted an informant who said that touching money, instead of looking at them, was the best way to know. According to her, a counterfeit coin was too smooth on the surface and rough on the edges while the note is rather coarse.

It may well be that good and bad counterfeits reflected the machine, the expertise available to the forger, and the materials that were used to create impressions. While good counterfeits spread with ease, the bad ones also entered into circulation. Good or bad forged money circulated very well because it was not always easy to distinguish them from legal ones. Even some government staff admitted to this, when they were interrogated as to why they obtained counterfeits from members of the public.[64]

How illegal money was distributed is also difficult to reconstruct at any great length from official sources, again because colonial officers and the police knew little about it. Six people confessed in 1937 that after making the money they would give it to their women agents to spend in markets in other towns.[65] This official source was corroborated in oral accounts: forgers are believed to fall upon their wives, hawkers, and traders to distribute their bad money.[66] One courier was arrested in 1933, hiding a lot of money, tied in a cloth, under his armpit.[67] Forgers did not have to profit from transactions in goods, since what they needed was legal money. Exchanging their counterfeits for legal money was possible in two ways. One, the women could buy goods for resale, thus collecting good money in the process or they could spend counterfeits of higher denominations in order to receive change in legal currency.[68] Counterfeit money could also be sold to agents or other dealers at half their face value.[69] At Ibadan in 1935, the D.O. reported that preventing the spread of counterfeits was difficult because they were refused if tendered at face value but "the petty traders in the market will, I understand, accept them gladly at a discount of 6d. in the 1s." A frustrated resident was to conclude negatively that if counterfeits could freely circulate at a discount of 50 percent, the government could look for little or no support from the people in its campaign against it.[70]

In a 1921 report written at Ijebu-Ode, an administrative officer discovered that forged money was sold to cattle dealers, who in turn sent them to other dealers in the northern towns of Ilorin and Kano for circulation. The cattle dealers passed through Ibadan on their way to the north. He was able to list the names of seven major dealers in Ijebu-

Ode.[71] This important piece of evidence is corroborated elsewhere. There was a traffic in illegal currency between the southwest and the north, associated with Hausa traders in cattle or those residing in the Sabo quarters. The important study by Abner Cohen has demonstrated that part of the make-up of the Hausa communities in the south was a small group of people who engaged in malpractices, notably stealing.[72] Another study confirmed this conclusion.[73] Stealing, however, was not the only illegal thing. Prostitution, trade in Indian hemp, and distribution of bad money were some others. There was a strong belief in southern Nigeria, supported by some British officers, that there were many villages in the north with people (especially nomads) who did not discriminate between good money and counterfeits. Even when official money had ceased to be legal tender, they still continued to exchange it among themselves. In addition, worn coins were never rejected.

Another common technique of circulating counterfeits was to use them to pay fees and fines demanded by the government. This would probably explain why bad money found its way to tax offices and courts. Two informants alleged that there was a collusion between forgers and public officials who deliberately accepted bad money for a commission.[74]

In 1936, the D.O. of Ife/Ilesa reported a case that offered yet an additional information on how bad money spread.[75] An accused person tendered two bad shillings in an Ilesa market and twenty-two other counterfeit coins were found on him. His story was that he had two friends living near Effon in the Ekiti country who were manufacturers. It was during a visit to his friends that he was offered a partnership if he could pay them a £5 "entrance fee." When the accused expressed his doubts as to the safety of the money, his friends gave him twenty-two newly made coins that he was to take back to Ede where he lived and worked as a shop clerk. He was instructed to bury the money in the ground in order to tone down their new color. The outcome would convince him as to the ease with which counterfeit money could be passed and the economic merit of becoming a partner.

The evidence shows that counterfeiters could recruit new people in order to find a way of circulating their product. But the data reveals more than this. It shows, for instance, how a new recruit could be made. The reference to the collection of £5 "entrance" fee shows another way by which forgers could make additional money. It was not unusual for new recruits into such a practice to pay for membership and information. However, many con men sought out people to deceive by promising that they could offer lessons in money making.[76] As early as 1923, one person was arrested at Abeokuta for telling gullible people that he could convert cardboard discs to coins.[77] Counterfeiters, money doublers, and fake magicians all resorted to the similar trick of selling fake information to make money.

Joy and Trouble

Archival sources are rich on the troubles of currency forgers for the simple reason that they got caught and were punished. We shall discuss the troubles later on. However, official sources do admit that not all counterfeiters could be arrested. Indeed, cases of arrest in the market place and other daily transactions were so limited that it can be concluded that the government itself was unlikely to know the extent of forgery or determine the amount of fake money in circulation. Since not all counterfeiters were arrested, oral sources are correct in saying that many got away with it and made "some good money."

The amount of what they got away with and how this affected their lives is difficult to determine. Official sources are virtually silent on this except in one instance when an agent was able to report that five men were able to make £16 in three days at an approximate cost of £1 12s. 6d.[78] There are two positions derived from information on counterfeiting and individual wealth. One is to exaggerate such gains, and to insinuate that rich or politically successful people derived their money in some dubious ways. Stories abound on fraudulent people, how they spent their money and stashed the excesses away in the new banks or in the ancient way of burying them in pots.[79] That there were rich people, there can be no doubt, but it is difficult to attribute their wealth to counterfeiting. Official sources yielded the names of only six people who probably made fortunes from counterfeiting.[80] When the sources of wealth of someone were unknown, it was common among the Yoruba to seek an explanation either in fraud, charms, or destiny. It was also usual to warn wealth seekers that: "*Isale oro l'egbin,*" that is, "the source of wealth is humiliating," no doubt an indication of the worries, troubles, and challenges that had to be overcome to succeed.

The second position is to diminish the gains made by counterfeiters by saying that the money they acquired was dissipated and they ended up being poor. Again there are too many stories of "from rich-to-rags" people (including counterfeiters). Such stories are often didactic, to comfort the poor or to extol the virtues of hard work. The theme of such stories is a common one: individuals could only profit and prosper for long on the basis of accumulation derived from honest means. When a misfortune befell a rich person, some would enjoin others not to sympathize because they did not know the basis of his wealth.

Without finding many people who would admit to having counterfeited, it is difficult to reconcile these two positions or even attempt a reconstruction of their lives. Perhaps oral sources point to real cases of counterfeiters who were rich for a short duration, but who became poor because they lacked the knowledge to invest or to sustain money production on a continuous basis. Perhaps the big-time counterfeiters were not even Nigerians, and the ones among the Yoruba were small operators with rudimentary techniques that could not transform their lives.

If the success of counterfeiters is difficult to reconstruct, the same is not true of their troubles. Whenever there was a suspicion or discovery, the forger had to go underground. There were cases of those who fled into the bush when questioned on the roadside as to the sources of their bad money, passengers who jumped out of moving vehicles to escape arrest, and people who relocated to other places when they feared that their secrets would leak.[81] Every arrest was accompanied by troubles: they were harassed and tortured by the police; their houses and those of their relatives were searched in broad daylight; they were treated as criminals and locked up in cells; and if prosecution was successful, they were jailed with hard labor. After the jail term, the shame was such that many never returned home, but disappeared somewhere else—usually a big city—where no one would know them or their previous history.

The tragedy of counterfeiting is that many innocent people also suffered. False accusations were made to settle other scores or destroy business rivals. In 1937, one Adeyemo Omolaja of Ojo village was arrested by an Inspector of the Motor Traffic Union for having told another person that he had lots of forged shillings. After a series of searches and interrogation the police found nothing and the High Court discharged him. But Omolaja suffered in the process; he was humiliated, and he lost his money while defending his good name.[82] There was also the case of a man arrested at Ilorin who led the police to Ila Orangun where he falsely accused some people of possessing money machines. Again, although no machine was found, innocent people were dragged into trouble. Letters were written to administrative officers and the police alleged that certain people were manufacturing money and that they should be investigated. While many of these were anonymous, a few were not. One case in point is that written by one Samuel O. Ola of Ibadan against Oni of Sukuru village, who he accused of hiding two persons on his cocoa farm as money makers. Samuel Ola even provided details, as if he himself was an insider to the operation, by alleging that at least £20 a day was manufactured on this farm and cleverly distributed as genuine money.[83] When Oni's farm was searched, nothing incriminating was found, but the man suffered a great humiliation. In a similar case reported at Osu, a man was not only falsely accused, but £5 6s. 6d. counterfeit coins were planted on his farm just to destroy him.[84]

There were cases when informers to the Criminal Investigation Department (C.I.D.) of the Nigerian Police Force misled the police and administrative officers about people. The informers deliberately led the police to innocent people. The D.O. of Ijebu Ode warned the police in 1933 to be careful of informers, and dismissed one agent who had misled him on many occasions. This particular informer had been convicted four times of various offences and he had lied against several people. The D.O. thought that he was interested in money and manipulating the police and detectives by appearing with them to make arrests in order to boost his own ego in the community.[85]

The nightmare for an innocent citizen was to be accused of possessing counterfeit money by the Native Authority Police (NAPF or the Akoda and Olopa in the records). In April 1937, the D.O. of Ilesa made one major report on this:

> Four Akoda, including the Head Akoda, have been arrested on various charges of taking money from people in order not to report coining offences to the District Officer. In some instances, the charges for which "hush" money is alleged to have been accepted seem to have been fabricated by means of "planting" counterfeit coins. In other instances, the offences which have been concealed may have been genuine but either way the Native Administration Akodas appear to have been extorting sums of money ranging from £2 10s. to £20 from various people.[86]

Accusing innocent people of possessing counterfeits or moulds to make money became a clever way by the agents of the state to extort money and abuse their power.

"Prevention and Cure": The Response of the State

The colonial government was clear as to its reaction: currency forgery was bad for the economy and society, and all necessary steps had to be taken to prevent its occurrence or rid the country of counterfeiters. In 1935, the Secretary of Southern Provinces issued a memorandum to outline the dangers of counterfeiting to the administration and society. Many of his points were to be repeated throughout the country:

> Circulation of counterfeit coins is a serious offence against the community. This coin can not be used for payment of tax, court fees, and fines or for the purchase of goods. Its existence leads to people suspecting one another of attempting to pass bad money and to a general lack of confidence in all transactions involving the use of Nigeria coinage.[87]

Officials expressed three main ideas for their opposition. One, counterfeiting was a case of bad money driving away the good. The government admitted from time to time that forgery undermined confidence in good money. The second view, more appealing to the public, was that counterfeiting had a negative impact on work ethic: honest people would be frustrated if the bad ones can thrive. Third, many senior officers regarded the problem as a case of administrative lapse at the lower level of government since the police and District Officers should be able to stamp it out.

In fighting counterfeiting, the state resorted to five interrelated measures. The first one was to use propaganda to discredit forged money, arrest offenders, and stop its circulation. Many statements, circulars, and notices were issued to alert the public and solicit their support. The chiefs and tax collectors were constantly told to be vigilant. In the early 1940s a number of collectors were warned that they stood to lose their pay and allowances if they were careless enough to collect forged money. Propaganda was mounted at grassroots levels to warn people about receiving counterfeits. Political and police officers occasionally attended markets to inform traders of the problems of receiving counterfeits. Proclamations were issued from time to time and read in native courts to alert the public of the "evil" of bad money. In the 1930s, the Chiefs and Council of Ibadan issued public statements on how to deal with the problem, an approach that was adopted in many other places. The local authorities urged the public to take seven steps:

1. If someone offers you a bad coin in payment for any debt or service you must give it back.
2. Call on the nearest person in authority, an Olopa or Akoda, your Bale, your Head of compound or the Elders in the market and show him the bad money.
3. If you are offered more than one bad coin raise an immediate alarm. The person offering the bad coins should be taken at once to the nearest person in authority.
4. All bales, village elders or heads of compounds and others to whom any complaint is made must take possession of the bad money at once and send it to the

nearest Native Court with a report of how it was found and name of the person in whose possession the bad money was found. If any person is found in possession of more than one bad coin that person must be sent to the nearest Native Court to explain how he got the bad money.

5. The Native Court will keep a record of all complaints made to them and it will send the record and all bad coins which are brought to them to the District Officer.
6. Any person, particularly any stranger who is found in possession of more that one bad coin and who cannot give an entirely satisfactory explanation of how he got the bad money must be sent to the District Officers.
7. In no circumstances should any bad money be returned to the person who has tried to use it as good money.[88]

Propaganda was not enough, however, thus necessitating the second measure. Informers were recruited to fish out forgers. Informers could be volunteers or those already persecuted for counterfeiting or any other offence. In most of the cases, informers were wrong about people, as nothing incriminating was found on them. Informers relied on rumors and some of them were men of dubious character.

The third measure was to arrest and punish counterfeiters. Counterfeiting was regarded as an offence of "extreme gravity."[89] To achieve this, occasional raiding expeditions were conducted to suspected areas and households. The targets were coin money manufacturers, followed by those who had access to large amounts of counterfeits. Special anticounterfeiting squads were suggested in the mid-1930s, but this was not approved. Instead, the CID took it upon itself to hunt counterfeiters. In many areas, the responsibility fell on the NAP, but senior officers realized in the 1940s that local policemen were either incompetent or corrupt to deal with the problem. Increasingly, the use of men of the Nigerian Police Force (NPF) became a better alternative. Suggestions were always made to expand the NPF, and move its men to villages and neighborhoods with "money factories." To encourage the police to be active, they were occasionally rewarded with bonuses for detecting counterfeiters. In some rare cases, political officers were able to successfully plant an agent among counterfeiters to learn the trade and effect arrest. For instance in 1935, the D.O. of Ibadan was able to arrest ten manufacturers and a considerable amount of apparatus and counterfeits.[90]

Those caught with forged money were arrested and prosecuted. Records of prosecution are less revealing of the widespread nature of counterfeiting, but do confirm many of the points made above on prevalence. Those prosecuted were usually sentenced to between three months and ten years in prison with hard labor. The criminal code provided for a maximum penalty of imprisonment for life, but this was usually reserved for currency forgers and not just those caught with the money.

A fourth measure relates to the disposal of seized money. All counterfeits discovered by the governments and banks were subsequently destroyed. Without exception, all the cases reported in Tables 1 through 4 were destroyed. In many cases, the counterfeits already had been used for transactions. From time to time, disposal procedures were issued by the Secretariat in Lagos, either as fresh guidelines or reminders to political officers. Until the mid-1940s, banks and local governments were allowed to destroy the coins or dispose of them the way they wanted. After 1940 however, Lagos issued a guideline for all the provinces in order to maintain consistency and ensure that fraudulent people did not recirculate seized money. Four steps were adopted in the disposal of counterfeit money:

1. When a coin which has the appearance of being counterfeit is tendered by a member of the public to any Revenue Collector or Sub-Accountant, it should be withdrawn from the tenderer and, if the accepting officer has no prima facie reason for believing that the utterance was willful, it should be broken or otherwise mutilated and the pieces returned to the tenderer. If there is reason to believe that the tenderer had knowledge that the coin was counterfeit, the Police should be informed and the coin handed over to them for enquiry. If there is any uncertainty as to whether the coin is spurious or not it should be sent to the Treasury, Lagos for a decision by the currency officer. If it is declared genuine the Treasury or Revenue Officer concerned will be authorized to refund the amount to its owner. If it is declared counterfeit it will be retained here for destruction.
2. Whenever a claim for a refund arising out of shortages caused by the presence of counterfeit coin in remittances is put forward, the coins themselves should accompany the claim. If they have been destroyed a certificate to the effect should accompany the claim, but the normal transmitted to the Treasury for examination.
3. Counterfeit coins received in remittances for which no claim against Government is likely to be preferred should be broken or mutilated and then destroyed. Any specially good specimens should be sent to the Treasury for inspection.
4. Any stocks of counterfeit coin now in possession of any Revenue Collector of Sub-Treasury should be sent to the Treasury, Lagos for disposal.[91]

The final step revolved around proposals to change the currency that was easy to forge. Many officers and police suggested in the 1930s and 1940s that any money that was easy to duplicate should be changed, to catch counterfeiters by surprise and throw them out of business. Complicated designs, concave edges, and rare colors were suggested to make duplication difficult. A popular suggestion was to revert to silver coinage, which was more difficult to counterfeit.[92] The trouble with this proposal was that the West African Currency Board had concluded in the 1920s that silver coins were expensive to make and they reduced their profits considerably. Yet another suggestion was to make coins from stainless steel or any base metal that was difficult to obtain locally. Withdrawing older coins without heavy expenses on the government and creating a currency instability in the minds of the public were used to counter such a change. To improve the money and make it more difficult to counterfeit, the corrugated security edge was introduced in 1939. In 1943, brass coins were introduced, with a change of color from previous ones. However, forgers were still able to counterfeit brass and to adjust the edges. One implementation of the proposal to change came in the 1950s, when a recommendation was accepted by the West African Currency Board to introduce new 20s. and 10s. currency notes with improved designs incorporating features that would present greater difficulties for currency forgers. Although crime prevention was not the only reason for the currency change, the anticipation of what forgers would do dominated the discussion and the final shape of the money. The West African Currency Board considered antiforgery proposals from regional treasurers, which included, among others, a design that would adopt a good and large watermark, a thread insertion, and numbers located in corners that could not easily be destroyed by folding. Others were two direct plate printings and two lithographic tint printings on the front of the notes, and the inclusion of a portrait.[93] The new notes introduced in 1953 were much smaller in both length and width than the old notes. The basic colorings of red for the 20s. note and green for the 10s. note were retained though the shades were deeper. A pictorial design was incorporated on the back of the notes, that on the 20s. depicting the cocoa industry while on the 10s. note the groundnut industry was illustrated. The paper was of better quality and the notes embodied a visible "security" line (a strip of metal woven in paper). The watermark was of an elephant's head, the numbers appeared in the top right and bottom left corner, while the Arabic characters indicating the values appeared on the face of the notes instead of the backs.

Limits of State Power

While the government was very active in preventing forgery, its actions were limited by the fact that it was more concerned with transactions that involved payment to its agencies and private banks. There were other reasons that limited the efforts to check the activities of counterfeiters.

One, counterfeiters were always ready to break the law. They could forge new notes and coins, relocate to places that were less policed, and distribute counterfeits to areas where the people were less discerning. The Assistant Commissioner of Police of Oyo Province reported in 1936 that he had a feeling that there was "quite a large number of active counterfeiters whose products, or the greater part of their products, are being circulated in other provinces."[94] He had guessed right: counterfeits moved across the southwest and other parts of Nigeria.

Yet another reason for the failure to put an end to the problem was that the police and lower-ranking officers of the government could take bribes or collude with offenders to ensure their freedom. The N.A. police had too many corrupt men, and a few were also arrested for manufacturing counterfeits or for planting counterfeits in the homes of innocent people in order to arrest and convict them. Administrators admitted that the activities of the N. A. police in detecting and prosecuting counterfeiters were impaired by their corruption, and they were at a loss to find out a fool-proof way of bringing offenders to book.

In some cases where arrests were made, convictions could not be obtained because of shoddy investigation by the police or the inability to provide evidence against the defendants. One interesting illustration of this was the failure to successfully prosecute four people arrested on May 23, 1937 at Osogbo for possessing £6 9s. counterfeit coins and moulds to make money.[95] All the accused were committed for trial in the High Court, in a case that became known as "Rex versus Daniel Ojo and three others." In August, the trial judge ruled and acquitted all the four accused on all counts. To the judge, the preliminary police work was badly handled by the N.A. police. In explaining his decision to the D.O. in a private correspondence, he blamed the police:

> If the accused really were the makers of the counterfeit money it ought (judging by what came out in evidence…) to have been fairly easy to obtain enough admissible and reliable evidence to have proved it indeed with a little cunning and patience it might have been possible to have deluded them and set a trap to catch them (or whoever else it may have been) while actually counterfeiting.[96]

The judgement provided a great insight into police investigation. Unable to do any thorough investigation, the N. A. police assumed that all that was necessary was to get one of the accused to mention the names of others who were then arrested and forced to make a statement that implicated them.

A final limitation was the difficulty of dealing with the N.A. staff and indigenous chiefs who were involved or implicated in the circulation of counterfeits. In such cases, it was always difficult to trace the source of counterfeits and to prosecute. The best example of this occurred at Ijebu Igbo, which generated perhaps the best documented case. On August 24, 1944, the Assistant Superintendent of Police (ASP) of Ijebu-Ode reported to the D.O. that two weeks earlier he received information that some money, put in different bags, was deposited to the Bank by the Ijebu-Igbo N. A. Treasury.[97] In one of these bags, a sum of £3 10s. counterfeit coins in 1s. pieces were discovered. On August 11, he went to the bank to talk to the manager who handed him the counterfeit coins found as part of a bag containing £100 deposited by the N. A. Treasurer. With the permission of the ADO, the ASP sent for the Treasurer, J. O. Banjo. This began a probe into what later turned out to be a case that became public, with all sorts of rumors about government workers, rich people, and the police.

J. O. Banjo did not deny the discovery made by the bank. However, he absolved himself of blame by saying that the particular bag was brought to his office in July 1944 by one Gabriel I. Wemimo, the Tax Clerk of the Oke Sopin quarters in Ijebu-Igbo. Banjo admitted that the money was checked in his presence, placed in the bag and sealed by Wemimo before he (Banjo) placed it in the strong room and that this seal was intact when the money was brought to the bank. When asked whether he tested the coins, he replied that he did not test everything because it was difficult to differentiate genuine money from fake ones, and the testing board was useless. According to him, the bank had a better machine to discover bad coins.

In his own evidence,[98] Wemimo said that he and other tax collectors usually paid tax money every fortnight to the Treasury. According to the procedure, the Treasurer checked the money with each tax clerk. "Sometimes the Treasurer used to test the coins with wood-block prepared for testing counterfeiting coins." He admitted paying a sum of £384 on July 28, 1944, at about the same time with three other clerks. His money was counted by Banjo, who checked everything, found it correct, and ordered it to be placed in bags. Of this amount, Banjo tested £184, all of which he found to be genuine. He was then ordered to seal the bags and initial the labels to complete his own transactions. Wemimo denied any knowledge of knowing how the counterfeit coins got into the bag, asserted that all the money he paid was genuine, and that he used the testing board to determine genuineness during collection. The bank also made its own testimony, written by the bank manager, who confirmed that the bank received the coins, all in one bag checked in his presence.[99] The counterfeits were examined by him and the N.A. Treasurer.

The ASP did not recommend any criminal action against either Banjo or Wemimo because he thought that any prosecution would fail on the following grounds:

> The amount was paid to the N.A. Treasurer since July, 1944.
>
> The N.A. Treasurer, although he did not test the money, was satisfied that they were all genuine coins.
>
> The seal on the bags bore no special mark and was only done with ordinary sealing wax.
>
> The amount was all the time in the possession of the N.A. Treasurer until the 1st August.
>
> The seal was not broken in the presence of the tax collector.

However, the A.S.P. recommended that the NA Treasurer should be asked to refund £3 10s. because he made himself liable in as much as he failed to test the money and ascertain that it was genuine.[100] Before the ASP made this recommendation and the D.O. could act, the N.A. Treasurer had reached his own verdict: Wemimo was guilty. He therefore went ahead to recover the money from Wemimo, and assumed that the case was over.[101]

The Treasurer was mistaken. On September 6, 1944, the D.O. reported the matter to the *Awujale* of Ijebuland, the king in whose area the "trouble" occurred.[102] He suggested that the issue be investigated by the King's Discipline Committee with a recommendation to changing the tax clerk if he was found responsible, and punishing the treasurer, too, in an appropriate manner should he too have had a hand in it.

It was not until October 2 that the Discipline Committee was able to convene. The Committee was comprised high-ranking chiefs; also in attendance was Chief Gbadamosi Kone, the *Otunba* of Oke Sopin, the boss of Wemimo.[103] The Committee started by requesting Chief Kone, responsible for tax collection at Oke Sopin, to describe the collection methods and how tax money was handled. Like everyone else, the Chief attempted to remove himself from the trouble by blaming the tax clerk and attributing his poor supervision to old age and bad eyes.

The Committee's decisions were based on the need to share the blame among all the parties involved and prevent a future occurrence. Tax money was no longer to be kept in the hands of the clerk for too long a time and would henceforth be paid to the subtreasury every Saturday. Wemimo should be dismissed, and Chief Kone should appoint another tax clerk at once. If not, the allowance paid in respect of the clerk should be suspended. Wemimo was found incompetent and guilty because he admitted that not all the money was tested by the treasurer and he made no effort to show that the bag containing the counterfeit coins were not his. The Committee was of the view that the treasurer deserved to be punished for negligence by imposing a fine of 10s. Chief Kone was not spared by the Committee either:

> As he is in the eyes of the authorities and of the law responsible for shortages or spurious coins, we recommend that he should refund £3.10s. to Mr. Wemimo, the tax clerk.

The Discipline Committee was not concerned with finding out how the counterfeit coins made their way to the bag and who could be responsible. Rather, the Committee resorted to the age-old Yoruba way of resolving conflict: apportion blame to all. But the Committee took a step further: it sacrificed Wemimo, the poorest and weakest of all the culprits. Wemimo was, however, not happy with his termination. In a long petition to the Resident of the province, the D.O., and the Awujale, he protested the findings of the Discipline Committee.[104] The D.O. was not impressed, and he dismissed the petition on the ground that Wemimo was not an employee of the N.A. but a personal clerk of Chief Kone.

This counterfeit fraud damaged the relations between Chief Kone and many people in the town who believed that he knew about forged money, and made tax collection difficult for some weeks because the new clerk failed to enjoy the support of many people. The case revealed how difficult it was to trace the source of counterfeit and to even prosecute offenders who denied any charges of wrongdoing. And in spite of petitions to the D.O. by some citizens alleging that Chief Kone and his son knew about counterfeit deals, the government did no investigation perhaps for fear of alienating indigenous chiefs.

Summary

At the beginning of colonial rule, there was much praise for the people of southwestern Nigeria for being law abiding.[105] Crime was seen as very low, and no administrator ever thought or contemplated that these law-abiding subjects would have among them counterfeiters and their willing collaborators. By the end of colonial rule, the picture had changed: the crime rate had increased, and counterfeiting offences were part of a long list of old and new crimes. Colonial rule created counterfeiting crime in two ways: the currency that it introduced was amenable to forgery; and the monetization of society pressured individuals to seek opportunities to enrich themselves in both legal and illegal ways. In dealing with counterfeiting as a crime, the victims included those poor people at the receiving end who did not know how money was manufactured or controlled by the state. As the case of Wemimo, the Tax Clerk of Oke Sopin in Ijebu-Igbo demonstrates, the "small man" might carry the burden of some discoveries. The majority of investigations and convictions affected those who had on them or spent counterfeits and not those who manufactured them. Currency manufacturers were generally smart enough to evade the authorities or to bribe their way out of trouble.

In resorting to the legal system to end counterfeiting, there were some problems. Very few ever confessed to knowing that they possessed counterfeits. In an interesting case in Ijebu-Ode in 1933, a man caught with 100 shillings counterfeits pleaded that he had defective eyesight.[106] The most common alibi was ignorance: that is, that they could not distinguish fake money from real money. Blame could be shifted to others who gave them the money in the course of ordinary transactions. A few denied ever being caught with counterfeits, thereby accusing those who arrested them of deliberate lies. The government itself was less critical of chiefs and senior Nigerian members of the administration even if their behaviour raised suspicion, as in the case of Chief Kone of Oke Sopin. Similar to the Ijebu Igbo case was rampant collection of counterfeits by Iseyin chiefs (near Oyo) in 1938, but again, the "big men" were left unpunished, only warned.[107] Wealthy people or those with regular wage income could justify possession of counterfeits by arguing that their agents or "boys" collected them in their various transactions.[108] To take another example, in spite of many insinuations by Nigerians, Indian and Lebanese traders were never investigated. It may thus be that there was a small core of influential people who were big-time counterfeiters or couriers of bad money who escaped police detective work.

Counterfeiting was not just a comment on colonial law and order. In a sense, it revealed yet another dimension of the pursuit of wealth in a colonial society. The reasons for seeking wealth have been highlighted elsewhere,[109] but in general, many took to legally and culturally approved ways of enriching themselves. However, there were other means that fuelled borrowing at excessive interest rates and which encouraged criminal or dubious activities. Counterfeiting was a quick way of making money; it was risky but profitable, and counterfeiters did not see themselves as thieves. Not all regarded themselves as criminals either; many rejected the position of the state that the circulation of counterfeits was bad both for the economy and the monetary system. With such a positive attitude and the high potentials for profit, counterfeiters were hard to drive out of business.

Notes

1. National Archives, Ibadan (NAI), Iba Div 1/1/1557, Counterfeit Coins, Quarterly Return Of. Except otherwise stated, all archival sources were derived at NAI.
2. See Ije Prof 4/J.433, Vol. I, Counterfeit Coining; Oyo Prof 2/3/C.23, Counterfeiting and offences relating to coin.
3. *Ibid.*
4. Ije Prof 4/J. 433, Vol. I, Counterfeiting.
5. Oyo Prof 1/623, Vol. IV, West African Currency Circulation of.
6. Oyo Prof 1/623 Vol IV, West African Currency Circulation of.
7. For the post-independence cases, see for instance, O. Aboyade and A. A. Ayida, "The War Economy in Perspective," *Nigerian Journal of Economic and Social Studies*, 13,1, 1971; and Tom Forrest, *Politics and Economic Development in Nigeria* (Bouder, CO: Westview, 1992). In spite of the prevalence of forgeries of local and international currencies, prevention laws in Nigeria remain undeveloped and few people have been prosecuted.
8. On the nature of post-colonial change and the value system, see Tunde Lawuyi and Toyin Falola, "The Instability of the Naira and Social Payment Among the Yoruba," *Journal of Asian and African Studies*, XXVII, 3-4, 1992, pp. 216–28.
9. For accounts of these changes, see for instance, R. O. Ekundare, *An Economic History of Nigeria, 1860–1960* (London: Methuen, 1973); and Toyin Falola, ed., *Nigeria and Britain: Exploitation or Development?* (London: Zed, 1987).
10. On the introduction of new money, see chapter 2 in those books. Also, see T. N. Tamuno, *The Evolution of the Nigerian State: the Southern Phase, 1898–1914* (London: Longman, 1972); A. G. Hopkins, "The Currency Revolution in Southern Nigeria in the late 19th century," *Journal of the Historical Society of Nigeria*, 3, 3, 1966, pp. 471–83; G. I. Jones, "Native and Trade Currencies in Southern Nigeria during the Eighteenth and Nineteenth Centuries," *Africa*, Vol. 28, No. 1, January 1958, pp. 43–54; and A. H. M. Kirk-Greene, "The Major Currencies in Nigerian History," *Journal of the Historical Society of Nigeria*, Vol. 2. No. 1, December 1960.
11. See for instance, W. I. Ofonagoro, "From Traditional to British Currency in Southern Nigeria: Analysis of a Currency Revolution, 1880–1948," *Journal of Economic History*, 39, 3, 1979, pp. 623–54.
12. See for instance, S. Johnson, *The History of the Yorubas* (Lagos: C.M.S., 1921) p. 119; *The Lagos Weekly Record*, May 26, 1984; I. B. Akinyele, *Iwe Itan Ibadan* (England: self-printed, 3rd edition, 1950), p. 124.
13. Oyo Prof 1/623 Vol. II, West African Currency Circulation of.
14. *Ibid*; Osun Div 1/2/OS.64, Nickel Coinage and Currency General.

15. Oyo Prof 1/623, Vol. IV, West African Currency Circulation of.
16. Originally, money was imported to Nigeria from the United Kingdom, but a West African Currency Board was created in 1912 to issue money for British West Africa. The Board issued its own money, with different designs. Its silver coins issued in 1913 had a palm tree on the reverse and the British king on the obverse. In 1916, it issued paper notes in units of 10 shillings, 2 shillings, and 1 shilling. The coin denominations were: florins (2 shillings); shillings (1s.); sixpence (6d), and one-tenth penny (issued in 1918/9). For pictures and information on fineness, see Ekpo Eyo, *Nigeria and the Evolution of Money* (Lagos: The Federal Department of Antiquities for the Central Bank of Nigeria, 1979), pp. 94–97.
17. On cowry, see chapter 2 in this book. Also, see the study by M. Johnson and J. Hogendorn, *The Shell Money of the Slave Trade* (Cambridge: CUP, 1986).
18. See for instance, R. R. Law, "Slaves, Trade and Taxes: The Material Basis of Political Power in Pre-colonial West Africa," *Research in Economic Anthropology*, 1, 1978; and Toyin Falola, "Money and informal Credit Institutions in Colonial Western Nigeria" in J. Guyer, ed., *Money Matters* (Heinemann, 1995, forthcoming).
19. Falola, *The Political Economy of a Pre-colonial African State, Ibadan, 1830–1900* (Ile-Ife: University of Ife Press, 1984), p.166; *Lagos Observer*, September 3 and 9, 1887.
20. See for instance, *Lagos Annual Report*, 1899, p. 85; and Iba Prof 3/10, Correspondence Book, Letter No. 103/09, 30 April, 1909.
21. Hopkins, "The Currency Revolution."
22. On these values and characteristics, see Toyin Falola and Tunde Lawuyi, "Not Just a Currency: The Cowry in Nigerian Culture," in D. Henige and T. C. McCaskie, eds., *West African Economic and Social History: Studies in memory of Marion Johnson* (Wisconsin-Madison: African Studies Program, 1990), pp. 29–36.
23. Oral Interviews: Chief Ojo, *Bada* of Saki (90+), Saki, 1991; Chief A. A. Oloko (80+), Ibadan, 1991; and Chief S. Lasebikan (70+), Ede, 1991.
24. Oral Interviews: Oladosu Ajimoke (age 76) Kaduna, 1991.
25. Oral Interviews: Babajide Olawale (74), Zaria, 1991; Omowumi Layode (87), Osogbo,1987.
26. Oral Interviews: Ebenezer Ojo (85+), Lagos, 1991.
27. Since the use of metal currency, counterfeiting had been reported in Britain at various times. See for instance two rare documents, H. Chamberlain, *A Collection of Some Papers Writ Upon Several Occasions Concerning Clipt and Counterfeit Money, and Trade so far as it Relates to the Exportation of Bullion* (London: Printed for Benj. Tooke, 1696); and Joseph Aickin, *The Mysteries of Counterfeiting of the Coin* (London: Printed by William Downing for the author, 1696).
28. Oral Interviews: Ebenezer Ojo; Adenuga Oyekan (80+), Lagos, 1985, 1991.
29. Oyo Prof 1/1592.
30. On Asians and their problems, see Toyin Falola, "Lebanese Traders in Southwestern Nigeria, 1900–1960," *African Affairs*, Vol. 89, October 1990, pp. 523–53.
31. Oyo Prof 1 /1592.
32. On the history of coins and paper money, see for instance, J. B. Loynes, *The West African Currency Board, 1912–1962* (London, 1962).
33. We owe this section of the chapter to information derived from field work, notably from extensive discussions with Chief Ojo, the *Bada* of Saki, a distinguished

local historian; Mr. Laja of Abeokuta, a community leader and former long-distance trader; and Mr. O. Adesanya, a local historian and trader based in Lagos.

34. Oyo Prof 1 /1592.
35. This remark was in reference to the secrecy that surrounded the production of iron ore among the Yoruba.
36. Oral Interviews: M. Adeyemi (75+) June 1990; P. Alabi (80+), June 1990.
37. Oyo Prof 1.1592.
38. Oyo Prof 2/3/C.23.
39. Oyo Prof. 2/3/C.23.
40. Oyo Prof 1/1592, Vol. I.
41. Oyo Prof 1/1592, Vol II, Counterfeit Coinage: Correspondence Re.
42. Oyo Prof 1/1592.
43. *Ibid.*
44. *Ibid.*
45. Oyo Prof 2/3/C.23.
46. Oyo Prof 1/1592.
47. *Ibid.*
48. Oyo Prof 2/3/ C.23.
49. *Ibid.*
50. Oyo Prof 1/C.23 Vol. II, West African Currency Circulation of.
51. E. O. Akeredolu-Ale, "A Sociohistorical study of the Development of Entrepreneurship among the Ijebu of Western Nigeria," *African Studies Review*, XVI, 3, 1983, pp. 347–64.
52. Oyo Prof 1/1592.
53. Oyo Prof 2/3/C.23.
54. *Ibid.*
55. *Ibid.*
56. Oral Interviews: A. Babayemi (83) Owo, 1992; E. Ajibodu (78), Ikare, 1991 June.
57. Oyo Prof 1/1592, Counterfeit Coinage Correspondence Re.
58. Oyo Prof 1/1592.
58. *Ibid.*
60. Oyo Prof 2/3/C.23.
61. Ije Prof 4/J.433 Vol. I.
62. Ije Prof 1/1592.
63. Oyo Prof 1/1592.
64. See for instance, Ije Prof 4/J.433 Vol. II, Counterfeit Coining.
65. *Ibid.*
66. *Ibid.*
67. Ije Prof 4/J433, Vol. I.
68. Oral Interviews: L. Ayinla, Ilobu (63) 1991; Alhaja Ajibike (81) Osogbo, 1992.
69. Oyo Prof 1/1592.
70. Oyo Prof 2/3/C.23.
71. Oyo Prof 2/3/C.23.
72. Abner Cohen, *Custom and Politics in Urban Africa: A Study of Hausa Migrants in Yoruba Towns* (Berkeley: University of California Press, 1969), chaps. 2 and 4.
73. Toyin Falola, "Migrant Settlers in Ife Society, 1830–1960," *The Calabar Historical Journal*, 3,1, 1985, pp. 18–35.
74. Oral Interviews: Taju Owoseni, alias Kabiyesi (82), Ijebu-Igbo, August, 1993; Morunfolu Oni (81) Ijebu-Ode, 1993.
75. Oyo Prof 1/1592.

76. Oral Interviews: Owoseni and Oni.
77. Oyo Prof 2/3/C.23, Counterfeiting and offences relating to coin.
78. Oyo Prof 2/3/C.23.
79. Oral Interviews: Owoseni, Oni and Taiwo Ajadi (69) Moniya, 1993.
80. These are listed in Ije Prof. 4/J. 433.
81. Oral Interviews: Ajadi, Oni; Oyo Prof 1/1592.
82. Oyo Prof 1/1592.
83. *Ibid.*
84. *Ibid.*
85. Ije Prof 4/J.433, Vol. I.
86. Oyo Prof 1/1592.
87. *Ibid.*
88. Oyo Prof 1/1592.
89. Ije Prof 4/J.433 Vol. I.
90. Oyo Prof. 2/3/C.23.
91. *Ibid.*
92. Oyo Prof 1/1592.
93. Oyo Prof 1/623, Vol. IV, West African Currency Circulation of.
94. Oyo Prof 1/1592.
95. Oyo Prof 1/1592.
96. *Ibid.*
97. Ije Prof 4/J.4.433 Vol. II, Counterfeiting Coining. [From Asst. Superintendent of Police Ijebu Ode to District Officer Ijebu Ode 24th August, 1944].
98. Ije Prof 4/J.4.433 Vol. II, Counterfeiting Coining. [From Gabriel I. Wemimo, Tax Clerk, Oke Sopin, Ijebu Igbo to the Asst. Superintendent of Police, Ijebu Ode, 23/8/44].
99. *Ibid.* [From D.L.G. Davies, Bank Manager, Ijebu-Ode to the Asst. Superintendent of Police Ijebu-Ode 12 Aug. 1944].
100. Ije Prof 4/J.4.433 Vol. II, Counterfeiting Coining. [From Asst. Superintendent of Police Ijebu Ode to District Officer Ijebu Ode 24 August, 1944].
101. *Ibid.* [From J. O. Banjo, Treasurer Ijebu-Igbo to the Asst. Superintendent of Police Ijebu-Ode Station, 21/8/44].
102. *Ibid.* [From the District Officer Ijebu-Ode to the Awujale of Ijebuland 6th September, 1944].
103. *Ibid.* [Minutes of Meeting of a Discipline Committee on Banjo (Treasurer, Ijebu-Ode) and Gabriel I. Wemimo (Tax Clerk, Oke Sopin, Ijebu Igbo) 1st August, 1944.
104. *Ibid.* [From Wemimo, G.I. Igboayire Township, Ijebu-Igbo to the Resident, District Office and the Awujale of Ijebuland. 16th October 1944].
105. See for instance, N. A. I., C.S.O. 26/06076, Notes on Customs and Superstitions of the Indigenous (Yoruba) Inhabitants of Oyo Province, by Captain A. Ross, C.M.G., paragraph 247.
106. Ije Prof 4/J433.
107. Oyo Prof 1/1592, Vol. II.
108. *Ibid.*
109. Toyin Falola, "Money and Informal Credit Institutions."

11

Money and Criminality: Corruption

To those who have power and are greedy for money, the abuse of power provided enormous possibilities to make money. The postindependent Nigerian civil service is now discredited largely because of corruption, and reforming it has become part of the general problems of underdevelopment and political instability. The political and military elite that is supposed to supervise and reform it is even worse. While scholarly attention on corruption in Africa is largely concerned with the postindependence period,[1] the root of the contemporary crisis goes back in time to the traditional conception of power, how the colonial civil service profited from a dominant control of authority, and how an emerging elite exploited available opportunities for selfish advantage. By the mid–1940s, so endemic had corruption become in many departments that leading representatives of the government began to express serious concerns about it. Rather than abate, corruption intensified in scale, and after colonial rule it became institutionalized as a legitimate practice. In this pioneer study on a period that is neglected in the literature and drawing data mainly from southwestern Nigeria, we locate the understanding of corruption in the attempts of the colonial civil service to use power for accumulation, how the indigenous power elite continued some age-old practices to legitimize corruption, and how the new educated elite exploited the transfer of power to great advantage. The primary focus is on Nigerians, although a number of British officers were also found guilty of corrupt practices during the same period.

For most of the colonial period, senior British officers and the operators of major commercial houses were fond of complaining about the ethical lapses among the Nigerian members of the public service. In the early years of British rule, there were complaints that emirs in the north and chiefs elsewhere were difficult to trust with money, that guards stole money and fled, and that local clerks were unreliable.[2] Very quickly the administration anticipated corruption, and issued a proclamation on how to deal with it, which was essentially that corrupt officers would have their appointments terminated and go to jail.[3] Detailed accounting and auditing guidelines were also circulated to assist and warn all officers. On many occasions in the 1920s and 1930s, grave doubts were expressed about the integrity of the Nigerian staff. To cite one example, in 1922, the Comptroller of Customs wrote to the Chief Secretary to the Government in Lagos that

> it is desirable to remember that most of the clerical work at the West African customs is done by Africans, many of whom unfortunately have not acquired that sense of responsibility and integrity which is usually found amongst Government Civil Servants. It is undoubtedly a fact that documents of a private and confidential nature, dealing with the intimate details of importers and exporters business cannot with impunity be left in the care and under the control of the West African Customs. As years go on, and the civil service atmosphere and tradition is acquired, this point may become of less importance.[4]

Indigenous chiefs were also accused of taking bribes, in spite of the fact that a number of them were entitled to regular salaries.[5] By the 1940s, senior officers of the colonial administration had come to accept that the civil service was rife with corruption. Many had to swallow their previous words, which had painted a good picture of the service. At the highest level of administration in Lagos, the governor and the secretary expressed the concern in the 1940s that corruption had permeated every branch of the civil service and was undermining the activities of the government.[6] "One of the curses of this country," declared the governor in 1946, was "bribery and until there exists a national conscience which will condemn the practice and an individual one which will neither offer nor accept a bribe, no real progress can be made."[7] Ten years later, the Western regional government noted with alarm the increasing scale of corruption and began to warn all its civil servants that the twin evils of bribery and corruption, unless they were checked, would destroy the structure of society. During the 1940s and 1950s, civil servants, especially the junior ones, were constantly reminded to read the General Orders dealing with corruption in the service. In the 1950s, political corruption was enhanced in status as the most damaging of all evils, and the British officers began to doubt the need for self-government. Just as the European belief of the "primitive Africans" was used to justify the conquest of the continent, so too was the idea of "corrupt Africans" used to argue against the transfer of power to Africans.[8]

Examples of corrupt practice and actions were legion. They can be divided into three major categories, in line with how the colonial government defined corruption. First, there was bribery, which simply involved giving money or goods to obtain a favor. This might be to facilitate service, or to influence the judgment of someone in a position of authority. Confidential information was sold pertaining to such issues as contracts, custom duties, new job openings, and the like. Promises of jobs were made to applicants or job seekers after receiving money from them. Nurses and other hospital staff collected payments for services that should have been freely rendered. Forestry inspectors, after collecting generous bribes, allowed contractors to fell trees either without permits or with forged permits. The administration of justice at the local level was very much affected by bribery. Justice was offered to the highest bidder. Court clerks were notorious for their unscrupulous behavior, and a few were dismissed for corrupt practices.[9] Kings, chiefs, and village elders expected gifts for rendering all forms of services, including those that the government had paid them to do. In October 1952, one Jacob Aina, a member of the public in the Akoko District, wrote to the District Officer (D.O.), to offer a major complaint and plead that the "poor and needy" be saved from corruption. His grammar may be lacking, but his idea is straightforward:

> Akoko has been turned to a corrupt District. Bribe is the motto of the day. Before a woman is allowed to divorce her husband, the head chief of the village would take money not less than £5. Akala[10] of Ikaram would take £7 to £10. The court clerk takes £2.10s., the policeman who serves the summons takes £1.10s. This is how slave trade is once again introduced to Akoko.
>
> There is corruption in engaging people to any office under the Native Administration. As though the counselors pretended to engage by examination, money is the machinery of their engaging people to the N.A. staff. The policemen, before they are engaged, pay £10.10s. The other people in other section with better rates in salary do pay more than the sum of money mentioned. This evil practice should cease. There are many corruption that is reigning in the District, the policemen (N.A.) are very avaricious. When they go to investigate into any matter, they often turn the matter upside down when their palms are greased. It is high time there is investigation sent to find and check the evils that are domesticated both by the Obas and the so-called counselors who take crowns of pride in sharing bribes extorted from the people as booty among themselves.[11]

Similar complaints were made by citizens in different parts of the country.

A second category of corruption was misappropriation, usually of public funds for private end. Many officers collected mileage allowances for trips that they did not make, and overtime allowances when they were not in fact working in their offices. Tax collectors collected money without issuing receipts, treasury clerks embezzled funds, firms and customs officers colluded to avoid the payment of duties, and chiefs refused to render proper accounts on tax and market dues. Studies on the Nigerian financial system strongly indicate that there were losses of public funds attributable to corrupt officials.[12] There was hardly a department that did not report losses of money, from small to large sums, attributed to officers of different categories, experiences, and nationalities. During the 1950s when Nigerians inherited political power and many occupied important positions in the regional bureaucracies, corruption became the fastest means of enriching individuals and political parties. All the major political parties devised the means to cleverly divert public money to party accounts. Notable politicians and civil servants became wealthy by stealing public money. To these people, stealing from the government was a "privilege" granted by access to money and, as a very popular saying put it, "the government does not abhor stealing; it is only the thief who is careless enough to be caught that the law descends heavily upon."

The third category was nepotism, bestowing patronage on the basis of ethnic or subethnic identities. As common as nepotism was, especially in the 1950s with intense regional competition, it was not treated as corruption by the elite. Rather, it was considered a legitimate political practice to reward members of a network, buy support, or ensure loyalty. As many politicians argued in the 1950s, nepotism (justified by ethnicity and regionalism) was part of the development process. When Nigerians began to control many departments, lobbying for positions and promotions and to escape punishments became accepted as a legitimate behavior. Characterized as "long leg," the belief was that connection with the right person could bring any desired results. Connections did work! Patronage was an effective means of survival in the 1950s and beyond, when the number of educated people had substantially increased, jobs were inadequate, and opportunities for mobility had reduced.

The police were the most visible beneficiaries of bribes, because they normally did so openly, were expected to receive bribes by cynical members of the public, and were always uncooperative in investigating allegations of corruption. The Native Authority (NA) police was particularly notorious, turning every case to an opportunity to make money. Prisoners and accused people were allowed to escape after arranging suitable payments, and people even had to bribe officers to ensure the prosecution of offenders.[13] There were a few cases when some towns called for the reposting or removal of policemen who were known to have colluded with thieves and robbers.[14] Operators of commercial vehicles paid regular bribes to avoid checks, carry more passengers than allowed, and obtain their permits on the roadworthiness of their vehicles. When a demand for a bribe was declined, the police could be rough, threatening false charges, lock up, and sometimes searching people's pockets and homes for money.[15]

The Prevalence of Corruption

An effort to explain corruption during the period reveals a number of issues on law and order, power, status, and prestige in a colonial situation. In explaining corruption as an established practice, the government described it as an "African phenomenon," a character problem: "Africans still are inclined to take bribery as a matter of course and at best look on it as a necessary evil."[16] This view probably encouraged the belief that corruption would disappear with some moral preaching by "honest senior officers" and the spread of Western education, with a curriculum stressing integrity and service.

Focussing primarily on "character," as the colonial officers did, does not enable a comprehensive understanding of the causes of corruption. This line of thinking yielded little or nothing on the relationship between the political and economic structures and the activities of individuals. In yet another sense, it took away blame from the colonial state and put it squarely on the citizens. However, it is difficult not to consider the economic and political conditions created by colonialism that promoted the spread of corruption both in its public service and the society at large.

Colonial officers first saw the evidence of corruption in the palaces of chiefs and kings, and in the customary courts presided over by them. There is massive data that chiefs and kings collected "bribes" from those who went to them for all kinds of reasons, including the resolution of conflicts.[17] To these chiefs and kings, the line between bribe and gifts was rather thin. Chiefs expected gifts, as of right or in remuneration for services rendered. In precolonial societies, such gifts were not regarded as "bribes" or corruption, but normal "payments" by the subjects to those in power.[18] Kings and chiefs received no salaries, and relied on gifts, booty, tributes, levies, and such. Also, there was practically no division between the private and the public purse.

Colonial rule provided the conditions for the chiefs and kings to continue to receive "bribes." To start with, those who assisted the British in conquering the country and maintaining their control were rewarded with regular salaries and incorporation to the colonial system. Thus, collaboration paid off. Then, there was the problem of adjustments to new political situations. Before the British administration, the chiefs and kings were the most wealthy and privileged in society, thanks to a good revenue base. Colonial rule undermined or destroyed the indigenous revenue base. Internal wars ceased, tributes ended or were severely cut back, toll gates were closed, and gifts reduced as citizens began to use new agencies created by the colonial governments. The urgent necessity to augment lost income promoted alternative searches, which included the use of power for corruption. To those who received income from the government, the money was never enough to meet their traditional obligations. Very quickly, they learned how to use gifts, whether legitimate or not, to augment their salaries. They also learned that new colonial laws, like those on taxation and legal system, offered ample opportunities to enrich oneself.

After 1918 when the system of Indirect Rule was extended to Yorubaland, the chiefs and kings immediately profited from it, by behaving as "civil servants" and maximizing the opportunities it provided as tax collectors for the government and native court judges. Kings and chiefs became members of Native Authorities (NA), with administrative power over districts. The NA had other related agencies, such as the Native Court, NA Prison, and NA Treasury. More importantly, it had the power to levy direct taxation. By recruiting chiefs as judges for the Native Court, it empowered them and opened the door to illegal revenues. Direct taxation also made money available to pay the chiefs, but equally empowered them as tax collectors. No doubt, Indirect Rule brought power, and the chiefs were quick to exploit this for both legal and illegal revenues. Since the amount of tax collected determined the salaries and emoluments of chiefs, they performed this job well, if only to benefit materially. The chiefs were also able to cheat on revenues, including such malpractice as forcing survivors of dead persons to pay taxes. They also manipulated the power granted by Indirect Rule to justify "irregular exactions," including the collection of death duties, "levied at a most ruinous rate."[19] For the chiefs to maintain their own economic standing, they had to disregard the interests of their own people—they acquired the characteristics of the "distant public service."

The interpretation of gifts as bribery tended to have criminalized the custom, and over time, turned it into a "disease." There were situations in the precolonial setting where gift giving was not negative. During the colonial period, many chiefs continued to receive gifts as before, occasionally getting into trouble with the government. The British authorities turned many cases of gift giving into a moral issue—a corrupt behavior—and effectively used their power to claim the higher ground. One of the earliest cases was in 1904 when a high ranking chief of Ilesa, the *Losi*, was accused of receiving a bribe for adjudicating a case. He was threatened with removal and imprisonment.[20] In the same year, the *Owa*, the king of the city, was accused of taking a bribe. These incidents put the chiefs on a collision course with the government. The Travelling Commissioner, the early colonial officer in charge of the area, was high handed. He called for "drastic measures" to prevent "extortion."[21] To the *Owa* and the other chiefs so accused, this was nothing but false charges, as they received money for services they had rendered or were capable of rendering. In Ilesa and elsewhere, chiefs and judges continued to receive gifts either to give judgement in favor or against.[22] "Wicked chiefs," "corrupt chiefs," and "bad judges" were some of the rather insulting descriptions that members of the public used for chiefs who forced them to give bribes.[23] The *Elese* (king) of Ese, a town near Ogbagi in the Akoko District, was reported to the D.O. for not allowing any person in his town "to do anything without receiving money from him."[24] In the 1950s, such accusations were rather common, and helped to diminish both the relevance of chieftaincy and the reputation of title holders. In one case at Ugheli, the chiefs were accused of not working to the satisfaction of the public, of corrupting the Native Courts, and that "their oppressions [we]re too great."[25] The colonial administration reconciled itself to the fact that indigenous chiefs and judges would receive gifts in kind and cash for favor, thus indirectly telling the public that it would not curtail the practice or even punish those who were reported. Thus, on the one hand, it "criminalized" the practice; yet on the other hand it was unable to put an end to it because both the chiefs and the public either refused to cooperate or interpret their actions as corrupt.

If resistance to colonial rule carried no reward, the lack of access to power created a situation that was no better. Except at the lower level, Nigerians were denied political power until the years of decolonization. Ambitious people had to resort to a variety of alternatives. Many sought the means to participate in the new import-export economy. Some struggled to receive education to gain access to wage labor. Irrespective of the strategy, colonial rule generated creative ways to attain social mobility and power. Not all the means were decent, and not everybody could succeed. Competition tended to have been rather intense for access to power and wealth, creating the need to resort to corruption. Within the cities, the emergence of ethnic unions allowed nepotism to thrive, as individuals manipulated ethnic networks for a variety of opportunities.

Leaving aside the traditional elite, and moving to the civil service, there were more problems. Perhaps the foremost problem, one that official records failed to recognize, was that in popular thinking the new civil service was regarded to be similar in many ways to the indigenous bureaucracy and kingship. The civil servants were the "masters of the public," in people's thinking, and not the "servants of the people," as the British intended. A District Officer was a "king," not an "obedient servant," and his staff were like the palace officials with power and prestige. Even inconsequential persons, like the gardener and the cook, who served white colonial officers, were seen to be important officials, conveniently located in the corridors of power. Members of the public who wanted to see the D.O. had to bribe his staff. The center of political power shifted from the traditional elite to the new colonial bureaucrats and officers. Wealth followed power, as the new elite grew richer than the chiefs and began to make money "far in excess of what all but the most favored of the kings received."[26] This shift in the balance of power, as well as the very conception of power, affected what the civil servants did with their privileges. The police could deny someone his freedom, the clerk could collect tax by force, the sanitary inspector could make a big case out of an unclean kitchen pot. All these were possible because the people believed that these officers had the power and "the right" to do so. Where they had the right and power, they used those to the maximum, and where they did not have both, they manipulated the public belief that they had power for selfish motives.

To the British, their Nigerian officers were expected to serve the interests of the colonial power, discharging their duties honestly in line with the colonial objectives. The administrative guidelines all over the country stressed the public orientation of the service. Civil servants were not expected to receive gratification. As many NA manuals stated, a civil servant would be summarily dismissed if "he corruptly accept[ed] or obtain[ed], or agree[d] to accept or attempt[ed] to obtain from any person, for himself or for any other person, any gift or consideration (other than the emoluments and allowances paid by the council) as an inducement or reward for doing or forbearing to do any act in relation to the council's affairs or business, or for showing or forbearing to show favour or disfavour in relation to the council's affairs or business."[27] The trouble with this and other guidelines is that only a few respected their words.

Except in the propaganda literature, civil servants hardly regarded themselves as "servants" of the public. It was a job that carried power, prestige, status, and attention, all of which were manipulable to receive bribe or attention. Bribery could be direct, as in the case of the police using their power to harass and cheat. It could be indirect, as in the case of postal workers whose services did not require the public from giving bribes, but who devised other means. They could cheat on time, by opening the counters rather late and closing one hour early. They could tamper with mail, to remove money. Or, as in one major complaint, cheat in a crude manner:

> The public is being cheated if a fairly large sum of money is to be used in purchasing postal orders, stamps, etc the clerk will play some fowl means in counting the sum of money, and will confidently argue with the purchaser by saying that the money is incorrect. Sometimes if an illiterate man or woman brings either postal order or money order the clerk will ask the person that how much do you want to claim forgetting that the person is an illiterate and somehow wants to play upon the mistake of the person wishing to claim money.[28]

Power was displayed in a most visible manner. Senior officers were authoritarian and liked to be treated as kings; the junior ones such as clerks and messengers bullied the members of the public.

Many writers have raised the important issue of a lack of commitment to the colonial state both by the public and the civil servants, a condition that highly promoted corruption. In this thinking, the government did not exist for the people; the state was not for its citizens but for the power elite. Those with power and privileges were not promoting any public good or policies to benefit everyone, but themselves. This idea of distancing from the government was the philosophy of the majority of the Nigerian civil servants, clearly expressed in the commonly recited "motto": *a ki sise ijoba laagun*—one does not have to work hard (lit. sweat profusely) for the government. The job was to provide a ready and stable income and offer prestige. While this attitude did not encourage a strong work ethic, it also promoted the idea that individuals could legitimately profit from the government.

There was also the problem of conflict of interest, an issue which the Western region exemplified in the 1950s:

> Suppose for instance that a civil servant owes a lot to a money-lender and that during the course of his duties he has to deal with the money-lender's application

> for a license to sell petrol or to acquire land. Suppose too that the civil servant knows facts which do not support the money-lender's application. Clearly, the applications would be rejected by an impartial official but how can an official be impartial towards a man who can exercise financial pressure on him? Similarly, if a civil servant has considerable shares in a firm, can he be impartial towards the firm's dealings with Government if his impartiality will affect the firm adversely? Obviously he will be strongly tempted to favour the firm in which he has an interest. For equally good reasons a civil servant is not allowed to be an official of any political party or to address public meetings except with the prior approval of the Governor. He must be impartial, he must subordinate his private interests to those of the Government he serves. Like any other citizen he has a vote and may favour a political party but he should not express his opinions openly in public because, if he did and his views are opposed to the policy of the Government he is serving, the public are entitled to ask whether he performs his duty with zeal if it conflicts with his deepest feelings. Such question may well lead to his dismissal.[29]

What the Western regional government failed to add was that civil servants and politicians deliberately created situations that led to "conflict of interests." Given their access to public information, the astute ones were in a position to manipulate policies to great advantage. They knew ahead of time what the government wanted to buy and they set up a business to sell the item or they gave the contract to a relation or trusted friend. Furthermore, the civil servant interested in business knew that the secretariat offered a leading opportunity to reach customers with great buying powers. Retail activities went on in offices, as such items as clothes, foodstuffs, and wrist watches were circulated. The traders could sell to their colleagues on credit and run around to collect their money during the regular pay periods.

Corruption also raises issues of law. New colonial laws and changes were interpreted in ways that promoted corrupt practices. To ensure the success of colonial objectives, many new laws were enacted. Some of these laws went against age-old practices. Thus for instance, someone with a certain kind of tree on his farm could not cut it without permission, or a trader could not cross the international boundaries without paper work. One area where corruption was noted on a wide scale was in divorce, simplified by new colonial laws. Divorce had to be sanctioned in native courts to become legal, thus encouraging judges and court staff to demand heavy bribes from the new husbands. More money would be paid if a man took as wife a woman not properly divorced, as the police became involved and used their power to demand "worriness payment," a crude way of requesting bribe for arresting or bringing someone before the court.[30] Using the police and courts to settle conflicts involving child custody, debt payment and others was to give opportunities to the police and civil servants to enrich themselves.

The administration of justice, in general, was a source of corruption. In the native courts, it became a "legitimate rule" that bribes must be offered to have access to justice and to purchase favorable judgements. Those who wanted to transact any form of business or receive summons had to give bribes to officials. Court clerks received money to assure complainants that cases would be settled in their favor.

To a number of contemporary observers, the need to accumulate wealth and flaunt it was the sole reason for corruption. "Many people wanted the good things of life and did not want to wait for long."[31] The colonial society provided other markers of distinction: education and all the elite occupations associated with it. As important as these were, they provided the successful elite with symbols of wealth. If the traditional elite had engaged in ostentatious living, the new elite also wanted to acquire wealth and use it. The new elite, whether civil servants or politicians, drew their lessons in success and social stratification from traditional sources. The successful person must have a big house in his town, buy good cars, send his children to good schools, establish a business for his wife, be generous with his money, help his relations and friends, and use all occasions to celebrate success, with lavish parties.[32] A good position in government, with access to money, provided the opportunities. People's job preferences clearly showed the connection between positions, corruption and status—the leading departments of choice were those of the police, tax, forestry, produce, and customs simply because they provided enormous opportunities for corruption.

Ethnicity and ethnic conflicts promoted corruption. Colonial rule engendered ethnic politics.[33] Ethnicity in turn enabled corruption to thrive and escalate. After 1945, with the program of transfer of power, Nigerians began to occupy important positions, thus adding political power to the bureaucracy. Political parties emerged, organised largely on ethnic/regional lines. Very quickly, political parties became powerful agencies of corruption. One party accused the other of excesses, thus helping to bring to light many corrupt practices or allegations of corruption. The 1950s was perhaps the most intense period in regional politics. Commitment to one's region and ethnic group became more important than commitment to the nation. Whoever had power or access to those who had it became a useful community resource to their people. Ethnicity allowed civil servants and politicians to obtain positions and support. It enabled ambitious people to circumvent requirements of merit and education to get what they wanted, by demanding quotas. It mediated competition among civil servants and others, as each person tried to manipulate a network to his advantage. Ethnicity allowed the notable representatives of groups to use power to accumulate capital, sometimes pretending to be so doing on behalf of the group. Through projects such as construction of buildings and roads, and many contracts, civil servants, and politicians were able to acquire money illegally. Investments had to be distorted to enable the power elite to engage in fraudulent practices. The NAs became centers of corruption. Politicians struggled to become council members to gain access to public treasuries. Council staff used their offices to embezzle market dues, local tax, and inflate contracts.

When civil servants and politicians were accused of wrongdoing, ethnicity provided a kind of defense: one should not be ridiculed because of what other representatives of other ethnic groups would say, or that the "enemy" (from a different group or town) was magnifying the problem. This was also a period when the civil service began to expand by recruiting Nigerians, and as a consequence generating competition and making use of nepotism and corruption to ensure recruitment. As more civil servants were recruited, so too did corruption increase in scale. No sooner did Nigerians take over that many members of the public began to notice corruption at an unprecedented scale. In 1954, one woman, Adunni Oluwole, formed the Nigerian Commoners Party, partly to complain about corruption among the members of the major political parties and called on the British not to grant independence to the country.[34] She gained an instant fame, and her message resonated well among the rural people who were themselves complaining about heavy taxation.[35]

Political parties became the means to put ethnicity into practice and engage in prebendalism. Ethnicity was manipulated to consolidate political power and rig elections. Patronage became both legitimate and justifiable to reward members and punish opponents and enemies. The post–1945 transfer of power and the regional politics of the 1950s made corruption possible, more accessible and difficult to punish. Relying on the analysis of Colin Leys, Nigeria entered the stage of "new states" with three conditions that could promote corruption:

1. The idea of the national interest is weak because the idea of a nation is new. .To many people the "state" and its organs were identified with alien rule and were proper objects of plunder...
2. The incentive to corrupt whatever official purposes public institutions are agreed to have is especially great in conditions of extreme inequality and poverty. The benefits of holding an office—any office—are relatively enormous; by com-

parison the penalties for attempting to obtain one bribery are fairly modest, in relation to the low standard of living of the would-be office holder, or in relation to the pressure of relatives' claims on his existing standard of living. Generally, corruption seems to be inseparable from great inequality;

3. Corruption is generally easy to conceal in the new states. Partly this is because people are generally not too clear about what the official rules are, or what (really) constitutes breaking them; or if they are clear, it may be because they do not greatly resent their being broken, and so are not zealous to prevent corruption. Partly it is because the law is ineffectively enforced and the police themselves may not be immune from corruption.[36]

Politicians learned to make money in dubious ways. Members of political parties were made directors of government corporations to be able to reward themselves and their associates. The party leader became the distributor of largess, from political appointments to money. He was expected to care for notable party members by giving them money when they requested it,[37] use development projects as rewards,[38] and overlook the misappropriation of funds by party members. Corruption became a means to fund and consolidate political parties. New indigenous banks survived through state patronage, and the banks in turn awarded loans to party members with little or no collateral.[39] An insider recounted the case of the Action Group, in relation to the formation of the Nigerian Investment Company (NIPC), the major regional holding:

> This company was devised as a conduit pipe to siphon government funds to the party coffers. It was a creation of Chief Awolowo when he was first leader of government business, and later the Premier in the Western Region. ...The company was founded by a few party leaders (four members) and large sums of money were made available on loan to the company by the government. These the company used to acquire properties for its real estate business...Government lands, known by then as crown lands, were allocated to the company both in Lagos and Ibadan...This company was to finance the Party. Some funds were paid directly to the company, and the company paid such funds straight into the coffers of the party without deducting a penny...A landed property which was bought for about £50,000 was escalated to £750,000 and sold to the government by the N.I.P.C. in order to pay the party's debt to the National Bank of Nigeria Limited.[40]

Corruption extended to the lower levels of administration. As administrative and constitutional reforms allowed the educated elite and political parties to control the Native Authorities after 1945, they converted the opportunity to a "money machine." Chairs and members of NAs were forced to align with the parties, reward party members, and enrich themselves. While it became public knowledge that local funds were embezzled, some notable cases came into the open. Perhaps, the most celebrated one was the charge of corruption leveled against the notable

Ibadan politician, Alhaji Adegoke Adelabu, in the 1950s. This allegation warranted a major administrative inquiry[41] that led to his downfall as a federal minister. Adelabu, as Chair of the Ibadan City Council, was alleged to have demanded a bribe before offering a job, inflated contracts, and stole money.[42] Similar inquiries during the same period in other councils revealed a series of cases of corruption. The one on the Lagos Council showed how the payment of bribes had become a requirement to obtain any service.[43]

Politicians justified corruption on the demands of their followers for patronage, the need for money to hold on to political power and campaign, and the maintenance of an aristocratic life style. When they were caught, they mobilized their followers to organize protests to save them from the hands of their "detractors." In a system based on clientelism, such a mobilization was never difficult. Ordinary people had come to depend on the civil servants and politicians for favor, and politics at the lower level tended to become the use of clientelism to penetrate centers of political power.[44] To those who have benefited from civil servants and politicians, nepotism was not a corrupt behavior, but the right thing to do by someone who loved his people.

The Anticorruption Crusade

Both the government and some members of the public regarded corruption as a problem demanding a vigorous attack. In some cases officers were sent to trial, and those found guilty ordered to pay a fine or go to jail. From the early years of the colonial administration, the administrative methods to deal with corruption was to establish a board of enquiry, with judicial powers, to investigate and recommend appropriate punishment which could include a refund, loss of job, suspension, and imprisonment.

In the 1950s, a few people presented anticorruption as a crusade to save the country. The strategy of the government was to investigate a case and prosecute an offender. The government began to request punishment, and examined the means to prevent culprits from getting away with crime. The stress was on discipline, and a good administration of justice. In 1947, Lagos decided that judges should stop accepting gifts from chiefs, an hitherto established practice. To avoid offending the chiefs whose gifts were rejected by visiting judges, the Resident was asked to explain the new decision and request the chiefs not to embarrass judges and other officers with gifts that they were bound to refuse.[45]

In June 1950, a few students of the King's College, Lagos, a high school, formed a club known as the League of Bribe Scorners, with the objective never to give or receive bribes for the rest of their lives. The government quickly supported the club and requested branches to be established in provincial and divisional headquarters, with a senior officer as the chairman. Many anticorruption societies sprung up. Rules and regulations declared abhorrence for corruption. Some clubs issued membership cards and asked their members to police one another to ensure that no one collected bribes. One reason for the rise of these clubs was the belief in government circles that the youth could be influenced to shun corruption. "Our best hope for the future," wrote a senior administrator in the 1950s, "lies not in the older generation whose ways often remain rooted in the traditions of the past but in the youth of the country whose minds can be educated to regard public immorality with scorn."[46] In Lagos, the Anti-Bribery and Corruption Society of Nigeria was active in the mid-1950s.[47] The various branches of the league probably achieved little. In one instance, the president of a branch was accused of embezzling membership dues.[48] In a few instances, a league would try to investigate the allegation of corruption against a public officer, but it lacked the power of prosecution. The police also ignored most of the complaints coming from members of the league.

In 1952, the western regional government had to establish a special committee to look into ways of curtailing corruption. The committee never doubted the prevalence of corruption, but only suggested the appointment of an officer to deal with cases as they arose. In 1955, the government established a new post of Anti-Corruption Officer to look at the problem of corruption in the civil service and recommend ways of stamping it out.[49] The Officer would investigate those cases that Heads of Departments would not have time for and those that were not specific enough to invite the intervention of the police. He was to educate the public and government staff on the evils of corruption, and to investigate complaints.[50] The officer went to work immediately. Four anticorruption posters were issued and pasted on the notice boards of different offices.[51] The regional government intensified its anticorruption campaigns, through the activities of the officer and many memoranda to staff. Civil servants were told to work for the good of the public, to be faithful, impartial, diligent, and honest. "It would indeed be tragic," warned one memo, "if you should jeopardise your career, your self-respect and your good name, for some temporary personal gain such as a bribe which can afford you no lasting satisfaction."[52] Whether in the

Western region or elsewhere, the official response was to describe corruption as undesirable because

> those corrupt officials who demand a bribe before they will perform a function which it is their duty to perform are making the public pay twice over for their services. Every adult citizen who pays his tax has paid his share of the revenue which is used to pay the salaries of Government officials. It follows that if the official who has been paid his salary demands extra money from the public for himself he is corrupt and should be reported to the Anti-corruption Officer. It is also clear the citizen who bribes an official instead of reporting him is as much an enemy of civilised society as the corrupt official himself because he is the man who encourages the bribe-taker and who makes it more difficult for the Government to ensure that the tax-paying citizen is served by trustworthy, honest public servants.[53]

Parents and school teachers were to be drafted to preach morality to the youth.

Whether at the federal, regional, or local level, the government campaign yielded limited results. It was a case of too late and too little. There was also no attempt to initiate political reforms to deal with the causes of corruption. A few arrests, all involving officers who stole small sums of money, were made. Few notable politician or senior bureaucrats suffered humiliation or loss of status. Corruption was treated as the disease of the junior civil servants, although the big sums were associated with the senior ones. While many cases were reported, allegations were generally difficult to establish. Only a few cases were successfully investigated and prosecuted in court. There were many cases of investigation. The accused would deny the charges, and the onus was on the person making the allegation to prove the case. In many instances, civil servants would cover one another, refusing to cooperate with the police or investigators. In units where everyone shared in the gains of corruption, accusing one staff members would lead to nothing, as the others would prevent an investigation. A smart person would not keep all the loot to himself or engage in a major fraud without relying on corrupt transactions with others in the same department or related departments. Senior officers were generally covered, staying in their offices to collect their share from the junior ones.[54] When the cases involved the police, it was even more difficult, as members of the public did not always cooperate, for fear that other officers would later victimize them. During the 1950s, when it was fashionable for one political party to accuse the other of corruption, it became even easier to get away with charges. As the party making the allegation was usually the one not in power, accused people would quickly blame it on party rivalry or a political plotting to discredit them, even when the charges were accurate.

The mechanisms to control the general public were rather weak. Other than to preach, there were few effective public policies or sanctions to deal with those who gave bribes. By the 1950s, giving bribes to civil servants and the police had become an entrenched practice. The practical measure that the government could take was to always remind members of the public to request receipts for all the money demanded by any agency and to report civil servants who failed to issue receipts.

It would certainly appear as if the public had an ambivalent attitude to corruption—they were tolerant and critical of all forms of corrupt practices. That members of the public always gave bribes and expected certain favors to which they might not be entitled cannot be denied. It is equally true that the members of the public complained to higher political authorities as the D.O. and Resident about corrupt officers and chiefs. While people in general complained about corruption, and occasionally reported incidents to the government, they would seem to have accepted the practice as the behavior of civil servants and politicians. The public did not appear to resent corrupt officials or organised to demand a civil service based on honesty and integrity. In private discussions, such activities were condemned, but not consistently so in public.

A resolution of whether or not to give bribes was not easy for many individuals. A number of questions had to be posed and answered as a moral dilemma. How could the members of the public organize access to funds and jobs without bribery? It was difficult, unless one had the right connections to help. In what ways should the acquisition of wealth and its display be condemned? Indeed, many wanted to be wealthy and envied the rich, but they would say that one must not be a thief, stealing from others. The trouble is that corruption was not regarded as theft. Indeed, some members of the public contrasted *riba* (corruption) with *ole* (theft), and condemned the latter. How should the public define morality if civil servants were highly regarded politically? This was hard, as the job was associated with privileges. When civil servants deliberately created delays to get things done, how could the members of the public accelerate the pace? This was difficult, unless one had the means to reach other officers who could help. Should the members of the public not provide gifts for chiefs, kings and elders, even in circumstances when they were seeking favor? Many would rather prefer to give gifts or bribes and talk ill of the recipients behind them, to avoid victimization. What about using illegal means to overcome poverty? Poverty was a "disease" that everybody wanted to be cured of. Thus on the one hand, there was a "moral opposition" to corruption, expressed in private discussions and there were many anti-corruption messages, especially to school children. Yet on the other hand, many people would not think twice to offer bribes or gifts to get whatever they wanted. An Owo chief, while reporting another chief who collected bribes, would appear to have captured this ambivalent attitude:

> Bribe receiving may sometimes bring shame when its receiver completely failed to render an assistance or help towards what he has received.[55]

This chief expected bribes to produce results. Whether it could bring shame or not would appear to depend on the status of the recipient. Yet another opinion, expressed in the 1960s but with relevance to the period under consideration, is that the society corrupted the people, by praising, rather than condemning, those whose fame rested on corruption and those with money, irrespective of how they came about it. Excessive hero worship encouraged ambitious individuals to seek all available means to succeed.[56]

Summary

Ridding Nigerian society, including its public service, of corruption has not been achieved since the 1940s. The situation appears to be worse from one year to another. A foundation of moral integrity has not been established either. From studies on postcolonial Africa, it is clear that corruption is widespread and on a scale that is destroying the fabric of society and generating political instability. Both the civil service and the government have lost the trust of the people, as one scandal follows another. The analyses of contemporary corruption have focussed on the problems of politics and poverty in general, the inability of rational rules to take root in new nations, the desire for extravagant living, and the shortage of leaders with strong moral values.[57] Given the pervasiveness of corruption, some analysts are beginning to turn their attention to its so-called positive impact, arguing that perhaps it facilitates access to power, and allows clientelism to function in a situation where credible political alternatives have not emerged.[58] This line of thinking has received a critical condemnation.[59]

While the devastating impact of corruption in the postcolonial society appears to be clear, it is difficult to say the same of the colonial period.[60] For one thing, it was not until the 1950s that Nigerians began to exercise greater political control that enabled an emerging political elite to gain access to state resources. Thanks to the interest of the media and numerous commissions of inquiry, data on the postindependence period is also more massive and readily available than those of the colonial era.

The patterns that emerged during the period can be reiterated. The civil service was the sphere of prestige, affluence, and authority, providing great opportunities for corruption. An entrance to this sphere was desirable, thus instigating the need to compete for it and for ambitious people to do whatever it took to get a place. The freedom and discretion of many civil service jobs offered opportunities for abuse: one could favor members of the network (relations, ethnic members, church members, etc.) at the expense of others. One could also extort, especially the farmers and poor people who needed services. The slow pace of civil service work encouraged members of the public who wanted quick results to bribe. Second, there were sanctions to deal with corrupt officials, although these failed to produce significant results. There is no evidence to suggest that corrupt officials wanted to be caught, or that they were secure about it. This point is in contrast with the postindependent period when corruption becomes "legitimate" and no one has to be polite about it or to explain the sources of his wealth. Third, until regional politicians and top bureaucrats acquired power in the 1950s, the amount involved in corruption was probably low. Many cases involved individuals acting alone, in small cases of fraud, theft, or collection of bribes. In the 1950s, political parties made it possible to build extensive transactions, thus enabling the increase in scale and scope, as many could cooperate for criminal purposes and avoid detection. Those on the right side of politics, with their parties in power, did get away with corrupt practice or, when caught, received only a slap on the wrist. Neither was stolen capital taken out of the country, as happened after 1960. Fourth, the colonial government was able to devise the means to punish those who were proven to have engaged in corruption, by dismissing them from service. Even the powerful politician as Alhaji Adegoke Adelabu was removed as a federal minister because of allegations of malpractice as the Chairman of the Ibadan Council. The device to punish offenders, in spite of its limitations, has not been a feature of postcolonial Nigeria. Finally, there is no evidence that corruption undermined the objectives of the colonial government and its capacity to function. However, the increasing scale of corruption in the

1950s (the last decade of colonial rule) continued after independence, to the point that local and foreign observers became worried.[61] It was one of the factors that led to the fall of the first republic and the emergence of the military in 1966.[62]

Notes

1. See for instance, Colin Leys, "What Is The problem About Corruption?" *The Journal of Modern African Studies*, 3,2, 1965, pp. 215–30; and Herbert H. Werlin, "The Roots of Corruption—the Ghanian Enquiry," *The Journal of Modern African Studies,* 10, 2, 1972, pp. 247–66.
2. For many of these allegations, see for instance, C. L. Temple, *Native Races and their Rulers* (London, 1918); and Robert Hesler, *The British in Northern Nigeria* (London, 1968).
3. *Ibid.* For various references to anticorruption devices, see pp. 36–161.
4. CSO 26/50341, Attempted Bribery of Customs Officer at Degema.
5. CSO 16/6/123.
6. National Archives, Ibadan (NAI) Kuku Div 2/KD 998, Bribery and Corruption, 1946–56.
7. *Ibid.* Circular No. 14/1946.
8. See for instance, Robert L. Tignor, "Political Corruption in Nigeria Before Independence," *Journal of Modern African Studies,* 31, 2, 1993, pp. 175–202.
9. Owo Div 1/865, Bribery and Corruption, 1946–56.
10. The *Akala* is the title of the king of Ikaram.
11. Owo Div 1/865.
12. See for instance, Margery Perham, *Native Administration in Nigeria* (London, 1937); and Walter R. Crocker, *Nigeria. A Critique of British Colonial Administration* (New York: 1971); and a short essay focussing only on British officers by A. A. Lawal, "Anatomy of Corruption in the British Colonial Service in Nigeria," *ODU: A Journal of West African Studies,* 31, January 1987, pp. 92–103.
13. Okiti Div 3/OWC8/1929, Mr. W.E. Mowarin, Sobo Interpreter charged with official corruption, Contra Section 116 of the C.C.
14. Owo Div 1/865.
15. Owo Div 1/865.
16. Owo Div 1/865.
17. See for instance, CSO 16/6/C58/1904, The Ilesa Council convicted the Owa of taking brie from a prisoner committed for trial; and CSO 16/6/C. 162/1904, Report that Chief Loro a member of the Ilesa Council has pleaded guilty to accepting 3 bribes of 5/- each from aina and Jalugbo of Ipetu.; Ije Prof. 4/J.679, J.N.A. vs. Obi Oyesanya: charged bribery (Uishan N.C. Case No. 21/34); and Oyo Prof 1/4310, Bribery & corruption.
18. See for instance, M.G. Smith, "Historical and Cultural Conditions of Political Corruption among the Hausa," *Comparative Studies in Society and History,* January 1964, pp. 164–98.
19. N.A. Fadipe, *The Sociology of the Yoruba*, p. 217.
20. C.S.O. 16/6/123.
21. C.S.O. 16/6/40.
22. See for instance, Owo Div 1/865.
23. Owo Div 1/865.
24. Owo Div 1/865.

25. War Prof 1/W.P. 859, Bribery and Corruption 1946–56.
26. N.A. Fadipe, *The Sociology of the Yoruba* , p. 215.
27. Owo Div 1/865.
28. Owo Div 1/865.
29. Agbor Dist. 1 AG 513, Anti-corruption, 1955.
30. Owo Div 1/865.
31. Oral Interview: A Salako, Ibadan, June 1992.
32. On the nature of Yoruba social stratification and wealth, see for instance, J. S. Eades, *The Yoruba Today* (Cambridge: Cambridge University Press), chap. 7. For an interesting characterization of the behavior of the "big man," see Karin Barber, *I Could Speak Until Tomorrow: Oriki, Women and the Past in a Yoruba Society* (Edinburgh: Edinburgh University Press for the International African Institute), 1991, chap. 6.
33. See for instance, O. Nnoli, *Ethnic Politics in Nigeria* (Enugu: Fourth Dimension, 1978).
34. On the brief career of this party, see Richard L. Sklar, *Nigerian Political Parties: Power in an Emergent African Nation* (Princeton: Princeton University Press, 1963), p. 257.
35. See for instance an eyewitness account of the successful activities of this lady in S. A. Tinubu, *S. L. Akintola: His Politics and His Nation. The Reminiscence of one of his associates* (Ibadan: The African Digest, 1992), p. 34.
36. Leys, "What is the problem about corruption," pp. 224–25.
37. See for instance Tinubu, *S.L. Akintola*, p. 52.
38. *Ibid*, p. 56.
39. P.N.C. Okigbo, *Nigeria's Financial System: Structure and Growth* (London: Longman, 1981), chap. 5. For some cases of banking scandals involving politicians, see Eme O. Awa, *Federal Government in Nigeria* (Berkeley & Los Angeles: University of California Press, 1964); and *Report of the Tribunal appointed to inquire into allegations reflecting on the Official Conduct of the Premier of, and certain persons holding Ministerial and other Public Offices in, the Eastern Region of Nigeria* (London, 1963).
40. Tinubu, *S. L. Akintola,* pp. 78–79.
41. See E. W. J. Nicholson, *Report of the Commission of Enquiry into the Administration of the Ibadan District Council* (Ibadan: Western Region Government, 1956).
42. Kenneth W. J. Post and George D. Jenkins, *The Price of Liberty: Personality and Politics in Colonial Nigeria* (Cambridge: C.U.P., 1973).
43. N.A.I., Storey Report, *Commission of Inquiry into the Administration of Lagos Town Council, 1953* (Lagos, 1954). See also *Report of the Commission of Enquiry into the Working of Port Harcourt Town Council, 1955.*
44. For one case study of the politics of clientelism and how it ensures access to officials and politicians, see Sandra T. Barnes, *Patrons and Power: Creating a Political Community in Metropolitan Lagos* (London: Manchester University Press for the International African Institute, 1986).
45. Kuku Div 2/KD 998, Circular 4541/16 of March 31, 1947.
46. Agbor Dist. 1, AG 513.
47. C.S.O. 26/38322/S.843, Anti Bribery & Corruption Society.
48. War Prof. 1/WP 859, Bribery & Corruption, 1946/56.
49. Okiti Div 1./OK 1922, Bribery and Corruption, 1955/57.
50. *Ibid.* Memo by the Deputy Governor, December, 1955.
51. Oyo Prof 1/4310, Bribery & Corruption.
52. Agbor Dist. 1/AG 513, Anti-corruption, 1955

53. Agbor Dist. 1, AG 513.
54. See for instance a case reported in the Public Works Department Water Works, Auchi, in Kuku Div 2/KD 998.
55. Owo Div. 1/865.
56. Labanji Bolaji, *Anatomy of Corruption in Nigeria* (Ibadan: Daystar, 1970), pp. 30–36.
57. See such studies as Bolaji, *Anatomy;* Robert Williams, *Political Corruption in Africa* (Dorset: Blackmore, 1987); Arnold J. Heidenheimer, Michael Johnston, and Victor T. LeVine, *Political Corruption* (New Brunswick, NJ: Transaction Publishers, 1989); Hyacinthe Sarassoro, *La Corruption des Fonctionnaires en Afrique* (Paris: Economica, 1979); Ken C. Kotecha and Robert W. Adams, *The Corruption of Power: African Politics* (Washington D.C.: University Press of America, 1981); and Shaukat Ali, *Corruption: A Third World Perspective* (Lahore, Pakistan: Aziz, 1985).
58. This line of thinking has been credited to scholars who adopt the "functionalist approach." See for instance, Arnold J. Heidenheimer, *Political Corruption: readings in comparative analysis* (New York, 1970).
59. See for instance, Herbert H. Werlin, "The Roots of Corruption"; and Syed Hussein Alatas, *The Sociology of Corruption. The Nature, Function, Causes and Prevention of Corruption* (Singapore: Donald Moore Press, 1968).
60. One analyst believed that the case of political corruption was exaggerated by the British to portray Nigerian politicians in a bad light. See Tignor, "Political Corruption."
61. See for instance, Ronald Wraith and Edgar Simpkins, *Corruption in Developing Countries* (London, 1963).
62. Corruption was top on the list of the reasons used to justify the coup. See for instance, Toyin Falola, *et al*, *The Military Factor in Nigeria* (New York: Edwin Melen, 1994), chap. 1.

Part 3

Money and the Oil Economy

12

"Time of Plenty": The Oil Boom and Money Supply

From the colonial era, the history and political economy of Yorubaland have largely become subsumed in the general history of Nigeria. This has implications for the development of Yoruba economy: its features and fortunes depended on the character and performance of the Nigerian economy as a whole. It was in this context that Yorubaland, while not an oil-producing region, experienced economic boom like the rest of Nigeria in the "time of plenty." This chapter discusses the "oil boom" of the 1970s and examines the role of petroleum in Nigeria's public finance during the 1970s and 1980s. It also examines the impact of the oil boom on Yoruba economy and society. This sets the stage for the next chapter, which focuses on the social and cultural crisis in Yorubaland following the adoption of Structural Adjustment Program (SAP) in the late 1980s.[1]

Of the many sectors of the Nigerian economy, none has had such a decisive effect on the economy as petroleum. In examining the oil sector, we also include information on agriculture, manufacturing, international trade, and other sectors. And in evaluating the disbursement of oil revenues, we examine the banking and other financial institutions and attempt to determine the phenomenal rise in money supply and the amount of currency in circulation. We use this data to illustrate the impact of the changing quantity of money on investment and consumption habits and changes in cultural values. Moreover, we evaluate the system of revenue allocation to also determine how oil revenues were shared among the states of the federation. This becomes especially useful in demonstrating how (not how much) a nonoil-producing region such as Yorubaland shared in the country's oil wealth.

Petroleum in Nigeria

Petroleum exploration in Nigeria began in 1908.[2] That year, a German company, Bitumen (Nigeria) Corporation, found quantities of petroleum in fourteen wells drilled around Lagos. The company's further exploration works were halted by the outbreak of World War I. Since Germany lost the war, its oil company was denied permission to resume work in the British colony of Nigeria. In 1937, a consortium known as Shell D'Arcy, jointly owned by the Royal Dutch Shell and British Petroleum, obtained oil exploration license from the British colonial government. World War II again interrupted the company's work, but after the war, Shell D'Arcy (renamed Shell-BP Petroleum Development Corporation) resumed oil prospecting operations, and in 1956 it found crude petroleum at commercial quantities at Oloibiri in the present Rivers State. In 1958, the company exported crude oil from Nigeria at the production rate of about 6,000 barrels per day (bpd).

As a result of its pioneering work in the field, Shell-BP enjoyed a monopoly of the Nigerian petroleum industry for almost a decade. It chose for its operations the best-known fields, and the areas where drilling and export could be done at minimum costs. By 1967, on the eve of the Nigerian Civil War, Shell-BP was responsible for 85 percent of Nigeria's total crude oil production, at an average of 350,000 bpd. In 1975, at the peak of the oil boom, Shell-BP was exporting 1.06 million bpd, representing 62 percent of Nigeria's total export that year.[3] In 1978, when the company's monopoly would seem to have been broken, and shortly before the nationalization of the petroleum products marketing arm of the company[4] Shell-BP was still dominant in Nigeria's petroleum industry, accounting for about 56 percent of the country's total crude oil production. Indeed, to students of MNCs, the involvement of Shell-BP in the Nigerian Civil War should be an interesting subject. A.H.M. Kirk-Green[5] has made useful references to the manner in which, caught in the spider's web of the Nigerian crisis in 1967, Shell-BP pitted its tent with the secessionist (Biafra) government to which it paid the necessary royalties and taxes.

Meanwhile, other oil companies had begun arriving in Nigerian petroleum industry. Mobil secured an oil-prospecting license under the departing colonial administration in 1957, but it could not do much exploration work until the 1960s. By then, other companies had joined in what amounted to an "oil rush." By 1962, Gulf, AGIP, SAFRAP, and Tenneco oil companies had begun exploration work. By 1975, the number of companies had increased to fifteen. These companies gave Shell-BP a keen competition in the main on-shore oil producing areas located in the present Bendel, Rivers, and Cross River States. Shell-

BP has continued to dominate the industry, especially the offshore locations.

The foregoing discussion on the coming of the "Oil Majors" into the Nigerian oil industry is relevant as a build-up toward establishing the fact that the country's oil industry is foreign dominated, capital intensive, and an enclave of MNCs. Later in this section we will demonstrate how the Federal Military Government (FMG) in the 1970s made futile efforts to wrest the control of the industry from the multinationals, and also examine the activity of the institution government created for indigenising the oil sector—the Nigerian National Petroleum Corporation (NNPC). It is necessary first to turn our attention to the expansion in oil revenues in the 1970s.

The Oil Boom

Oil production and export increased with the number of oil companies. Those who have followed the development of the oil industry[6] have shown that petroleum became the dominant export commodity in the Nigerian economy in the 1970s (also see Table 1). At the beginning of the civil war in 1967, oil production figures had risen from 6,000 bpd in 1958 to 319,324 bpd. The civil war affected production and export. But by 1970 production figures had risen to 1.08 million bpd, from there to 2.05 million bpd in 1973, and finally to 2.3 million bpd in 1979. Due to the economic recession and the oil glut of the early 1980s, production figures declined. Subsequently, Nigeria's production levels were determined at OPEC meetings as a part of that organization's effort to stabilize oil prices, regulate the volume of petroleum pumped into the consumer countries, and protect producer countries from the vagaries and shocks of the market. Nigeria has been reported and reprimanded several times for exceeding this quota. Consequently, production and export figures were not regularly published. In spite of OPEC production ceiling, the oil glut, and the falling prices, oil production in Nigeria was still as high as 1.355 million bpd in 1988. This proves that the oil industry has been firmly established in Nigeria, whether the market was in boom or in glut.

Nigeria strolled into the oil boom in the mid–1970s. Before 1973, Nigeria was only an average oil producer and exporter, selling petroleum at the prices dictated by Euro-American purchasers. Things changed at the end of that year and Nigeria was never the same again. The change resulted from the Arab-Israeli War of 1973–74 when Arab oil exporters decided to use oil as a weapon.[7] They cut back production, increased petroleum prices, and embargoed oil sales to Western supporters of Israel. These positively affected Nigeria: although her production level only increased slightly, her crude oil was now in high demand, and the prices (at four times the 1972 level) have never been so good. Table 1 demonstrates this boldly. Oil production increased slightly from 1.7 million barrels per day (mbpd) in 1972 to 2.2 mbpd in 1974, but revenue receipts from oil sales rose from N576.2 million ($1152.4 million) in 1972 to N4,138.8 million ($8,277.6 million) in 1974. The boom had begun.

From the oil boom period crude petroleum has become Nigeria's prime revenue earner. Petroleum revenue (consisting of petroleum profit tax, mining rents and royalties, and NNPC sales) accounted for the largest proportion of total Federal Government revenue. By extension, petroleum revenue became the basis of state government finances, since they depended on statutory allocations from federally-collected revenue. Tables 1 and 2 clearly demonstrate the growth and extent of this dependence. From a mere one percent in 1960, the share of petroleum revenue in total federally collected revenue only climbed to 26 percent in 1970 at the end of the Civil War. It stood at 54 percent in 1973, but soon jumped to 82 percent in 1974. This share fluctuated in the rest of the 1970s, but in the 1980s it ranged from 70 to 82 percent.

In addition to crude petroleum, Nigeria has potentials to produce three different types of gas. These are liquefied natural gas (LNG), dome gas, and liquefied petroleum gas (LPG). Until 1986, only LPG, which constitutes about 20 percent of the proven gas deposit, was being exploited. Its exploitation was associated with the production and refining of crude petroleum. Being accidental, therefore, the exploitation of gas has not been done commercially. It is reported that more than 95 percent of LPG produced is flared up, wasted in the course of petroleum production. Negotiations for the commercial exploitation of LNG began as soon as natural gas was discovered in the course of petroleum exploration, but nothing concrete was achieved until the late 1970s when the FMG entered into a partnership with Shell, BP, AGIP, ELF, and Phillips for the joint exploitation of LNG. The main problem had initially been the nonavailability of a large market for the product both in Nigeria and abroad. To promote internal market, a gas cylinder company was established and the government began advertising for domestic usage of gas in urban centers. The number of retailers of cooking and industrial gas also increased. However, the domestic market in cook-

TABLE 1
Oil Production, Export, and Revenue, 1958–1979

Units:
a. Quantity in thousand barrels per day
b. Revenue in million Naira

Year	Oil Production	Oil Export	Oil Revenue	Total Federal Government Revenue	Oil Revenue as % of Total Revenue
1958	5.14	4.99	0.2	154.6	0.10
1959	11.22	10.84	3.3	177.6	1.80
1960	17.40	17.06	2.5	223.7	1.08
1961	46.03	45.22	17.1	229.0	7.45
1962	67.46	67.45	16.9	231.6	7.31
1963	76.47	75.89	11.0	249.2	4.43
1964	120.21	118.67	16.1	299.1	5.38
1965	272.20	265.71	29.2	321.9	9.06
1966	417.61	381.28	37.7	339.2	11.10
1967	319.32	299.38	41.2	300.0	13.70
1968	141.82	139.70	23.3	299.9	7.80
1969	540.29	540.25	72.5	435.9	16.60
1970	1084.48	1050.56	196.4	633.2	26.20
1971	1530.63	1486.43	740.1	1169.0	43.60
1972	1757.40	1751.31	576.2	1404.8	54.40
1973	2056.42	1981.68	1461.4	1695.3	59.90
1974	2255.67	2180.03	4138.8	4537.0	82.10
1975	1784.95	1719.56	4611.7	5514.7	77.50
1976	2071.20	2013.18	5548.5	6765.9	79.30
1977	2098.78	2039.49	5821.5	8080.6	75.20
1978	1896.63	1828.46	4654.1	7371.1	63.10
1979	2308.15	2229.39	8880.9	10913.1	81.40

Sources: Federal Office of Statistics (FOS), *Annual Abstract of Statistics,* 1970. CBN, *Economic and Financial Review,* 1975. NNPC, *Annual Report,* 1979.

Currency conversion rate: N1 ≅ $2

ing and industrial gas utilized only a small fraction of the available gas. Moreover, the international market was more important as foreign exchange earner. The search for foreign market was intensified, and success was made in the late 1980s when markets were secured in Europe for 2.8 milliard cubic meters. Market for the balance was assured in the USA.[8] These assurances necessitated the signing of the LNG agree-

TABLE 2
Oil Revenue and Federal Government Revenue, 1983–1990

Revenue Type	1983	1984	1985	1986	1987	1988	1989	1990
Oil Revenue	**7,253.0**	**8,209.7**	**10,915.1**	**8,107.3**	**19,027.0**	**20,933.8**	**41,334.4**	**54,713.2**
Petroleum Profit Tax	3,746.9	4,761.4	6,711.0	4,811.0	12,504.0	12,496.5	24,161.7	26,909.0
Mining Rent & Royalties	3,506.1	3,448.3	4,204.1	3,002.5	6,242.2	8,435.6	17,172.7	27,804.2
Other (NERF)	—	—	—	293.8	280.8	1.7	—	—
Non-Oil Revenue	**3,255.7**	**2,924.0**	**3,691.0**	**4,194.7**	**6,072.8**	**6,377.0**	**8,937.7**	**12,182.2**
Customs & Excise Duties	1,984.1	1,612.7	2,063.3	1,728.2	3,540.8	4,264.1	5,950.2	8,724.6
Other	1,271.6	1,311.3	1,627.7	2,466.5	2,532.0	2,112.9	2,987.5	3,457.6
Total Revenue	**10,508.7**	**11,133.7**	**14,606.1**	**12,302.0**	**25,099.8**	**27,310.8**	**50,272.1**	**66,895.4**
Oil Revenue as % of Total Revenue	**69.02**	**73.74**	**74.73**	**65.90**	**75.80**	**76.65**	**82.22**	**81.79**

Sources: CBN, *Annual Report and Statement of Accounts*, various years
Currency conversion rate: N1 ≅ $1 in 1985; N11.5 ≅ $1 in 1990

ment that set up a LNG plant in 1988. The major partner in the project was the NNPC (60 percent of the share capital), and the other partners were Shell (20 percent) and Elf (10 percent). Work progressed in 1988 in the areas of fiscal arrangements, project organization, and shareholder's agreement. Construction work was expected to begin in 1991, test runs to be carried out by October 1994, and the first shipment of LNG was to be delivered to customers by January 1995.

This agreement had not progressed much further than the paper stage as of April 1998. The main problem was the economic crisis that deepened in the 1990s and the mismanagement of funds, corruption, and lack of interest in the project by successive military administrations. Owing to this crisis and to many other factors, including probably the lack of interest by the technical partners in the project, Nigeria was no way near the realization of her dream of a virile and buoyant gas industry.[9] The "gas boom" has, therefore, been delayed.

The petroleum industry contributed immensely to Nigeria's economic growth. Available information (see Table 1) shows the oil industry has strengthened government revenue and expenditure, provided employment, contributed to the dream of transfer of technology, and financed social development. On the other hand, the overall performance of the oil industry within the economy has been generally unimpressive.[10] Nigerian governments (military and civilian) have neither developed the expertise, nor gained the necessary experience, to integrate the industry as a whole, and the rising oil wealth in particular, into the local economy. Thus, the more oil wealth was injected into the economy, the greater the condition of inequality and underdevelopment in the society. In other words, rather than domesticate the oil industry, the industry had increased the rate at which the economy was integrated into the international division of labor and Third World impoverishment.

The available data shows that in the 1970s the Nigerian economy had become molded into a dual system, each part existing almost separately. The oil sector was smaller, even though it provided the bulk of the country's source of finance. It was highly capital intensive. Therefore, it employed only a small, skilled proportion of the Nigerian labor force, a good number of its employees being highly skilled expatriates. The other sector was agriculture. It employed a larger proportion of the country's unskilled (or traditionally skilled) labor force but contributed less and less to government revenue and expenditure. One of the main problems facing governments in the 1970s was how to domesticate the oil sector and make it Nigerian in essence, location, and ownership.

The history of the management of the oil industry in Nigeria dates much earlier than the 1970s.[11] There were colonial ordinances and acts of the Nigerian legislature between 1959 and 1966 that set out the relationship between the oil companies and the Federal Government, especially with regard to profit sharing and concession holding. The emphasis of the legislation was principally on making the pioneering companies reap the full benefit of their investments and risk taking. It was also part of the neocolonial structure bequeathed at independence by which only British companies (or companies from a specified number of western countries) had access to the resources of the neocolony. The profit-sharing procedure was as exploitative as the colonial structure that informed it. By the arrangement, government received 50 percent of the profit after the cost of production and marketing of the crude petroleum had been discounted. The injustice in this profit-sharing scheme became apparent, and this exploitative system was gradually rectified as government adopted more favorable fiscal measures (see Table 3).

TABLE 3
Royalty and Petroleum Profit Tax Rates

A. Royalties

Period	Onshore	Offshore
1950	12.5%	40k per ton of crude oil
March 1967 – June 1974	12.5%	10%
July 1974 – September 1974	14.5%	14.25%
October 1974 – March 1975	16.67%	16.67%
April 1975 – March 1977	20%	20%
April 1977 – to 1990	20%	18.25% up to 100 meter of water depth 16.67% above 100 meter of water depth

B. Petroleum Profit Tax (PPT)

Period	Rate
From inception – 19 March 1971	50%
20 March – 30 September 1974	55%
1st October 1974 – 30 November 1974	60.78%
1st December 1974 – 31 March 1975	65.75%
1st April 1975 to 1990	85%

These fiscal measures, together with the establishment of posted prices for Nigerian crude oil in 1967, increased the government's earnings from the oil industry. Then in 1968 a further step was taken by the Companies Decrees, which required all oil companies operating in the country to be registered and come under Nigerian laws. In 1969, a landmark was made when the government promulgated the Petroleum Decree, which reduced the length of concession period to twenty years and provided that within ten years (i.e., by 1979) oil producing companies must *Nigerianize* up to 75 percent of their senior administrative and management positions. The comment must be made here that in all these laws, the government was adopting policies already being introduced in the oil industry in the Middle East. It is, therefore, only a matter of formality when in 1971 Nigeria became a member of the Organization of Petroleum Exporting Countries (OPEC). The advantages and demerits of Nigeria's membership of OPEC were not matters for considerable debate at that time. Indeed, throughout the 1970s Nigeria's membership was mutually beneficial. The matter began to generate controversy as a result of the glut in the oil market that began in the 1980s. Since then, the opinion has been expressed that in order to avoid the OPEC quota, to sell at whatever price the country chooses, and to deal with the country's economic ills independently, Nigeria should pull out of OPEC.[12]

Another step taken in 1975/74 by the Federal Government was to purchase 55 percent shareholding in oil companies operating in Nigeria. This was in line with the indigenization policy of the Gowon Administration.[13] Curiously, Shell-BP, the company that pioneered the exploitation of Nigeria's oil resources, and which was controlling the oil industry, was given preferential treatment. Government's indigenization did not affect the company until 1973; even then, only 35 percent of the company's shares were taken over. It was the Murtala/Obasanjo regime that eventually brought Shell-BP in line with other companies in 1979, and also increased Nigerian interest in the companies to 60 percent. At the same time, the government acquired all the interests in the petroleum products marketing arms of Esso, BP, and Shell and renamed them Unipetrol, African Petroleum (AP), and National, respectively. On the surface, therefore, by 1979 oil companies operating in the country were *Nigerianized.*

A sharp and critical look at this indigenization policy will reveal that the acquisition of ownership was not the same as the achievement of management and technical control. Indeed, the former could take place without being accompanied by a corresponding transfer of the management of the companies. For instance, the number of Nigerians in management cadres of the companies was very low. Moreover, the type of positions they occupied and services they performed was such as would not give them access to vital company information. Nigerian managers in these companies were usually given positions in personnel management and administration where they dealt with files rather than have useful contact with vital oil deals and technology. The hope that the petroleum industry would lead to a transfer of technological and managerial know-how thus remained elusive.

Apart from indigenization, the government invested directly in the oil industry in the 1970s. By Decree No.18 of 1971, the government established the Nigerian National Oil Corporation (NNOC), which was empowered to engage in all phases of the oil industry such as exploration, production, transportation, refining, marketing, training, service, and research. It was anticipated that through a gradual process of learning and participation the country would eventually take control of the commanding heights of the economy. This was also a policy borrowed from the Middle East and Persian Gulf oil producers. There were certain defects in the NNOC decree that became apparent in the mid–1970s. By Decree No.33 of April 1977, the government established the NNPC to replace the NNOC. This decree gave the NNPC a Managing Director and a seven-man Board of Directors whose chairman would also be the Federal Commissioner (Minister) of Petroleum. A Petroleum Inspectorate Division was also set up under the NNPC.

A number of studies have been conducted on the activities and capabilities of the NNPC. B.A. Osuno,[14] the Corporation's exploration manager in 1978, had examined the role of the NNPC in Nigeria's oil industry. In that study, he painted a glossy picture of the NNPC's activities. He concluded that the NNPC was very effective in protecting Nigeria's interest in the oil industry through its monitoring of the petroleum reserves and supply of regular and vital information on the oil industry. This rather official position on the ability of the NNPC is grossly misleading. Nothing in its suggests that it had sufficient information on the activities of the "Oil Majors" and on the situation in the international oil market. In fact, shortly after the NPN Administration took office in 1979, the allegation was made public that oil revenue worth about N2.8 billion appeared to have been missing and NNPC auditors could not trace it. Although the Crude Oil Sales Tribunal (COST) set up by President Shehu Shagari under Justice Ayo Irikefe could not establish this allegation, the Tribunal nevertheless revealed that the NNPC was incapable of effectively managing Nigeria's oil industry and of monitoring the activities of the oil companies.[15] In essence, even direct government institutional involvement in the oil industry did not result in the desired domestication of the industry.

The injection of oil revenues into the economy soon began to affect Nigerians in many different ways. The popular culture blossomed, the taste for imported basic and luxury goods heightened, and the work ethic experienced remarkable shift. Oil wealth was injected into the economy through wage increases beginning with the Udoji recommendations, the payment of arrears in 1974, the boom in the construction industry in the mid–1970s, and the fraud in the public sector. In general, domestic consumer prices and the cost of living rose, and inflation was in the double digits. Vehicles were imported in large numbers, and assembly plants were established to make available to the populace the Peugeot, Volkswagen, and Landrover brands very popular in the country. All these increased the demand for petroleum products such as motor fuel, engine oil, brake fluids, and diesel oil. Moreover, road construction raised the demand for tar which, because the Nigerian petroleum is light, had to be imported from sources of heavy crude oil like Kuwait and Venezuela. Nigeria in essence was not just an oil exporter, it became a huge consumer of petroleum products as well.

Consumption of fuel, for example, rose astronomically from a modest 60,000 bpd in 1971 to 235,000 bpd in 1978. As a result of this sharp increase, existing refining and distribution networks were over tasked and could not meet domestic demand. Shortages were recorded in the mid–1970s and early 1980s. To satisfy this demand, the government did three things. First, it increased the number of refineries to three—Port-Harcourt refinery, which had been built in 1965; Warri refinery, opened in 1978; and Kaduna refinery in 1980.[16] Secondly, there was an increase in the number of service stations (or gas stations). The Shagari Administration so relaxed the regulations governing the operation of petroleum products marketing stations that indigenous "money bags" could own their filling stations. This resulted in the unfortunate development of piracy, known by Nigerians as "illegal bunkering," by which petroleum products were sold indiscriminately by the road side and were smuggled to neighboring countries by people who had no such license and who probably got the products through illegal means. The Buhari/Idiagbon regime in 1984 successfully cracked down on these illegal operators by imposing death penalty on anyone caught tampering with NNPC pipelines.

The third way the government dealt with the problem of shortage of petroleum product was the construction of about 3,000 km multipurpose pipelines. This conveyed crude oil from the oil fields to the refineries, and refined products from the refineries to petroleum product depots constructed in each of the then nineteen states of the Federation. When they were fully operational, the storage capacity of these depots was 1.83 million metric tons, considered sufficient to supply the country for ninety days in case of an interruption in the operation of the refineries. The pipeline distribution network had five systems: 2A, 2B, 2C, 2D, and 2E.[17] 2A carried petroleum products from Warri via Benin and Ore to Mosimi depot near Sagamu; 2B from Mosimi to Murtala Mohammed Airport, Ikeja and to Ilorin via Ibadan depots; 2C carried crude oil from Warri to Kaduna refinery; 2D carried petroleum products from Kaduna refinery to Kano and Gusau depots, and another arm of 2D from Kaduna to Maiduguri via Jos and Gombe depots; and 2E carried petroleum products from Port-Harcourt to Makurdi via Aba and Enugu depots.

These efforts were made with the good intention of ensuring an uninterrupted supply of petroleum products, especially motor oil. Moreover, Kaduna refinery was designed to process heavy crude oil imported from Kuwait and to produce heavy products required in the construction industry. The implementation of these laudable projects and schemes was, however fraught with problems of mismanagement, sabotage, and official bungling. In spite of the availability of retail outlets, pipelines, and depots, there has been no year since 1980 when there was no shortage of petroleum products.[18]

Throughout this section, the emphasis has been on the petroleum industry itself. It should suffice to say that when considered on its own a significant development took place in the oil industry in the 1970s and 1980s. Oil revenue increased, government revenue received a boost, and there was some promise of economic prosperity. When related to the whole economy, however, the oil industry had deepened Nigeria's social inequality and worsened the structure of the economy by making it more dependent on one product—oil export.

Oil Revenue, Money Supply, and the Growth of Banking

In the euphoria of the oil boom, the head of state, General Yakubu Gowon, was believed to have carelessly stated that money was not Nigeria's problem, but how to spend it. Utilizing proceeds from the oil industry seemed to have posed a problem to this once cash-strapped nation. Oil revenue brought new optimism and enabled a new spending frenzy. National development plans were more ambitious, capital projects were more grandiose, and several social service programs were promised. The frequency and size of such noneconomic, cultural programs as the national sports festival and national cultural festivals increased. Nigeria hosted continental sporting engagements and capped this with the World Black Arts Festival (FESTAC) in 1977.

Government expenditure pumped oil money into the economy. Money supply rose sharply from 1974. The Central Bank of Nigeria (CBN) analysis on money supply in the period between 1974 and 1977 reveals that

> in the four-year period, increases in M_1 ranged between 42.5 and 73.5 percent and averaged 48.1 percent while increases in M_2 ranged between 33.7 and 68.0 percent and averaged 50.0 percent.[19]

This was a phenomenal growth in money supply. To demonstrate these increases in plain terms, one might call attention to the windfall in salary increases in 1975 when workers' salaries not only doubled, but such

TABLE 4
Money Supply, 1978–1990

Unit: N million

Month/ Year	Quasi Money	Money Supply	Currency outside banks	Private demand deposits	Total monetary liabilities	Interest Rate %
Dec. 1978	2,601.6	5,098.7	2,157.2	2,932.5	7,691.3	7.0
Dec. 1979	3,702.1	6,146.6	2,350.8	3,795.8	9,848.7	7.0
Dec. 1980	5,163.2	9,226.8	3,185.9	6,040.9	14,390.0	7.5
Dec. 1981	5,796.1	9,744.9	3,861.9	5,883.0	15,541.0	7.5
Dec. 1982	6,838.3	10,048.5	4,222.4	5,826.1	16,886.8	10.5
Dec. 1983	8,082.8	11,282.4	4,842.8	6,439.6	19,365.2	10.0
Dec. 1984	9,391.3	12,204.1	4,883.5	7,320.6	21,595.4	10.0
Dec. 1985	10,550.8	13,267.8	4,909.9	8,357.9	23,818.6	10.0
Dec. 1986	11,487.8	12,728.3	5,177.9	7,55.4	24,216.1	11.0
Dec. 1987	17,366.6	14,726.2	6,298.6	8,427.6	32,092.8	11.5
Dec. 1988	21,631.7	21,148.6	9,412.3	11,736.3	42,780.3	16.5
Dec. 1989	20,525.3	25,697.6	11,688.4	14,009.2	46,222.9	25.5
Dec. 1990	27,699.0	37,233.7	14,940.6	22,293.1	64,902.7	26.0

Sources: CBN, *Annual Report and Statement of Accounts*, various years.

increases applied retroactively from the year before. The money supplied through the "Udoji award," as those salary arrears were called, went into the purchase of imported and locally produced manufactures, many of them of poor quality but at exorbitant prices.

Economic theory accepts an increase in money supply in a period of economic growth—as was the case in the 1970s (at least in general terms). It is not economically healthy, however, when money supply continues to increase in lean years, as was the case in the mid–1980s. It is also economically unsound to have money supply and interest rates move in the same direction—upwards. Dotun Phillips has described this situation as a "paradox."[20] Table 4 clearly shows the continued increase in money supply throughout the 1980s. It also shows the rise in interest rates—from about 10 percent in 1985 to 26 percent in 1990. Part of the explanation for this paradox could be found in the continued central position of the federal, state, and local government expenditure in the economy. Another reason is the currency devaluation that followed the adoption of the Structural Adjustment Program (SAP). Thus, whereas there was a lot of money in circulation (see Table 5), the pat-

Table 5
Currency in Circulation, 1982–1986

Unit: N million

Month/ Year	Notes	Coins	Total Currency in circulation	Cash held by Banks in vaults	Total outside Banks
Dec. 1982	4,652.4	76.4	4,728.8	506.4	4,222.4
Dec. 1983	5,219.3	80.0	5,299.3	456.5	4,842.8
Dec. 1984	5,260.9	86.2	5,347.1	463.6	4,883.5
Dec. 1985	5,288.6	86.4	5,375.0	465.1	4,909.9
Dec. 1986	5,594.0	102.3	5,696.3	514.3	5,182.0
Dec. 1987	6,742.6	112.3	6,854.9	556.3	6,298.6
Dec. 1988	10,091.0	119.5	10,210.5	798.2	9,412.3
Dec. 1989	12,972.4	137.9	13,110.3	966.0	12,144.3
June 1990	12,429.9	138.1	12,568.0	741.5	11,826.4

Sources: CBN, *Annual Report and Statement of Accounts*, various years. CBN, *Economic and Financial Review*, various monthly issues.

terns of income distribution ensured that only a few had access to the money. In Dotun Phillips' words:

> The increasing deregulation of the money and foreign exchange markets in recent years has had only one major consequence, namely, the unmitigated sharp increases in the prices that prevail in these markets.... The consequence on the general price level, investment, output, and employment have been largely negative.... So much damage had been done in these areas that when the authorities capped interest rates at 21 percent in 1991, the investment market understandably failed to respond.[21]

The point that we intend to stress here is that the oil boom increased official spending, money supply, the amount of currency in circulation, and the rate of interest and inflation. Another way to prove this phenomenon is by examining the situation in the banking sector. After all, the financial system occupied a central position in the formal sectors of the country's economy. Within this financial system, the banking sector constitutes the pivot on which all financial transactions were anchored.

Banks in Nigeria have come a long way.[22] In addition to the commercial banks examined in chapter 6, the oil boom era witnessed the growth of specialized banking. Most were established by the FMG and the new state governments, but others were privately owned and operated. We examine a few of them here.

Merchant banking activities began in Nigeria in 1960 when Phillip Hill (Nig.) Ltd. was established. In 1969, this company was taken over by the Nigerian Acceptances Ltd. The economic boom of the 1970s provided the favorable climate for the establishment of merchant banks, and by 1976 there were already five merchant banks operating mostly in Lagos and other key cities where industrial and commercial activities were concentrated. These were the Nigerian Acceptances Limited (which changed its name to Nal Merchant Bank), the Nigerian Merchant Bank, the International Merchant Bank, the Chase Bank, and the ICON Merchant Bank. Like commercial banking, the number of merchant banks increased in the few years following the adoption of the Second-tier Foreign Exchange Market (SFEM). By 1988, the number had increased to 24.[23]

Unlike commercial banks, which were "retail bankers," merchant banks were wholesale bankers operating large deposits and granting large, long-term loans to their customers. Loans were made to businessmen and companies, and they utilized their funds by accepting bills of exchange to finance trade.[24] Merchant banks provided long-term credit to finance agriculture and real estate businesses, dealt in foreign exchange, and provided financial advice to companies. On the latter, they advised companies on how to raise capital for expansion and development, and offered advice on mergers, acquisitions, and capital reconstruction. They floated state government loan stocks.

Another banking institution established by the government to perform specialized functions in the economy was the Federal Savings Bank of Nigeria (FSBN). Formerly known as the Post Office Savings Bank, the FSBN started in 1886 when the Treasury Savings Bank was established. The main objective of the FSBN since its establishment was to stimulate the saving habit of Nigerians. The bank accepted deposits as low as 10 kobo (approximately 10 cents) from individuals, churches, thrift societies, and trade unions. Owners of the account could draw on their savings anywhere in the country in which the bank has a branch, that is, at any Nigerian post office. This had an advantage over other banking institutions in that rural banking services were automatically provided by the FSBN. On the other hand, as far as most Nigerians were concerned, a Post Office was a post office, not a bank. Moreover, it did not lend money to its customers.

Nigerian Industrial Development Bank (NIDB) was another specialized bank, established in 1964 with an initial capital of N8.50 million ($17 million). In September 1978 the resources of the bank had grown to about N693.7 million ($1,387.4 million). The bank was established with the objective of providing long- and medium-term loans for industrial development. It financed manufacturing, nonpetroleum mining, and tourism industries. In 1988 alone, the bank approved loans and investments totaling N171.3 million ($35 million) for 21 projects. Of this, loans to four textile industries absorbed N105.2 million ($21 million) equivalent to 62.6 percent.

For agriculture, the FMG under General Gowon established the Nigerian Agricultural and Co-operative Bank (NACB) in 1972. The objective of the bank was to finance agricultural development, and this included production, storage, and marketing of agricultural products, and enhancing the level and quality of horticulture, poultry farming, pig breeding, fisheries, forestry, timber production, animal husbandry, and other types of farming.[25] The bank, in pursuing these goals, dealt with a special class of borrowers, including state governments, farmers' cooperatives and "credit worthy individuals." In other words, although in name it was an agricultural bank, and although it extended credit toward the development of agriculture and related activities, peasant farmers who constituted the mass of agricultural producers had little access to the bank. Most peasants lacked the kind of collaterals NACB demanded even to obtain a small loan fund of N5,000 (about $1,000) and, going by the highest figure of individual beneficiaries in 1988, 29,000 "farmers" represented a very small proportion of millions of peasants who required credit.

The Nigerian Bank for Commerce and Industry (NBCI) was established in 1973 with an authorized capital of N50 million ($100 million) of which N10 million ($20million) was paid up. By 1978 the paid-up capital of the bank had grown to N45 million ($90 million), and by December 1988 the total assets of the bank stood at N572.5 million (about $114 million, owing to currency devaluation). The bank was established principally to provide equity capital and loan funds to Nigerians and Nigerian institutions for long- and medium-term investments in commerce and industry. For all practical purposes, it was established to meet the demands of indigenization. It was also empowered to perform all aspects of merchant and other banking businesses, and to assist indigenous businessmen in identifying viable projects, preparing feasibility studies, and advising on technical and management matters.

The Federal Mortgage Bank of Nigeria (FMBN) was established in 1977 to provide Nigerians with loan funds to buy or build their own houses, and to encourage the habit of saving among the people. It began operation effectively at a time the priority of the Federal Government under the NPN was "housing for all." By 1986, however, the bank had run into serious problems, and had to close down temporarily. At the end of September 1988, the bank had a total assets/liabilities of N753.9 million (about $151 million). At the same time, total mortgage loans and advances outstanding stood at N572.2 million (about $115 million). Also, savings outstanding with the bank totaled N180.4 million (about $36 million).

Insurance companies are financial institutions whose operation and function are fairly different from banking institutions. They nevertheless deal in money; and, like banks, lend money to their customers at interest rates favorable to the companies. Describing what constitutes the activities of insurance companies in financial accumulation and disbursement, Oyejide and Soyode have written:

> A typical insurance firm collects a premium of relatively small magnitude from a policy-holder, and pools such over many policy holders with an understanding to pay relatively large compensation to victims if and when there are fortuitous occurrences. There is a time-lag between premium collections and payment of compensation. At any particular time, therefore, the insurance company is in possession of sums of money which it has to make available to the policy-holder at one time or the other, but of which it temporarily has the use.[26]

At any particular time, therefore, the monetary assets of insurance companies, and the use to which they are put, are of interest to the company itself whose "primary goal is to ensure decent profits for their owners." They are also of interest to the policy holder, who must be paid compensation when due; the government, which ensures that the companies conduct their business properly, remain solvent, and positively contribute to national economic development; and the third party wherever applicable.[27]

The number of insurance companies in Nigeria grew rapidly from 1976 when the first attempt at bringing them under strict government control was made.[28] That year, the Insurance Companies Regulation Decree was promulgated, creating an Inspectorate Division in the Federal Ministry of Finance to which all insurance companies must submit a number of returns including their balance sheet, profit and loss accounts, and revenue accounts. The number of companies grew from twenty-four in 1969 to fifty-five in 1971 and to seventy-one in 1973. One of the reasons why the insurance business sustained higher rate of growth than the banking sector is the fact the government regulation on financial requirement before insurance companies are established were much lower: N50,000 ($100,000) for general insurance, and N100,000 ($200,000) for general and life insurance. In 1976, a new Insurance Decree was promulgated which raised this paid-up capital from N50,000 ($100,000) to N300,000 ($600,000), and from N100,000 ($200,000) to N500,000 ($1 million), respectively.

Prior to the promulgation of the Nigerian Enterprises Promotion Decree of 1971, and the establishment of the National Reinsurance Corporation, the bulk of the investible funds accumulated by insurance companies were transferred abroad for investment.[29] The Nigerian Enterprises Promotion Decree altered this structure. It decreed that no less than 40 percent of nonlife premiums, and 100 percent of premiums on life insurance business, were to be invested in Nigeria. Also, as a result of this indigenization decree, the Federal Government acquired 60 percent of the equity of all foreign insurance companies. This was in addition to those that were wholly owned by the Federal and State governments.[30]

One comment necessary here with regard to insurance companies is that many of them did not render audited accounts to the government. As at 1979, there were seventy-three registered insurance companies, and only thirty-five of them had published accounts. In 1980, only twenty-seven of them again reported. The situation had not improved as of 1987 and 1988. In the former year, of the eighty-seven registered insurance companies operating in the country, only forty-three reported, and in 1988, seventy-three companies reported. On the basis of the 1988 returns, the CBN reported on the insurance companies as follows:

> Insurance funds accruing to the reporting companies was N850.5 million out of which life insurance policies accounted for N644.3 million or 75.7 percent. The balance—N206.2 million or 24.3 percent—accrued from non-life insurance business. Their gross premium receipts amounted to N542.2 million and constituted 27.1 percent of their total liabilities. The funds were utilized for loans and investments. Aggregate loans granted by the companies stood at N102.4 million at the end of September, with only three of the insurance companies contributing N91.7 million or 61.0 percent of the total. Total investments stood an N522.0 million at the end of September 1988. Out of this amount, N283.5 million or 54.3 percent were invested in private sector securities, mainly debenture stocks. The balance—N238.5 million or 45.7 percent—was held in Government debt instruments.[31]

These banking and financial institutions did not operate without some form of state control. The Central Bank of Nigeria (CBN) established in 1959 represented the interest of the government in these institutions. It also monitored the activities of banks and other financial institutions.

A lot has already been written about the origin of the CBN.[32] Mr. J. Mars first drew the attention of the colonial administration to the need for a state bank in Nigeria in 1948 in his article published as part of the collection by Margery Perham.[33] Opinion in academic circles was divided on the "desirability" and "practicability" of central banking in the country. Mr. J. L. Fisher, an adviser to the Bank of England appointed in 1952 to advise the government of Nigeria, was of the opinion that Nigeria did not possess the sound economic base for central banking.[34] T. Newlyn and D. C. Rowan, in their own study, supported the idea of central banking which, in a developing economy like Nigeria's, should perform developmental functions. Naturally, the colonial administration accepted the Fisher report until the wave of nationalist activity made a reconsideration of the issues inevitable. Arguing his motion in the House of Representatives, Hon. K.O. Mbadiwe urged the government to establish a Central Bank immediately.[35] Although Mbadiwe's motion was amended, the point had been well made. Soon after, the World Bank Mission of 1953[36] commented on the Central Bank issue and supported its establishment in view of the country's march toward independence.[37] Government had to move fast between 1957 and 1959 to ensure that a Central Bank was established before independence. It appointed Mr. J. B. Loynes, also of the Bank of England, to make detailed recommendations on the establishment of a Nigerian Central Bank. The Loynes Report[38] formed the basis for the drafting of CBN Ordinance of 1958 and the CBN Bylaws of 1959. On July 1, 1959, the CBN came into full operation.

The principal objectives of the Central Bank have remained as they were stated in the 1958 Ordinance. These are:

1. issuance of legal tender currency in Nigeria,
2. maintenance of external reserve in order to safeguard the international value of the currency.
3. promotion of monetary stability and sound financial structure,
4. serving as banker and financial adviser to the Federal Government of Nigeria, and
5. serving as banker to other banks in Nigeria and abroad.

The capability of the Central Bank has, however, increased with regard to the performance of these functions. At the time of its establishment, the financial institutions of the country were underdeveloped. The CBN was expected to induce the development of "sound financial structure." This was the classical case of building the economy from the top, which Fisher had earlier advised against. In this circumstance, the CBN inevitably had to face serious difficulties in the early 1960s.

The development of its resources, expertise, and power over the economy was based on the series of amendments to the Banking Ordinance passed in 1962 and 1969. More importantly, the CBN's hold on the economy was further assured by the emergency powers granted to it by the Federal Government during the Civil War. O. Teriba has aptly concluded that the 1967–69 amendments to the Banking Ordinance were largely responsible for the development of the CBN's capacity to perform its functions.[39] The oil boom of the 1970s also assured CBN the resources to perform developmental roles in the economy. Many banks and financial institutions (examined above) were promoted by the CBN for the development of agriculture, commerce and industry in the period. The situation has since changed in the 1980s. Although CBN continued to perform its functions, the resources had dwindled and, like the country itself, CBN has fallen prey to the foreign (World Bank, IMF, etc.) prescriptions on the Nigerian economic recovery.

The CBN's functions relating to the development of the domestic economy, and those affecting the external economic and monetary relations have been examined.[40] One issue that is of interest to this study is the quality of reports and data emanating from the CBN on the economy. More than any other institution in Nigeria, even more than the Federal Ministries of Finance and Economic Development, the CBN publishes up-to-date reports and reviews of the economy. It is the first, and perhaps the final, source of reliable data on the country's economy. As an establishment source, however, CBN does not engage in a critical review of government policies, and this generally weakens the quality of the report. Often, the reports themselves bemoan difficulties in obtaining data on certain aspects of the economy.

To conclude discussion in this section, it is necessary to examine in general some of the main defects in the Nigerian banking and financial system. As in most sectors of the economy, the modern has not sufficiently replaced (nor found good use for) the traditional system in banking and finance. Thus, both for good and evil, the *esusu* and *ajo* systems have continued to occupy an important place in the financial system. This is itself a mirror of the inefficiency of the modern financial system and its inability to command enough confidence among the people.

In addition, the Nigerian financial system has serious structural weaknesses. S. B. Falegan has identified some of them: lack of supervision over nonbank financial institutions chartered outside the Banking Decree; underdevelopment of the financial market; nonfunctioning of the open market operations; rigid insistence on collateral before loans are approved; congestion of banking halls (itself an indication of the backwardness of the operations of the banks); concentration of banks in the urban centers, especially Lagos; and the underdevelopment of the securities market.[41] As Falegan has pointed out, solutions to these problems and structural weaknesses must be located within the general economy. The CBN also has a significant role to play, since it is the "hub around which the development of additional (financial) institutions will revolve."[42]

Revenue Allocation: The Sharing of Oil Revenue

In all federations (and that includes Nigeria), revenue sharing performs many functions, including regulatory, incentive, resource enlargement, and redistributive functions.[43] However, each federation, and a federation at different times, gives priority to only a few of these functions. In Nigeria, the redistributive functions have been emphasized since the inception of regional administrations in 1946. The issue of equitable distribution of federally collected revenues has also been emphasized at the expense of fiscal efficiency. In other words, revenue sharing in the Nigerian federation revolves around the key issues of ensuring equitable distribution of revenue among the federal, regional/state and local governments and between the geopolitical divisions of North-South, East-West, and North-East-West.

It is impossible to ascertain how much of the money is spent in any part of the country. This section will only briefly examine the share of the Yoruba-speaking parts of Nigeria in federally collected oil revenue, and it will focus only on the revenue sharing principles, formulas, and allocations. Nigerian political elites and scholars have struggled with this issue of regional and ethnic balance/fairness in the allocation of revenue. This is not our intention here. Rather, it is to evaluate the impact of oil revenue on the Yoruba economy.

Perhaps it is important to state that revenue sharing in Nigeria has had some interesting features. First, ad-hoc "commissions of experts" have considered the problems of revenue sharing. Since independence, there have been five revenue allocation commissions, namely, Raisman-Tress, 1958[44]; Binns, 1964[45]; Dina, 1968 (unpublished); Aboyade, 1977[46]; and Okigbo 1979[47]. The respective commissioning governments accepted the recommendations, except those of the Dina and Aboyade commissions. Usually, they were operated for a few years, their defects were manifested, a new clamor would be made for revision, and another commission would be appointed. This soon became a revolving cycle.[48]

Second, revenue sharing has been characterized by the employment of a number of principles and formulas. These have been unstable, as it was impossible to permanently satisfy all the conflicting interests and positions. Since independence, several principles have been tried and discarded, and many more (such as the special problems of erosion and desertification, and the length of federal roads) have been suggested by those interested in the debate. These principles could be viewed as "knives" with which to cut a slice of the "national cake," and the longer one's knife the bigger the slice.

It was in 1970 that the government got around the problem by producing a very simple formula via decree No.13 of 1970 that took effect retroactively from 1969. The background to the Decree was the various conferences of Finance Commissioners where the allocation of revenue from the oil industry was debated. The Commissioners from the oil producing states—then known as Mid West and Rivers states—wanted the continuation of existing derivation principle by which they received 50 percent of oil rents and royalties. But oil exploration had expanded in 1969, and the government's earnings in the oil industry were rapidly rising. Commissioners from the nonoil-producing states, therefore, sought to reduce the influence of derivation. The Decree sided with the majority (the nonoil producing states), enlarged the composition of the Distributable Pool Account (DPA), and altered the formula for allocating the funds in this Account. According to Decree No.13 of 1970, "one half shall be divided equally among the states, and the other half shall be divided...proportionately to the population of each state."

The Decree strengthened the hand of the Federal Government, and achieved much the same effect as the rejected Dina Commission report had sought to do. The breakdown of the revenues that accrued to each of the state governments is presented in Table 6. Perhaps what was of greater significance is the fact that each of the twelve states was now treated on its own merit, not as a member of the "block of states" or region from where it had been created. The immediate result was that the Northern states between them accounted for 51.8 percent of the DPA, 9.8 percent greater than what they used to receive before 1969. In addition, the states created out of the former Western Region received 12.7 percent of the DPA, 6.6 percent lower than what was recommended by the Dina Commission, and 5.3 percent less than what the region used to receive before 1969.

Among other things, Decree No.13 of 1970 (combined with No.9 of 1971) awarded the highest yielding taxes—off-shore mining rents and royalties and petroleum profit tax—to the Federal Government. The effect of this became apparent in the mid-1970s when the oil prices quadrupled and production figures soared. With this financial boom, the FMG began to make nonstatutory grants and loans to the state governments. Between 1962 and 1968, the regional governments had received a total of N19.2 million ($38.4 million) as grants.[49] This system of grants became a handy tool to the FMG in the 1970s and in 1974–75 alone it had increased to N364 million ($728 million). Along with these grants grew the power of the FMG over the state governments, a situation that could not successfully be reversed after 1979.

It must be stressed, therefore, that the share of Yoruba-speaking parts of Nigeria in federally collected oil revenue was made possible by the simple formula adopted by the military government. Like other nonoil producing states of the federation, Yoruba-speaking states were in the forefront of the clamor to remove the derivation principle by which oil-producing states would have had the largest share of revenue. This was a 180-degree turn, a complete negation of the region's position in the period before oil revenue.

The reduction in the application of derivation, which was embodied in the 1970 decree, was further reviewed in 1975. The immediate cause of this review was the share of the 1974–75 windfall of oil revenue that went to oil-producing states. This share heightened the jealousy of elites from the nonoil producing states. Mid-Western and Rivers states between them accounted for 47.6 percent of the allocated revenue. This was evidently inequitable, and it was necessary to reexamine the derivation principle. Gowon promised to appoint a fiscal review commission, but he temporized. He issued Decree No.6 of 1975, which dealt significantly with the oil revenue component allocated by derivation and DPA. Thenceforth, 20 percent, not 45 percent, of onshore oil rents and royalties were returned to the states by derivation. The new DPA was now composed of the full proceeds from export duties on produce and hides and skins, import duties on tobacco, and motor fuel, 35 percent of all other import duties, 50 percent of all excise duties, 80 percent of onshore rents and royalties, and 100 percent of offshore rents and royalties.[50] The formula for sharing the DPA funds remained unchanged. The immediate impact of the Decree when it was operated in 1976–77 was a marked reduction in the share of the oil-producing states, which then accounted 19.24% of the allocated revenue. In spite of this reduction, the two states' share was still the highest per capita.

In short, with oil wealth at stake in the mid–1970s, the ruling class in each state criticized the revenue-sharing formula. The creation of more states in 1976 occasioned another series of problems that the simple formula used in allocating the DPA funds could not adequately solve. In 1977, the military government appointed the Technical Committee on Revenue Allocation to study these issues. Although its report was not accepted, the committee proposed a certain number of innovative principles that subsequent committees could not ignore.

The one remarkable contribution of the Aboyade Committee was its effort to abolish the DPA and to replace it with a system by which all federally collected revenue would be paid into the Federation Account. Funds in this Account would then be shared out among the federal government (60 percent), state government (30 percent), and local government (10 percent). In other words, there would no longer be any need to treat federal tax revenue differently, and all contests would now shift to the states' 30 percent share of the Federation Account. This was the first time a single account was created for the Federation. It was this recommendation that even the Presidential Commission could not discount.

Dr. Pius Okigbo's Presidential Commission on Revenue Allocation recommended that the Federal Account be shared between the federal government (53 percent), state governments (30 percent), and local governments (10 percent). But a Special Fund (7 percent) was created which the federal government should allocate as follows: 2.5 percent for the Federal Capital Territory, 2 percent for mineral producing states, one percent for other ecological problems, and 1.5 percent as revenue equalization fund. The principles for allocating the funds in the States' Joint Account (SJA) also combined the existing practice with some principles of fiscal efficiency and tax efforts.

The above recommendations were accepted in principle, but the percentages and the procedure were the subject of a bitter controversy that raged throughout 1980 and 1981.[51] At the end of the debate in the National Assembly the Revenue Allocation Act was passed. In sharing out funds in the Federation Account, the Act made the following provisions: the federal government 55 percent, state governments 35 percent, local governments 10 percent. The states' shares were divided as follows: 30.5 percent to States' Joint Account (SJA); 2 percent to oil producing states by derivation, 1.5 percent to be administered by the Federal Government for the development of mineral producing areas.

The funds in the SJA were to be shared according to the following principles: equality of states 40 percent, population 40 percent, social development factor 15 percent, and internal revenue effort 5 percent.

Although many principles have been adopted over the years, the most controversial have been derivation, population, and equality of states. Derivation has had the most turbulent history. It began in 1946 as the only principle used in sharing 100 percent of the revenue available among the regional governments. At that time agricultural export was the main source of public revenue. Derivation continued to gain appeal throughout the 1960s when oil revenue was still minimal, but it lost appeal from the mid–1970s when the oil boom started and agricultural export had declined. Even in mineral revenue, derivation was employed initially to allocate 50 percent of the funds. By 1970, however, the great changes had begun: the prospect for increased oil production and export was high after the war, and the application of derivation was seriously challenged by the nonoil-producing states. It is not surprising that the Decree issued that year reduced derivation form 50 percent to 20 percent. Finally, in 1981, derivation was reduced to insignificance, being applied to only 2 percent of the SJA, which itself constituted only 35 percent of the Federation Account.

The origin of the population principle, on the other hand, can be traced to 1949 when it was specifically demanded by the Northern Regional elites. The principle was not accepted then, but it was cleverly brought in when the Hicks-Phillipson Commission called it "Needs"—in the belief that the needs of all citizen were the same. The population principle lost favor in 1953, it reappeared in 1958, and waxed stronger in 1970 when it was used to allocate 50 percent of the funds in the DPA. Although this declined to 40 percent in 1981, and further to 30 percent in 1989 when the Federal Military Government introduced 10 percent for "land mass," it has been one of the country's most enduring principles of revenue allocation. The only drawback is the absence of a reliable population census.

The principle of the equality of states was the brainchild of the Gowon regime in 1970. On the other hand, the number of states has increased virtually every decade: from three regions in the 1950s, to twelve states in the late 1960s, to nineteen states in the mid–1970s, and to twenty-one in 1987. Creation of mores states continued in the 1990s and was actually done twice. Thus, the Nigerian federation acquired a thirty-state structure in 1991, and in 1996 six additional states were created to give the structure thirty-six states. Each of these states was created by splitting existing states or by merging parts of two or more states. Each of them was held in principle to be equal. "Equality of states" became a necessary tool in the political economy to assure all "old" and "new" states legal, political, and fiscal equality. It masks the fact that, in reality, these states were neither equal nor equally endowed: many were neither populous nor oil rich. "Equality of states" as a revenue sharing principle proceeds from the simple logic that all states are constitutionally created equal in status, have the same responsibilities to the citizens, possess all the paraphernalia of state, and maintain an administration. Although it began as a hit-or-miss effort, it has remained on the chart, now being used to allocate 40 percent of the funds in the SJA.

What conclusions could we reach on the allocation of revenue collected by the Federal Government?[52] First, it made revenue—including oil revenues—available to other tiers of government. This in turn increased money supply as those governments awarded contracts, paid salaries, and undertook a number of development projects. Second, the oil-producing areas of the country have continued to protest the pattern of revenue allocation, the manner of federal government expenditure, and the activities of the "Oil Majors." They feel they have been unfairly treated by the allocation principles, and left at the mercy of oil companies who took little or no interest in their conditions.[53] Third, revenue sharing ensured that Yoruba-speaking (and other nonoil-producing) parts of the country had a share of the oil revenues.

The Oil Boom in Yoruba Economy and Society

Yorubaland was not an oil-producing area, but the oil wealth into which Nigeria strolled in the 1970s had tremendous impact on the society and culture. Government spending and private investments increased, and these increases further promoted growth in both the modern and the traditional sectors of the economy. The first part of this section catalogs visible evidence of this growth. The second part discusses the phenomenon of private accumulation in the wake of the oil boom. It must be emphasized that these findings on oil and society in Yoruba-speaking states are true for the rest of Nigeria as well.

At the beginning of the oil boom, the Yoruba-speaking part comprised of Lagos State, Western State, and a large part of Kwara State. The city of Lagos itself was the federal capital until 1976 when Abuja was selected as the new federal capital.[54] The states creation exercise of 1976 in the middle of the oil boom increased the number to five, namely,

Lagos, Ogun, Ondo, Oyo, and Kwara states. The most recent two administrative changes were the creation of Osun State in 1991 and Ekiti State in 1996. Public expenditures by these state governments, along with federal and local government expenditures, brought the oil wealth into the Yoruba-speaking parts of Nigeria.

Government projects were numerous. The rate of construction was unprecedented. Roads, houses, hospitals, schools, airports, and the like were being constructed in the 1970s. To provide labor for these projects unskilled, daily paid workers came from all parts of Yorubaland. This increased the rate of rural-urban migration and put pressure on social amenities in the cities. More workers had to be brought in from neighboring Togo and Ghana.

Government projects were implemented through contracts. The main contractors were usually foreign, but the managers, shareholders, and workers were Yoruba and other Nigerians. Most of all, Yoruba-owned companies were often the subcontractors and consultants. This opened up avenues for the participation of the indigenous people in many areas of the economy. Many members of the business elite used this position to develop their businesses.

Educational opportunities were expanded to provide skilled workers and specialists needed in the various sectors of the expanding economy. Admission into middle-level teacher training institutions that award the National Certificate of Education (NCE) diplomas were expanded. Graduates of these institutions were expected to teach in primary and secondary schools, as the number of students in these schools was also rising. Admission into universities increased, and the federal government expanded the number of universities in Yoruba-speaking areas by opening the University of Ilorin in 1976. Many students in these higher educational institutions received federal government scholarships and loans, and others received state scholarships and bursaries. Tuition was free, food was cheap, and books were available. In 1976 the federal government also introduced the universal free primary education (UPE). It was a decade of expansion in education.

The oil boom era also witnessed an increase in the number of people that acquired skills using the traditional process of apprenticeship. Many young men who were too old to start school (following the free education program) entered into these apprenticeship program to learn a trade. With government construction projects everywhere requiring labor, training in such trades as carpentry, bricklaying, plumbing, and electrical works were popular. So were tailoring, motor mechanic, and electronic repair services because of the pattern and scale of expenditure of the people on clothes, automobiles, and electronics. Young women also received training in sewing, catering, hair dressing, and "nursing." These led to the establishment of several small-scale businesses in big cities and small towns. Although E. Akeredolu-Ale has aptly concluded that these businesses were underdeveloped,[55] there is no doubt that they filled the vacuum in the provision of those basic semiskilled services. It was also important that through these businesses the oil wealth trickled down to farmers, laborers, and other people who were not engaged in the formal sectors of the economy.

At the sociocultural levels, Yoruba society was the place to be in the 1970s. Leisure became an art. Opportunity for recreation was almost endless. For the elite there were exclusive clubs that required membership, and for the rest of the population there were beer parlors for drinking and partying. The number of breweries increased, giving the populace choices in alcoholic consumption. There were amusement parks for children and the family. Theater came of age with several travelling theater groups performing Yoruba plays to the delight of the people. This signified the beginning of the end for the traditional masked performer, the *eegun alare*. As the reading public increased, Yoruba language magazines and comic books were everywhere.[56]

A form of renaissance occurred in art, particularly following FESTAC in 1977. Traditional and modern painters and sculptors received government and private sector patronage. Music probably received the biggest boost. It was in this period that a new musical genre, the *Fuji*, was born. The older repertoire of *Juju*, *Apala*, and *Sakara* also received a boost. Growth in the music industry was further promoted by the affordability and availability of electronics equipment, such as the new three-in-one sets (with radio, tape, and record decks). Radio and television became household items in many homes.

Weekends in Yorubaland in the late 1970s and early 1980s were especially interesting. Whole cities would go agog for wedding, funeral, and other ceremonies. Parties were huge as people came from far and near. Celebrants received gifts, and were "sprayed" with mint-condition Naira notes when they danced. Guests were served good food and plenty of drinks, and sometimes were allowed some "take-homes" such as plastic containers, yard-length clothes, or live goats. To fund these parties celebrants might take loans from banks, friends, *esusu* society, or *s'ogun-d'ogoji*. Access to loan funds were relatively easy because there was optimism that the borrower would soon receive his/her salary or wage, make a big sale, land a big contract, receive a large payment from government, or just simply come by some big money.

The oil revenue impacted the Yoruba society in other ways, too. Revenues meant for government services and works were diverted into other ventures outside public circles. This suggests that when some sections of the Yoruba elite clamored for a change in the revenue allocation formula, they were concerned about the proportion of federal revenue to which they would have access. Segun Osoba has called attention to this pattern of accumulation.[57] In his view, as a result of their participation in government decision-making processes from 1952 onward, the elites formulated and executed policies beneficial to their class. The governments became much bigger as a result of the oil wealth, and patronage covered a wide range of areas, such as increased salaries and wages, award of contracts, business promotion, and issuance of import and export licenses.

In addition to government patronage, the indigenization of foreign enterprises also aided elite accumulation.[58] The Indigenization Decree of 1977 was issued by the military to enable Nigerians to take control of the "commanding heights of the economy." The decree achieved this purpose, particularly in the area of transfer of ownership and by allowing indigenous majority shareholding. It also made available to members of the business and political elites throughout the country additional avenues for investing the money they had looted in the period of the oil boom. For, according to Billy Dudley, "resources from bank loans and 'kickbacks' from the award of contracts went into the purchase of stocks and shares in on-going enterprises—made possible under the indigenization program..."[59] Many members of the Nigerian elite, particularly those that lived in Lagos, became agents, directors, shareholders, and "fronts" for multinational corporations (MNCs).

An interesting narrative on this point comes from an unexpected source. J. L. Brandler was a British timber magnate who began business in Nigeria in the colonial period. His memoirs,[60] published in 1993, is a mine of information on the Nigerian state and society, and on the wheeling and dealing that went on in Lagos business and governmental circles. In 1976 his company, Brandler & Rylke Timber Company, was lured into the oil business by a London-based company, Parazone Petroleum Ltd., which then needed a Nigerian agent or front. Here is Mr. Brandler's story, the story of Lagos elites and the oil money:

> At the urging of a cousin, himself an oilman, to whom I was under obligation, I had been invited by Parazone Petroleum Ltd, an important London oil trading concern,

to meet them and discuss their quest for Nigerian crude oil. Berry had given me an outline of their business, and how they had built up an important enterprise since starting in the 1920s.

"My Chairman, Mr. Edgar, will have told you who we are and what we are doing. I am in charge of crude oil trading. We handle large quantities, about 150,000 barrels daily, which we buy and sell all over the world. Dealing with Nigeria has so far escaped us; our direct approaches to the government oil agency have been rebuffed. We've had many people call here promising to help us enter the market, well-spoken Nigerians, and others. Most of them insisted that money was needed to get into this business and asked for large amounts which they would repay by deductions from commissions once a contract was signed. We don't pay such money up front, Mr. Brandler, I must be clear about that. I understand you know Nigeria well and may be able to assist us."

He went on to say that they would like to do business with the Nigerian National Petroleum Corporation (NNPC), but that they had become wary of the visitors who called promising to facilitate an approach, all of whom wanted money before they could move, and of whom nothing was ever heard again. He explained that...Nigeria interested them because of the grade of oil she produced...

I took his brochures with their impressive figures and said good-bye.

Back in Lagos, I mentioned the matter to my secretary, Ekaite, a well-connected young woman. I could see her alert brain go into top gear. "Oil, sir, is where all the money is these days. If you have a good company, surely we must find ways and means to bring them here."

A few days later, Ekaite turned up in great excitement. "Sir, I think I have found a man who can get your friends into NNPC."

"Who is that?"

"A lawyer I met socially. He told me he had every chance to get oil if he brought the right buyers."

"Very well, let's see him."

So we met lawyer Negus who informed us that he had been promised oil from the highest quarters if he could bring the right company to buy it....I showed him the brochures and he was impressed. His lawyer's training went to work. "If you want me to act for you..."

"Them," I corrected.

"Them. Then I must have a letter from the company appointing me as their exclusive agent for a minimum period to be agreed, along with some indication of what I, and my friends, would receive as fee or commission. We know the going rate," he added.

"Thank you, Mr. Negus. I'll report to London and get back to you."

"Don't leave it too long. These things come and go."

"We will act promptly," I assured him and he left.

"How well do you know this man?" I asked Ekaite.

"I know him quite well. He has the connections all right."

I sent a note to Berry...

It was agreed that an application be made by the company to the NNPC. A letter was given to Mr. Negus appointing him as exclusive agent for three months in the first place, which would be ratified on a contract being signed within that period for as long as the contract ran. Negus went to work.[61]

Mr. Negus might not be a Yoruba but his profile fit the profile of so-called directors, agents, and "arrangees" of Lagos business community.

It would be safe to say that many Nigerian government officials at all levels stole money, especially those that had access to government funds. This phenomenon has been known by many names: "kleptocracy," "graft, bribery, peculation and straightforward looting of the public treasury."[62] Kleptocracy became rampart in the 1970s. Embezzlement, diversion of public funds, and other corrupt practices thrived well under military regimes as well as in the civilian administration. According to Billy Dudley, with a high degree of centralization of political power and the absence of any form of public accountability characteristic of military rule, "the exploitation of office-holding for personal, private ends becomes inevitable and inseparable."[63] This was indeed the case in 1973–83, a period when the oil wealth was flowing into the private pockets of the military governors and other elite groups close to them.[64]

Cases of corruption and illegal enrichment by the elites were so numerous that we cannot refer to them all here. A few actually hit the headlines and were investigated,[65] but several others are only rumored and never probed. Many more were not even discovered.

With the massive increase in oil production and prices, government revenues soared to unprecedented heights and government public services were expanded. The creation of more states and local government reforms also assisted in increasing the number of governments and bringing the governments (and the revenues) closer to the elite. The avenues for financial misappropriation were thus enlarged. The impact of oil revenues on governmental expenditure and waste, and on property relations, cannot be overemphasized.

Thus enriched, the Yoruba power and business elites flaunted this wealth by their conspicuous and ostentatious styles of living. While this lifestyle was not unusual, the prosperity did not permeate through all the classes. It is not surprising that the rich had to hire private security systems (including guard dogs) to protect themselves and to guard the symbols of their wealth: huge mansions, expensive cars, clothes, and jewelry. It is also interesting that the paradoxical result of the oil wealth was armed robbery and burglary.

There are several ways through which Yoruba top government official—military governors, commissioners, permanent secretaries, engineers, accountants, and so forth—benefited from the oil boom. There were official salaries, allowances, and other benefits which, as we have stated above, increased tremendously in 1974 with arrears. In addition there was bribery. Many public officials demanded money before a contract was awarded. Officers who received and processed applications and tenders, and those that short-listed contractors, have been known to use this method. Another was "kickback," usually worked out in percentages of commission either on gross cost or on profit. Such kickbacks were directly responsible for the inflation of contract costs. Kickbacks were obtained by a very small circle of officials, usually those that had the authority to sign contract papers on behalf of government. Another means that officials devised in the oil boom days of enriching themselves was to award the contract to themselves or to their blood relations, in-laws, friends, and business partners. The rules of conflict of interest usually went unheeded.

The foregoing reveals a few of the destinations of the increased money supply examined earlier in this chapter. These public revenues were meant for the provision and expansion of amenities such as water, electricity, housing, roads, and hospitals. They were released under the various national development plans to fund specific projects in the economic and social development of the country. The federal, state, and local governments released these funds, but only a small proportion actually went into the implementation of the projects. Much of it ended in the private pockets and businesses of the members of the ruling class.

Summary

This chapter has examined several issues that this summary now attempts to tie together in a few sentences. Classical theories hold money as an enabler, a catalyst. This chapter has shown clearly how money—the oil boom—has impacted the pace of development in Nigeria (and indeed in Yorubaland). It impacted upon public finance, which in turn promoted the growth of banking and financial institutions. The increase in the number of governments through states creation and local government reforms, and increase in government spending in the 1970s, all transformed Nigerian (and Yoruba) economy and society. State-sponsored programs were bigger and more ambitious than before the oil boom. Corruption entered every aspect of public life. The amount of money in circulation increased. Among the Yoruba, more money was spent on social engagements and rites of passage, such as naming, wedding, and funeral ceremonies. Indeed, it was all about money—oil money.

Notes

1. For analytical purpose, we close the data and other pieces of information for this chapter in 1990. The oil boom was already over and it was four years since the

adoption of Structural Adjustment Program (SAP). However, the impact of the oil boom continued to be felt up until that year. In later years, Nigeria's economic conditions grew worse.

2. Scott R. Pearson, *Petroleum and the Nigerian Economy* (Stanford, CA: Stanford University Press, 1970); L. H. Schatzl, *Petroleum in Nigeria* (Ibadan: Nigerian Institute of Social and Economic Research,1969).
3. A. G. Adebayo, "Petroleum and Nigeria's Foreign Policy, 1970–79," M.A. Thesis, University of Ife, 1982.
4. The nationalization was part of Nigeria's strategy for persuading Britain to take seriously the negotiations for the independence of Zimbabwe.
5. A.H.M. Kirk-Greene, *Crisis and Conflict in Nigeria: A Documentary Sourcebook* (London: Oxford University Press, 1971), Vol. 1, pp. 89–93.
6. See Akin Iwayemi, "The Military and the Economy," in Oyediran, O. (ed.), *Nigerian Government and Politics under Military Rule* (London: Oxford University Press, 1979); S. A. Madujibeya, "Oil and Nigeria's Economic Development," *African Affairs*, Vol. 75, No. 300, 1976; Adebayo Adejugbe, "Multinational Oil Corporation and the Development of Nigeria's Economy," *Oil and the New International Economic Order* (Ibadan: NES Conference Proceedings, 1980).
7. An excellent source on Arab-Israeli wars up to the Yom Kippur War of 1973–74 is T. N. Dupuy, *Elusive Victory: The Arab-Israeli Wars, 1947–74* (New York: Harper & Row, 1978).
8. Central Bank of Nigeria (CBN), *Annual Report and Statement of Accounts* (Lagos: CBN, 1988), p.37.
9. *Guardian*, 8 April 1990, 18 May 1990; *Sunday Tribune*, 8 April 1990.
10. S. B. Falegan, *Redesigning Nigeria's Financial System* (Ibadan: UPL, 1970); S. B. Falegan and G. O. Okah, "The Contribution of Petroleum to Nigeria's Economy," *Oil and the NIEO* (Ibadan: NES, Annual Conference Proceedings, 1980).
11. P. C. Asiodu, *Nigeria and the Oil Question* (Lagos: NES, 1979).
12. *Nationswealth*, March/April 1990.
13. O. Aboyade, "Indigenising Foreign Enterprises: Some Lessons from the Nigerian Enterprises Promotion Decree," in Teriba, O. and Kayode, M.O. (eds.), *Industrial Development in Nigeria* (Ibadan: IUP, 1977); R. O. Soetan, "Ownership and Control of British Joint Ventures in Nigeria," *Quarterly Journal of Administration* (*QJA*), Vol. XIX, Nos. 3 & 4, April/July 1985.
14. B. A. Osuno, "The Role of the NNPC in Nigeria's Oil Industry," NIJ, 7th Annual Oil Seminar, 1978; Emman O. Osuji, *The Role of Petroleum Inspectorate of the NNPC as the "Guardian" of the Nigerian Oil Industry* (Lagos: NNPC, 1984).
15. Nigeria, *Crude Oil Sales Tribunal Report* (Lagos: Government Printer, 1980); Shehu Shagari, *The Challenge of Change: Collected Speeches of President Shehu Shagari* (Lagos: Office of the President, 1982).
16. J. O. Onah, "Uniform Pricing and Retailing of Petroleum in Nigeria," *Oil and the NIEO* (Ibadan: NES, Annual Conference Proceedings, 1980).
17. NNPC, *Petroleum Exploration and Development in Nigeria* (Lagos: NNPC, 1986), p. 27.
18. The situation has since worsened. At the time of revising this chapter (August 1998), the whole of Nigeria was facing acute shortage partly because all refineries broke down.
19. CBN, *Annual Report and Statement of Accounts* (Lagos: CBN, 1980), p. 40. According to CBN, Annual Report, 1981, p. 35, "M1 is defined as currency in circulation outside the banks plus private sector demand deposits in the commercial banks. M2 is comprised of M1 and savings and time deposits at the commercial banks."

20. Dotun Phillips, *The Nominalization of the Nigerian Economy* (Ibadan: NISER Occasional Paper No. 3, 1992), p. 20.
21. *Ibid.*, p. 21.
22. See chapter 6 of this book.
23. CBN, *Annual Report and Statement of Accounts* (Lagos: CBN, 1988).
24. S. I. Ajayi, and O. O. Ojo, *Money and Banking Analysis and Policy in the Nigerian Context* (London: George Allen and Unwin, 1981), p. 56.
25. G. E. Okurume, "Nigerian Agriculture Bank, Its Function and Prospects," *The Bullion*, Vol. 2, Nos 3 and 4, 1977.
26. T. A. Oyejide and A. Soyode, "Capital Earnings in the Insurance Industry: The Case of Nigeria," *QJA*, Vol. IX, No. 4, July 1978.
27. *Ibid.*
28. S. O. Asabia, "Impact of the Nigerian Enterprises Promotion Decrees on the Banks and Other Financial Markets," *QJA*, Vol. XVI, Nos 3 & 4, April/July 1982.
29. *Ibid.*, p. 139.
30. For more details, see J. O. Irukwu, *Insurance Management in Africa* (Ibadan: Caxton, n.d.); S. E. Omoruyi and C.A. Demuren, "The Growth of Insurance Business in Nigeria, 1969–78," *EFR*, Vol. 18, No. 1, June 1980.
31. CBN, Annual Report and Statement of Accounts (Lagos: CBN, 1988), pp. 80–81.
32. See J. O. Olakanpo, *Central Banking in the Commonwealth* (Calcutta, 1965); P. C. Okigbo, *Nigerian Financial System* (London: Longman, 1981); S. I. Ajayi and O. O. Ojo, *Money and Banking Analysis*, op. cit.
33. J. Mars "The Monetary and Banking System and Loan Market of Nigeria," in M. Perham (ed.), *Mining, Commerce and Finance in Nigeria* (London: Faber, 1948).
34. J. L. Fisher, *Report on the Desirability and Practicability of Establishing a Central Bank in Nigeria for Promotion the Economic Development of the Country* (Lagos: Government Printer, 1953).
35. Nigeria, *House of Representatives Debates* (Lagos: Government Printer, 1953), pp. 1172–83.
36. IBRD (World Bank), *The Economic Development of Nigeria: Report of a Mission* (Baltimore: Johns Hopkins University Press, 1955).
37. CBN, *Twenty Years of Central Banking in Nigeria* (Lagos: CBN, 1979).
38. J. B. Loynes, *Report on the Establishment of a Nigerian Central Bank, the Introduction of a Nigerian Currency and Other Associated Matters* (Lagos: Government Printer, 1957).
39. O. Teriba, "The 1967–69 Banking Amendment in Nigeria: An Appraisal of Financial Adaptation in an Underdeveloped Economy," *NJESS*, Vol. 12, No. 1, March 1970; A. E. Ekukinam, "Administration of Nigeria Monetary Policy," *QJA*, Vol. III, 1968.
40. See J. O. Olakanpo, *Central Banking in the Commonwealth*, op. cit.; CBN, *Twenty Years of Central Banking*, op. cit.; O. Olashore, "Evolution of Banking Operation in Nigeria and the System of Control," *CBN Newsletter*, Vol. 2, Nos. 2 & 3, Feb/March, 1972.
41. S. B. Falegan, *Redesigning Nigeria's Financial System* (Ibadan: UPL, 1970).
42. F.U. Ezeuduji, Review of S.B. Falegan's book in *Economic and Financial Review*, Vol. 26, No. 1, March 1988.
43. Sam Aluko, "Financing Federal Systems: Suggestions for Revenue Sharing," in R. Olaniyan (ed.), *Federalism in a Changing World* (Lagos: The Presidency, 1988).
44. Nigeria, *Fiscal Commission, 1957–58: Report* (London: HMSO, 1958).
45. Nigeria, *Fiscal Review Commission: Report* (Lagos: Government Printer, 1964).
46. Nigeria, *Report of the Technical Committee on Revenue Allocation under the Military* (Lagos: Government Printer, 1979).

47. Nigeria, *Report of the Presidential Commission on Revenue Allocation* (Lagos: Government Printer, 1980), 4 vols.
48. See A. G. Adebayo, *Embattled Federalism: A History of Revenue Allocation in Nigeria* (New York: Peter Lang, 1993).
49. David G. Offensend, "Centralization and Fiscal Arrangement in Nigeria," *Journal of Modern African Studies*, Vol. 14, No. 3, September 1976.
50. A. O. Phillips, "Three decades of Intergovernmental Financial Relationship in the Federation of Nigeria," *QJA*, Vol. XIV, No. 2, January 1980.
51. A. G. Adebayo, *Embattled Federalism*, pp. 165–75.
52. It would be worthwhile to be able to determine the share of the Yoruba-speaking parts of Nigeria in the federally allocated revenue. However, this is not our goal here. It is certainly difficult to specify how much money the Federal Government spent on a particular region. In addition to statutory allocation from the Federation Account (or the DPA), there were direct federal transfers to Local Governments, and direct federal investment spending in the states (such as through the siting of industries). There were loans from the federal to state and local governments as well. Moreover, there were federal expenditures on social services, such as hospitals, schools and universities, roads, hotels, and tourism. These are impossible to quantify with accuracy. Those interested in pursuing an analysis of how fair or unfair the revenue allocation system has been could begin with the data on revenue allocation we have supplied in Tables 6 and 7.
53. Cyril I. Obi, "The Impact of Oil on Nigeria's Revenue Allocation System: Problems and Prospects for National Reconstruction," in Kunle Amuwo *et al.* (eds.), *Federalism and Political Restructuring in Nigeria* (Ibadan: Spectrum Books, 1998).
54. The actual transfer of federal ministries and institutions did not begin until the 1990s and has not been completed. Lagos has remained Nigeria's entrepot and major commercial and business center.
55. E. O. Akeredolu-Ale, *The Underdevelopment of Indigenous Entrepreneurship in Nigeria* (Ibadan: IUP, 1975).
56. Examples were *Atoka*, *Aworerin*.
57. S. O. Osoba, "The Nigerian Power Elite, 1952–65" in P.C.W. Gutkind and Peter Waterman (eds.), *African Social Studies: A Radical Reader* (London: Heinemann, 1977), pp. 368–78.
58. A. G. Adebayo, *Embattled Federalism*, p. 123.
59. Billy Dudley, *An Introduction to Nigerian Government and Politics* (London: Longman, 1982), pp. 119.
60. J. L. Brandler, *Out of Nigeria: Witness to a Giant's Toils* (London: The Radcliffe Press, 1993).
61. *Ibid.*, pp. 307–09. The deal with Mr. Negus got Parazone an interview with the NNPC, but the company was unsuccessful partly because its management was not familiar with "how they do business" in Nigeria. For instance, Mr. Berry lost his temper when he was kept waiting for almost an hour. Mr. Brandler explained the outcome philosophically: "It was only much later that I discovered the cause of the debacle. Negus had many friends and many enemies, and the latter prevailed when they found out that he was about to clinch a deal." Parazone eventually got into the Nigerian crude oil business. Mr. Brandler found another "agent," Mr. Lisan, who clinched the deal.
62. Osoba, *op. cit.*, p. 378.
63. Dudley, *op. cit.*
64. The investigation ordered by the Murtala regime into the assets of state governors under General Gowon's administration surprisingly found the governors of

Lagos and Western states clean. This does not detract from our position here that the Yoruba power elite, like the rest of their Nigerian counterparts, enriched themselves through their direct access to governmental funds.

65. They include Nigeria, *Report of the Federal Assets Investigation Panel* (Lagos: FMOI, 1976); *Report of the Special Panel on the Farms of Alhaji Audu Bako and Mr. S. O. Ogbemudia* (Lagos: FMOI, 1976); *Federal Military Government's Views on the Report of the Federal Assets Investigation Panel* (Lagos: FMOI, 1976); Benue-Plateau State, *Government Decisions on the Report of the Panel of Inquiry into the Benue-Plateau State Houses and Contract Procedure* (Jos: Government Printer, 1975); Borno State, *Government's Views on the Report of the Judicial Commission of Inquiry into the Suspended Damaturu Local Government* (Maiduguri: Government Printer, 1978).

TABLE 6
Statutory Allocation of Revenue to State Governments, 1970/71–1974/75

Unit: Naira

STATES	1970–71		1971–72		1972–73		1973–74		1974–75	
	(Naira)	%	(Naira)	%	(Naira)	%	(Naira)	%	(Naira)	%
BENUE-PLATEAU	17,057,506	6.0	19,979,480	6.1	19,987,874	6.2	19,687,627	5.4	37,165,045	4.5
EAST-CENTRAL	25,723,558	9.0	30,860,744	9.4	31,645,292	9.8	36,068,488	10.0	72,097,715	8.7
KANO	24,245,604	8.5	25,929,040	7.9	26,210,896	8.1	22,517,559	6.2	43,190,387	5.2
KWARA	13,342,066	4.7	16,111,048	4.9	15,712,195	4.9	15,108,788	4.2	28,940,069	3.5
LAGOS	13,995,322	4.9	15,554,140	4.8	13,692,047	4.3	13,209,824	3.6	32,321,170	3.9
MID-WESTERN	38,456,600	13.4	44,304,596	13.6	46,718,004	14.5	84,892,664	23.5	253,645,660	28.0
NORTH-CENTRAL	16,849,192	5.9	19,546,672	6.0	19,528,879	6.1	18,582,438	5.1	35,945,246	4.3
NORTH-EASTERN	23,721,956	8.5	27,662,790	8.5	27,548,612	8.6	26,438,804	7.3	50,797,171	6.1
NORTH-WESTERN	19,257,272	6.7	23,038,550	7.1	23,052,163	7.2	22,064,740	6.1	42,031,566	5.0
RIVERS	22,531,290	7.9	33,075,840	10.1	30,640,708	9.5	47,385,821	13.1	163,242,042	19.6
SOUTH-EASTERN	20,714,898	7.2	18,898,370	5.8	20,947,372	6.5	22,530,647	6.2	34,713,131	4.2
WESTERN	50,078,608	17.5	51,660,374	15.8	46,084,667	14.3	33,413,404	9.3	59,348,936	7.1
TOTAL	285,973,872	100	326,621,644	100	321,768,709	100	361,900,804	100	833,438,337	100

Sources: Nigeria, *Estimates* (various years); Nigeria, *Accountant-General's Report with Financial Statements* (various years). Nigeria, *Official Gazettes* (various years); Federal Office of Statistics, *Annual Abstracts of Statistics* (various years).

Currency conversion rate: N1 ≅ $2

TABLE 7

Statutory Revenue Allocation to State Governments, 1976/77–1990

Units: %; N million

States	1976/77	1977/78	1978/79	1980	1981	1982	1983	1984	1985	1986	1987	1988	1989	1990
Akwa Ibom	—	—	—	—	—	—	—	—	—	—	1.6	4.0	4.3	4.5
Anambra	5.1	5.2	5.3	5.5	5.2	5.5	5.5	5.5	5.5	5.2	5.4	5.6	5.7	5.4
Bauchi	4.2	4.2	4.4	4.1	4.5	4.3	4.3	4.4	4.5	5.0	4.4	4.2	4.1	4.4
Bendel	11.1	8.9	8.8	8.9	8.1	7.0	7.0	7.0	6.8	6.8	6.6	6.2	6.7	6.1
Benue	4.2	4.3	4.4	4.8	4.5	4.4	4.5	4.3	4.1	3.9	4.3	4.3	3.6	4.3
Borno	5.2	4.7	4.8	4.8	5.4	5.0	4.9	5.1	5.2	5.5	5.2	5.0	5.0	5.4
Cross-River	5.1	6.3	5.2	5.5	5.2	5.3	5.3	5.4	5.1	5.0	4.3	2.8	3.0	3.7
Gongola	4.3	4.5	4.5	4.3	4.6	4.5	4.5	4.4	4.6	4.6	4.5	4.4	4.2	4.9
Imo	5.9	6.3	6.1	6.5	6.0	5.9	6.1	5.3	5.6	5.2	5.7	5.6	5.7	5.3
Kaduna	5.8	5.6	5.7	5.7	5.8	6.0	5.9	6.3	6.6	6.8	5.3	3.5	3.0	3.9
Kano	6.8	7.0	7.1	6.8	6.8	7.5	7.4	8.0	8.4	8.7	7.9	7.7	7.8	6.8
Katsina	—	—	—	—	—	—	—	—	—	—	1.7	4.4	4.1	4.1
Kwara	3.6	3.7	3.8	3.8	4.1	3.6	3.6	3.6	3.8	2.9	3.2	3.3	3.3	4.1
Lagos	3.4	3.5	3.6	3.5	3.4	4.0	4.0	4.0	4.2	4.8	4.3	4.1	4.2	3.9
Niger	3.2	3.3	3.4	3.2	3.6	3.1	3.1	2.7	2.9	3.1	3.0	2.8	2.9	3.5
Ogun	3.5	3.6	3.6	3.4	3.6	3.5	3.5	3.6	3.5	3.8	3.7	3.4	3.3	3.8
Ondo	4.4	4.5	4.6	4.4	4.5	4.7	4.7	4.2	4.1	3.6	4.2	4.3	4.3	4.5
Oyo	6.3	6.5	6.6	6.7	6.5	6.9	6.8	6.9	7.2	7.4	6.9	6.9	6.9	6.2
Plateau	3.9	4.0	4.1	3.9	4.2	3.8	3.9	3.4	2.9	2.7	3.2	3.6	3.8	4.0
Rivers	8.1	8.9	8.1	8.4	7.9	6.8	6.8	7.1	6.2	5.9	6.1	5.9	6.1	5.4
Sokoto	5.8	6.0	6.1	5.6	6.3	6.2	6.3	6.2	6.5	6.6	6.5	6.2	6.1	5.9
FCT Abuja	—	—	—	—	—	2.0	1.9	2.3	2.5	2.5	2.0	1.8	1.9	—
Total %	100.0	100.0	100.0	100.0	100.0	100.0	100.0	100.0	100.0	100.0	100.0	100.0	100.0	100.0
Total Revenue	1,415	1,796	1,631	4,165	3,826	3,312	3,240	2,865	3,344	2,916	6,324	8,333	10,091	13,510

Sources: CBN, *Annual Report and Statement of Accounts*, various years; Nigeria, *Estimates*, various years.
Currency conversion rates: 1970s N1 ≡ \$2; 1980–85 N1 ≡ \$1.50; 1986–1990 N1 ≡ \$5

13

"Hard Times": Currency Devaluation and Changing Lifestyle

Ohun ti i tan ni odun eegun
Bi o ba ya Omo Alagbaa yio fi oojo mu'ko.
(Nothing lasts forever: All the feasting
by the Chief Priest's son terminates
after the masquerade festival).

Nothing lasts forever, indeed! The oil boom lasted only a few years. Arab producers were back in the oil market in 1974 after the Yom Kippur War. Oil prices stabilized. Western economies recovered. The oil crisis ended. As for Nigeria, the boom times were over. The crunch times were here, a time of belt-tightening measures and external borrowing. The "hard times" had begun.

In Yorubaland the hard times were quickly manifested in the scarcity of money. Money was scarce to the majority of the population, but abundant to a few with connection to state power and corruption. Not that money scarcity was a new phenomenon, but the prolonged inflation and the collapse of productive agriculture had created more poor people than at any other time during the century. Objects of status became largely Western—expensive cars, satellite dishes, grandiose architectural buildings, and the like. Traditional ways of demonstrating status had equally survived—lavish parties, excessive consumption habits, expensive clothes and jewelry, and so forth. The Yoruba society underwent profound changes and tensions in the way the people related to poverty, wealth, materialism, and globalization. In this chapter, we examine the attempts to adjust to declining fortunes associated with the Structural Adjustment Program (SAP) initiated by the military in the mid-1980s. While it has brought a decline in fortunes to many people, the society has moved more in the direction of materialism and in the worship of money. We bring together what we consider the major analytical points on price shifts, title taking, club membership, and social payments in the contemporary Yoruba society.

The historical period is the 1980s, when the government introduced first a series of "austerity measures"[1] and second the SAP. To illustrate more general points we focus on the impact of SAP on leisure and the ways in which the Yoruba adjust their expectations to fluctuations in income. To connect with some of the issues in the preceding chapters we bring together the major analytical points on price shifts, title taking, club membership, and social payments in the contemporary society.

The discussion deals with changing lifestyles, adaptations, and patterns of tension among groups and between individuals by contrasting interests and values in a modern stratified society. The individual or collective reaction to SAP could varied from outright acceptance, passivity, narrowly self-serving interests, and manipulation of divisive forces, to one of outright condemnation and rejection. Since we deal with a plural society much under the influence of neocolonial forces and institutions, these reactions often necessitated a situation whereby individuals and groups were variously adjusting and/or contending in order to ensure their survival or progress.

The settings that are assumed here include two interrelated social orders. The first is the stratified order—the class system—and its contrastive and contrasting value systems. The second is the internal-external relations (external to the Yoruba and other Nigerians at large) which, on the one hand, are partly responsible for the neocolonial programs imposed on the people and, on the other hand, have introduced bourgeois capitalism that further expands the gap between the indigenous social classes. Values within this development often have ambiguous, complex, and subtle meanings in the society.

Two main theses emerge in this discussion. The first is that before and after the introduction of SAP in 1986, there has been a gradual destruction of collective values. A mix-match of cultures and attitudes was in place, so mosaic and so vague as to confuse the general observer of the Yoruba society. The preceding years of plenty, the oil boom era, had dealt a heavy blow on the postcolonial balance and synthesis. New "money men" emerged, but not many new productive enterprises to justify and sustain their wealth. Many began to aspire to be rich, not through work but through corruption and other dubious means. The second thesis is that shifting cultural-psychological identifications and social mobility are increasingly important and valuable—as forces for social change—among the Yoruba people.

By focusing on the Yoruba, we are treating a national issue like an ethnic one. Of course, the emphasis here is on reactions to a national program; indeed, to an imposed condition. Our attention is not on a national response but on specific values and behaviors. Both values and behavior are often related: for instance, the introduction of new values and the questioning of old values can generate crisis in moral or political behavior. At the moment, the Nigerian crisis illuminates entitlements and motivates actions to contend the legitimacy and power of the ruling elite. It is assumed here that the Yoruba elite (to be specific) would see SAP as consistent with their "superior" values but that the individuals and subgroups within the subordinate collectivities, possessing the least power and property, would seek to resist the new values and protest their increasing marginalization. The ensuing tension and struggles may contain enormous potential to destroy the traditional culture or reorganize it in a radically new way.

"Hard Times": The Structure Adjustment Program (SAP)[2]

The hard times were usually associated with the Shagari (NPN) administration, but they began earlier. The Shagari and Buhari administrations tried unsuccessfully to tackle the problems with draconian, authoritarian measures. The Babangida regime decided to do it differently. The regime's economic experts diagnosed that the problem of the economy was basically structural; and that "adjustments" had to be made to the structure and nature of the state, the size of government, its expenditure, its functions, and control over the economy. It was believed that such adjustments would have a positive effect on the depressed economy and result in the promotion of free enterprise under the control of market forces. Economic planners further reasoned that the inauguration of this structural adjustment would have to precede any discussions on the nature of the Fifth National Development Plan.[3] Thus, the SAP was introduced in 1986 while the introduction of the Fifth Plan was postponed.

Unlike the usual national development plans, SAP was not embodied in any widely publicized and coherently written government guideline or statement.[4] In addition, the general theory on which SAP was based was not entirely homespun. Rather, it was a concept originally developed in the advanced industrialized economies and brought to Third

World countries by international financial organizations, the World Bank and the International Monetary Fund (IMF). Ostensibly, the program was designed to put the dislocated economies of the Third World back on course, not so much as a humanitarian endeavor but in order to enable them to perform their proper role in the international division of labor. In short, SAP could be described as a form of short- and medium-term programs for economic recovery to be adopted by developing nations, including Nigeria, so that they would be better able to pay their debt. This is why SAP is constantly being reviewed at every forum where debt rescheduling and negotiations are made as well as within the individual countries where the program is being executed. It is necessary to begin our consideration of the Nigerian experience under SAP with a brief survey of Nigeria's political economy after the toppling of the military administration of General Muhammadu Buhari.

Shortly after taking over the reins of government in August 1985, the military administration of President Ibrahim Babangida initiated a public debate over whether or not the country should take an IMF loan. The FMG then revealed part of the IMF *conditionalities*, which included currency devaluation, removal of government subsidies on social services, privatization and commercialization of government corporations, deregulation and trade liberalization, and generally a significant reduction in government spending. Between October and December 1985, the public debated the issues involved. The popular decision reached was that the loan should be rejected and that Nigerians were resolved to seek internal solutions to salvage the economy. Government accepted this verdict; but contrary to the expectation of all those who participated in the debate, the FMG accepted the IMF conditions for implementation. In June 1986, the SAP package was introduced.

Unlike earlier development plans, and unlike regular government programs, the objectives of SAP were not clearly stated. Indeed, it was doubtful if the government itself was fully aware of the full, immediate, and long-term implications of the various policies that were eventually introduced under SAP. The objectives of SAP can only be compiled from scattered government publications and other writings.[5] They included:

1. to restore the country to a healthy balance of payments position;
2. to diversify the productive base of the economy;
3. to alter and realign aggregate domestic expenditure with production and consumption patter;
4. to minimize the country's dependence on the oil sector and imported inputs; and

5. to thrust the economy onto the path of noninflationary and sustainable growth and development.

Thus, like the Economic Stabilization Act of 1982, SAP was designed as a short-term measure to redress the problems of the economy. However, as the economic crisis deepened, more medium-term measures were taken under SAP.[6] A comprehensive discussion of these measures is impossible here, but reference will be made to nine of them here.

1. Devaluation of the Currency: This was done through the Second-tier Foreign Exchange Market (SFEM), later called Foreign Exchange Market (FEM). It succeeded in combating the problem of issuance of import licenses, a process that was thoroughly abused during the Second Republic. On the other hand, it also succeeded in turning the Naira into virtually worthless paper. For instance, by December 1989 one US dollar was being exchanged for N7.5. This fell to N20 by May 1992, and fell further to N85 on the "black market" by August 1998.

2. Trade Liberalization: The earliest form of this was the elimination of the Produce Marketing Boards in 1986. It was believed that this would remove one of the biggest impediments to international trade and eliminate import licenses and other foreign exchange controls. It had a positive effect in raising the income of farmers, especially the producers of cash crops like cocoa, cotton, and rubber. But since these goods are also being consumed in Nigeria either directly or as industrial raw materials, prices were bound to go up to reflect the current exchange rates. This has been the case with cocoa-based beverages, cotton-piece goods, and rubber products. In addition, since the producers of these commodities are generally illiterate peasants, they possessed little knowledge of the wider Nigerian market and much less information about the conditions of the international market for their goods. The elimination of the marketing boards merely left them open to the vagaries of the international market and to exploitation by dubious middlemen.

3. Balancing the Budget: This was an ambitious program. The government sought to reduce budget deficit through staff reduction and retrenchment, expenditure rationalization, and a better tax administration. This came at a high social cost. More and more people joined the already glutted labor market. The number of the unemployed increased phenomenally. Efforts at creating jobs—through the National Directorate of Employment—did not yield significant success. The NDE stepped up campaign that job seekers should consider self-employment in farming, small-scale businesses, and petty trading. The campaign failed to acknowledge the problem of availability of land, capital, and managerial abilities and experiences. Where money was provided by the NDE, these were generally too little to start the business and many beneficiaries lacked appropriate skills and enterprise to run a successful business.

4. Promotion of Agriculture: The federal and state governments were enjoined to promote agricultural production through higher producer prices, better organized extension services, and prohibition of importation of certain foods that could be produced in the country. The result has been an increase in agricultural production but it also came at a cost. Increase in agricultural yield was at the expense of the small-scale producers who lacked access to capital and who were losing their traditional titles to land to richer urban dwellers actively purchasing farmlands in rural areas.

5. Industrialization: Industrial growth was promoted by encouraging higher rates of utilization of installed capacity, local sourcing of raw materials, maintenance of plants, and the participation of medium- and small-scale enterprises in the country's industrial development. Also, the government changed the import substitution approach to industrialization to what became termed as import replacement.

6. Privatization: The debate over privatization has been lively and heated.[7] Proponents of SAP—especially technocrats and leading members of the Babangida administration—argued that through privatization the efficiency of businesses hitherto run by government would increase, more profit would be made, and the financial burden on public finance (in term of subsides and subventions to these corporations) would cease. Antagonists argued that privatization would widen the gap between the rich and the poor, since the rich also have access to financial resources with which to buy government's shares in these businesses. The government seemed committed to this program, and shares in many government-owned businesses were offered for sale to the public. To mute the voice of opposition, some state governments offered their workers loans with which to purchase these shares. Progress toward privatization has been slow, unlike many other programs of SAP.

7. Removal of Subsidy on Government Services: The government embarked on appropriate pricing policies, especially the removal of subsidies on petroleum products and public enterprises. The effect of these on members of the public has been very severe. Many Nigerians found it difficult to understand why they were paying higher prices for petroleum products when the country is an oil producer and at a time the international price of crude oil was falling. The removal of subsidy in other areas—such as agricultural inputs, health services, and education—was also being pursued. For instance, in many states students were required to bring their desks and chairs to school, as the government was no longer supplying them.

8. Special Reflationary Expenditure: The Central Bank recalled from the banks the Naira value of rescheduled external commercial debts. The funds would then be utilized to pay off the debts when they fall due. What this meant was that the federal government had borrowed these funds from the banks at zero interest to meet "special" expenditure obligations. In strict terms, reflation is designed to promote growth by expanding the utilization of existing and idle capacity and expanding the scope of productive employment.[8] In 1987 alone, the government spent N2.5 million (about $625,000) for repair and maintenance of school and health facilities, N100 million ($25 million) for computer literacy, N40 million ($10 million) for rehabilitation of Youth Development Centres, and N60 million ($15 million) for rehabilitation of Federal Hospitals. These constituted about 35 percent of the reflationary fund. The larger percentage was to be expended abroad, largely on importation, thereby depleting the foreign exchange. Among them, N700 million (about $175 million) would be spent on mass transportation; N350 million (487.5 million) on flat steel production, NEPA, and the like, N120 million ($30 million) for special equipment for the Police, and N160 million ($40 million) for the purchase of special equipment for the Ministry of External Affairs. Pius Okigbo has aptly stated that these expenditures were actually not "special"—they were the "normal nonrevenue generating capital expenditure" and should not constitute reflation.[9]

9. Debt Rescheduling: Since 1984/85, Nigeria has begun to service her external debts, which kept growing annually. As at December 1985, the debt stood at $18,348 billion; by October 1987 it had increased to $23,445 billion. (Other figures quoted in the same month ranged from $26 billion to $27 billion.) The federal government's approach to the debt problem was to reschedule the existing stock of debt and have part of it cancelled. Rescheduling had two advantages: the repayment period was lengthened and the interest rate was reduced. On the other hand, rescheduling was a tedious exercise, wasted time and money, and lowered the dignity of the debtor country before creditor countries (Paris Club) and creditor banks (London Club). A corollary to rescheduling which the country also attempted was the debt-equity swap. Many people outside government circles suggested total repudiation of these debts because they have been crippling public finance. For instance, in 1988 the provision in Nigeria's federal government budget for debt service was $1.711 billion, representing 23.1 percent of gross earning of $7.4 billion, or 25 percent of net earnings of $6.82 billion. This situation would certainly not promote growth in the economy.

The foregoing fairly summarizes the short- and medium-term objectives and measures under the rubrics of SAP. There is no doubt that the World Bank and IMF were actively involved in the formulation of these programs. It is also possible that these international organizations were acting as proxies for Nigeria's creditors. A number of studies have appraised the achievements of SAP since its introduction. Most of the establishment writings have extolled the gains of SAP[10] while the radical literature has been critical of its objectives, policies, programs, and operation. On the other hand, a few cautious remarks have been made in more conservative analyses.[11] In any case there is no denying the hardship that the policies and programs pursued under SAP held for the average Nigerian, and the improbability of any quick solutions to these problems.

The impact of SAP on Yoruba society is examined in the rest of this chapter. But first, in the next section we establish the theoretical framework for our analysis of changes in values and in interpersonal and intergroup relations in the face of declining money supply.

Dominant Values and Intergroup Relations

Specifically, in terms of the orientation of the debate, we can discern two positions in the sources: the liberal and Marxist scholars. These two orientations share certain things in common. First, they are interested in the conditions of the poor and the underprivileged, however they also inadvertently focus on the values of the dominant groups. As they seek to answer the issue of stratification, they also answer the question of how access to wealth and power is regularized; how groups achieve specific adaptations to each other; "and how intergroup relations evolve along general and specific trajectories as determined by general and specific conditions."[12]

A second issue is that state-society relations have increasingly been on a collision course. The state actively promoted conflict through the denial of citizen's rights, through the state's increasing distance from the concerns and expectations of its plural society, through the massive buildup of coercive instruments to deal with internal agitation, and through the operation of an exploitative economy. The reaction of the civil society has been equally strong: there is an increase in armed robbery, intensified competition, and rampant religious conflict.[13] Marxists have attempted to rationalize the development as an inevitable product of, first, cultural specificities derived from traditions associated with alien sociocultural systems; and second, the internal stratification in their own right (classes that are) analogous to or even parallel with the power structure of the national leadership. In terms of the latter perspective, Bade Onimode, an avowed Nigerian Marxist scholar, expressed the role of ethnic strategy for the emergent bourgeoisie in Nigeria in the following words:

> [T]he power exercised by leaders of major political parties would appear to derive mainly from the class and communal foundations of those parties and their unofficial ancillary structures. Communal interest groups generally accept the leadership of emergent and dominant class interest groups.[14]

What has motivated and sustained the acceptance of the new dominant class is not clearly explained by Onimode, but one gets the impression that sociocultural differentiation is not of itself a sufficient reason for accepting a leadership that is violent and insensitive. Indeed, we also note that protests against the policies of the ruling elite cut across ethnic boundaries. We therefore think that the overall significance of this paradigm of cultural difference must be understood as part of an evolved system of stratification which is not "natural," but imposed. Indeed, to accept cultural difference as *sine qua non* to violence implies that ethnic pluralism negates development. Examples from other parts of the world, notably from the Western societies, do not support this viewpoint. We must, therefore, reject this position.

This is not to deny, however, that there is an overlap between indigenous and modern stratification systems. Rather, the specific characters of the indigenous classes and cultures are themselves a response to the character of the modern stratification that was created and nurtured by the colonial regimes; they did not evolve directly from the creativity of the people. According to Karl Polanyi, there is, however, a rider:

> [T]he fate of classes is much more often determined by the needs of society than the fate of society is determined by the needs of classes. Given a definite structure of society, the class theory works; but what if that structure itself undergoes change? A class that has become functionless may disintegrate and be supplanted overnight by a new class or classes. Also, the chances of classes in a struggle will depend upon their ability to win support from outside their own membership, which, again, will depend upon their fulfillment of tasks set by interests wider than their own. Thus, neither the birth nor the death of classes, neither their cooperations nor their antagonisms can be understood apart from the situation of society as a whole.[15]

Polanyi does not see a society that is exclusive from the dynamics of its internal and external relations. The needs within the society are as much conditioned by changes in the world economic order as by a change in local climate. The essential role played by class interests in social change is in the nature of things; it inheres in the process of initiating and responding to change. Whether the source of the change be war, trade imbalance, external debt, or startling inventions, all sections of the society must respond; they must adjust their interests or seek to consolidate their positions. The "challenge" is to society as a whole; the response comes through groups, sections, and classes.[16]

The challenge to the Nigerian nation is to replace its "subsistence economy" with a "cash economy." Within this scheme, rural Nigerians could acquire cash with which to buy the goods they want through two main methods: either by growing a cash crop on their lands or, where this is impracticable, by selling their labor. Among the Yoruba, the radical change into the modern economy started as late as the nineteenth century with the introduction of cocoa and the establishment of colonial rule. The acceptance of a cash economy is not, however, the issue; rather, the modes of operation require skills, organization, and dynamism that are not fully grasped. The result is that rural and urban dwellers sell their labor directly to the international market through employment with the multinational corporations, or to the national market through employment in public or private services. Yet, labor does not translate into capital accumulation, nor are commodities controlled in such a way as to yield the maximum benefits they are capable of. Their earning power is invariably substantially influenced by the operation of the free market system in which external factors participate. The differential income, if any, is a factor of production and of a mode of distribution well controlled by the multinational corporations and their national agents.

By the 1970s, a substantial increase in oil production also meant an increase in the revenue earning capacity of the nation, and also of personal incomes. But corruption during the oil boom led to fiscal maladministration. It also led to mismanagement of public funds, and to the formulation of interventionist policies designed to encourage economic development. Economic development itself was no more than the maximum flow of human and material resources consistent with minimum consumption requirement—with reasonable economic stability in the face of long-run inflationary pressure and short-run international price movements.[17] The conditions under which the government had to intervene in the market economy in the 1980s had much to do with an unsteady oil price, heavy external debt, poor mobility of factors, nonoptimal income distribution, low economic efficiency, and monopoly under technological externality.[18] Two possibilities were open: the production sector could either be arranged so that a satisfactory income distribution was achieved at the expense of economic efficiency, or economic efficiency through allocational efficiency and a satisfactory income distribution.[19] The latter would lead to welfare maximization.

But the government was less enthusiastic about more welfare programs that could only increase external debt. As such, redistribution aimed at altering the pattern of consumption favored a change in production techniques and in consumption habits and tastes. It was reasoned that the best arrangement for realizing these ends was to subject public management to the play of market forces. In other words, "to adjust the exchange rate via the Foreign Exchange Market (FEM), liberalize the exchange and trade system, remove controls throughout the economy and on prices, improve the fiscal balance by tightening monetary and fiscal policies, promote non-oil exports as well as improve the country's balance of payments position."[20]

The historical current that led to the introduction of SAP is already examined above.[21] The implication of the policy has received equally wide attention, although the liberals' and Marxists' positions seem to differ. To begin with, all the scholars would agree that some interventionist policies were necessary to save the economy from its inefficient performance. But the Marxists see SAP as an attempt to expand the capitalist conspiracy to defraud the poor in the interests of big business. Marxists further consider SAP a protectionist measure as a program that primarily serves the interests of the upper classes. However, the liberals consider SAP as essential to status mobility and the expansion of the elite membership. To them, the advantages of SAP include an increase in price of cash crops and the transformation of Nigeria from a credit-based trading company to a cash-and-carry one on the basis of easy accessibility to foreign exchange from the banks.[22] It is also argued that foreign exchange is now allocated more efficiently to the raw material sourcing and that locally produced materials enjoy greater patronage. The national currency, the Naira, is now correctly valued[23] and the public service is more efficient.[24] Also, the consumption patterns and tastes are said to be realistically in tune with the local level of production.[25] The liberals would also admit that the SAP produced an increase in inflationary pressure, and a redistribution of income from workers to businessmen. They think that these disadvantages are less damaging to the economy.

From either the liberal or the Marxist position, the overall significance of SAP is that existing class relations must be understood as part of an imposed system of economy. In essence, SAP is as much politically rooted in expanding Western economy as in a declining local productive ability. The impact is to be felt in the deteriorating conditions of life, in the decrease in wage earnings, in the absence of vital food and material supplies, and in the failure to respond to challenges. To restate the issue more clearly: the point of contention is that the liberals and the Marxists write—without thinking much about it, no doubt—as if they are examining the social universe from somewhere near a moral center. From this standpoint, all exceptions to the established order of social structure and supporting values appear irrelevant or marginal—be they the mobility of the lower class or the change in taste and consumption patterns. Nothing obscures their social vision as effectively as their economic prejudice. They ignore issues of cultural degradation. As Karl Polanyi noted,

> Yet it is precisely this emphasis put on exploitation that tends to hide from our view the even greater issue of cultural degeneration. If exploitation is defined in strictly economic terms as a permanent inadequacy of ratios of exchange, it is doubtful whether, as a matter of fact, there was exploitation. The catastrophe of the native community is a direct result of the rapid and violent disruption of the basic institutions of the victim.... These institutions are disrupted by the very fact that a market economy is foisted upon an entirely differently organized community: labor and land are made into commodities, which, again, is only a short formula for the liquidation of every and any cultural institution in an organic society...[26]

Next, we turn to the impact of SAP on consumption patterns, focusing on the specific example of consumption in leisure. The quality of this section is further enhanced by insightful comments in local and national daily newspaper, magazines, and journals.

The Culture of Leisure

Traditional Yoruba society makes a distinction between "liminality" and "liminoid," as time away from work directed by different actors to the pursuit of society's creative agenda. There is really no confusion in their minds regarding what each stands for. Hence, while the rituals and festivities are directed by religious leaders, leisure, as aspect of the liminoid, is the time that is understood as being free of religious dogma, taboos, or leadership. This, then, is the time to play *ayo,* to drink palmwine (that is, wine from palm trees), to engage in debates, to organize wrestling competitions, to visit friends, and to date. Both the liminal and the liminoid activities do coexist in the society, although from all indications the liminality is much more elaborate, time consuming, and challenging than the liminoid. It is even possibly more threatening to the social order since the consumption of alcohol tolerated during leisure is disapproved in the liminal condition where, without the intoxicants, law and order are easily subverted by physical aggression.

With the process of modernization, the structure of liminality in traditional rituals and festivals has been assaulted and eroded by Christianity and Islam, but the liminoid sphere has expanded to include tourism, overseas holidays, and modern games such as squash and table tennis, video shows, and movies. The liminoid has become more expensive with increasing sensitivity to Western tastes and values; it has become more educational, but yet not as creative as traditional liminal contexts. However, it is no less equally threatening to the social order since, as suggested by a former police officer, the Nigerian military plan their coups during leisure, while consuming "pepper soup."

Several points of similarity do exist in leisure, as we know, before the advent of colonialism and thereafter until the introduction of SAP. First, it is less communal but tailored to the expression of individualistic artistry or expression. Second, it involves huge expenditures on entertainment, quite often invested in alcohol, food, and delicatessen. However, the lower class can still afford it through savings or, alternatively, by becoming involved in the production of entertainment materials. Third, there is little or no attempt to "privatize" the affairs since it involves audience-actor participation. Therefore, the artistry can be seen by everybody and critically assessed. Fourth, they are quite often monitored by agents of the state to ensure that order prevails, and also to collect information to ensure the stability of the state. Fifth, the context of activity is rarely changed so as not to disrupt public/participant expectations. Sixth, it is an atmosphere charged by rivalry and competition, by attempts to ensure conformity to rules, and by failure to satisfy needs and wants. In short, there is always the possibility of conflict, even if this is not expressed. It all depends on the limit set to deviance.

With the introduction of SAP, some aspects of leisure have been modified. The consumption pattern has changed and only the rich can afford to satisfy the demands of the culture of leisure. For example, at the beer parlors, hotels, and recreation centers, the lower and middle class no longer engage in gift drink ritual as they did before 1986. That is, they neither buy drinks for the man sitting next to them nor for friends who may accidentally stroll into the bar. Because of the high cost of beer, most people buy for themselves only. Also, since they cannot afford to buy many, they just "rush" their beer and go, there being little or no time for extensive talk over drinks and no strong in-group feeling. With the element of sociability reduced, the bar is supposedly a spot for contacting social diseases; that is, for interacting with an "ideology that encodes class-related biases in a presumably medical way and which thus makes certain groups possess behaviors that are pathological and require a cure."[27] Those who visit the bar then pass to the relevant publics as "the drunkards," "the a-religious," and "the depressed." It would definitely not be correct to assert that this social stereotyping began with SAP. However, the image is lent credibility with SAP in that most people have either stopped or minimized entertaining themselves, their friends, or their families at recreation centers.

Indeed, the rise of voluntary associations between 1986 and 1990 was not partly unconnected with attempts by the upper class to distance itself from this social typing, thus bringing honour to their leisure. Today, the visibility of the Rotary Club, Lions Club, Zonta, Soroptomist, Full Gospel Businessmen's Fellowship, and ethnic associations are linked with a search for honor. The existence of these clubs is informed by the same tradition that governs their establishment elsewhere:

> As soon as several of the inhabitants...have taken up an opinion or a feeling which they wish to promote in the world, they look out for mutual assistance; and as soon as they have found one another out, they combine. From that moment on they are no longer isolated men, but a power seen from far, whose actions serve for an example and whose language is listened to.[28]

In voluntary associations, leisure is no longer a moment of freedom and it is no longer a "transcendental" experience (that is, one that cuts across social classes in its membership). It is unlike the real leisure, which is distinguished by that "simultaneous sublimation and dilution in which the heavily freighted forces of reality are felt only as from a distance, their weight fleeting in a charm."[29] The time is spent discussing and associational rules, and entertainment is not really "open" but closed to outsiders. For a leisure to function, those persons gathering together need not share the same identity or class, but they must act as if there is equality.

A Cultural Dilemma

The discussion above leads to one major issue: the individual in the middle and lower classes can hardly pay back services or appreciate love (as between husband and wife) or friendship through leisure, as much as they would have desired. There has been considerable cutback in spending, and luxurious items rarely "trickle down" anymore but are circulated mostly within the elite. The cultural dilemma, since SAP began, has been how to respond to appreciable encounters. In many cases, debts of cash or of kind accumulate. For instance, in the past, invitations were sent to friends to attend naming ceremonies, funeral services, weddings, and social clubs. The individual invitee then responded with gifts, with gift drink ritual, with visits, and with sponsorship for overseas holidays. But now, people either visit their friends and cut down on the entertainment expenses which the visits demand, or send some money to the celebrant and keep away. And, judged against an earlier background in which people not only visit but also exhibit high spending, some kinds of debts are invariably incurred.

The capital investment in social outings has also diminished considerably. This has forced a cutback in entertainment, and in status-supporting items like dress, mortuary price, and night parties. Table 1 shows the contraction in funeral ceremonies in the period between 1970 and 1980. First of all, much like the scenario painted for leisure, there is as yet no substantial attack on the uses of money for social payments. Second—and this is contradictory of the first—there is an attempt to find the means to contract social payments by incorporating cost-saving devices by borrowing from external practices (e.g., Western and Islamic) for legitimation. For instance, the traditional dimension of paying the chiefs some token amount, for their maintenance of law and order in the town, and/or for their social visits to the family of the deceased, all of that is now discontinued in conformity with Christian or Islamic practices which forbid recognition of such traditional "rituals."

Third, there is a circulation of old goods and second-hand items, all in the attempt to minimize new expenditures or reduce costs in fulfilling social payments. In fact, second-hand markets now flourish to sell all sorts of items or to barter old items with new. This exchange is extended to social payments; for example, gifts of old clothes, shoes, bags, and furniture. In some cases, those attending weddings or naming ceremonies simply pick from the collection of their own wedding or naming ceremony gifts.

TABLE 1
Funeral Presentations (Yoruba Christians): 1970s and 1980s Compared

1970s	1980s
1. Corpse stayed in the mortuary for months to allow for burial preparation. Entertainment and gifts commenced.	Corpse stayed in the mortuary for several days or weeks. Entertainment and gifts reduced.
2. Advertisement of announcement of death with instruction to await further announcement of funeral programs.	Announcement of death and program of burial at the same time.
3. Ceremony accompanies the collection of the corpse at the mortuary.	Collection of corpse without ceremony.
4. Wake-keeping ceremonies at the temporary and permanent residence of the deceased, with lavish entertainment, printed programs, and musical band in attendance.	One wake-keeping ceremony and light entertainment (usually tea and *akara*).
5. Traditional (non-Christian) ceremonies involving huge payments to chiefs.	Avoided or minimized.
6. Elaborate church service, with crowd overflowing outside of the church; fanciful program; different choirs in attendance.	The scale was reduced.
7. Elaborate feeding of guests, officiating ministers and choirs.	The scale was reduced.
8. Involvement and feeding of the whole town (in small communities) or big neighborhoods in big towns.	Feeding of invited guests only.
9. All-night party after burial, several musical bands invited; assorted foods and drinks served.	Night parties minimized in preference for a reception that ended by 6 p.m.
10. *Aso ebi*: imported and expensive clothes were worn.	*Aso ebi*: preference for cheap clothes.
11. Gifts to guests at the night parties (livestock, jewelry, spirits, etc.).	Gifts were minimized and items became inexpensive.
12. Thanksgiving service a week after burial with special service and another round of entertainment.	Thanksgiving service held on the following day, as part of the normal service; entertainment avoided.
13. Advertisement on radio and newspaper to thank all guests.	This became rare.
14. Months later: "turning the coffin" ceremony with entertainment.	This was avoided.
15. Annual celebrations with obituaries in the media.	This was avoided or reduced.
16. Gifts to the celebrant at every major phase.	A once-and-for-all gift.

We must not give the impression that when expenses at leisure, funeral, naming, or wedding ceremonies are reduced or old goods are circulated the individual accepts this as a new culture and, therefore, morally acceptable. Rather, those who indulge in this mode of social payment do often lament the lack of culture and do have misgivings about their actions. In other words, they would lament their inability to attend a friend's party and blame SAP for making them so poor as to not be able to afford the price of new items. It is as if a gift, a social visit, or a potluck embodies social expectations of commitment, loyalty, endurance, and consistency. Social payments are metaphors of good conduct or character. "The object of the exchange was to produce a friendly feeling between the two persons concerned, and unless it did this it failed of its purpose."[30]

We have, thus, pointed to changes: all to meet expectations rather than create new or revolutionary structures. This is much evident in Table 1, which reveals no new structures of social relations or calls attention to fundamental changes in styles and tastes. Rather, the desire to meet expectations intrinsically linked to old forms of stratification and prestige ratings leads to false self-presentations designed to soothe or massage a crippled ego. Thus, the amount of financial gifts in social functions is exaggerated, sometimes beyond imaginable proportion. For example, a chairman at a wedding reception may announce a gift of $5,000 to the new couple when, in actual fact, only $500 was given. To further boost his ego, the same chairman could promise to pay for the residential apartment of the couple for two years. He would, of course, receive an immediate applause, although the promise may never be fulfilled.

In all, at the root of the present cultural dilemma are the values attached to the concept of *Omoluabi*. When a person fails to make appropriate repayment, when he makes false declarations, when he sounds boastful or feels relatively weak and powerless in his efforts to redefine his social obligations, he unconsciously reckons with the attributes of an *Omoluabi:*

> To be an *Omoluabi* is to be of good character in all its ramifications. Good character, in the Yoruba sense, includes respect for old age, loyalty to one's parents and local traditions, honesty in all public and private dealings, devotion to duty, readiness to assist the needy and the infirm, sympathy, sociability, courage, and an itching desire for work and many other desirable qualities.[31]

Some of the attributes are presently under assault by consciousness of status, materially inspired. As Theophilus Danjuma, the country's chief of army staff from 1975 to 1979, noted,

> we've always had corruption in this country, as indeed the world over. But now, it is so abrasive, so flagrant and pervasive, that it is frightening.... Young military officers are living obviously above their means and nobody is asking questions.[32]

No longer is honesty a key value in the understanding of an *Omoluabi*. And, as we have noted, a good character may not hinge on respect for local traditions. Nevertheless, age, sex, status, space, matter, cause, relation, human nature, and society itself are social products that the society has produced to account for exchange. They serve to sustain the sense of reality and of good conducts. But they are not immutable products; they change, particularly in the ways and manners they are combined to produce an assessment of persons, behaviors, or situations. The root verb of *Omoluabi, wa,* supplies the cannon of this change. *Wa* is to be, to exist; all things that are exist insofar as they are beings-in-potential. When they cease to express their innate potentials, they cease to exist. When they manifest new potentials they change attitudes to their being.

The form of life that is most appropriate to a thing is one that allows the full efflorescence of the thing's essence. *Wa* is thus an axiological standard by which we apply moral epithets to human behavior:

> A form of life in which a thing's *iwa* (being) coincides with its essence is the best form of life of the thing. The greater the gulf between a thing and its essence, the less suited is its form of life to its essence. Thus, if we know the erga of a thing, the more its *iwa* is not an embodiment of these erga, the more we will say that its *iwa* is not good and vice versa.[33]

In the SAP culture, this blindness to the social basis of essential and justifiable behaviors makes a social reading of supposedly economic relations—*ipso facto,* one that is rational—deeply perplexing. This is due to the peculiar character of the abstraction associated with the economic exchange. Essential qualities of human beings and the means and mode of exchange are intricately interwoven such that goods and labor are representations of character, and character is the means of appreciating the worth of goods and labor. Take, for example, the false declaration of a gift of $5,000 instead of $500. The individual intends by this act to meet an expectation intrinsic to the essential character of a man of status: assistance to the needy and the infirm, generosity, and sociability. Had he donated less than this amount, he would hardly have drawn an applause from the audience, or, had he gotten one, he would be met inside or outside the hall by those who were disenchanted with his miserly, undignifying, and insulting donation.

The point is that the concept of *Omoluabi* interposes itself between persons, mediating direct awareness of social relations by the abstract principles of character. The Yoruba, even in SAP, live in this system of social relations that is aimed at the satisfaction of social bonds through an array of qualitatively defined needs. As such, debt repayments are not subject only to the whims of the market economy but to the criteria of moral assessment. The consequence is that social relations are never between things but between persons. Hence, it is morally acceptable to blame a rich man for not overlooking a debt, or a "small" balance in repayment. It is also acceptable in some fashion to reproach a man for not wanting to pay up the debt. Both are likely to damage a relationship whose potential usefulness goes beyond the present. The Yoruba themselves put it this way: "*a ni ohun pupo ti a o ba ara wa se*" ("we have many things that we would do for each other"). The laments about the absence or degeneration of culture invariably and inevitably do touch on the issue of how relations can endure and be invested with quality meaning.

Summary

SAP has been an ogre, a real monster, yet without a face. The comparisons made in this chapter between the oil boom and SAP decades are real enough, but the situation has declined even further in this decade. The important question, therefore, is: Why have social payments persisted in spite of SAP and the collapse of the Naira? Perhaps the first answer is that Nigerians are yet to reach the bottom line of their survival strategies. Many, especially the battered middle class, continue to argue that there is still much money but that the bulk circulates among the rich. Those who have access to those who have can thus nurse the hope of a better tomorrow. Second, those with access to power continue to enjoy a limitless access to wealth. The traditional access—salaries, gifts, and bribes—is not just extant but has widened in scope. Allowances are high, and more gifts come from those who benefit from contacts with the power elite. Indeed, corruption is on the increase; and new devices for collecting donations, such as the award of honorary chieftaincy titles and degrees, are in vogue.

A third answer is that social payments have become ideological and institutionalized. The ruptures to society by contacts with the outside world have not led to the jettisoning of child-naming, marriage, and funeral ceremonies, cult membership, and chieftaincy. These institutions have all become part of the elite values and aspirations. They are forums, through and by which individuals seek to repay their social debts.

The positive view of the social ceremonies is shaped by the sheer extravagance of sound, smell, and activity which characterize them. The decade of the 1980s has seen a dramatic shift in perception, although this is not strong enough to completely obliterate them. There is, of course, among the Yoruba culture, a significant relation between exchange and character of the persons involved in the exchange. By paying attention to the characters, and not the money or goods in circulation, the Yoruba tacitly express their commitment to those values which the ceremonies maintain, that is, human hierarchy and old patterns of exchange. Otherwise stated, in socioeconomic exchange the Yoruba continually reproduce among themselves the ideology necessary for the legitimation of a social system of structured inequality.

Notes

1. These were the belt-tightening measures introduced under the civilian administration of Alhaji Shehu Shagari (NPN) and the Buhari/Idiagbon military regime. The measures included cutback in import of essential commodities and the banning of the importation and consumption of certain luxury goods.
2. The analysis here focuses on the period between 1985 and 1992—approximately the era of Babangida. The economic crises had deepened since 1992, and in many ways things have grown worse. The Abacha government did little to alleviate people's suffering as a result of SAP. Rather, our thesis here holds true: the deepening economic crisis produced opportunists who grew rich from SAP.
3. For a discussion of the national development plans, see P. C. Okigbo, *National Development Planning in Nigeria, 1900–92* (London: James Currey, 1989); Julius O. Ihonvbere and Timothy M. Shaw, *Towards a Political Economy of Nigeria* (Aldershot: Avebury, 1988); E. Dean, *Plan Implementation in Nigeria, 1962–66* (Ibadan: OUP, 1972).
4. Some information is, however, contained in Nigeria, *SAP for Nigeria, July 1986–June 1988* (Lagos: Government Printer, 1986).
5. This was before he was appointed to head the ill-fated interim government. See E. O. Shonekan, "The Place of Foreign Investments in Nigeria's Foreign Policy," in G.O. Olusanya et al. (eds.), *Economic Development and Foreign Policy in Nigeria* (Lagos: NIIA, 1988).
6. See Efiong Essien, *Nigeria Under Structural Adjustment* (Ibadan: Fountain Publications, 1990); M. O. Ojo, "An Appraisal of the Socio-Economic Impact of SAP in Nigeria," *Economic and Financial Review,* Vol. 27, No. 1, March, 1989; Eghosa Onagie, "Operating SFEM in the Nigerian Setting," *NJESS*, Vol. 28, No. 1, 1987; *idem*, "The IMF the World Bank in Nigeria's Economic Recovery," Paper presented at the Conference on Nigeria's International Economic Relations,

NIIA, 9–11 December, 1987; and *idem*, "A Survey of the Nigerian Economy since Independence," in Olusanya, G.O. et al. (eds.), *Economic Development and Foreign Policy in Nigeria* (Lagos: NIIA, 1988); S. E. Omoruyi, "A Review of SAP: The Foreign Exchange Market and Trade Policies in Nigeria," *EFR*, Vol. 25, No. 4, December, 1987.

7. A. O. Sanda, "Justification and Strategies for the Selective Privatisation of State-Owned Enterprises," *QJA*, Vol. XXI, Nos. 3 & 4, April/July, 1987; A. F. Olajide, "A Framework for Evaluating the Performance of Nigerian Public Enterprises: Implication for Privatisation," *QJA*, Vol. XXI, Nos. 3 and 4, April/July, 1987.
8. P. C. Okigbo, *National Development Planning in Nigeria*, p. 179.
9. *Ibid.*
10. V. A. Odozi, "The Nigerian Experience of SAP: A Central Bank Perspective," *Economic and Financial Review*, Vol. 26, No. 3, September, 1988; F. O. Orestotu, "Foreign Investment and Nigeria's Economic Recovery: Issues and Prospects," *EFR*, Vol. 26, No. 1, March, 1988; A. Ahmed, "Strategies for Foreign Investments in Nigeria: A Central Bank Perspective," *Economic and Financial Review*, Vol. 26, No. 1, March, 1988; J. O. Sanusi, "Deregulating the Nigerian Economy: Achievements and Prospects," *EFR*, Vol. 26, No. 4, December, 1988; Omo Omo Omoruyi, "Beyond the Local Government Reform of 1976," in Adamolekun, L. (ed.), *Nigerian Public Administration, 1960–80: Perspectives and Prospects* (Ibadan: Heinemann, 1985).
11. NES, *SAP and the Nigerian Economy* (Ibadan: NES, Proceedings of Annual Conference, 1988).
12. M. Harris, "Race Relations, Review of Michael Banton," *Current Anthropology*, No. 10, 1969, pp. 103–04.
13. See D. Rothchild and N. Chazan, *State and Society in Africa* (London: Westview Press, 1988).
14. B. Onimode, "Class Struggle as a Reality in Nigerian Development," in O. Nnoli (ed.), *Path to Nigerian Development* (Dakar: Codesria Book Series), p. 163.
15. G. Dalton (ed.), *Primitive, Archaic and Modern Economics* (Boston, MA: Beacon Press, 1968), p. 39.
16. *Ibid.*
17. S. M. Adesola, "Fiscal Management in Nigeria: A Prescription for the Third Republic," *Quarterly Journal of Administration*, Vol. XXIII, Nos. 1 & 2, 1989, p. 80.
18. Ojo, "Foreign Exchange Market in Nigeria," *Quarterly Journal of Administration*, Vol. XXI, Nos. 3 & 4, 1987, pp. 111–26.
19. J. O. Odufalu, "Market Failures and Government Intervention in the Nigerian Economy: A Comment," *Quarterly Journal of Administration*, Vol. XII, No. 1, 1977, pp. 87–98.
20. E. A. Aladejare, "The Institutional Structure and Operation of the Second Tier Foreign Exchange Market," *Quarterly Journal of Administration*, Vol. XXI, Nos. 3 & 4, 1987, p. 108.
21. See also Toyin Falola and Julius Ihonvbere, *The Rise and Fall of Nigeria's Second Republic* (London: Zed, 1984).
22. O. O. Ojo, "Foreign Exchange Market in Nigeria," *Quarterly Journal of Administration*, Vol. XXI, Nos. 3 & 4, 1987, pp. 111–26.
23. E. A. Aladejare, "Institutional Structure and Operation of the Second Tier Foreign Exchange Market," pp. 107–09, 127–56.
24. D. Olowu, "Economic Liberalization and the Nigerian Public Service," *Quarterly Journal of Administration*, Vol. XXI, Nos. 3 & 4, 1987, pp. 157–72.
25. A. F. Odejide, "A Framework for Evaluating the Performance of Nigeria Public

Enterprises: Implication for Privatization," *Quarterly Journal of Administration*, Vol. XXI, Nos. 3 & 4, 1987, pp. 190–208.

26. G. Dalton, *Primitive, Archaic and Modern Economics* (Boston: Beacon Press, 1968), p. 49.
27. R. Fox, "Commentary," *Medical Anthropology*, No. 214, 1978, p. 54.
28. A. Tocqueville, *Democracy in America* (New York: Alfred A. Knopf, 1954), pp. 117–18.
29. G. Simmel, *On Individuality and Social Forms* (Chicago, IL: University of Chicago Press, 1971), p. 140.
30. M. Mauss, *The Gift* (W. W. Norton & Company, 1967), p. 18.
31. T. A. Awoniyi, "*Omoluabi*: The Fundamental Basis of Yoruba Education," in W. Abimbola (ed.), *Yoruba Oral Tradition* (Ibadan: Ibadan University Press, 1975), pp. 364–65.
32. *African Concord*, 30th April 1990, p. 28.
33. O. B. Lawuyi and O. Taiwo, "Towards an African Sociological Tradition: A Rejoinder to Akiwowo and Makinde," *International Sociology*, Vol. 5, No. 1, 1990, p. 70.

14

Overview and Conclusion

The central thesis of this book is that money has played a transformative role in Yoruba economy, politics, and culture. Out of this comes four interrelated conclusions. First, monetization occurred very early in Yorubaland, as early as the fifteenth century. Second, the monetization altered the nature and course of social stratification, and constantly changed the composition of the elite. Third, the concept of money has been dynamic with the dominant view being that money is indispensable in social and economic relations. Fourth, increased monetization combined with several other factors to promote criminality, such as theft, counterfeiting, and corruption. From the nineteenth century through the colonial era to the present, people would do almost anything to acquire money.

The number of occasions that requires the use of money has grown phenomenally.[1] In addition to economic exchange which, as should be expected, required the use of money, political and social payments have also been conducted in cash. The transition to wage economy toward the end of the nineteenth century, together with the capitalization and expansion of the economy consequent to the British colonization, all increased the use of money. This book demonstrates that from its humble beginning in cowry shells around the fifteenth century, the role of money in Yorubaland has expanded. Cowries had other uses in rituals and as a means of nonverbal communication, but they were primarily the means of exchange. They had advantages of being scarce, imperishable, and portable. Counting the cowries even enriched the system of numeration. But cowries had the disadvantage of being bulky, heavy in large quantities, and dependent on external sources.

Colonialism introduced new currencies to replace the old cowries, integrated Yoruba economy into the modern Nigerian and world markets, and enhanced the exchangeability of Nigerian currency in international financial markets. This process was continued after independence when Nigeria introduced its own currency, the Naira. The amount of money in circulation increased dramatically during the oil boom years. By the end of the oil boom the monetization of the economy had been thorough. It is probably not without foundation that the Yoruba say: *Oro t'owo ba se ti, ile l'o ngbe*. That is, "whatever problem money cannot solve is to be left alone," probably because it is unsolvable or impossible.[2] This has been the case since the late 1980s, when the country's economic conditions worsened. With the currency devaluation and inflation, every transaction required the use of a lot of cash. As we have demonstrated in chapter 13, the scale of expenditure has decreased but the notion of using money in these transactions has not.

One of the first results of monetization was the transformation of social relationships. We could begin with the family setting. The transformative power of money is borne out in the following saying: *Owo to s'egbon d'aburo lo tun s'aburo d'egbon*. Literally, this means that "money turns the older brother into the junior brother." A deeper interpretation is necessary. As a gerontocratic society, the Yoruba placed great emphasis on age in the allocation of status and power in the family. Even the fact that the man (father or husband) is the head of the household could be explained in part by age: most times the man is older than his wife. Monetization interfered with this chronological arrangement. Thus, the one who has money has an elevated status irrespective of age.[3] An older person without money would defer to his younger but richer brother, but it is up to the richer one to not rub this deference in.

Thus, money has had a great impact on social stratification. This book demonstrates that before monetization stratification was mostly by ascription but the society had some room for ranking by age, physical strength, spiritual gifts, and wealth in knowledge and property. The traditional upper class comprised kings, princes, aristocrats, or chiefs. They derived their position by birth, but their status was enhanced by access to such revenue-yielding avenues as the tolls on long-distance trade. As we have shown in chapter 5, these tolls could be paid in cash or in kind. With increased monetization, however, a new class of the nouveaux riches came into the mix. One pertinent observation in this book (chapter 4) is the way the membership of the nouveaux riches has been enlarged over time. In the period of the Atlantic trade, for instance, the class of nouveaux riche was composed of warrior nobles, who raided outlying towns and villages for slaves, and merchants who sold these war captives and condemned prisoners to European slave traders. The membership of this class changed upon the abolition of slave trade. Those who were smart among the merchants quickly changed their wares from slaves to raw materials and continued to trade under the colonial political and economic dispensation. Warrior nobles also participated in legitimate trade by producing palm oil and other produce on their farms. The work force was often made up of the slaves they had acquired from war.

Gradually, new members were added to the nouveaux riche. The first crop were the "Returnees,"[4] the educated elite who settled in Lagos, Badagry, and Abeokuta, and who funded and organized the trade in legitimate commodities. They also constituted the nucleus of the Yoruba middle class. As educational opportunities expanded in the colonial and postcolonial era, the next crop was added to the nouveaux riche. These were several Yoruba businessmen and professionals such as teachers, accountants, physicians, engineers, and lawyers. Their membership qualifications were further enhanced by their salaries, position of authority, and access to government funds. A related development was the admission of a new group of "warrior nobles," the military officers, who have also made their money by their access to or involvement in a military regime. The point here is that the family background and social origins of members of the nouveaux riches have constantly changed.

Another interesting element in the culture of money as it pertains to the Yoruba system of stratification is the position and treatment of strangers (migrants or refugees). In Oyo-Ile, the capital of the Old Oyo Empire, recent immigrants were strangers, *ara oko*, and were ranked lower than slaves. Their position only became elevated after imbibing Oyo culture and integrating into Oyo society. Other Yoruba cities and kingdoms had similar cadres for migrants in the social stratification. In Ile-Ife they were called *elu* and in Lagos they were known as *sesede* (the one who just arrived) or derisively as *JJC* (Johnny just come). These migrants initially faced hard times: learning the language or dialect of their hosts, understanding how the social system operates, and generally becoming streetwise. All such derogatory references to—and demeaning treatments of—them vanished the moment the migrant integrated into the host community, usually by learning to speak the language, by business success, or by marriage.[5] King Sunny Ade, in a mid-1980s song, counseled the newcomer to Lagos to be careful[6]:

> My friend, the-one-who-has-just-arrived-in-the-city (Sesede), be careful
> There is Adamu-Orisa in Lagos
> That teaches the fool a lesson.

If you work hard you will be rich
When you have money still be careful
There is a lot of fraud in Lagos:
Like selling one house to eight people

In other words, a stranger could be very successful but only needs to learn the culture (and the tricks) of the host community. Successful strangers, such as the Lebanese and Hausa traders, are not only integrated into the community but they also receive chieftaincy titles. Other guests, such as foreign scholars and missionaries, whose works have been of immense benefit to the community, are awarded chieftaincy titles.

Although membership in the nouveaux riche has widened substantially, the character of the Yoruba elite has not changed much. Many of them seek traditional symbols of power and elitism, such as chieftaincy titles, membership in a secret society or cult and, for the men, having many wives and children. The knack for ostentation and open display of wealth has not diminished, neither has the propensity for the rich to oppress the poor. On the streets of Lagos the other name for the rich is "oppressor." The wide gap between the rich and poor is not recent. Neither is the oppression of the poor by the rich. In fact, money seemed to have been causing troubles from its inception. A Yoruba saying seems to capture the negative impact of monetization: *Oran t'owo ma a da s'ile apa owo o ni le ka*. That is, "money will cause trouble that money itself would be unable to solve." It is difficult to ascertain the origin and age of this saying, but the austere times of the 1980s has brought it into sharp focus. King Sunny Ade also played a big role in popularizing the saying and elaborating upon it thus[7]:

The troubles that [the reckless search for] money will cause in this world
[The realization of] money itself may not be enough to overcome them.

Examine my statement critically:
What is going on these days
Only God almighty could fathom it.

The wife is taking command over the husband
The husband is escorting the wife to her boyfriend's place
In order to earn money for food!
The husband knows what is right and what is befitting of a man
He knows what he is supposed to do in the circumstance
But his poverty turns him into a fool.
What a catastrophe!

The changes [we are witnessing in] society is like the blunt edge of the cutlass
Which in turn has been made into a knife:
The poor man's wife is someone else's.
The poor man's child is someone else's.

God, please don't afflict me with poverty,
Let me have authority in my household.

[My listeners] say "Amen" to these prayers:
That I would have money to build houses—*Amen*
That I would have money to provide for my wife—*Amen*
That I would have money to provide for my child—*Amen*
That I would [have money to] buy the latest automobile—*Amen*
[God] do not let me marry a lazy woman—*Amen*
Do not let me have a lazy child—*Amen*
Do not give me diseases in abundance—*Amen*
[But] bless me with money so that my status would be enhanced—*Amen*
Give me money with which to enjoy my time on earth—*Amen*
Give me money so that my enemies would not know my secrets—*Amen*

Do not afflict me with poverty, God Almighty
Bless me with the money to live my life to the fullest.

In this piece, King Sunny Ade is singing about prostitution, spousal abuse, and child neglect, a few of the contemporary outcomes of the emphasis on money in Yoruba society and the people's reckless search for it. He is also concerned that, given the economic conditions of the country, by the time a man realized his goals for money it might be too late to redress the damage done to family values, spousal relations, and cultural ethos.

Therefore, the key to success (or even to merely getting by) is to have money. This could mean approaching banks and other credit institutions. The traditional systems were the *ajo* and *esusu* institutions, which have continued to function alongside the modern banking and credit systems introduced under colonial rule and since independence. Commercial, merchant, rural, and other specialized banks have spread the culture of banking throughout Yorubaland. Although they may not be doing a lot of business in recent years because of the economic crisis, and they may not be patronized by the vast proportion of the population in rural areas, banks have limped along and have been counted among the indicators of a community's development.

Bank loans were accessible to only a few, usually the literate businessmen and professionals who resided in the urban centers and engaged in the formal sector of the economy. For the majority of the people, access to credit was through the *s'ogund'ogoji*. We consider the culture of money lending and loan repayment so pertinent that we have devoted two chapters (7 and 8) to it. We analyze the traditional moneylenders, the *s'ogund'ogoji*, as usurious lenders who not only made loans at a high (at least 100 percent) interest rate but also harassed and abused the borrowers. Their lending practices were a cause for concern to the borrower and to the Nigerian colonial administration. The *s'ogund'ogoji* practice survived into the postindependence period, despite the efforts of the colonial administration to reform it. Perhaps because postcolonial governments did not do much to regulate it, *s'ogund'ogoji* continued to thrive well into the oil boom era and has only been weakened by economic austerity, the Structural Adjustment Program, and the establishment of community and other grassroots banks.

Avenues for enrichment were not limited to the legitimate but long route of hard work. Access to money was also not limited to the rough and painful route of borrowing from traditional and modern financial institutions. Chapters 9 and 10 present information on enrichment through criminal shortcuts[8]—theft and counterfeiting. Theft is not a new phenomenon in Yoruba society, although there were periods when it was not very prevalent. We evaluated the situation in the colonial era and observed cases of theft everywhere. This is in part the result of increased monetization, taxation, and materialism under colonial rule. The thieves were the professional underworld. Mostly they stole cash; but they also stole goods that could easily be unloaded for cash. Theft has assumed an alarming proportion since the oil boom years, and with the emergence of armed robbery. This has, indeed, impacted the esthetics of modern Nigerian architecture. Iron bars adorn the gates, entrances, and windows of many homes and businesses. Called "burglary proofs," these barricades are usually produced by craftsmen with some artistic talent. The fact that they are not concealed gives modern Nigerian (and Yoruba) architecture the look of a society under siege—the siege of armed robbers. It also indicates the extent to which the rich would go in protecting their property, and the extent some professional thieves would go in having money.

Counterfeiting emerged partly because the metallic and paper currencies introduced by European traders in the nineteenth century and by British colonialism in the twentieth century could be forged. Counterfeiting did not precede European rule in Yorubaland because cowries, the precolonial currency, could not be forged. Cases of counterfeiting or "making money without sweat" were widespread. Colonial officials recovered thousands of counterfeited coins and made numerous rules to protect governmental agencies and banks from being paid in bad money. A smart counterfeiter generally avoided the formal sectors but continued to thrive in rural, nonformal markets. Counterfeiting has continued in Nigeria. In the early 1980s, following the civilian administration of Alhaji Shehu Shagari, so much counterfeited Naira notes were in circulation that the new military administration decided to change the currency. The point here is that money has assumed such indispensable dimensions that some would go to the extent of making it illegally.

The government has been the most steady source of money. It should not be surprising that another illegal shortcut to money is by taking it from government coffers. Known worldwide as corruption, this subject is examined in chapter 11 and in parts of chapter 12. In the precolonial era, the kings and chiefs did not differentiate between state and personal revenues. In fact, they considered state revenues theirs, and had unlimited access to tributes and other funds collected from their subjects. In addition, they appropriated the loot from wars, such as money, movable property, captives, potent charms, and amulets. In their early encounters, colonial officials noticed that kings and chiefs were taking bribes from those who went before them for any number of reasons, an old practice depicted in the statement: *ati ojebi ati ojare ni yio san'wo opa*. That is, "both the guilty and the not guilty would be charged with the cost of the trial."

At first, colonial rule provided the opportunity by which chiefs and kings could continue their precolonial privileges. Those who assisted the British in the conquest of the country received salaries from the colonial state and headed the customary courts where they continued to receive bribes. Later, after they had consolidated their powers, colonial officials tried to teach a different lesson by separating public and private revenues and removing the ultimate decision about public revenues from the kings. This new approach benefited members of the new class of the nouveaux riche who have been attracted into the service. Some were inconsequential persons such as cooks, gardeners, and messengers of the colonial officers. Others were in more elevated positions in the public service, such as accounts clerks, policemen, bureaucrats, and later politicians and professionals. They devised the most ingenious methods of accessing and appropriating public revenues.

The scale of corruption has grown since the colonial times. Bribery, for instance, is no longer *owo eyin* (meaning money behind the scenes) but *egunje* (literally, the sweet forbidden fruit). It is openly demanded and collected by gun-totting policemen at checkpoints, by customs and immigration officers at the ports, and by officials of such public parastatals as those in charge of the supply of electricity (NEPA) and telephone (NITEL). *Egunje* is built into the cost of social services provided by government, such as electricity, water, and telephone. Most services carry two prices: the official and the real cost. To have telephone service connected to a home or business, for instance, a prospective subscriber has to pay the official price (the one that appears on the receipt) plus an undetermined unofficial price (the *egunje*). Therefore, the real cost of a service to a subscriber is the official price plus this unofficial price. An interview in June 1998 yielded another interesting example. Our informant who already paid *egunje* to have electricity connected to his home had to pay further *egunje* to NEPA for a meter, to have the meter read, and to receive monthly bills on his energy consumption.[9] In other words, he had to bribe NEPA for the supply and use of the equipment, having literally to pay in order to be billed. Corruption has assumed a whole new proportion. It is blatant, accepted, and expected. To this extent, it is those that oppose corruption (rather than those that condone and do it) that are given a bad name. The following contemporary Yoruba sayings bear this out:

> *Eni ifa o kan ni i pe e ni riba*
> To the one not so lucky to receive it, a mere tip is bribery.
>
> *B'owo omode ko ba ba ijadu*
> *A ni, "Kosi ohun ti a o je ti ki i tan."*
> When a young man is unable to grab a bigger share
> He consoles himself that, "Nothing lasts forever."

Money is good to have! It is indispensable in economic and social relations. Money intervenes in the ideology of social system, and mediates in the existing class divisions. Large quantities of cowries were required for survival and ego in the distant past; today one still needs large quantities of Naira and foreign currencies, notably the US dollar or the British pound Sterling, to function and acquire prominence. In 1997, King Sunny Ade, the celebrated Yoruba musician whose work has been cited twice already, devoted a song in praise of money—and of course a Yoruba "money bag"—in a way that captures the situation today and supports our careful choice of *kose-e-mani* as the Yoruba concept to organize the ideas in this book. We wish to quote a few lines from King Sunny Ade and use his song to bring this book to a close[10]:

> Good morning money
> Good afternoon money
> Good evening money
> Money, please come, to make me successful.
>
> Iyiola appears from a distance, manifesting the accomplishments of money
> The rich is elegant
> I see you and pray to God to make me like him

I desire money
Money brings fame
Let me have money to adorn myself.

Money, I call you with all respect
I plead with God to have you in abundance
To have you to spend as I wish
Like Iyiola Omisore, the tree that produces money.

Here is a great song, a brilliant celebration of money and the person who has it in abundance. As King Sunny Ade says, when Iyiola calls, one must hurry to answer. Iyiola has many chieftaincy titles from principal Yoruba cities, friends in high places, known to all traditional kings, a business magnate, a generous spender, a socialite, and one who has money to the limit that he needs. In raising his hero to this peak King Sunny Ade, himself a rich person, has shown how money goes into the definition of the modern successful Yoruba. He demonstrates that money regulates inter-group relations, connects people with power, and inevitably intrudes into the consciousness, prayer, and aspirations of the struggling poor and the middle-class aspiring to climb up in the social hierarchy.

Notes

1. It must be stated from the onset that money has not completely supplanted the values placed on good character and personal involvement in social relations and interactions. In other words, crass materialism has not replaced the community spirit, and people still relate to each other as people, not as objects that have prices. Not every aspect of social relations has been quantified. The Yoruba situation has not reached the level at which money would, according to Georg Simmel, reduce "all quality and individuality to the question: How much?" See Georg Simmel, *The Philosophy of Money* (London: Routledge, 1990; first published 1900, translated by Tom Bottomore and David Frisby), pp. 120–25. Friends, relations, co-workers, and business partners often prefer "company" to money on certain occasions. For example, one does not just send money or gift to a friend who is getting married. It would be considered impolite, impersonal, and curt. Rather, one has to be present at the occasion and assist the celebrant by serving as an usher, receiving and seating other guests, and serving them food and drinks. This issue is best captured by the statement: *na'wo na'ra*. This term comes from *na,* which means to spend or to use. *Na'wo* combines *na* and *owo*, that is, to spend money. *Na'ra* combines *na* and *ara*, and literally this translates as to use one's body. Contextually, however, *na'ra* refers to the act of putting one's energy, labor, and spiritual gifts to the service of another. A celebrant's friend could compensate for the lack of money by throwing himself into the occasion, cheerfully performing menial tasks and paying meticulous attention to details that his friend might overlook in the pomp of the celebration. For some occasions money just isn't enough.
2. On the surface this statement seems to contradict the concept of *na'wo na'ra* (note 1, above), that money isn't everything. The contradiction is easily resolved

by the recognition that *na'wo na'ra* only refers to specific types of social responsibility and payments whereas one requires money for all manner of economic transactions and several types of social payments.

3. Mr. A. A. Adediran, personal interview, Ilesa, June 21, 1998.
4. "Returnees" were recaptured slaves, freed, settled, and educated in Sierra Leone in the nineteenth century, and who "returned" to the approximate country of origin. Most were missionaries, traders, and physicians.
5. One exception seemed to be the Modakeke refugees in Ile-Ife. These were Oyo people who had considered themselves the most civilized of all Yoruba groups. They had come to settle in Ife as a result of the collapse of the Old Oyo Empire in the 1830s. Now the table had turned: they were the strangers, the *elu*, in another society. They were forced to settle in Modakeke, separate from the Ife. As their number increased because of the influx of more Oyo refugees throughout the nineteenth century, Modakeke became a powerful settlement without integrating into the Ife society. The settlement not only participated in the Yoruba civil wars as an autonomous entity but it has been the source of constant and persistent threat to its host. The most recent crisis is the two-year-old civil strife that started in 1997 over the creation of a local government and the nonsiting of its headquarters in Modakeke. For information on Modakeke-Ife crises, see S. A. Akintoye, "Ife's sad century: The nineteenth century," *Nigeria Magazine*, No. 104, 1970, pp. 34–39.
6. King Sunny Ade, "Sweet Banana" (Lagos: Master Disk Ltd., ca. 1985), track entitled "Sesede ko rora se."
7. King Sunny Ade, "The Merciful God" (Lagos: Sigma Disk Ltd., ca. 1986), track entitled "Pagidari." There were other problems than Sunny Ade identified in this piece. A recent study also reports on the increase in the number of beggars in Yoruba society. "Most of them had been begging for 13 years to avoid starvation," says the report. See "Beggars in Nigeria," *Global Aging Report*, Vol. 3, No. 4, July/August 1998, p. 4.
8. The Yoruba word for process is a metaphor, *ona* (meaning "road"). The long process is the long route, and the short process is the shortcut. There are also the easy way and the difficult way.
9. Dauda Nasiru, personal interview, Lagos, June 11, 1998.
10. King Sunny Ade, "Glory" (KSA label, 1998).

Bibliography

I. Primary Sources

1. Archival Sources: Nigerian National Archives, Ibadan and Public Record Office, London

C.M.S. CA1/087, S. Crowther to Major Straith, 22 February 1837.

C.M.S. CA1/089, S. Crowther to Major Straith, 22 February 1837.

C.M.S. CA2/019, W. S. Allen's Journal Extracts for half-year ending June 1879.

C.M.S. CA2/049, Journal of David Hinderer.

C.M.S. CA2/056, Letters and Journals of James Johnson, Native Pastor, 21 March 1877.

C.M.S. CA2/066, Journal of Rev. A. Mann, 1852–1880.

C.M.S. CA2/068, J. A. Maser, *Letters and Journals,* 1853–1879.

C.M.S. CA2/07, Correspondence between the Colonial Government and Native Authorities, 1851–1872.

C.M.S. CA2/083, Journal of J. Smith, 27 June 1865.

C.M.S. CA2/085 (a), Townsend to Venn, 30 August 1852.

C.O. 147/149. MacGregor to Colonial Office Conf., 17 June 1900.

C.O. 147/166, MacGregor to Colonial Office Conf., 22 July I903, enclosure.

C.O. 147/186, Colonial Office to MacGregor, telegram, 18 June 1903.

C.O. 879/333, Alvan Millson to the Colonial Secretary, enclosure I in No. 23 of 14 February 1890.

Ibadan City Council, Letter Book No. 92 of 31 March 1903, enclosure, Elgee to the Alaafin of Oyo.

Ibadan Municipal Papers, Minutes of Council Meetings, 13 and 30 October, 1906 and 23 May 1907.

N.A.I., Ab Prof /342 D. O. Egba Div. to Resident, Abeokuta, 4 December 1933.

N.A.I., Ab Prof 2/ABO 342/1 Cpt. Scot's report on robbery, 1930.

N.A.I., Ab Prof 2/ABP 342222/1, D.O. Ilaro Division to the Resident, Abeokuta, April 1930.

N.A.I., Abe Prof /ABP 342 Robberies in the Ilaro Division Jackson to Resident, Abeokuta, 12 June 1933.

N.A.I., Abe Prof 1/ 2nd. Acc. Rex vs. Yaya Sokoto & Seven Others Charge: Armed Robbery contra.

N.A.I., Abe Prof 2/342, Bale of Maun village and thirty others to the D.O. Ilaro, 29 August, 1954.
N.A.I., Abe Prof 2/ABP 342, Jackson to Resident, Abeokuta, 22 June 1933.
N.A.I., Abe Prof 2/ABP 342/1; Assistant Commissioner of Police, Ilaro to the Resident, Abeokuta Province, 24 March 1930.
N.A.I., Agbo Dist. 1/ AG 530, Money Lenders Ordinance.
N.A.I., Agbor Dist. 1 AG 513, Anti-corruption, 1955.
N.A.I., AK Div Co 1/166.
N.A.I., Ak Div Co 9/450. Money Lenders 1961.
N.A.I., Ben Prof 1/BP 1423, Money Lenders Ordinance.
N.A.I., Ben Prof. l/B.P.2982, Armed Burglars in Benin.
N.A.I., C.S.O. 12/10/11–2441/100.
N.A.I., C.S.O. 12/19/11–2441/1900, Resident Ibadan, supplying information re Tolls.
N.A.I., C.S.O. 12/21/15–C1011/1902, Forwards Tariff of Proposed Tolls of the Railway (Iddo) gate.
N.A.I., C.S.O. 12/22/ 34–3172/1903, Estimates, Province of Ibadan December 1903–March 1904–April 1904–March 1905.
N.A.I., C.S.O. 12/24/25–3038/1905, Letter from the Oni of Ife on the question of the boundary between Ibadan and Ife, and the establishment of a toll house at Apomu, submitted.
N.A.I., C.S.O. 14/2/5–A4170/10, Preparation requested of Short Precis of the Ibadan Financial Arrangements Showing the Development, etc. from 1903.
N.A.I., C.S.O. 14/2/5–A4170/10.
N.A.I., C.S.O. 147/161, MacGregor to Colonial Office, Conf., 7 July 1903.
N.A.I., C.S.O. 147/166, MacGregor to the Colonial Office.
N.A.I., C.S.O. 147/75 Conf., *Lagos Weekly Record,* 16 January 1904.
N.A.I., C.S.O. 16/3/47, Confidential 97, 1901, Ibadan Estimates.
N.A.I., C.S.O. 16/5/34 c.80/1903.
N.A.I., C.S.O. 16/5/35–c.80/1903, suspension of arrangements for collecting tolls at Ibadan.
N.A.I., C.S.O. 16/5/49 Conf. 115/1903 Tolls.
N.A.I., C.S.O. 16/5/60. Proposals as to tolls.
N.A.I., C.S.O. 16/5/61 c. 37/1903. Request instructions on the date upon which the collection of tolls should commence.
N.A.I., C.S.O. 16/5/74 c. 160/1903, Estimates of Revenues and Expenditure, Ibadan, for period from 1 September 1903 to 31 March 1904–onward.
N.A.I., C.S.O. 16/5/77–c. 166/ 1903, Minutes of the Ibadan Council held at the Bale's House on 7 September 1903 onward.
N.A.I., C.S.O. 16/5/94, Infringing the toll regulations charge against Mr. Chersworth agents of P & Z.
N.A.I., C.S.O. 16/5/95, Fine imposed on a clerk of Messrs PZ for false declaration of the contents of certain packages imported into Ibadan.

N.A.I., C.S.O. 16/6/1905 279–1904, Bills of J. P. Jackson for Stationery for Ibadan Tolls Service—disputed by Ag. Resident Ibadan.
N.A.I., C.S.O. 16/6/2, Tolls at Oyo (1904).
N.A.I., C.S.O. 16/6/6. Application for appointment of Collector of Customs.
N.A.I., C.S.O. 16/6/64, Report by Mr. Lambert, Assistant Auditor, on the accounts of Mr. Henwood, Late Inspector of Tolls, Ibadan.
N.A.I., C.S.O. 16/6/76–241/1904, Estimates for financial year 1905–1906.
N.A.I., C.S.O. 16/6/C. 162/1904, Report that Chief Loro a member of the Ilesa Council.
N.A.I., C.S.O. 16/6/C58/1904, The Ilesa Council convicted the Owa of taking brie from a prisoner committed for trial.
N.A.I., C.S.O. 16/7/22/630/05, Report on Ibadan and Egba Tolls.
N.A.I., C.S.O. 16/7/28 42/05, Report of Commercial Intelligence Office on Illicit Transit Tolls at Lanlate.
N.A.I., C.S.O. 16/7/39, Egba Tolls at Otta.
N.A.I., C.S.O. 16/7/52, enclosure, Letter from C. H. Elgee, Resident, Ibadan to the Honourable Colonial Secretary, Lagos on 7 April 1905.
N.A.I., C.S.O. 16/7/72–104/1905, The Collection of Transit Tolls in the Interior.
N.A.I., C.S.O. 16/7/95–142/1905, Estimates Ibadan Station 1905–1906, submitted.
N.A.I., C.S.O. 16/728–42/05, enclosure, C.I.O. to Colonial Secretary, 7 June 1905.
N.A.I., C.S.O. 18/3/14, Correspondence on the levying of tolls, 1903.
N.A.I., C.S.O. 19/7–N/871/1919 and War Prof. 3/10 Burglary at Ase.
N.A.I., C.S.O. 19/9–N3027/1921, Cases of robberies and burglaries in Lagos-Return of-asks for.
N.A.I., C.S.O. 26/06076, Notes on Customs and Superstitions of the Indigenous (Yoruba) Inhabitants of Oyo Province, by Capt. A. Ross, C.M.G., paragraph 247.
N.A.I., C.S.O. 26/19/9/N.3027/1921; and Ije Prof. 1/925, Pick Pockets Raiding Markets.
N.A.I., C.S.O. 26/21351/S.167, Ikot Ekan Government School Store-Burglary At.
N.A.I., C.S.O. 26/21351/S.169 Umuahia Government College-Burglary At; and War Prof 3/10/130/28 Burglary at Ase.
N.A.I., C.S.O. 26/21351/S.173 Government School, Owerri, Burglary At.
N.A.I., C.S.O. 26/21351/S.88 Burglary at the Onitsha Forestry Office.
N.A.I., C.S.O. 26/30315 Vol. I.
N.A.I., C.S.O. 26/30315 Vol. II [Memo by the Governor General].
N.A.I., C.S.O. 26/30315 Vol. II, [Clerk, Executive Council to the Ex. Co.].
N.A.I., C.S.O. 26/30315 Vol. III, [Nigerian Moneylenders Association to the Governor of Nigeria].
N.A.I., C.S.O. 26/30315 Vol. I, Police Magistrate to Chief Registrar of Supreme Cort, 26 August 1935.

N.A.I., C.S.O. 26/30315 Vol. I.
N.A.I., C.S.O. 26/30315 Vol. II, Money Lenders Amendment Ordinance 1935.
N.A.I., C.S.O. 26/30315 Vol. III, Money Lenders Amendment Ordinances 1935 [Williams to The Acting Chief Secretary to the Government, 26 August 1938].
N.A.I., C.S.O. 26/38322/S.843, Anti Bribery & Corruption Society.
N.A.I., C.S.O. 26/4/30172, Intelligence Report Of Ondo District (by A. F. B. Bridges), 18.
N.A.I., C.S.O. 26/50341, Attempted Bribery of Customs Officer at Degema.
N.A.I., C.S.O. 446/46 Reg. No. 38925, Wallace to Secretary of State 7 October 1905, enclosing Resident's responses to questionnaire on collection of tolls.
N.A.I., Com Col 1/553, Indebtedness of Mrs. Hilda Hamilton to Lagos Money Lender.
N.A.I., Iba Div 1/.1331, Vol. IV Money Lenders Licenses.
N.A.I., Iba Div 1/1/1557, Counterfeit Coins, Quarterly Return Of. Except otherwise stated, all archival sources were derived at N.A.I.
N.A.I., Iba Prof. 3/10, Correspondence Book, Letter No. 103/09, 30 April, 1909.
N.A.I., Iba Prof. 3/6, The Resident's Travel Journal, 1897–1899, entries relating to tolls.
N.A.I., Iba. Div l/l, Robbers-Ibadan Div. in re.
N.A.I., Ijaw W. 4/W.1 167 Vol. 1 Money Lenders License—Matters Re 1937/48.
N.A.I., Ije Prof 4/458, Rex vs. David Oloyede of Abeokuta, charged with burglary.
N.A.I., Ije Prof 4/7.679 Money Lenders Ordinance CAP. 147 Corresp. Re.
N.A.I., Ije Prof 4/956 Vol. 1, Money Lenders Ordinance Cap 147 Corresp. in re 1929/44. [Petition of Mrs Gbolade Dele to the District Officer, June 29, 1941].
N.A.I., Ije Prof 4/J.433,Vol. 1, Counterfeit Coining; Oyo Prof 2/3/C.23, Counterfeiting and offences relating to coin.
N.A.I., Ije Prof 4/J.458, Rex vs. David Oloyede of Abeokuta, charged with robbery.
N.A.I., Ije Prof 4/J.459 Rex vs. Imoru of Ilorin, charged with burglary.
N.A.I., Ije Prof 4/J.626 Rex vs. Lasisi Oyebanjo, charged with burglary.
N.A.I., Ije Prof 4/J.679 Money Lenders Ordinance Cap 147 Corresp in re. 1929/44.
N.A.I., Ije Prof.4/J.474, Rex vs. Folabi, Olayemi charged with receiving stolen goods.
N.A.I., Ije. Prof.4/J.1225, Highway Robbery and Murder at Ode Oko.
N.A.I., Kuku Div 2/KD 998, Bribery and Corruption, 1946–1956.
N.A.I., Kuku Div. 2/K.D. 1401, Burglary.

N.A.I., Kuku Div.2 KD 928, Money Lenders Re.
N.A.I., Okiti Div 1./OK 1922, Bribery and Corruption, 1955/57.
N.A.I., Okiti Div 1/1/OK 1238, Money Lenders Ordinance Cap 136 [Application letter of M. Emmanuel to the District Officer, 28 August 1953].
N.A.I., Okiti Div 3/OWC8/1929, Mr. W. E. Mowarin, Sobo Interpreter charged with official corruption, Contra Section 116 of the C.C.
N.A.I., Ondo Prof 1/1/570 Money Lenders Ordinance Corresp. Re.
N.A.I., Oshun Div.1/1/196 Vol. 1, Burglaries, Oshogbo District.
N.A.I., Osun Div 1/2/OS.64, Nickel Coinage and Currency General.
N.A.I., Owo Div 1/865, Bribery and Corruption, 1946–56.
N.A.I., Oyo Div. 1/1, Escaped Prisoners.
N.A.I., Oyo Prof 1/1175, Burglaries in Oyo Province: Reports on.
N.A.I., Oyo Prof 1/1175, D.O. Oshogbo to Senior Resident, Ibadan 24 January 1931.
N.A.I., Oyo Prof 1/1477 Vol. II, Money Lenders Amendment Ordinance 1935 [Petition by A Sanni].
N.A.I., Oyo Prof 1/1477, Vol. I, Money Lenders Ordinance: Corresp. Re. and Vol. 2., Money Lenders Ordinance Corresp. Re.
N.A.I., Oyo Prof 1/1592, Vol. II, Counterfeit Coinage: Correspondence Re.
N.A.I., Oyo Prof 1/2971 Arrest of four Native Admin. Constables at Ilesa.
N.A.I., Oyo Prof 1/4310, Bribery & Corruption.
N.A.I., Oyo Prof 1/623 Vol. II, West African Currency Circulation of.
N.A.I., Oyo Prof 2/3/C.23.
N.A.I., Storey Report, 1954 *Commission of Inquiry into the Administration of Lagos Town Council, 1953* (Lagos: Government Printer).
N.A.I., Ugheli Dist. 1/322, Rex vs. Ogunade and two others involved in burglary.
N.A.I., War Prof 1/W.P. 859, Bribery and Corruption 1946–56.
N.A.I., West African Lands Committee, *Papers and Correspondence* (London: Colonial Office, 1916), Questions 7,538–63.
P.R.O., C.O. 147/166, MacGregor to Colonial Office, Conf. 7 July 1903, enclosure, appendix 8.
P.R.O., FO 2132, Glover to Baikie, 20 July 1895, enclosure in Baikie to Malmesbury, 6 August 1895.
Rhodes House Mss Afr. 5958, Report on Ilorin, July 1902.

II. Newspapers (selected as needed)

African Concord
Daily Sketch
Daily Times
Daily Tribune
Iwe Irohin

Lagos Observer
The Guardian
The Lagos Weekly Record
West Africa
Global Aging Report, Vol. 3, No. 4, July/August 1998, "Beggars in Nigeria," p. 4.

III. Government Publications

Benue-Plateau State. 1975. *Government Decisions on the Report of the Panel of Inquiry into the Benue-Plateau State Houses and Contract Procedure* (Jos: Government Printer).

Borno State. 1978. *Government's Views on the Report of the Judicial Commission of Inquiry into the Suspended Damaturu Local Government* (Maiduguri: Government Printer).

Central Bank of Nigeria. *Annual Report and Statement of Accounts* (Lagos: CBN, various years).

Central Bank of Nigeria. *Economic and Financial Review* (Lagos: CBN, various years).

Colonial Office. 1963. *Report of the Tribunal appointed to inquire into allegations reflecting on the Official Conduct of the Premier of, and certain persons holding Ministerial and other Public Offices in, the Eastern Region of Nigeria.* London.

Nigeria, *Estimates of Revenue and Expenditure* (Lagos: Government Printer, various years).

Nigeria. 1953. *House of Representatives Debates* (Lagos: Government Printer).

Nigeria. 1955. *Report of the Commission of Enquiry into the Working of Port Harcourt Town Council* (Lagos: Government Printer).

Nigeria. 1958. *Fiscal Commission, 1957–58: Report* (London: HMSO).

Nigeria. 1964. *Fiscal Review Commission: Report* (Lagos: Government Printer).

Nigeria. 1976. *Federal Military Government's Views on the Report of the Federal Assets Investigation Panel* (Lagos: FMOI).

Nigeria. 1976. *Report of the Federal Assets Investigation Panel* (Lagos: FMOI).

Nigeria. 1976. *Report of the Special Panel on the Farms of Alhaji Audu Bako and Mr. S. O. Ogbemudia* (Lagos: FMOI).

Nigeria. 1979. *Report of the Technical Committee on Revenue Allocation under the Military* (Lagos: Government Printer), 2 volumes.

Nigeria. 1980. *Crude Oil Sales Tribunal Report* (Lagos: Government Printer).

Nigeria. 1980. *Report of the Presidential Commission on Revenue Allocation* (Lagos: Government Printer), 4 vols.

NNPC. *Annual Report* (Lagos: NNPC, various years)

Western Regional Government. 1954. "Tax Collection in the Western Region, 1953–54," Paper laid on the Table of the Western House of Assembly by the Chief Secretary, February 1954 (Lagos: Government Printer).

2. Oral Interviews

Name	Age	Place of Residence	Date of Interview
A. Babayemi	83	Owo	1992
Adenuga Oyekan	80+	Lagos	1985, 1991
Adeyemo Ojo	60+	Obamoro	February 1993
Alhaja Ajibike	81	Osogbo	1992
Babajide Olawale	74	Zaria	1991
E. Ajibodu	78	Ikare	June 1991
Ebenezer Ojo	85+	Lagos	1991
L. Ayinla	63	Ilobu	1991
M. Adeyemi	75+	Ibadan	June 1990
Misitura Yusuf	90+	Iwo	16 December, 1991
Morunfolu Oni	81	Ijebu-Ode	1993
Oladosu Ajimoke	76	Kaduna	1991
Omowumi Layode	87	Osogbo	1987
P. Alabi	80+	Ibadan	June 1990
Taiwo Ajadi	69	Moniya	1993
A. A. Adediran	45+	Ilesa	1998
Danda Nasiru	40+	Lagos	1998
Taju Owoseni alias Kabiyesi	82	Ijebu-Igbo	August 1993

IV. Secondary Sources

Abimbola, Wande. 1976. *Ifa: An Exposition of Ifa Literary Corpus* (Ibadan: OUP).

———. 1977. *Ifa Divination Poetry* (New York: Nok Publishers).

Aboyade, O. 1977. "Indigenising Foreign Enterprises: Some Lessons from the Nigerian Enterprises Promotion Decree," in Teriba, O. and Kayode, M.O. (eds.), *Industrial Development in Nigeria* (Ibadan: Ibadan University Press).

Aboyade, O. and A. A. Ayida. 1971. "The War Economy in Perspective," *Nigerian Journal of Economic and Social Studies,* 13, 1.

Achebe, Chinua. 1959. *Things Fall Apart* (New York: Astor-Honor).

Ade, King Sunny. 1985. "Sweet Banana" (Lagos: Master Disk Ltd.)

——. 1986. "The Merciful God," (Lagos: Sigma Disk Ltd.)

——. 1998. "Glory" (Lagos: KSA label).

Adebayo, A. G. 1982. "Petroleum and Nigeria's Foreign Policy, 1970–79," (M.A. Thesis, University of Ife).

——. 1983. "Origin and Development of Iwo," *The African Historian,* x.

——. 1992. "The Production and Export of Hides and Skins in Colonial Northern Nigeria, 1900–45," *Journal of African History,* 33.

——. 1993. *Embattled Federalism: A History of Revenue Allocation in Nigeria* (New York: Peter Lang).

Adebayo, A. G. and M. M. Fasheke. MS. "Social Transformation, Colonial Government Intervention and the Rise of the Urban Crisis."

Adebayo, A. G. and Toyin Falola. 1986. "Intergroup Relations in Nigeria," in Toyin Falola and Biodun Adediran (eds.), *Nigeria: Peoples, States and Cultures before 1800* (Lagos: John West).

Adediran, Biodun. 1978/79. "Yoruba Ethnic Groups or a Yoruba Ethnic Group?" *History Department Seminar Series, University of Ife,* late published in Africa (Sao Paulo).

Adediran, Biodun. Forthcoming. "The 19th century Wars and Yoruba Royalty," in I. A. Akinjogbin et al. (eds.), *War and Peace in Yorubaland, 1793–1893* (Ibadan: Heinemann).

Adegbite, Ademola M. 1978. "Oriki: A Study in Yoruba Musical and Social Perception," Ph.D. Thesis, University of Pittsburgh.

Adegboye, R. O. 1983. "Procuring Loans by Pledging Cocoa Trees," in J. D. von Piscke et al. (eds.), *Rural Financial Markets in Developing Countries* (Baltimore, MD: Johns Hopkins University Press).

Adejugbe, Adebayo. 1980. "Multinational Oil Corporation and the Development of Nigeria's Economy," *Oil and the New International Economic Order* (Ibadan: NES Conference Proceedings).

Adelowo, E. Dada. 1988. "A Comparative Look at the Phenomena of Death (Iku), Burial and Funeral Rites (Isinku) in Yorubaland," *Odu: A Journal of West African Studies,* 33.

Adesola, S. M. 1989. "Fiscal Management in Nigeria: A Prescription for the Third Republic," *Quarterly Journal of Administration,* XXIII, 1 & 2.

Adewoye, O. 1970. "The Legal Profession in Southern Nigeria, 1863–1943," Ph.D. dissertation, Columbia University.

Aickin, Joseph. 1969. *The Mysteries of Counterfeiting of the Coin* (London: Printed by William Downing for the author).

Ajayi, J. F. Ade. 1975. "The Aftermath of the Fall of Old Oyo," in J. F. Ade Ajayi and Michael Crowder (eds.), *History of West Africa, II* (London: Longman).

Ajayi, S. I. and O. O. Ojo. 1981. *Money and Banking Analysis and Policy in the Nigerian Context* (London: George Allen and Unwin).

Ajisafe, A. K. 1964. *A History of Abeokuta* (self-published by author, Fola Bookshop, Abeokuta, 1916, revised edition).

Akeredolu-Ale, E. O. 1975. *The Underdevelopment of Indigenous Entrepreneurship in Nigeria* (Ibadan: Ibadan University Press).

——. 1983. "A Sociohistorical study of the Development of Entrepreneurship among the Ijebu of Western Nigeria," *African Studies Review,* XVI, 3.

Akerlof, George. 1971. "The Market for Lemons: Qualitative Uncertainty and Market Mechanism," *The Quarterly Journal of Economics,* Vol. LXXXIV.

Akinjogbin, I. A. 1965. "The Prelude to the Yoruba Civil Wars," *Odu: A Journal of West African Studies,* I, 2.

—— 1967. *Dahomey and Its Neighbours, 1708–1818* (Cambridge: CUP).

——. 1978/79. "The *Ebi* System Reconsidered," *Department of History Seminar Papers* (Ile-Ife, University of Ife).

——. Forthcoming. "The Causes of the 19th Century Yoruba Civil Wars," in I. A. Akinjogbin et al. (eds.), *War and Peace in Yorubaland* (Ibadan: Heineman).

Akintoye, S. A. 1970. "Ife's Sad Century: The nineteenth century," *Nigeria Magazine,* No. 104.

——. 1971. *Revolution and Power Politics in Yorubaland, 1840–1893* (London: Longman).

Akinyele, I. B. 1950. *Iwe Itan Ibadan* (England: self-printed, 3rd edition).

Aladejare, E. A. 1987. "The Institutional Structure and Operation of the Second Tier Foreign Exchange Market," *Quarterly Journal of Administration,* XXI, 3 & 4.

Ale, A. 1984. *The Underdevelopment of Indigenous Entrepreneurship in Nigeria* (Ibadan: Ibadan University Press).

Alexander, F. and W. Healey. 1969. *Roots of Crime* (New Jersey: Patterson Smith).

Ali, Shaukat. 1985. *Corruption: A Third World Perspective* (Lahore, Pakistan: Aziz).

Aluko, Sam. 1988. "Financing Federal Systems: Suggestions for Revenue Sharing," in R. Olaniyan, *Federalism in a Changing World* (Lagos: The Presidency).

Appadurai, Arjun. 1986. "Introduction: Commodities and the Politics of value," in Arjun Appadurai (ed.), *The Social Life of Things: Commodities in Cultural Perspective* (Cambridge: Cambridge University Press).

Ardener, Shirley. 1964. "The Comparative Study of Rotating Credit Associations," *Journal of the Royal Anthropological Institute,* xciv.

Ardener, Shirley and Sandra Burman. 1995. *Money-Go-Rounds: The Importance of Rotating Savings and Credit Associations for Women* (Oxford: Berg).

Asabia, S. O. 1982. "Impact of the Nigerian Enterprises Promotion Decrees on the Banks and Other Financial Markets," *QJA,* Vol. XVI, Nos. 3 & 4, April/July.

Asiodu, P. C. 1979. *Nigeria and the Oil Question* (Lagos: NES).

Atanda, J. A. 1973. *The New Oyo Empire: Indirect Rule and Change in Western Nigeria, 1894–1934* (London: Longman).

Awa, Eme O. 1964. *Federal Government in Nigeria* (Berkeley & Los Angeles: University of California Press).

Awoniyi, T. A. 1975. "Omoluabi: The Fundamental Basis of Yoruba Education," in W. Abimbola (ed.), *Yoruba Oral Tradition* (Ibadan: Ibadan University Press).

Ayantuga, O. O. 1965. "Ijebu and its Neighbours, 1851–1914," Ph.D. thesis, University of London.

Babatunde, Emmanuel D. 1992. *A Critical Study of Bini and Yoruba Value Systems of Nigeria in Change: Culture, Religion, and the Self* (Lewiston: The Edwin Mellen Press).

Baier, Stephen. 1980. *An Economic History of Central Niger* (London: Clarendon).

Banerjee, Abhijit and Eric S. Maskin. 1996. "A Walrasian Theory of Money and Barter," *The Quarterly Journal of Economics,* Vol. 111.

Banuazizi, Ali. 1984. *Social Stratification in the Middle East and North Africa: A Bibliographical Survey* (London: Mansell).

Barber, Karin. 1991. *I Could Speak until Tomorrow: Oriki, Women and the Past in a Yoruba Town* (Edinburgh: Edinburgh University Press for International African Institute).

Barber, Karin. 1995. "Money, Self-Realization, and the Person in Yoruba Texts," in Jane I. Guyer (ed.), *Money Matters: Instability, Values and Social Payments in the Modern History of West African Communities* (Portsmouth, NH: Heinemann).

Barnes, R. H. and Ruth Barnes. 1989. "Barter and Money: In and Indonesian Village Economy," *Man,* Vol. 24, Sept.

Barnes, Sandra T. 1986. *Patrons and Power: Creating a Political Community in Metropolitan Lagos* (London: Manchester University Press for the International African Institute).

Bascom, W. R. 1955 "Urbanisation among the Yoruba," *The American Journal of Sociology,* lx, 5.

Bascom, William R. 1951. "Social Status, Wealth and Individual Differences among the Yoruba," *American Anthropologist,* 53, 4.

———. 1952. "The Esusu: A Credit Institution of the Yoruba," *Journal of the Royal Anthropological Institute,* lxxxii, 1.

———. 1969. *Ifa Divination: Communication between Gods and Men in West Africa* (Bloomington: Indiana University Press).

———. 1969. *The Yoruba of Southwestern Nigeria. Prospect Heights: Waveland, 1984;* first edition.

Beier, Ulli. 1980. *Yoruba Myths* (Cambridge: Cambridge University Press).

Belasco, Bernard I. 1980. *The Entrepreneur as Culture Hero: Preadaptations in Nigerian Economic Development* (New York, Praeger).

Berry, Sara. 1985. *Fathers Work for their sons: Accumulation, Mobility, and Class Formation in an Extended Yoruba Community* (Berkeley: University of California Press).

Biobaku, S. O. 1957. *The Egba and Their Neighbours, 1842–1872* (Oxford: Clarendon).

Bolaji, Labanji. 1970. *Anatomy of Corruption in Nigeria* (Ibadan: Daystar).

Bowen, T. J. 1969. *Adventures and Missionary Labours in Several Countries in the Interior of Africa From 1849–1956* (New York, reprint; originally published in 1857 by the Southern Baptist Publication Society).

Brandler, J. L. 1993. *Out of Nigeria: Witness to a Giant's Toils* (London: The Radcliffe Press).

Calvert, Peter. 1982. *The Concept of Class* (New York: St. Martin's Press).

Campbell, R. 1861. *A Pilgrimage To My Motherland* (New York:).

Central Bank of Nigeria. 1979. *Twenty Years of Central Banking In Nigeria* (Lagos: CBN).

Chamberlain, H. 1969. *A Collection of Some Papers Writ Upon Several Occasions Concerning Clipt and Counterfeit Money, and Trade so far as it Relates to the Exportation of Bullion* (London: Printed for Benj. Tooke).

Clapperton, H. 1829. *Journal of a Second Expedition into the Interior of Africa* (London: Murray).

Clarke, W. H. 1972. *Travels and Explorations In Yorubaland, 1854–1858*, in J. A. Atanda (ed.) (Ibadan: Ibadan University Press).

Cohen, Abner. 1969. *Custom and Politics in Urban Africa: A Study of Hausa Migrants in Yoruba Towns* (Berkeley: University of California Press).

Coker, G.B.A. 1966. *Family Property among the Yorubas* (London: Sweet and Maxwell).

Cottrell, Allin. 1984. *Social Classes in Marxist Theory* (London: Routledge & Kegan Paul).

Crocker, Walter R. 1971. *Nigeria. A Critique of British Colonial Administration* (Freeport, NY: Books for Libraries Press).

Crummey, D. 1986. (ed.) *Banditry, Rebellion and Social Protest in Africa* (London and New Hampshire: James Currey and Heinemann).

Curtin, P. D. 1967. (ed.) *Africa Remembered: Narratives by West Africans from the Era of the Slave Trade* (Madison, WI: University of Wisconsin Press).

Dalton, G. 1968. *Primitive, Archaic and Modern Economics* (Boston: Beacon Press).

Dalton, George. 1971. *Traditional Tribal and Peasant Economies. An Introductory Survey of Economic Anthropology* (Reading, MA: Addison-Wesley).

Damachi, Ukandi G. and Hans Dieter Seibel. 1973. (eds.) *Social Change and Economic Development in Nigeria* (New York: Praeger).

Davidson, Paul. 1985. "Money," in Adam Kuper and Jessica Kuper, *The Social Science Encyclopedia* (London: Routledge & Kegan Paul).

Delano, Isaac O. 1955. *Aiye D'aiye Oyinbo* (London: Nelson).

Dudley, Billy. 1982. *An Introduction to Nigerian Government and Politics* (London: Longman).

Durkheim, E. 1973 repr. *The Division of Labour in Society* (New York: The Free Press).

Durkheim, Emile and Marcel Mauss. 1963. *Primitive Classification* (Chicago, IL: Chicago University Press).

Eades, J. S. 1980. *The Yoruba Today* (Cambridge: Cambridge University Press).

Eisenstadt, S. N. 1971. *Social Differentiation and Stratification* (Glenview, IL: Scott, Foresman & Company).

Ekukinam, A. E. 1968. "Administration of Nigeria Monetary Policy," *QJA*, Vol. III.

Ekundare, R. O. 1973. *An Economic History of Nigeria, 1860–1960* (London: Methuen).

Elgee, C. H. 1914. *The Evolution of Ibadan* (Lagos: Government Printer).

Eliade, Mircea. 1962. *Images and Symbols* (New York: Sheed & Ward).

Engineer, Merwan and Dan Bernhardt. 1991. "Money, Barter, and the Optimality of Legal Restrictions," *Journal of Political Economy*, Vol. 99, August.

Epega, Afolabi A. 1995. *The Sacred Ifa Oracle* (San Francisco, CA: Harper).

Es'Andah, Bassey W. 1975. "An Archaeological View of the Urbanization Process in the Earliest West African States," *Journal of the Historical Society of Nigeria (JHSN)*, VIII.

Eyo, Ekpo. 1979. *Nigeria and the Evolution of Money* (Lagos: Central Bank of Nigeria).

Fabiyi, Y. L. 1979. "Land Tenure Reform in Nigeria: Implications of the Land Use Decree for Africultural Development," *Ife Journal of Agriculture*, I, 2.

Fadipe, N. A. 1970. *The Sociology of the Yoruba*, F.O. and O.O. Okediji (eds.) (Ibadan: Ibadan University Press).

Falegan, S. B. 1970. *Redesigning Nigeria's Financial System* (Ibadan: UPL).

Falegan, S. B. and G. O. Okah. 1980. "The Contribution of Petroleum to Nigeria's Economy," *Oil and the NIEO* (Ibadan: NES, Annual Conference Proceedings).

Falola, Toyin. 1978. "The Place of Women in the Yoruba Pre-Colonial Domestic Economy," Seminar Paper, History Department, University of Ife.

———. 1984. *The Political Economy of a Pre-Colonial African State: Ibadan, 1830–1900* (Ile-Ife, University of Ife Press).

———. 1985. "Migrant Settlers in Ife Society, 1830–1960," *The Calabar Historical Journal*, 3, 1.

———. 1985–86. "Brigandage and Piracy In 19th Century Yorubaland," *Journal of the Historical Society of Nigeria*, XIII, 1 & 2.

———. 1987. (ed.), *Nigeria and Britain : Exploitation or Development?* (London: Zed).

———. 1990. "Lebanese Traders in Southwestern Nigeria, 1900–1960," *African Affairs*, Vol. 89, October.

———. 1991. "The Yoruba Caravan System of the 19th Century," *International Journal of African Historical Studies*, 24, 1.

———. 1995. "Money and Informal Credit Institutions in Colonial Western Nigeria," in Jane I. Guyer, *Money Matters: Instability, Values and Social Payments in the Modern History of West African Communities* (Portsmouth, NH: Heinemann).

Falola, Toyin. forthcoming. (ed.) *Oil and Nigerian Economy and Society* (Lagos: Longman).

Falola, Toyin and Ann O'Hear. forthcoming. (eds.) *The Economic History of Nigeria During the 19th Century* (ms.).

Falola, Toyin and Julius Ihonvbere, 1984. *The Rise and Fall of Nigeria's Second Republic* (London: Zed).

Falola, Toyin and Paul Lovejoy. 1994. (eds.) *Pawnship in Africa* (Colorado: Westview).

Falola, Toyin and S. A. Olanrewaju. 1986. (eds.) *Transport Systems in Nigeria* (Syracuse, NY: Maxwell School of Citizenship and Public Affairs).

Falola, Toyin and Tunde Lawuyi. 1990. "Not Just a Currency: The Cowry in Nigerian Culture," in D. Henige and T. C. McCaskie (eds.), *West African Economic and Social History: Studies in Memory of Marion Johnson* (Madison, WI: African Studies Program).

Falola, Toyin, et al.** 1994. *The Military Factor in Nigeria* (New York: Edwin Melen).

Ferber, Robert. 1964. "Saving," in Julius Gould and William Kolb, *A Dictionary of the Social Sciences* (New York: Free Press).

Fisher, J. L. 1953. *Report on the Desirability and Practicability of Establishing a Central Bank in Nigeria for Promotion the Economic Development of the Country* (Lagos: Government Printer).

Fitzgerald, Bruce. 1987. "Countertrade Reconsidered," *Finance and Development,* Vol. 24.

Forrest, Tom. 1992. *Politics and Economic Development in Nigeria* (Boulder, CO: Westview).

Fox, R. 1978. "Commentary," *Medical Anthropology,* 214.

Fuja, Abayomi. 1962. *Fourteen Hundred Cowrys: Traditional Stories of the Yoruba* (London: OUP).

Gbadamosi, Bakare and Ulli Beier. 1968. *Not even God is ripe enough: Yoruba Stories* (London: Heinemann).

Geertz, Clifford. 1962. "The Rotating Credit Association: A "Middle Rung" in Development," *Economic Development and Cultural Change,* x.

Gerth, H. and C. W. Mills. 1922. (eds.) *Max Weber: Essays in Sociology* (New York: J. B. Moler).

Goddard, S. 1965. "Town-Farm Relationships in Yorubaland: A Case Study from Oyo," *Africa,* xxxv, 1.

Guyer, Jane I. 1995. "Wealth in People, Wealth in Things—Introduction," *Journal of African History,* 36.

———. 1995. (ed.) *Money Matters: Instability, Values and Social Payments in the Modern History of West African Communities* (Portsmouth, NH: Heinemann).

Hammond, Grant. 1990. *Countertrade, Offsets and Barter in International Political Economy* (New York, St. Martin's Press).

Harris, M. 1969. "Race Relations, Review of Michael Banton," *Current Anthropology,* 10.

Hay, Douglas, et al. 1975. *Albion's Fatal Tree: Crime and Society in Eighteenth Century England* (London: Allen Lane).

Heidenheimer, Arnold J. 1970. *Political Corruption: Readings in Comparative Analysis* (New York: Holt Rinehart and Winston).

Heidenheimer, Arnold J., Michael Johnston, and Victor T. LeVine. 1989. *Political Corruption* (New Brunswick, NJ: Transaction Publishers).

Henn, Jeanne Koopman. 1988. "The Material Basis of Sexism: A Mode of Production Analysis," in Sharon B. Stichter and Jane L. Parpart (eds.), *Patriarchy and Class: African Women in the Home and the Workforce* (Boulder, CO: Westview Press).

Herbert, Eugenia W. 1973. "Aspects of the Use of Copper in Pre-Colonial West Africa," *JAH,* xiv.

Heussler, Robert. 1968. *The British in Northern Nigeria* (London: OUP).

Hinderer, A. 1872. *Seventeen Years in Yoruba Country* (London: Seeley, Jackson & Halliday).

Hiskett, M. 1966–1967. "Materials Relating to the Cowry Currency of the Western Sudan," *Bulletin of the SOAS*, xxix, 1, and xxx, 3.

Hodder, B. W. and U. 1. Ukwu. 1969. *Markets in West Africa: Studies of Markets and Trade among the Yoruba and Ibo* (Ibadan: Ibadan University Press).

Hoff, Karla and Joseph E. Stiglitz. 1990. "Introduction: Imperfect Information and Rural Credit Markets—Puzzles and Policy Perspectives," *The World Bank Economic Review,* iv, 3.

Hogendorn, Jan and Marion Johnson. 1968. *The Shell Money of the Slave Trade* (Cambridge: Cambridge University Press).

Holy, Ladislav and Milan Stuchlik. 1968. (eds.) *Social Stratification in Tribal Africa* (Prague: Academy of Sciences).

Hopkins, A. G. 1966. "The Currency Revolution in Southwest Nigeria in the late nineteenth Century," *Journal of the Historical Society of Nigeria,* Vol. 3, No. 3, December.

———. 1969. "A Report on the Yoruba, 1910," *Journal of the Historical Society of Nigeria,* V, 1, (December).

———. 1973. *An Economic History of West Africa* (New York: Columbia University Press).

Hosbawm, E. J. 1959. *Primitive Rebels: Studies in Archaic Forms of Social Movement in the 19th and 20th Centuries* (Manchester: Manchester University Press).

Hosbawm, E. J. 1981. *Bandits* (Harmondsworth: Penguin, 1972; 2nd ed.).

IBRD (World Bank). 1955. *The Economic Development of Nigeria: Report of a Mission* (Baltimore, MD: Johns Hopkins University Press).

Inikori, J. E. 1982. *Forced Migration* (London, Hutchinson).

Irukwu, J. O. N.d. *Insurance Management in Africa* (Ibadan: Caxton, n.d.).

Isola, Akinwumi. 1970. *Efunsetan Aniwura: Iyalode Ibadan* (Ibadan: OUP).
Johnson, Marion. 1968. "The Nineteenth-Century Gold 'Mithqal' in West and North Africa," *JAH,* ix, 4.
———. 1970. "The Cowry Currencies of West Africa," *Part I, Journal of African History,* xi, 1, pp. 17–49; *Part II, Journal of African History,* xi, 3.
Johnson, The Reverend Samuel. 1921. *The History of the Yorubas* (Lagos: C.M.S. Bookshops, 1921, reprinted 1976).
Jones, G. I. 1958. "Native and Trade Currencies in Southern Nigeria during the Eighteenth and Nineteenth Centuries," *Africa,* Vol. 28, No. 1, January.
Keynes, John M. 1936. *The General Theory of Employment, Interest and Money* (New York: Harcourt, Brace).
Khapoya, Vincent B. 1994. *The African Experience: An Introduction* (Englewood Cliffs, NJ: Prentice Hall).
Kirk-Greene, A. H. M. 1960. "The Major Currencies in Nigerian History," *Journal of the Historical Society of Nigeria,* Vol. 2. No. 1, December.
———. 1971. *Crisis and Conflict in Nigeria: A Documentary Source-book* (London: Oxford University Press) 2 Volumes.
Kopytoff, J. H. 1965. *Preface to Modern Nigeria: The "Sierra Leoneans" in Yoruba* (Madison: University of Wisconsin Press).
Kotecha, Ken C. and Robert W. Adams. 1981. *The Corruption of Power: African Politics* (Washington D.C.: University Press of America).
Kurtz, Donald V. 1973. "The Rotating Credit Association: An Adaptation to Poverty," *Human Organization,* 32.
Lander, R. 1830. *Record of Captain Clapperton's Last Expedition to Africa, I* (London: H. Colburn & R. Bentley).
Lander, R. and J. Lander. 1832. *Journal of an Expedition to explore the Course and Termination of the Niger,* 3 vols. (London: J. & J. Harper).
Latham, J. H. 1971. "Currency, Credit and Capitalism on the Cross River in the Pre-colonial Era," *JAH,* xii, 4.
Law, R. C. 1978. "Slaves, Trade and Taxes: The Material Basis of Political Power in Pre-colonial West Africa," *Research in Economic Anthropology,* 1.
Law, R.C.C. 1973. "Contemporary Written Sources," in S. O. Biobaku (ed.), *Sources of Yoruba History* (Oxford: Clarendon Press).
———. 1974. "The Owu War in Yoruba History," *JHSN,* VII.
Law, Robin. 1977. *The Oyo Empire, c. 1600—1836: A West African Imperialism in the Era of the Atlantic Slave Trade* (Oxford: Clarendon Press).
———. 1978. "Slaves, Trade and Taxes: The Material Basis of Political Power in Precolonial West Africa," *Research in Economic Anthropology,* I.
———. 1986. "Early European Sources Relating to the Kingdom of the Ijebu (1500—1700): A Critical Survey," *History in Africa,* 13.
Lawal, A. A. 1987. "Anatomy of Corruption in the British Colonial Service in Nigeria," *ODU: A Journal of West African Studies,* 31, January.

Lawuyi, O. B. and J. K. Olupona. 1987. "Making Sense of the Aje Festival: Wealth, Politics and the Status of Women Among the Ondo of Southwestern Nigeria," *Journal of Ritual Studies,* No. 1.

Lawuyi, O. B. and O. Taiwo. 1990. "Towards an African Sociological Tradition: A Rejoinder to Akiwowo and Makinde," *International Sociology,* 5, 1.

Lawuyi, Tunde and Toyin Falola. 1992. "The Instability of the Naira and Social Payment Among the Yoruba," *Journal of Asian and African Studies,* XXVII, 3–4.

Lewis, O. A. 1977. "Economic Performance Orientation and Problems of Small Scale Industries in Nigeria's Former Western State," *Quarterly Journal of Administration,* xii, 1.

Leys, Colin. 1965. "What is the Problem about Corruption?" *The Journal of Modern African Studies,* 3, 2.

Lloyd, P. C. 1962. *Yoruba Land Law* (London: Oxford University Press).

Lovejoy, Paul. 1982. *Transformations in Slavery* (Cambridge, CUP).

———. 1974. "Interregional Monetary Flows in the Precolonial Trade of Nigeria," *JAH,* xv, 4.

———. 1981. The Ideology of Slavery in Africa (Beverly Hills, CA: Sage).

Loynes, J. B. 1957. *Report on the Establishment of a Nigerian Central Bank, the Introduction of a Nigerian Currency and Other Associated Matters* (Lagos: Government Printer).

———. 1962. *The West African Currency Board, 1912–1962* (London: West African Currency Board).

Lucas, J. O. 1948. *The Religion of the Yoruba* (Lagos: C. M. S. Bookshop).

Mabogunje, A. L. 1962. *The Yoruba Town* (Ibadan: Ibadan University Press).

———. 1976. *Cities and African Development* (Ibadan: OUP).

Mabogunje, A. L. and J. D. Omer Cooper. 1971. *Owu in Yoruba History* (Ibadan: Ibadan University Press).

Mabogunje, Akin L. 1995. "The Capitalization of Money and Credit in the Development Process: The Case of Community Banking in Nigeria," in Jane Guyer, (ed.), *Money Matters: Instability, Values and Social Payments in the Modern History of West African Communities* (Portsmouth, NH: Heinemann).

Madujibeya, S. A. 1976. "Oil and Nigeria's Economic Development," *African Affairs,* Vol. 75, No. 300.

Malinowski, Bronislaw. 1922. *Argonauts of the Western Pacific* (New York: E. P. Dutton).

Mars, J. 1948. "The Monetary and Banking System and Loan Market of Nigeria," in M. Perham (ed.), *Mining, Commerce and Finance in Nigeria* (London: Faber).

Marx, Karl. 1967. *Capital* (New York: International Publishers), 3 Vols.

Mauss, M. 1967. *The Gift* (New York: Norton).

May, D. J. 1860. "Journey in the Yoruba and Nupe Countries in 1858," *Journal of the Royal Geographical Society,* xxx.

Mayer, Thomas. 1995. "Money," in *Grolier Multimedia Encyclopedia.*

McIver, R. M. 1931. *Society: Its Structures and Changes* (New York: R. Long & R. R. Smith).

Merton, R. K. 1969. *Social Theory And Social Structure* (New York: The Free Press).

Mitchel, N. C. 1961. "Yoruba Towns," in K. M. Barbour and R. M. Prothero (eds.), *Essays on African Population* (London: Routledge & Paul).

Morton-Williams, P. 1964. 'The Oyo Yoruba and the Atlantic Trade, 1670–1830," *Journal of the Historical Society of Nigeria,* III, 1, 41.

Morton-Williams, Peter. 1968. "The Fulani Penetration into Nupe and Yoruba in the 19th century," in I. M. Lewis (ed.), *History and Social Anthropology* (London: Tavistock).

Needham, Rodney. 1962. "Review of Falkenberg," *American Anthropologist,* No. 64

Nicholson, E.W.J. 1956. *Report of the Commission of Enquiry into the Administration of the Ibadan District Council* (Ibadan: Western Region Government).

Nnoli, O . 1978. *Ethnic Politics in Nigeria* (Enugu: Fourth Dimension).

Noberini, Mary Rose and Rochel U. Berman. 1983. "Barter to Beat Inflation: Neighborhood Network for Swapping Services on Behalf of the Aged," *The Gerontologist,* 23, 5.

O'Hear, Ann. 1997. *Power Relations in Nigeria: Ilorin Slaves and their Successors* (Rochester, NY: Rochester University Press).

Obayemi, Ade. 1971. "The Yoruba and Edo-speaking Peoples and their Neighbours before 1600," in J.F. Ade Ajayi and Michael Crowder (eds.), *History of West Africa* (London: Longman, second edition 1976).

Obbo, C. 1980. *African Women: Their Struggle for Economic Independence* (London: Zed).

Obi, Cyril I. 1998. "The Impact of Oil on Nigeria's Revenue Allocation System: Problems and Prospects for National Reconstruction," in Kunle Amuwo et al., *Federalism and Political Restructuring in Nigeria* (Ibadan: Spectrum Books).

Odejide, A. F. 1987. "A Framework for Evaluating the Performance of Nigeria Public Enterprises: Implication for Privatization," *Quarterly Journal of Administration,* XXI, 3 & 4.

Odufalu, J. O. 1977. "Market Failures and Government Intervention in the Nigerian Economy: A Comment," *Quarterly Journal of Administration,* XII, 1.

Offensend, David G. 1976. "Centralization and Fiscal Arrangement in Nigeria," *Journal of Modern African Studies,* Vol. 14, No. 3, September.

Ofonagoro, W. I. 1979. "From Traditional to British Currency in Southern Nigeria: Analysis of a Currency Revolution, 1880–1948," *Journal of Economic History,* 39, 3.

Ofonogaro, W. Ibeke. 1979. *Trade and Imperialism in Southern Nigeria 1881–1929* (New York: Nok Publishers).

Ogumefu, M. I. 1929. *Yoruba Legends* (London: The Sheldon Press).

Ogunremi, G. O. 1982. *Counting the Camels: The Economics of Transportation in Pre-Industrial Nigeria* (New York: Nok Publishers).

Ojo, Ade T. and W. Adewunmi. 1980. *Cooperative Banking in Nigeria: Evolution, Structure and Operations* (Lagos: University of Lagos Press).

Ojo, G. J. A. 1966. *Yoruba Culture: A Geographical Analysis* (London: University of London Press).

Ojo, O. 1983. "Rural Banking Scheme as a Strategy for Bank Location," *Ife Social Sciences Review,* vi, 1 & 2.

Ojo, O. O. 1987. "Foreign Exchange Market in Nigeria," *Quarterly Journal of Administration,* XXI, 3 & 4.

Okigbo, P. N. C. 1981. *Nigeria's Financial System: Structure and Growth* (Harlow: Longman).

Okurume, G. E. 1977. "Nigerian Agriculture Bank, Its Function and Prospects," *The Bullion,* Vol. 2, Nos. 3 and 4.

Olakanpo, J. O. 1965. *Central Banking in the Commonwealth* (Calcutta).

Olaniyan, R. A. and A. G. Adebayo. 1998. "Yoruba Intergroup Relations and Diplomacy," in Ogunremi, Deji and Adediran, Biodun (eds.), *Yoruba History and Culture: Essays in Honor of I. A. Akinjogbin* (Lagos: Rex Charles).

Olaniyan, Richard. 1975. "Elements of Yoruba Traditional Diplomacy: An Assessment," in Abimbola, Wande (ed.), *Yoruba Oral Traditions: Poetry in Music, Dance and Drama* (Ile-Ife: Department of African Languages and Literature).

Olashore, O. 1972. "Evolution of Banking Operation in Nigeria and the System of Control," *CBN Newsletter,* Vol. 2, Nos. 2 & 3, Feb/March.

Olomola, I. 1979. "Aroko: An Indigenous Yoruba Semiotic Device," *Odu,* No. 19.

Olowu, D. 1987. "Economic Liberalization and the Nigerian Public Service," *Quarterly Journal of Administration,* XXI, 3 & 4.

Oluwasanmi, H.A. and J. A. Alao. 1965. "The Role of Credit in the Transformation of Traditional Agriculture: The Nigerian Experience," *Nigerian Journal of Economic and Social Studies,* vii, 1.

Omoruyi, S. E. and C. A. Demuren. 1980. "The Growth of Insurance Business in Nigeria, 1969–78," *EFR,* Vol. 18, No. 1, June.

Onah, J. O. 1980. "Uniform Pricing and Retailing of Petroleum in Nigeria," *Oil and the NIEO* (Ibadan: NES, Annual Conference Proceedings).

Onimode, B. 1981. "Class Struggle as a Reality in Nigerian Development," in O. Nnoli (ed.), *Path to Nigerian Development* (Dakar: Codesria Book Series).

Oroge, E. A. 1971. "The Institution of Slavery in Yorubaland with Particular Reference to the Nineteenth Century," Ph.D. Dissertation, University of Birmingham.

Oroge, E. Adeniyi. 1985. "Iwofa: An Historical Survey of the Yoruba Institution of Indenture," *African Economic History,* 14.

Osoba, S. O. 1977. "The Nigerian Power Elite, 1952–65" in P.C.W. Gutkind and Peter Waterman (eds.), *African Social Studies: A Radical Reader* (London: Heinemann).

Osuji, Emman O. 1984. *The Role of Petroleum Inspectorate of the NNPC as the 'Guardian' of the Nigerian Oil Industry* (Lagos: NNPC).

Osuno, B. A. 1978. "The Role of the NNPC in Nigeria's Oil Industry," *NIJ*, 7th Annual Oil Seminar.

Oyediran, O. 1979. (ed.) *Nigerian Government and Politics under Military Rule* (London: Oxford University Press).

Oyejide, T. A. 1977. "A Structural Analysis of Some Institutionalised Saving Patterns in Nigeria, 1961–73," *Journal of Business and Social Studies*, I, 1.

Oyejide, T. A. and A. Soyode. 1978. "Capital Earnings in the Insurance Industry: The Case of Nigeria," *QJA*, Vol. IX, No. 4, July.

Pallinder-Law, A. 1973. "Government in Abeokuta 1830–1914, with special reference to the Egba United Government 1898–94" (Ph.D. thesis, University of Goteborg).

Payne, Otunba. n.d. *Payne's Lagos and West African Almanac, 1893*. London: J. S. Philips.

Pearson, Scott R. 1970. *Petroleum and the Nigerian Economy* (Stanford: Stanford University Press).

Peel, J.D.Y. 1983. *Ijesha and Nigerians: The Incorporation of a Yoruba Kingdom 1890s–1970s* (Cambridge: Cambridge University Press).

Perham, Margery. 1937. *Native Administration in Nigeria* (London: OUP).

Phillips, A. O. 1980. "Three decades of Intergovernmental Financial Relationship in the Federation of Nigeria," *QJA*, Vol. XIV, No. 2, January.

Phillips, Dotun. 1992. *The Nominalization of the Nigerian Economy* (Ibadan: NISER Occasional Paper No. 3).

Post, Kenneth W. J. and George D. Jenkins. 1973. *The Price of Liberty: Personality and Politics in Colonial Nigeria* (Cambridge: Cambridge University Press).

Ritter, Joseph A. 1995. "The Transition from Barter to Fiat Money," *The American Economic Review*, Vol. 85, March.

Robertson, Claire and Iris Berger. 1986. (eds.) *Women and Class in Africa* (New York: Africana Publishing Company).

Robertson, Ross M. 1964. "Money," in Gould, Julius and Kolb, William L. (eds.), *A Dictionary of the Social Sciences* (New York: The Free Press).

Rothchild, D. and N. Chazan. 1988. *State and Society in Africa* (London: Westview Press).

Ryan, Joan. 1983. "Silent Barter," *Omega*, Vol. 14, No. 2.

Sangree, Walter. 1965. "The Bantu Tiriki of Western Kenya," in James L. Gibbs (ed.), *Peoples of Africa* (New York: Holt, Rinehart & Winston).

Sarassoro, Hyacinthe. 1979. *La Corruption des Fonctionnaires en Afrique* (Paris: Economica).

Schatzl, L. H. 1969. *Petroleum in Nigeria* (Ibadan: Nigerian Institute of Social and Economic Research).

Shagari, Shehu. 1982. *The Challenge of Change: Collected Speeches of President Shehu Shagari* (Lagos: Office of the President).

Siamwalla, Ammar, et al. 1990. "The Thai Rural Credit System: Public Subsidies, Private Information and Segmented Markets," *The World Bank Economic Review,* iv, 3.

Simmel, Georg. 1950. *The Sociology of Georg Simmel* (London: The Free Press of Glencoe, translated by Kurt H. Wolff).

———. 1971. *On Individuality and Social Forms* (Chicago, IL: University of Chicago Press).

———. 1990. *The Philosophy of Money* (London: Routledge; first published 1900, translated by Tom Bottomore and David Frisby), pp.120–25

Sklar, Richard L. 1963. *Nigerian Political Parties: Power in an Emergent African Nation* (Princeton, NJ: Princeton University Press).

Smith, M. G. 1964. "Historical and Cultural Conditions of Political Corruption among the Hausa," *Comparative Studies in Society and History,* January.

Smith, Robert. 1988. *Kingdoms of the Yoruba* (Madison: University of Wisconsin Press), 3rd edition.

Soetan, R. O. 1985. "Ownership and Control of British Joint Ventures in Nigeria" *Quarterly Journal of Administration (QJA),* Vol. XIX, Nos. 3 & 4, April/July.

Soyode, A. and T. A. Oyejide. 1975. "Branch network and Economic Performance: A Case Study of Nigeria's Commercial Banks," *NJESS,* Vol. 17, No. 2, July.

Steady, Filomina Chioma. 1981. (ed.) *The Black Woman Cross-Culturally* (Canbridge: Schenkman Publishing).

Stichter, Sharon B. and Jane L. Parpart. 1988. "Introduction: Towards a Materialist Perspective on African Women," in Sharon *B. Stichter and Jane L. Parpart (eds.),* Patriarchy and Class: African Women in the Home and the Workforce (Boulder, CO: Westview Press).

Stiglitz, Joseph. 1990. "Peer Monitoring and Credit Markets," *The World Bank Economic Review,* iv, 3, 1990.

Syed Hussein Alatas, *The Sociology of Corruption. The Nature, Function, Causes and Prevention of Corruption* (Singapore: Donald Moore Press).

Talbot, P. A. 1926. *Peoples of Southern Nigeria* (London: Frank Cass).

Tamuno, T. N. 1972. *The Evolution of the Nigerian State: the Southern Phase, 1898–1914* (London: Longman).

Temple, C. L. 1918. *Native Races and their Rulers* (London: Way & Co.).

Teriba, O. 1970. "The 1967–69 Banking Amendment in Nigeria: An Appraisal of Financial Adaptation in an Underdeveloped Economy," *NJESS,* Vol. 12, No. 1, March.

Tignor, Robert L. 1993. "Political Corruption in Nigeria Before Independence," *Journal of Modern African Studies,* 31, 2.

Tinubu, S. A. 1992. *S. L. Akintola: His Politics and His Nation. The Reminiscence of one of his Associates* (Ibadan: The African Digest).

Tobin, James. 1992. "Money," *The New Pelgrave Dictionary of Money and Finance* (London: The MacMillan Press), Vol. 2.

Tocqueville, A. 1954. *Democracy in America* (New York: Alfred A. Knopf).

Tucker, Reeve. 1948. *Abeokuta or Sunrise Within the Tropics: An Outline Of the Progress of the Yoruba Mission* (London: Carter & Bros.), 2nd edition.

Tuden, Arthur and Leonard Plotnikov. 1970. (eds.), *Social Stratification in Africa* (New York: The Free Press).

Udry, Christopher. 1990. "Credit Markets in Northern Nigeria: Credit as Insurance in a Rural Economy," *The World Bank Economic Review,* iv, 3.

Weber, Max. 1965. *The Theory of Social and Economic Organization* (New York: The Free Press).

Werlin, Herbert H. 1972. "The Roots of Corruption-the Ghanaian Enquiry," *The Journal of Modern African Studies,* 10, 2.

Wiliamson, Steve and Randall Wright. 1994. "Barter and Monetary Exchange under Private Information," *The American Economic Review,* Vol. 84, March.

Williams, Robert. 1987. *Political Corruption in Africa* (Dorset: Blackmore).

Wraith, Ronald and Edgar Simpkins. 1963. *Corruption in Developing Countries* (New York: Norton).

Zaslavsky, Claudia. 1983. "The Yoruba Number System," in Ivan Van Sertima (ed.), *Blacks in Science: Ancient and Modern* (New Brunswick, NJ: Transaction Publishers).

Zelizer, Viviana. 1992. "Money," *Encyclopedia of Sociology* (New York: Macmillan), Vol. 3.

Index